# E A R L
# B R O W D E R

# EARL
# BROWDER

■

*The Failure of*
*American Communism*

JAMES  G.  RYAN

The University of Alabama Press
*Tuscaloosa and London*

Copyright © 1997
The University of Alabama Press
Tuscaloosa, Alabama 35487-0380
All rights reserved
Manufactured in the United States of America

∞

The paper on which this book is printed meets the minimum requirements of
American National Standard for Information Science–Permanence of Paper for
Printed Library Materials, ANSI Z39.48-1984.

**Library of Congress Cataloging-in-Publication Data**

Ryan, James G., 1947–
Earl Browder : the failure of American communism / James G. Ryan.
p.    cm.
Includes bibliographical references and index.
ISBN 0-8173-0843-1 (cloth : alk. paper)
1. Browder, Earl, 1891–1973.   2. Communists—United States—Biography.
3. Communist Party of the United States of America—History—20th century.
4. Communism—United States—History—20th century.    I. Title.
HX84.B69R93   1997
335.43′092—dc20
[B]                                                                          96-25763

British Library Cataloguing-in-Publication Data available

1  2  3  4  5  6  7  8  9  10   /   06  05  04  03  02  01  00  99  98  97

FOR MY MOTHER
IN MEMORY OF MY FATHER

# CONTENTS

■

# ACKNOWLEDGMENTS

■

So many persons helped with this project that I list names with reluctance, fearing I might inadvertently omit someone.

This book had its earliest origins long ago in a University of Delaware research seminar with the late J. Joseph Huthmacher. He gently persuaded a shy young graduate student to locate, contact, and interview Earl Browder. The study was nurtured in dissertation form at the University of Notre Dame under Vincent P. De Santis. I owe him a special debt of gratitude for his tireless encouragement during the great academic depression of the 1980s. Over the nine long years that I spent teaching virtually around the clock as an itinerant scholar, little tangible progress on the project was made. Research began in earnest when I was appointed assistant professor at Texas A&M University at Galveston (TAMUG) in 1990.

I thank Robert J. Alexander, the late Earl Browder, the late Gladys Browder, Felix Browder, William Browder, Sam Darcy, Gil Green, Dorothy Healey, the late Philip J. Jaffe, A. B. Magil, and Junius Irving Scales for the patience and care with which they offered their recollections, and I thank John W. Roberts for discussing the history of the federal prison system with me.

Colleagues who kindly read portions of the manuscript at various stages, from a chapter to the entire text (in some cases more than once) include James R. Barrett, Robert A. Calvert, Joseph G. Dawson, Vincent P. De Santis, Theodore Draper, Gary Fink, David J. Garrow, John Earl Haynes, Larry D. Hill, Edward P. Johanningsmeier, Harvey Klehr, Niko Pfund, Herbert Romerstein, Charlotte Sheedy, and Paul Wilson.

Editors at The University of Alabama Press have been a delight to work with; any errors or shortcomings in the text are, of course, due to my own stubbornness. I feel a special debt of gratitude to the director emeritus, Malcolm M. MacDonald, for his interest in this project.

TAMUG provided research grants in 1990, 1991, 1992, 1993, and 1995, as did Texas A&M's main campus in 1993. I am grateful for all of these monies, which helped fund archival enrichment from sources in locales as diverse as Palo Alto, Atlanta, Washington, New York, and Moscow. I thank archivists and their staffs at the Hoover Institution; Woodruff

Library, Emory University; Library of Congress; National Archives; Department of Justice; Department of State; Federal Bureau of Investigation; Immigration and Naturalization Service; Federal Bureau of Prisons; Office of the Pardon Attorney; Tamiment Library, New York University; Columbia Oral History Project; Franklin D. Roosevelt Library; Bird Library, Syracuse University; Indiana State Library; and King Library, University of Kentucky. Thanks go also to Robert J. Alexander, Hugo L. Black, Jr., and Theodore Draper for allowing me to examine their collections, and to Ken BeSaw for providing photographs from the archives of the *People's Weekly World.* I also thank the editors of the *Review of Politics* and the *Proceedings of the Indiana Academy of the Social Sciences* for allowing me to use material that first appeared, in different form, in their publications.

Making arrangements to live and study alone in Moscow when relatively few Western scholars had done so was difficult. It posed an especially daunting task for someone unfamiliar with overseas travel or the Russian language. Dan Leab and Harvey Klehr convinced me that the trip was essential, my misgivings notwithstanding. Ed Johanningsmeier and John Haynes provided contacts with English-speaking historians in Moscow and gave literally hours of encouragement over the telephone. Jonathan Coopersmith and Ann Todd Baum offered valuable advice. Arch Getty located comfortable, affordable housing near the Prospect Mira metro station. Effectively, Lisa Vernon warned me against becoming distracted on the trip.

Kirill M. Anderson, director of the Russian Center for the Preservation and Study of Documents of Recent History (RTsKhIDNI), and his staff provided cheerful and generous help to a stranger unfamiliar with their archive. Galina Khartulary explained the system, located promising files, translated daily, and found me an evening job teaching eager, advanced English students. She and her husband, Valery Klokov, familiarized me with central Moscow. Though significantly younger than I am, they both worried about me as parents might; I caused them great concern and a trip across town when I locked myself out of my apartment for many hours on my second night there. Dasha Lotareva translated additional materials, took me to beautiful places in Moscow and St. Petersburg after the archives closed, and later mailed copies of valuable files to Texas. When the passage of time forced me to return home, I left more than a dozen friends in Russia.

Back in the United States, Leon Luxemburg and Harry Walsh provided additional translations of Russian material. Herb Romerstein was very generous in sharing his own documents from the RTsKhIDNI. I appreciate all the help provided by the interlibrary loan departments at Rosenberg Library in Galveston and the Jack K. Williams Library at TAMUG. I thank TAMUG's Department of General Academics for partial release time and paying my typists. Christine Schmale, Pat Wallace, and Gretchen Stoltz put the revised manuscript on a word processor and made literally thousands of changes over several drafts. Gretchen also taught me Wordperfect, showing admirable forbearance.

Since my 1993 visit the Russian intelligence services have closed several important sections of the Comintern records. Hundreds of thousands of pages remain available, however. It is difficult to overstate the significance of these materials. They offer a perspective on American radicalism available nowhere else. I believe U.S. scholars have been slow to realize their relevance and richness and hope that every student of domestic Communism will make use of them in the future.

# ACRONYMS USED
# IN TEXT

■

| | |
|---|---|
| AAS | Anglo-American Secretariat |
| ACLU | American Civil Liberties Union |
| AFL | American Federation of Labor |
| CCNY | City College of New York |
| CI | Communist International |
| CIO | Committee for Industrial Organization |
| CP | Communist party |
| CPA | Communist Political Association |
| CPO | Communist party, USA (Opposition) |
| CPUSA | Communist party of the United States |
| ECCI | Executive Committee of the Communist International |
| EPIC | End Poverty in California program |
| FCC | Federal Communications Commission |
| HUAC | House Un-American Activities Committee |
| INS | Immigration and Naturalization Service |
| IWW | Industrial Workers of the World |
| NCPAC | National Citizens Political Action Committee |
| NIRA | National Industrial Recovery Act |
| NKVD | *Narodnyi Komissariat Vnutrennikh Del* [People's Commissariat of Internal Affairs] (Soviet secret police agency; later the KGB) |
| NRA | National Recovery Administration |
| PAC | Political Action Committee |
| PCF | French Communist Party |
| PCI | Italian Communist Party |
| RILU | Red International of Labor Unions (also known by the Russian abbreviation Profintern) |
| SI | Second International |
| SLP | Socialist Labor party |
| SP | Socialist party |
| TUEL | Trade Union Education League |
| TUUL | Trade Union Unity League |
| UAW | United Auto Workers |
| WPA | Works Progress Administration |
| YCL | Young Communist League |

# EARL
# BROWDER

# INTRODUCTION

■

## *The Man from Kansas*

Perhaps no single individual better illustrated the bifocal nature of the Communist party (CPUSA or CP), with its American and Russian concerns, than Earl Russell Browder. A wiry figure with sharp features, sandy hair, and magnetic light-blue eyes, he led the movement from 1932 to 1945. A product of rural poverty and the culture of a small nineteenth-century Great Plains city, Browder carried boyish good looks well into his forties. Self-educated, he overcame a shy temperament to become the greatest public relations expert in CPUSA history. Although his countrymen stereotyped Marxists as stocky, swarthy figures having thick Slavic accents, Browder, slender and ruddy-complected, made his Kansas twang the voice of American Communism. He invoked a 150-year domestic radical tradition. No previous CP head had ever seemed proud to be an American. Surrounding himself at rallies with Soviet and U.S. flags, he fascinated the press for over a decade.

Why should anyone today care about Earl Browder? As historian John Haynes has observed, much of the public and particularly students have the attitude that the Communist party was a joke. Books about it, some assume, are written by followers of the late Senator Joseph McCarthy, with their wild imaginations, or by Red-diaper babies (children of Communist families) seeking to reassert the patriotism of oft-vilified relatives.[1]

Actually, although it was never a major force, the CPUSA was once an important minor player in America's politics, labor movement, and cultural life. Under Browder's leadership the Communists attempted to use working-class Americanism, the proletarian response to dominant, conservative pressures toward loyalty and conformity (so ably described by historian Gary Gerstle) to build a mass radical movement. In the process the CPUSA achieved respectability previously unknown and now frequently forgotten. According to political scientist Harvey Klehr, Communists even enjoyed a "measure of prestige in some circles." Probably the best organized party left of Franklin D. Roosevelt's New Deal Democrats, they surpassed the declining Socialists. Their nearly 100,000 members' influence ranged far beyond party rolls. After 1935 they appeared in nearly every walk of life. The CPUSA, moreover, displayed an ability to "dominate organizations filled with non-Communists" such as the Congress of Industrial Organizations and Minnesota's Farmer-Labor party. Finally, at least some Congresspersons regarded the Communists seriously, "not, for a change as harbingers of violence but as a political force to be conciliated and addressed." During the mid-1930s and after 1941 Browder and his followers seemed close to achieving legitimacy. Why did they fail to attain it?[2]

Like the peace movement, also unsuccessful, American Communism was not insignificant. Its followers, after years of internecine conflict, developed a Leninist focus that gave them a detailed revolutionary blueprint. Victory in Russia created a government ruling one-sixth of the earth's surface. This seemed a magnificent beginning toward global working-class rule. Although looking to Moscow for basic strategy, the Communists in America soon proved innovative at adopting tactics suitable to the United States.

Interested as he was in redefining national heroes in a larger democratic context, Browder never restrained his admiration for Joseph Stalin. Although historians are now careful about using the term *Stalinist*, Browder employed it proudly throughout his entire career. As party chief he deliberately copied the Soviet dictator's false modesty and made certain everyone knew that Stalin, too, was a quiet person.

Behind Browder's gentle public demeanor lay dramatic family secrets. His sister, Margaret ("Marguerite"), worked for the foreign directorate of the Soviet agency NKVD, the KGB's forerunner, during the 1930s. (The NKVD included both internal security and external intelligence.) Browder's second wife, Raissa Luganovskaya, had played a role in the Russian civil war that Earl could not defend in the United States.

Who was this man from the Midwest? How did he rise to CPUSA leadership? Browder was no mere homegrown, corn-fed front figure for Soviet policies. He enjoyed a real degree of autonomy and tried to give Communism a native face during the mid-1930s, the years of the Popular Front or worldwide struggle for antifascist unity. Yet character flaws prevented him from acquiring a million followers as did Eugene V. Debs, the Socialists' perennial early twentieth-century presidential candidate. Browder's efforts make an excellent case study in American leftist politics during the years of Soviet ascendancy. Like many immigrants and blacks of the era, Browder was a first-generation urbanite who identified easily with the dispossessed. What is his place in history? His career prompts larger questions. Could an individual really be both a Communist and an indigenous radical? If one did not preclude the other, how could the USSR's form of Marxism be compatible with working-class Americanism? Finally, does the CPUSA's failure tell us anything about the larger anguish of the domestic left during the twentieth century?

# ONE

∎

## From Field to Office (1891–1930)

"Why don't you go back where you came from?" Earl Browder heard this taunt constantly after becoming a public figure. In response he hired a genealogist to find how deeply his roots extended. By 1936 bragging had replaced defensiveness, and a CPUSA pamphlet described him as "blood and bone of America."[1]

Browder's maternal Scottish-American ancestors, many of whom were miners, had no pedigree-conscious members. They could be traced back only a few generations and left few records. Browder's paternal lineage, however, led to three mid-seventeenth-century Welsh brothers who settled in Dinwiddie County, Virginia. They were restless Protestant religious dissenters, and their progeny carried the tradition to Kentucky. There numerous Browders helped build the Methodist Church, and others migrated to Illinois.

Earl's grandfather, born in 1790, fought in the War of 1812 and then became a circuit-riding minister. Earl's Illinois-native father, William, youngest of eighteen siblings, married Martha Hankins, his sixteen-year-old sweetheart, in the 1870s. Like most nineteenth-century midwesterners, both were imbued with the American dream of self-reliance and success; neither feared hard work. Carrying their worldly possessions in a covered wagon, they staked out a quarter section of virgin prairie near Medicine Lodge, Kansas, and attempted homesteading.[2]

### WE HAVE BEEN NAUGHT

Although William and Martha were young and strong, frontier life proved a crushing experience. The United States in the late nineteenth century was undergoing a corporate revolution that made subsistence farming especially difficult. The change started imperceptibly about 1820 when early factory owners recruited rural women and girl workers, and it quickly skewed resources. By 1860 the population's richest 10 percent possessed more than two-thirds of the nation's wealth.

The Civil War, bringing unprecedented demands for arms, munitions, and clothing, hastened the locomotive of industrialization. Congress stoked the engines by giving business credit and land. The judiciary greased the rails by allowing corporations to use the Fourteenth Amendment, designed to protect helpless southern freedmen, to avoid state governmental regulation. Although the early republic had few millionaires, five thousand existed by 1900. Twenty-five sat in the U.S. Senate alone. A typical family earned $500 annually in 1900, but steel magnate Andrew Carnegie received $40 million. Just five years earlier the Supreme Court had ruled a modest federal income tax unconstitutional.

The corporate revolution created far more paupers than entrepreneurs. It lured millions of immigrants to America's cities, along with rural whites and eventually African American refugees from the South. These workers toiled twelve-hour days in factories that literally threatened life and limb—when they could find work. Unprecedented numbers of poor, single women entered the legal and illegal labor force; according to historian Ruth Rosen, professional prostitution probably peaked just before 1900. Urbanites lived in tenements designed to crowd as many possible into the smallest space (fresh air, running water, and public services awaited a new century). A middle class of small property owners identified more with business than with those struggling to survive.[3]

Mercantilist economic policies raised America's tariff walls to protect manufacturing but not agriculture. Meanwhile the spread of railways and steamship lines and the opening of the Suez Canal in 1869 resulted in a world market for food products. American farmers, unable to control output, faced continually declining crop prices. Between 1870 and 1890 vast new tracts of Canadian, South American, and Australian land came under cultivation, and domestic grain prices skidded to record lows. Soon Kansas farmers were burning corn in their fireplaces for fuel.

The harsh Great Plains climate often seemed merciless to the Browders. William and Martha lived in a "dugout," lost two children to disease, and saw drought ruin their crops. They mortgaged their hut for living expenses. When they fell behind in payments, they forfeited it. Abandoning agriculture, they rented a modest dwelling in Wichita, labeled by historian Craig Miner as Kansas's "most Republican and probably most conservative city." The grinding poverty and loss of economic independence kindled a resentment that smoldered within them for the rest of their lives. Suffering also brought them closer to each other and their offspring. To the Browders a warm family life was one of the few buffers against a system they now saw as unjust. Their eighth child, Earl Russell, arrived on May 20, 1891; subsequently, Martha gave birth to two others.[4]

Earl spent his childhood years in a city that was undergoing a separate economic disaster. Wichita had begun in the 1860s as a frontier trading area on the Chisholm Trail, located at the junction of the Big and Little Arkansas rivers in south Kansas. It had been a boom town since the first Caucasian settlement. Over successive decades Wichita had grown through trade with the Indian Territory (now Oklahoma) just after the Civil War; the spending by Texas cowboys and the cattle industry during the 1870s; and finally a manic real estate speculation that attracted nationwide attention for most of the 1880s. In 1886 and 1887 one thousand new residents arrived per month. The municipality, however, displayed an inability to attract industries commensurate with its population growth, which peaked at thirty-four thousand. In early 1888 the precipitous type of decline that often follows speculative orgies began. Once land prices began to drop, the shrinking tax base could no longer sustain the urban amenities, such as all-night electric street lights, for which the local government had contracted during the boom. Within two years the population had shrunk to 23,500, a decrease of almost one-third. By 1896 the city that had made capital expenditures for 40,000 housed a mere 19,892, with unemployment and hunger rampant.[5]

At the same time the national farming crisis had made the state of Kansas a political earthquake's epicenter. Earlier agrarian self-help efforts had not sufficed. They had, however, spawned the People's party, which became arguably the largest third party in American history. Feeding on farm belt discontent over low prices and loss of autonomy, the party challenged the status quo politics of the Democrats and Republicans through a reform platform inclusive enough to target all the poor. The Populists sought a flexible national currency, graduated income tax, postal savings banks, and nationalization of railroads. They also tried to enlist urban workers through advocating publicly owned streetcar lines that would charge low fares, municipal power plants, and public housing projects. The Populists believed they could give American democracy a more pervasive definition.[6] In 1892 their presidential candidate, James B. Weaver, captured one million popular and twenty-two electoral votes. The new party secured three U.S. senators, three governors, and more than fifteen hundred members of state legislatures. When the national economy plunged into severe depression in 1893, the People's party began to smell victory.

It never arrived. The Populists held their own in 1894's Congressional elections but courted disaster two years later. They endorsed William Jennings Bryan, the Democratic nominee, although they named him to head a separate ticket with a Populist running mate. Bryan eschewed the People's party's broad platform, taking but a single plank, monetary inflation through unlimited silver coinage. His landslide defeat in 1896 brought down the national Populists with him. Browder gradually came to self-consciousness in a Kansas that had returned to her solidly Republican tradition, but not to prosperity.

In Wichita, William, whom Earl called "Paw," taught elementary school and espoused first Populism, then Socialism. His misery also made him a religious skeptic; soon he was known as the town infidel. In his home radical Congressman "Sockless Jerry" Simpson was a hero. Although young Earl hawked the Republican, pro-business *Wichita Eagle* by day, at night his father taught the "three r's" and class consciousness. "Maw" Browder displayed less interest in politics but bestowed an even stronger anticlericalism. She tutored her children from Thomas Paine's *Age of Reason* and displayed a broad love of literature. She urged them to publish their own tomes some day. Earl, an energetic yet frail boy, loved sports but suffered frequent injuries that included broken bones. While mending, he took to organizing games, which he did well. He also claimed entrepreneurial skills.

Late in life Browder boasted of having been present when the notorious Carry Nation, whom he described as "a dumpy little woman in widow's weeds," brought to town her one-person campaign to enforce the Kansas prohibition law. Her target was the Carey Hotel, with a luxurious long bar, $1,500 plate-glass mirror, and large canvas painting of a naked Cleopatra. Nostalgically Browder declared, "Before I could get to the scene, Carry's famous hatchet had smashed the windows, hacked the mahogany bar beyond repair together with the pyramids of bottles behind it, slashed the nude painting and ruined the mirrors." She "emerged from the ruins as I panted up and made a shrill little speech to the crowd. Nobody moved to touch her, and she drove off" in her buggy. "I grabbed some fragments of the broken glass for souvenirs; I could sell them for a dime apiece."[7]

If the nine-year-old Earl actually witnessed some of the excitement, he eventually confused the details. Nation, of nearby Medicine Lodge, did in fact invade the Carey House annex bar on December 27, 1900, using an iron rod and throwing rocks and billiard balls. She was arrested by city detective Park Massey after a vigorous struggle, however. Nation made a second raid on January 21, 1901, wielding a hatchet (to attract more publicity), and she was accompanied by two Wichita women, one of whom swung a wrench and the other of whom swung a cane. Yet one has difficulty understanding how a child could have perceived the six-foot, 185-pound Nation as small.[8]

It is far more certain that the iconoclastic Browder family found its own ways to resist community pressures. Although the Republican slogan "enrich yourself" had swept the state, family members considered corporate wealth immoral. They believed that life was an eternal struggle between the "haves" and the "have-nots," and they identified defiantly with the latter. Unlike many of the dispossessed, however, the Browders were voracious readers and scorned emotionally oriented religions. William led his family from Methodism into the Unitarian Church, although affluent property owners dominated its local congregation. The Browders' values complicated their lives considerably but made them tough, emotionally and intellectually. All of Earl's siblings eventually found themselves in or near the Communist party.[9] No direct evidence exists to explain their radicalization. One may surmise, however, that the brothers and sisters, possessing similar genetic makeup and facing the same family situation, shared many of Earl's feelings.

In 1900 William Browder became an invalid, possibly from a nervous breakdown.[10] This illness forced his sons to leave school. Earl became a department store errand boy before he could complete third grade. Later he delivered messages for Western Union. Educational deprivation had far-reaching psychological effects on him. As a youth he struggled to compensate through hard work and an unquenchable thirst for knowledge. He displayed a lifelong hostility toward the economic injustice that had cut short his childhood. Yet self-inculcation never fully relieved a private insecurity. Early on he developed an inner craving for public recognition of his intellect. William recovered eventually, living to age ninety-two. He never received another teaching position, however. He became an urban handyman and later an agricultural laborer. Earl joined the Socialist party at age fifteen in 1906.

Browder's formative years coincided with American Socialism's heyday. Marxist parties have had a problematic history in the United States. From 1890 to 1914 Daniel De Leon, a brilliant but dogmatic thinker, led a minuscule Socialist Labor party (SLP) that was dedicated to overthrowing the capitalist system completely. Scorning all reforms it sought a single proletarian goal, victory at the polls. Class-conscious industrial unions would make it possible through mass educational efforts. Outside the party, workers battled corporate forces violently in bloody strikes suppressed by state and federal troops at Homestead, Pennsylvania; Pullman, Illinois; and a half dozen Rocky Mountain mining towns. Yet the SLP's refusal to address immediate issues, such as the eight-hour day, kept its membership low. By contrast, growth spelled confidence for the Socialist party (SP), which was formed in 1901 from two smaller sects (one an SLP splinter group) that totaled barely seven thousand members. Nontheoretical, this party looked as much to George Bernard Shaw and Karl Kautsky as to Karl Marx. By 1908, under Eugene V. Debs, its charismatic midwestern presidential candidate, it had more than forty-one thousand dues-paying members in more than three thousand locals. The *Red Special*, an SP-owned railroad car, carried the Debs campaign across the land. Two years later the party had its first Congressman, Victor Berger of Wisconsin, and one thousand local elected officials. Socialist mayors soon appeared in Berkeley, Butte, Milwaukee, Reading, Schenectady, and other cities. A dozen party newspapers, led by Julius Wayland's highly successful *Appeal to Reason*, challenged capitalist hegemony.[11]

In and about the SP clustered cultural radicals, syndicalists, and foreign language federations. Harvard-educated journalist John Reed, Jewish students from New York's City College, and writers Upton Sinclair, Max Eastman, and others created an atmosphere in Greenwich Village not unlike that in the 1960s. Eastman, a handsome blond poet who taught philosophy at Columbia University and who would write some twenty books, was his generation's best-known literary leftist. Radical unionist "Big Bill" Haywood's Industrial Workers of the World (IWW, nicknamed the Wobblies), in loose affiliation, mixed words and action. Trying to organize those ignored by the crafts-oriented American Federation of Labor (AFL), it reached out to the unskilled, unemployed, immigrants, African Americans, and women. The IWW, strongest in logging camps, harvest fields, and among seamen, advocated slowdowns and the general strike to cripple capitalism. Its ideology resembled that of European syndicalism. Powerful in France, Italy, and Spain, syndicalists saw labor unions as revolutionary instruments. They, not political parties or governments, would control the new society. Syndicalist attitudes thrived among America's most militant leftists. Language federation members had the fewest inhibitions concerning Socialism's alleged incompatibility with American values.[12]

The SP belonged to a larger Second International (SI), a chiefly European organization itself ideologically untidy. It had been created in 1889 to replace the First International Workingmen's Association, a loose federation of sects and trade unions that had perished during Marx's life-time. Among the SI's member parties raged a controversy between revisionists and radicals. The former, a majority backed by trade unionists after 1906, was inspired by the writings of Germany's Eduard Bernstein. He called for evolutionary socialism, valued parliamentary means, and termed the ultimate goal "nothing to me." The radical minority, following Rosa Luxemburg and Karl Liebknecht, sought capitalism's destruction through a mass strike and condemned imperialism.[13]

Browder, a fair-haired adolescent, never rebelled against his parents' values. While other boys scanned the sports pages and talked about baseball heroes such as Honus Wagner and John McGraw, Browder peddled party periodicals and urged adults to elect Debs. For a small monthly fee he purchased fifty "Socialist classics" through a Chicago mail-order house. Typically he found Frederick Engels easier to grasp than Marx. Browder enjoyed Karl Kautsky's *Road to Power* most. Not surprisingly the spindly, curious youth who liked books went into office work. By age nineteen Browder toiled as an accountant. His early years, though difficult, did not embitter him. Instead he radiated the left's optimism.[14]

In 1912, at age twenty-one, he left home for Kansas City, Kansas, just as the party's appeal peaked. In that year's election Debs received 6 percent of the total popular vote—the highest ever polled by an American Socialist. Browder, recently married, felt no pressure to continue aiding his parents' large family. Hoping to play some modest role in radical politics, he sought employment that would provide free time. He entered a small partnership that manufactured and sold brooms, but the firm went bankrupt within nine months. Eventually he landed a pleasant position tending books for a Standard Oil trust subsidiary. A brisk worker, he learned to discharge his daily duties in just four hours. He used his remaining office time to study, completing a correspondence school law course in 1914. Browder had nights free for family and labor activities, although for a while he dabbled in evening courses in mathematics and Latin.[15]

American Socialism suffered a major reversal shortly after Browder ventured on his own. Back in 1910 two ironworkers, James and John McNamara, had bombed the *Los Angeles Times* building, killing twenty persons. Virtually the entire Socialist movement, believing protestations of innocence, rallied to the McNamaras' defense. The party entered the 1911 Los Angeles mayoralty race with an even chance of electing its nominee, Job Harriman. Then, five days before the polls opened, the McNamaras suddenly confessed, which brought predictable results. En-

Browder, circa 1910, age 19, Wichita, Kansas.
(From the Syracuse University Library, Department of
Special Collections, 600 Bird Library. Used by permission.)

raged moderate SP delegates to the 1912 convention amended the party constitution to expel anyone advocating sabotage. The outspoken Haywood, a syndicalist who sought to weaken capitalism through workers' power, just months earlier had endorsed direct action in the *International Socialist Review*. In February 1913 a recall election removed him from the SP's National Executive Committee.

Browder and thousands of other members left the party in protest, and many more departed because it had peaked as a municipal reform movement. Among them went John Reed, Columbia University graduate Max Eastman, and most Greenwich Village opinion makers, who took their popular journal, the *Masses*, with them. Many SP right-wingers began supporting President Woodrow Wilson's progressive administration.

A restless spirit, Browder roamed Kansas City political haunts. He declined an offer to join the Pendergast machine that would send future President Harry S. Truman to the U.S. Senate. Browder settled instead for the Workers' Educational League. It was the local affiliate of the Syndicalist League of North America, which was led by William Z. Foster. A tall, lean, mercurial figure raised in a teeming Philadelphia slum, Foster would soon become one of the nation's most feared labor organizers.

Browder analyzed current events for the group's monthly, the *Toiler*, edited it from 1913 to 1915, and had great success at selling subscriptions. During the same period he also served as local head of the Bookkeepers, Stenographers, and Accountants, an AFL union, representing it on the Kansas City (Missouri) Central Labor Council. He resigned from Standard Oil in 1916 and instead managed a nearby farmer's co-op, sat on the Cooperative League of North America's national council, and wrote occasionally for the league's journal.

Thus even by age twenty-six Browder had not found a political home. He had tried Socialism, syndicalism, trade unionism, and cooperativism, but he continued to drift.[16] He had escaped grinding poverty, which was no small achievement, but his dilettantism revealed immaturity. Beyond his business skills he had little to offer the left and, more important, had no particular ambition. Browder was merely one more discontented working-class provincial who rejected capitalist values but had no clear idea of what he supported.

And then World War I came to the United States. Its 1914 outbreak, pitting Britain, France, and Russia against Germany, the Austro-Hungarian empire, and the Ottoman Turkey, caused consternation among Socialists. The SI had pledged opposition to all armed conflicts save proletarian revolution, yet French, British, and German parties stampeded to support their respective governments' military actions. Only the Italians, English pacifists, and Russian Bolsheviks held to SI principles. Stunned, the American SP, three thousand miles from the battlefields, displayed indecisiveness and division. Officially it opposed the hostilities and U.S. preparedness. Yet many members feared German militarism, and others had become disillusioned by European socialism's failure to keep the peace. Nevertheless, although some people defected and began to support the Wilson administration's preparedness efforts, membership in the SP shot up quickly after 1915. As the only antiwar party, it attracted strong support among northern industrial workers and immigrants, especially those in foreign-language groups. As historian Nick Salvatore has noted, many had arrived too recently to possess the vote and "tended to disparage Socialist political action and gravitated instead toward revolutionary industrial unionism." Russian, Finnish, and Polish Socialists, under oppressive working conditions in the United States, supported orthodox Marxist theory. They despised those who wanted political rather than economic action—domestic revisionists such as Victor Berger and Morris Hillquit. By 1919 the federations comprised 53 percent of all party members and had reversed the post-1912 decline.[17]

At last the antiauthoritarian Browder had found a cause that inspired his passionate dedication. During the winter of 1916–1917 he joined a committee of about fifteen intellectuals, which called itself the "League for Democratic Control." A growing patriotic hysteria was sweeping the land, creating a bitter animus against Germans, immigrants, African Americans, class-conscious workers, and Socialists. Nevertheless, league members proselytized in Kansas and Missouri towns against American entry into the war. Authorities watched them closely.

President Wilson signed Congress's declaration against Imperial Germany on April 6, 1917. The SP took an unequivocal antiwar stand, although some intellectuals, trade unionists, and the *Appeal to Reason* supported the administration. A federal conscription bill was enacted on May 18; immediately Browder and his comrades began urging young men to resist it. On May 30 authorities in Olathe, Kansas, arrested him, his brother William, and a future brother-in-law, Thomas R. Sullivan, for conspiracy. In jail the men spurned an opportunity to register for the Selective Service. An indictment followed immediately. Their aged lawyer, a states' rights advocate, argued that the Selective Service Act was unconstitutional, but the court dismissed his motion. Therefore, the men posted bail and awaited their trials.[18]

They had little hope of obtaining legal or financial assistance. The Espionage Act in June and the Sedition Act the following May defined criminal disloyalty so broadly that some of the worst violations of civil liberties in American history ensued. The government harassed Socialist newspapers, the post office denied the SP use of the mails, and around the nation police began rounding up antiwar militants. Soon Eugene V. Debs and more than sixty IWW leaders faced indictments. Browder later recalled the situation succinctly: "A wave of mob violence against Socialist meetings and headquarters had struck in many cities. Few people

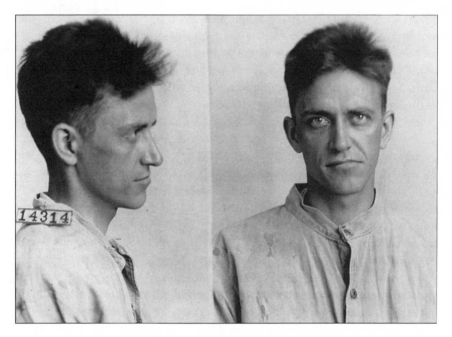

Browder in Kansas arrest photo, 1917.
(Courtesy of the National Archives.)

likely to be interested in our case were without similar cases closer to hand."[19]

In December 1917 juries convicted the Browders and Sullivan; each received a one-year sentence for nonregistration and two years for conspiracy. For the first crime they spent the next ten months in a small Platte County, Missouri, jail because of federal prison overcrowding. Earl Browder handled incarceration stoically, believing that it was the price paid for being an American radical. He later told journalist Milly Bennett that imprisonment provided his first taste of leisure. Never before had he been free from worrying "where the next meal was coming from." His jovial jailer, J. A. Vestal, happy to receive federal maintenance money and a bit of excitement in his small town, provided every privilege the law allowed. When friends visited the prisoners, he locked them in, lunch basket and all.[20] To fight boredom Earl wrote an accounting pamphlet.

In February of 1917 the bourgeois revolution in Russia surprised American radicals. November's Bolshevik takeover mesmerized them.

Most realistic Socialists had not expected a successful proletarian uprising in their lifetimes. Now the promised land loomed before them. According to Salvatore, many on the left became convinced that "all that stood between them and the establishment of American soviets was a purge of conservative leaders and the restructuring of the party on proper revolutionary principles along the Russian model."[21]

Within twelve months Europe ignited. Finland established a Socialist government, and Hungary erupted in revolt. Facing military defeat, the German emperor fled. The Communists shot the czar and his family. In March 1919 they created a Third International (Comintern), which ordered every SP to split. Only powerful left-wing movements would hasten revolution's spread. The U.S. government's decision to send soldiers to Archangel and Murmansk to aid the anti-Soviet White Army prompted liberals and Socialists alike to defend Russia.

Against 1919's European backdrop, American workers hit the streets in record numbers. They resented losing the recognition Wilson's administration had granted to pacify labor during the war. Sharp peacetime inflation enraged them, and demands for an eight-hour day inspired them. In all four million toilers walked off their jobs that year alone. They put the whiff of class warfare in the air as they closed New York's harbor and mounted a general strike in Seattle. More than 367,000 shut down U.S. Steel for four months. Even Boston's police force called a work stoppage. Repression of radicals and labor agitators continued.[22]

Browder, freed between October 1918 and the following July pending his conspiracy conviction's appeal, felt inspired by the Bolsheviks' unprecedented success and rejoined the Socialist party. His choice was a natural response to earthshaking events, not unlike that made by many others of his day. Victory in Russia appealed to the restless young dissenter who had looked for a political home among domestic groups that had made only marginal progress. Lenin's startling triumph provided a focus and optimism Browder had lacked previously, even though reports from the new workers' state remained sketchy. He, colleague James P. Cannon, and others tried to capture Kansas City's branch for its left wing. They began publishing the *Worker's World,* one of America's first pro-Communist papers outside New York. Every week Browder penned editorials endorsing proletarian dictatorship. Plagued by legal problems, the new organ did not survive the year. At one point its entire staff languished in prison. In July Browder, his brother, and Sullivan began their second sentences. Each served sixteen months at Leavenworth Penitentiary. Although leftist publications claimed that prison officials targeted draft resisters for special abuse, Browder's only mistreatment came from the capitalist media.[23]

Outside, the Socialist movement soon split into three organizations. On August 31, 1919, John Reed, Benjamin Gitlow, and eighty other English-speaking leftists formed the Communist Labor party, praising Russian workers' councils and calling the IWW a model for industrial unionism. The next day the foreign-language federations created the Communist party (CP). It was inspired by brilliant young theoretician Louis Fraina, who earlier had denounced the SP right-wing's timid "sausage socialism," led by humorless Charles Ruthenberg. Both new groups (which would soon unite at Soviet insistence, ultimately to become the CPUSA) offered a daring, sweeping critique of American life that grew out of labor, Populist, and Socialist experience.

By age twenty-eight Browder had achieved neither a following nor name recognition. He had done nothing noteworthy. Yet his early years constituted a decisive period. He had suffered, but he had also developed a keen understanding of American radical politics that never deserted him.

## A FOOTLOOSE RADICAL
## BECOMES AN APPARATCHIK

Naturally introverted, Browder rarely discussed personal affairs. He was doggedly reticent about his early, unsuccessful marriage. Longtime party leaders did not even know his wife's name. He had cause for maintaining the mystery. Browder met Gladys L. Groves around 1907, when his parents moved next door to her family. Both youths were about sixteen years old. Near the Browders' back porch stood the Groveses' buggy shed. Whenever Gladys hitched up her family's black mare, Lady, Browder would help her pull out the surrey. Soon it served as an excuse to go riding together frequently. The relationship grew, and in January 1911 they married at a Unitarian minister's parsonage in Independence. A year later they moved to Kansas City, Kansas, where Gladys gave birth to a son, Jay. Between 1912 and 1917 Browder balanced successfully his radical activities and family life; he and Gladys had a happy relationship despite modest circumstances.

During these serene days the youthful, handsome Browder displayed his ready wit. He liked to pass summer evenings outside his cottage playing little ballads on the flute. He also talked about poetry and wrote couplets.[24] Gladys was a kind young woman with a keen sense of humor that lasted a lifetime. She loved Earl deeply and was content to rear a family quietly in the Midwest, far from foreign revolutions. Her contentment concealed extreme vulnerability and emotional dependence on him.

On Earl's apprehension Gladys suffered a nervous breakdown. For years thereafter she experienced epileptic seizures, although occasionally her health permitted her to visit Earl in prison. His incarceration brought her severe financial distress. Lacking his income, she and five-year-old Jay moved in with her father and relocated several times. At one point even Earl's warden conceded that she probably suffered more than Earl. Gladys underwent more misfortune in July 1922 when an automobile accident killed her father.[25]

Browder entered Leavenworth Penitentiary on July 14, 1919, exactly two weeks before famed IWW idol and war resister Haywood, whom Browder termed a "hulking one-eyed monolith of a man," secured release. Several factors combined to make possible their contact. At the time the national law's rapidly expanding scope, the paucity of federal facilities, a low level of prison science, and dire underfunding caused severe overcrowding to be the norm. The modern practice of isolating new prisoners had not become standard. In 1919 arriving inmates faced a virtual next-available-bed policy; generally they received little more than a shower, uniform, rule book, and cell. Several times Browder played chess with Haywood, praising him and trying to start political conversations. The latter found Browder irritating and remained silent. Browder believed he got subsequent matches only because Leavenworth had few competent chess players.[26] Prison caused two fundamental changes in Browder's personality: one negative and temporary, the other positive and permanent.

First the grim stone environment, atop Browder's embitterment over reincarceration, produced a burning anger. His earlier commitment to Bolshevism had been intellectual and optimistic; by contrast Leavenworth instilled a resentment so fierce that the cause soon outweighed and distorted every other aspect of his life. He did not outgrow this mindset for several years. Browder, not known for understatement, termed Leavenworth a "tough place." It contrasted ferociously with the Platte County jail. Instead of the easy-going Mr. Vestal's boarding house, Browder now faced the strictest military regimentation, featuring twenty-four-hour guard surveillance. Leavenworth, normally home to five hundred convicts by the twentieth-century's end, housed two thousand inmates in huge bird-cage cell blocks five tiers high. Daily the men rose to a loud bell and silently marched in line everywhere: to breakfast in a massive dining room; to assigned workplaces; to lunch; to their cells; and later to dinner. They stood at attention four times a day while they were being counted and relaxed only during interminable lock-up hours.

They had rights merely to bread and water in an isolation cell's total darkness. Anything more constituted a privilege, revocable at the slightest infraction. Spirited prisoners worked in rough labor gangs; less grueling assignments awaited those whose attitudes improved. Leavenworth housed more than one hundred IWW members who opposed the war but espoused revolutionary violence. For them, noncooperation was a matter of honor. They endured backbreaking drudgery until their sentences ended. By contrast, the Browders, skilled office workers, offered no resistance whatever.[27]

Accordingly, Leavenworth hardly meant sixteen months of unabated agony. As the resourceful Browder later admitted, "For a year my 'work' was participation in the prison band and orchestra, which gave me unusual freedom and at least four extra hours a day for study and reading." The regulation that rigidly enforced silence allowed him to indulge totally his passion for self-education. Browder possessed a layman's knowledge of Christian theological controversies. He convinced the prison chaplain, who controlled the library, to allow him to receive books from outside to expand his understanding of religion and economics. The clergyman gave him carte blanche for tomes from "respectable" institutions. Having planned ahead, Browder had contacts at the Kansas City Public Library. A friend, Ralph Cheyney, whose father taught at the University of Pennsylvania, also offered help. So did Professor John C. Kennedy, a University of Chicago economist and Socialist alderman. According to Browder, the scheme enabled him to read "all the works of Marx and Engels available in English"; few translations of Lenin existed.[28]

Browder did not prove a happy student, however. Time weighed heavily. Exciting events filled the newspapers. John Reed's eyewitness account, *Ten Days That Shook the World,* gave Bolshevism a mystique to Americans. Two Communist parties seceded from the Socialists in late summer 1919. Isolated from U.S. masses, both sought proletarian dictatorship through armed uprisings when conditions ripened. Even the "reformist" SP, unwilling to work for these goals, applied for Third International membership with reservations and endorsed industrial unionism.

In January 1920 Attorney General A. Mitchell Palmer, an unannounced presidential candidate, responded to revolution's specter. After terrorist bombs killed three dozen and a mailed package addressed to him exploded and maimed his maid, he raided homes, union headquarters, and meeting halls. He arrested four thousand, holding many incommunicado for days, and ordered one thousand deported. A wave of xenophobia swept the land and encouraged vigilante attacks on IWW members, foreign-language clubs, and all things radical.

That same month the Comintern sent its first instructions to American Communists, setting an important precedent. It ordered both parties underground before the government could rule them illegal. In May Moscow forced them to amalgamate, producing the United Communist party, under power-hungry Charles Ruthenberg. In August the International issued twenty-one conditions for affiliation, effectively tying each member party to Soviet orders. From Atlanta Penitentiary Debs ran his final White House campaign. Although he polled an unprecedented 920,000 votes, the electorate had doubled because the recently passed Nineteenth Amendment had opened voting to women. Just days later the Third International rejected the SP's application.

Browder's parole date finally arrived on November 5, 1920. He emerged a twenty-nine-year-old enthusiast, seeking to devote all his time to promoting Leninism. Accompanying his zeal was an ability to rationalize. He concluded that his "jailbird" reputation doomed him to unemployment in Kansas and decided to move to a city with a big Communist movement. He tried to persuade Gladys to relocate. She, however, had spent her whole life in the state and wanted to remain near her relatives. Caught between his cause and his family, Browder chose the former.[29]

Callously he abandoned his wife and son and set off for New York. He used the excuse that Gladys was an invalid, thereby revealing brutal insensitivity. (Ironically she eventually recovered and outlived him.) She last saw Earl when he paid her a brief visit in 1924. Two years later he wrote a letter asking her to obtain a divorce. She did not do so until 1959, when she needed to be single to inherit her mother's property. For at least twenty years, however, Browder voluntarily paid her a relatively generous $50 monthly alimony through a Manhattan attorney.[30] By contrast, a number of CP cadres, including his brother-in-law Harrison George, abandoned families and paid nothing. Far more Communists, however (especially ethnic members), used extended kinship networks as a source of protection in a brutally competitive economy.

Leavenworth Penitentiary altered Browder's life in a second, more profound manner. Unlike the Platte County jail, it taught him the self-discipline necessary to champion a highly unpopular cause. Although he

William Browder, Sr., and Earl after the latter's
release from Leavenworth Penitentiary in 1920.
(Courtesy of *People's Weekly World*. Used by permission.)

was probably more interesting when youthful and fickle, Browder did
not display the traits necessary to persevere as an American Communist.
If prison killed the restless free spirit in him, it also gave birth to a more
robust, mature radicalism. The experience proved to Browder that he
could suffer enormously for the cause and persevere. Obsessed with a desire to strike back, he easily made the transition to being single and did
not miss his wife and son. Until his anger subsided, the revolution was
his work, his hobby, his mistress.

The early 1920s saw a sharp economic downturn, court decisions that

voided protective legislation for women and children, and private industry's "American Plan," a union-busting offensive. Samuel Gompers and
other AFL leaders became fearful and, as labor historian James R. Green
has noted, cautioned conservatism, preached anti-Communism, and
hoped progressives in government would protect collective bargaining
rights. Liberals, including philosopher John Dewey and economist Stuart
Chase, still hailed the Soviet Union as an industrial model. The *New York
Times*'s and the *Nation*'s correspondents Walter Duranty and Louis Fis-
cher praised the new society regularly. Most Socialists did not reject the
USSR, merely its predictions of uprisings in the United States. In North
Dakota, A. C. Townley built the Nonpartisan League and sold socialistic
ideas to Great Plains farmers: state-owned flour mills and grain eleva-
tors, hail insurance, and rural credit banks. The league's greatest innovation, capturing the traditionally dominant Republican party by bloc
voting in the direct primary, sent Lynn Frazier to the state house. Its success stimulated the Farmer-Labor and Progressive parties.[31]

In New York Browder soon met another Leavenworth veteran, now a
Communist (never identified by Browder), who offered to establish connections with the party underground. The enterprising Browder, despite
his felony convictions and a sharp postwar recession, had already found
employment. Indeed, he later declared, "It took me longer to find the
party than to get a job," a head bookkeeper's position at a Broadway
wholesale import-export company. Supervising twelve ledger clerks and
two cashiers, he received an excellent salary. In January 1921 the United
Communist party admitted him as a charter member, although in prison
he had missed the founding conventions.[32]

Browder's timing could not have been better. International Communism had recently undergone its first historic change of line. By 1920, V. I.
Lenin realized that, except in Russia, the world revolution had failed.
Abandoning extremist tactics, that spring he published *Left Wing Communism: An Infantile Disorder.* It demanded above-ground parties, rejected
syndicalism, and ordered members to infiltrate existing trade unions. Although the edict bewildered left-wing leaders and culture radicals such
as Haywood and Reed, it created an ideal situation for Browder. During
his incarceration, Communists had refused to deal with the AFL, instead
setting up competing or "dual" unions, a policy Browder opposed. A
translation arrived in January 1921. Chagrined, United Communist
party members found they had to bridge a chasm of ill-will separating
them from organized labor.[33]

Many Communists had come from the IWW or other revolutionary unions. One figure, James P. Cannon, concluded that Browder possessed more AFL experience than any other member. Cannon handed him a copy of *Left Wing Communism*. Browder considered the new strategy clever and welcomed it. Soon Cannon offered to introduce him to the leadership, and Browder leaped at the opportunity.[34]

By another coincidence, three representatives of American Communist factions in Moscow, Sen Katayama, Charles E. Scott, and Louis Fraina, were visiting the United States to recruit a delegation for the first Congress of the Red International of Labor Unions (RILU). Also known by the Russian abbreviation Profintern, the RILU began operations that July. Subordinate to the Comintern, it already had its own staff, funds, and networks in foreign countries.[35]

Liking Browder's midwestern and AFL background, the visitors asked him to join American representatives to the gathering as a delegate from Kansas's left-wing miners. Immediately Browder quit his job, although he had hoped to pay off moving debts. A convert given first recognition, he darted about the country enlisting delegates that had union support. Significantly all were genuine labor activists rather than professional revolutionaries, offering the movement a growth opportunity. Organizing this project did not make him America's top Communist, but it signaled his arrival to the second stratum of leaders.[36]

Steaming across the Atlantic Ocean aboard the Scandinavian liner *Oscar II*, Browder again encountered Haywood, freed from Leavenworth pending appeals shortly after Browder had arrived. He got to know his old hero under dubious circumstances. Haywood, long a symbol of militant working-class integrity, feared that more prison would kill him. Deserting his IWW comrades and other jailed radicals, he had jumped bail and was fleeing to the USSR. Browder's unqualified admiration now dimmed into ambiguity. He could not help thinking of the demoralized supporters who had put up funds and the declining cause Haywood had deserted. This was not the way people were supposed to become Communists.[37]

Browder's trip initiated a dangerous practice. Until the 1930s the State Department refused to grant passports to known Communists. Therefore, they attended international meetings on borrowed or fraudulent documents. Browder used the papers of Nicholas Dozenberg, a particularly unfortunate choice as he would later learn. The secretive Browder remained ready to flout laws to promote the cause.[38]

A provincial arriving in Moscow, he quickly caught the day's growing optimism. Despite widespread famine and military reverses, the Bolshe-

viks were nevertheless defeating a coalition of foreign and domestic opponents in the Russian civil war. The Soviets he met overwhelmed
him with their friendliness, education, and intellectual sophistication.
Their respectful attention, despite his lack of formal schooling and modest achievements, intoxicated him. Believing he now stood at a new
epoch's threshold, he felt he had come a long way from obscure begin-
nings.

The Moscow experience convinced Browder that his career move had
been a correct one. Eight years earlier as an accountant by day and radical
dilettante by night, he had enjoyed a material existence far more comfortable than he had ever known in childhood. Now, however, he had the
opportunity to play a role in helping remake the world. Instead of protesting feebly against capitalism, he could hasten its destruction.

The trip to Russia had another important result. Browder had invited
his old Syndicalist League associate William Z. Foster to come along as
an observer. During World War I Foster had helped bring Chicago's
packing-house workers' union a 1,000 percent membership growth and
an eight-hour day. He had also led 1919's unsuccessful Great Steel Strike
and had become America's leading left-wing unionist. His Trade Union
Educational League (TUEL) sought, as labor historian Harvey A. Levenstein has noted, "to stimulate militant, radical industrial unionism within existing unions." Foster now decided to become a Communist, and his
Chicago-based TUEL was soon the Profintern's American section. The
TUEL had, since its creation a year earlier, attempted to bore from within
the AFL, which had been losing members and represented mostly skilled
workers in only a few industries. With Moscow's financial backing, the
TUEL could now expect some success. Indeed, its power soon rivaled that
of Charles Ruthenberg's Communist political leadership in New York.
According to Levenstein, Foster's attitudes "shaped much of the Communist labor union work until 1929 and after 1935."[39]

Foster entered on his own terms; Browder became his assistant. Employing characteristic hyperbole, the latter tried to convince Lenin that
Foster led the AFL's left wing. He told Trotsky that 1919's strikes, where
Foster had played a major role, educated American workers far better
than anything the two Communist parties had done. At home Browder
edited the TUEL's paper, the *Labor Herald,* and served as liaison between
the CP's Chicago and New York factions. Although recognized as very
efficient, he of course came to resent being considered Foster's "man Fri-
day." Browder especially loathed Foster's anti-intellectualism. Working
under Foster taxed his self-restraint greatly. Foster's imperious attitude

increased the friction. James P. Cannon, by then a friend of neither, noted how Foster flattered those whom he needed and abused those who needed him. Browder accumulated many resentments. Yet Browder's first Moscow visit also initiated a long, auspicious friendship. Profintern head Solomon A. Lozovsky took a fancy to him. Without any particular effort, Browder developed an advantageous association Foster never enjoyed.[40]

The era 1922 to 1929 did not invite political activism. Much of the nation enjoyed unprecedented prosperity. Scientific management streamlined factories but increased exponentially the intensity of most jobs and eliminated many forms of shop-floor independence. Henry Ford perfected his assembly line; by late 1925 a new car emerged every ten seconds. Record productivity made possible welfare capitalism, replacing open suppression with relatively high pay and benefits designed to win workers' loyalty: recreational facilities, athletic teams, insurance plans, and stock purchase options. Four hundred firms maintained employer-dominated "company unions" to give workers the illusion of representation.

America's affluence was uneven, however. Depressed industries abounded. Workers in brewing, textiles, coal, and the needle trades faced desperation. Mechanization devastated entire crafts such as glassblowing. Timid, unimaginative William Green, who became AFL president in 1924, told unions to help make management policies "efficient." In the labor field the Communists missed many opportunities to grow.

As frequently happens during times of rapid change, race relations worsened badly. The Ku Klux Klan became a national movement, centered in the midwest. Its targets moved beyond African Americans to include Roman Catholics and Jews, and it supported the "American Plan," the employers' open-shop drive. The Eighteenth Amendment made Prohibition the law of the land and represented a blow at all things urban. The immigration restriction acts of 1921 and 1924 virtually closed the nation's gates to southern and eastern Europeans and signaled that industry would rely thereafter on black and white migrants from rural America as well as Mexicans.

During the 1920s dissent usually took social avenues. Young women imitated Clara Bow, the seductive red-haired silent film queen. Men found ways to purchase alcohol illegally. A "lost generation" of writers voiced its social alienation through cultural criticism. Believing prosperity permanent, artists decried the pursuit of wealth as meretricious.

A malaise settled on the left. Max Eastman visited the USSR, was well received, and was even befriended by civil war hero Leon Trotsky, Lenin's

presumptive heir. Eastman's confidence in the revolution ebbed nevertheless. John Reed, also disillusioned in Russia, died there before he could
make an open break. Anarchists Emma Goldman and Alexander Berk-
man, once devout supporters, looked on aghast as the Bolshevik government gunned down mutinous sailors at Kronstadt. On Lenin's death in
1924 Joseph Stalin, backed by a hoard of apparatchiks (Communist party
careerist bureaucrats), attacked leadership rivals. Trotsky gave Eastman
important documents and urged him to leave the country and tell the
world of the Soviet power struggle. The papers included Lenin's final
"Testament," dictated from his deathbed. It endorsed Trotsky, terming
Stalin too "rude" to hold even his current post as general secretary. Eastman published them in 1925. Historian John Patrick Diggins contends
that "Trotsky's subsequent failure to act upon those revelations and the
defeat of the opposition in Russia made the Stalinization of American
Communism a certainty."[41] By mid-decade many Socialists were openly
questioning Soviet human rights violations while defending the Soviet
Union's right to exist. Debs died. Former Presbyterian minister Norman
Thomas replaced him. He put forth a program of traditional progressive
reforms and a pacifism linking war to economic injustice, yet only intellectuals listened.

Historian Edward P. Johanningsmeier has observed that "To workers
confronted with the tribunes of modernity on the shop floor," the TUEL
offered the prospect of a stronger, more militant industrial unionism and
an end to "class collaboration." Foster began the campaign among railroad unions. Assisting him, Browder acted as if his position were an apprenticeship and seemed the model bureaucrat. Between 1922 and 1926
Foster considered him a reliable executive. A seemingly faceless organization man, Browder took on any task assigned him and, though learning, remained greatly underrated.[42] Always introverted, he became what
a later generation would label a "workaholic"—driven, compulsive overachiever who never seemed to tire. Throughout his life this trait receded
at times but always returned with new vigor.

During the mid-1920s Browder was very busy. He spent long hours behind the scenes writing and editing for the *Labor Herald*, maintained contact between Foster and the New York Communists, and was involved in
CP efforts to build a labor party in America. In short Browder did the
mundane, detailed work that Foster happily delegated to him.

As did most Chicago-based "trade union Communists," Browder
sought to liquidate the party's underground, a relic of the Palmer Raids.
He also worked to get Communists accepted into a broad-based, reform-

oriented Farmer-Labor party for national elections of 1924. The Communists enjoyed greatest success in the AFL's Chicago Federation of Labor, where they gained one-fifth of the seats. Working closely with its dominant personality, John Fitzpatrick, who admired Foster, the TUEL exercised considerable influence and enjoyed relative immunity from attack by Samuel Gompers and AFL conservatives. Browder tried to hold his comrades to an agreement not to dominate this effort, but he could not control his party's New York faction. Led by Comintern agent John Pepper, the CP flooded the Farmer-Labor party's 1923 convention with disguised delegates from paper organizations, thereby capturing control and creating a new Federated Farmer-Labor party under Communist leadership. Embittered, Fitzpatrick turned the Chicago Federation against the TUEL. Quickly thereafter the AFL banned TUEL membership, destroying the only Communist organization that had substantial labor movement influence. Despite the fiasco, Foster refused to speak out. At a CP leadership meeting, however, Browder boldly seized the microphone before the scheduled Pepper could reach the rostrum. He decried the split and proposed sending Pepper back to Europe. Browder's rashness hurt his standing badly; he received no invitation to the national convention that year.[43]

Another political disaster occurred in 1924. The domestic Communists tried to salvage a third-party movement by supporting the presidential campaign of Robert La Follette, an uncompromising progressive with a national following. When their delegation went to Moscow for an April–May plenum, however, it found itself swept up in Soviet politics. Lenin had died in January, and a succession struggle featured a troika of Gregory Zinoviev, Lev Kamenev, and Joseph Stalin opposing Leon Trotsky. The latter took a militant revolutionary stance and termed his opponents opportunists, singling out in particular their backing of American Communist participation in La Follette's campaign. Zinoviev tried to refute the charge by ordering a break with La Follette forces. A disappointed Foster brought the news back to the United States on June 1, only to find that La Follette had already learned of the Moscow decision and denounced the Communists on May 28. The change of line cost them their few remaining farmer-labor supporters.

Browder played no important role in that year's events; indeed he seemed destined to remain an apparatchik permanently. The years 1924 and 1925 proved the low point in his career. Compensating, he came to value Communist women as much as the Communist party. Past thirty,

Browder nevertheless retained his youthful good looks and sinewy build. Although most Leninists donned leather jackets to project a proletarian image, he continued to wear middle America's three-piece suit. His clean-cut, if rumpled, appearance contrasted sharply with that of his rougher comrades. Standing five feet seven inches tall and possessing sparkling azure eyes, he maintained his easy-going demeanor.[44] Women found him very attractive. By 1924 he had become such a playboy that rivals claimed that he enjoyed liaisons with Ella Reeve "Mother" Bloor, a friend twenty-eight years his senior.

When Browder did attend to his duties, he displayed his faith in revolution's inevitability. He churned out dreary editorials for the *Workers' Monthly*, which replaced the *Labor Herald* that November and later became the *Communist*.[45] Had his life continued this way, it would hold no historical interest whatever.

## AN OVERSEAS CONNECTION

A dramatic, unexpected turning point in Browder's life occurred in 1926. Soon international intrigue replaced his mundane routine as Foster's assistant. Browder met Communists of virtually every nationality. He traveled third class on Third World passenger trains and crossed oceans on tramp steamers. He consumed unwholesome food and slept on floors with the world's poorest people. Frequently he sat awake staring into the night, fearing armed violence.[46] Facing death transformed him from an unpolished party clerk into a respected Comintern veteran. It built up political IOUs in an organization that valued loyalty and service above all else save ideological correctness.

These hard, exciting growth years began unexpectedly in January. Earlier Foster had gone to Moscow to seek Comintern arbitration between the New York and Chicago factions. He cabled home, demanding his lieutenant's assistance. Browder arrived for the American commission's final session, also attended by Joseph Stalin, whom he had not yet met.[47]

Browder later claimed he had heard rumors of an impending Comintern policy shift. Therefore he tried to maintain a discreet silence throughout the discussions. At one point Stalin, who spoke no English, suddenly turned toward Browder and asked his opinion. As Browder listened to the translation, Foster, smelling victory, poked his ribs, frantically urging him to second their faction's position. Unsure which way to lean, the cautious Browder stood up and stuttered that his recent arrival left him unprepared to speak. This assertion of independence enraged Foster.[48]

The meeting proved the most important of Browder's life. He later declared, "From that evening I became a pupil of Stalin."[49] He added this devotion to his Great Plains radicalism, and they became the two pillars of his value system. He never considered that they might possibly clash. Thenceforth he followed the Soviet general secretary blindly, a highly rewarding move.

Why did Browder become and remain a self-proclaimed Stalinist? He never answered the question directly. Certainly he admired toughness and later contended he had predicted Stalin's victory over all Soviet rivals. In at least one way Browder's 1926 decision resembled his earlier endorsement of the Bolsheviks: he wanted to back an anticapitalist winner. To Browder ideology was not the most significant difference between Socialists and Communists. The latter controlled one-sixth of the earth's surface.

During the 1920s and 1930s Browder always did well in Moscow. No doubt having friends such as Lozovsky in high places helped him. But Browder was also a keen observer and a good listener. By now he was developing the quintessential Soviet survival skills: a strong intuitive grasp and the ability to anticipate changes in Russian politics. Browder manifested enough cynicism of his own to admire that of one of cynicism's greatest masters, Joseph Stalin.

This foreign loyalty also represented a way to begin building a political identity separate from that of Foster. Doubtlessly overseas adventure and the chance for glory were more appealing than enduring Foster's condescension on a daily basis. Still, Browder's decision was not totally unprincipled. During the 1920s Stalin, who had not yet killed millions of people, seemed more moderate than Trotsky. His position appeared more in accord with Lenin's *Left Wing Communism*, which had most inspired Browder.

Browder's conversion finalized his transformation, long in the making, from revolutionary to careerist. From 1926 on he identified the future of American Communism with the future of Earl Browder, much as the Soviet leader identified that of world Marxism with his own. Browder's new allegiance brought no immediate acknowledgment, however. Stalin disliked Communists who hedged, although he himself had refused to give Lenin military prognostications during the Russian civil war. He never again asked Browder to speak, much less meet with him.[50] The dictator's cold shoulder did not dampen Browder's enthusiasm, however.

After Browder's insubordination Foster had little desire to bring him home. He left him there to guard the Chicago faction's interests as America's Profintern delegate. Foster hoped to regain his loyalty eventually.

In Moscow Browder's good looks and fondness for women paid a considerable dividend. No longer 1921's awestruck country boy, Browder, now age thirty-five and well dressed, mingled comfortably in high-level Soviet circles. He quickly attracted the attention of a Profintern bureaucrat, Raissa Luganovskaya.

Luganovskaya, a flaxen-haired, hazel-eyed legal scholar who had been divorced less than two years, met Browder at a government social function. They became intimate quickly, and she also found his thirst for knowledge attractive. Thirty-one and pretty, she had an inner strength that fascinated him. Born into a Jewish white-collar family named Berkmann in the town of Marijampole (later Kapsukas) near the Baltic Sea, she, like Browder, had suffered grinding poverty. Her German father, Boris, had held a sales position in a small trading company. He did not do well, and her mother, Bertha, divorced him. At age two Raissa and three siblings were moved to their paternal grandparents' humble village on the Prussian border. Later their mother took all of them; Boris responded by sending money only irregularly. Raissa worked her way through the gymnasium (secondary school) by typing and tutoring in French and German. After graduating she sold the gold medal her talents had earned and went to St. Petersburg to study jurisprudence.

There in 1912 the seventeen-year-old Berkmann encountered the revolutionary movement. She became attracted to a Bolshevik veteran, a baker named Luganovsky, who helped edit the illegal newspaper *Pravda*. Within two years they had married; she became Luganovskaya (the name's feminine form) and accompanied him to Kharkov, a Ukrainian city where the czar's police had exiled him. Germany had invaded Russia in 1914. Soldiers suffered battlefield defeats, and civilians endured food shortages. Luganovskaya's academic career limped as she combined studying with working to survive. Still, she passed her graduation examinations in St. Petersburg in 1917 and joined the Communist party just weeks before the monarchy's collapse on March 15. Under the new provisional government the Bolsheviks were now legal but not part of the ruling coalition.

Luganovskaya did well in a proletarian party that had few lawyers. By

May she belonged to its Kharkov city committee, conducting agitation and propaganda (agitprop) efforts among youth and women. When the Communists seized power in November she organized sanitation detachments of women and men in different Red Guard companies. That winter, as the German army approached, she and her organization retreated to Moscow. There Luganovskaya did cultural service work for the army until it retook Kharkov.

Germany's surrender to the Western Allies in November 1918 did not bring peace. The Communists' opponents formed the White Army, launched a full-scale civil war, and ultimately received aid from troops of fourteen countries. Luganovskaya found herself appointed local commissar of justice. Despite her youth, she supervised Leninist judges known for their harshness. Later that year General A. I. Denikin's Whites captured the city. As the Bolsheviks retreated, Luganovskaya received "extraordinary powers," including that of ordering summary executions. There is no direct evidence that she ever decreed anyone's death, but civil wars do not encourage restraint. By 1919 she was in Moscow, a member of the People's Commissariat of Justice. Here her inexperience began to show, and her upward mobility ceased.

In 1920 as the Red Army approached victory, the Moscow party leadership had her teach a six-month jurisprudence course at Sverdlosk University to provide court workers for the new regime. Thereafter, her career took on a more clearly political nature. For the next two years she directed agitprop work in the capital. From 1922 until 1924, when she divorced her husband (but retained his name), she represented the Moscow Soviet in the struggle against the worst famine before Stalin's dictatorship. Lenin's food-requisitioning policies caused five million to die of starvation in the countryside. When Browder met Luganovskaya, she was serving as a secretary to the Profintern's executive committee. Although she became pregnant, they did not wed.[51]

Luganovskaya, known in RILU circles as a climber according to Communist youth leader Sam Darcy, pestered Solomon Lozovsky to give Browder a career break.[52] The Profintern chief, who already liked him, quickly found a suitable challenge. Noting his organizing experience in Kansas City and Chicago, the Soviets asked him to join an international labor commission to civil war–torn China. The Kuomintang, a nationalist party, had begun battling militarily to end warlord rule. By 1927 the Kuomintang itself had split into fighting factions: a right wing under Chiang Kai-shek in Nanking and a left wing under Wang Ching-wei in

Wuhan. Chiang's April 1927 war with the Communists (previously his allies) increased the bloodshed dramatically.

Of course, Browder leaped at the opportunity. Along with veteran British dockworkers' union leader Thomas Mann, Jacques Doriot, a French parliament member who spoke no English, and Sydor Stoler, the delegation's Russian-born secretary and translator, he left Moscow that December. Although Browder had known American poverty intimately, he never forgot some East Asian scenes. In Canton he saw "great heavy carts loaded high with cans bearing the 'Socony' (Standard Oil Co. of New York) label, being pulled through the streets by gangs of men, women, and children—evidently families, starved-looking, gaunt and exhausted, straining with all their might at the ropes—and earning an average of 15 cents each for twelve hours labor, to the greater profit of Standard Oil."[53]

Despite ubiquitous violence, the delegation toured much of the nation. In early 1927 a Pan-Pacific Trade Union Conference met in Hankow. The group entered the city to banners reading "Welcome the Earl of Browder." Chinese comrades thought an English noble had joined the cause. That March the conference created a permanent secretariat located first there and later at Shanghai. An illegal trade union center, it served seven countries and angered right-wing governments. Browder headed it and edited its underground journal, the *Pan-Pacific Monthly*, which circulated widely despite Chinese, Japanese, and Australian efforts to suppress it. He remained in East Asia for most of 1927 and 1928.[54]

As Harvey Klehr, John Haynes, and Fridrikh Firsov have shown, the secretive organization "intermingled overt and covert political organizing with a heavy dose of clandestine practices," justifiably in light of oppressive local conditions. It also eventually gave a significant number of Americans experience in undercover work. Veteran U.S. Communists Jim Dolson and Philip Aronberg, along with younger cadres Eugene Dennis, Steve Nelson, Margaret Undjus, and Undjus's husband, Charles Krumbein, all served the PPTUS at one time or another.[55]

Browder's tasks included creating Communist labor unions and politicizing workers. Wearing shabby clothes, living in a rough, cell-like room, and sleeping on a canvas army cot, he began to feel for the workers' plight. Although he tried to relate local problems to Western parallels, he also faced conditions uniquely Chinese. Corporations employed armed guards to protect their factories and intimidate strikers. In response the peasants' union maintained a militia for every local. Milly Bennett, an

American journalist there, noted how closely Browder monitored the spread of revolutionary ideas. He took special pride when a white-collar union appeared at Changsha. She quoted him as saying, "The bank clerk, the postal clerk, the little merchant has become a revolutionist along with the farmer, the seaman and the rickshawman."[56]

Tom Mann, in his seventies, added an amusing sidebar to Browder's duties. Browder tried to keep him in top condition for the trade union conference and other public functions. This was no small task because Mann loved to consume huge quantities of alcohol. Browder, who did not drink regularly but would not refuse if offered, tried to match him one night. Awakening the next day with a throbbing hangover, he found the aged Mann lying so still that Browder believed he had died in his sleep. Browder learned from the experience, but Mann did not. A few weeks later Bennett took him to Hankow's German beer garden. When they returned an irate Browder, sounding like a Bible Belt populist preacher, made the pedestrian observation that "booze was the downfall of the working class" and that she was ruining Mann.[57]

Amid international machinations, Browder found comfort in romance, even as Luganovskaya was giving birth to his son Felix on July 31, 1927. His partner was Katherine Harrison, a beautiful, young Canadian Comintern agent. Called "Kitty Harris," she stood five feet three inches tall and had thick brown hair. Her motives may have had as much to do with opportunism as attraction to Browder or even dedication to Marxism-Leninism. Sam Darcy, a friendly acquaintance of her two brothers, contended she was merely a poor working-class young woman seizing her first opportunity to travel overseas. She went as Browder's secretary, using a bogus American passport. She had joined the CPUSA in 1923 and was granted a transfer to the Soviet party, a special privilege, in 1927. They cohabitated in Shanghai the following year. Browder was always most secretive about Harrison, possibly because the affair disappointed him.[58]

One day as Harrison strolled down the Bund in Shanghai, she ran into Darcy and his wife Emma, whom she had known in Chicago. He, as a Young Communist International Executive Committee member, was traveling from Moscow to the Philippines to unite quarreling factions there. Harrison explained she was living in the French concession with Browder and invited them over for dinner. At one point Harrison told him she was unhappy because Browder allegedly wanted her to do things she did not do. Darcy did not ask and never discovered what they were. Eventually Harrison had other reasons to regret the China adventure.

Browder with Tom Mann in China, late 1920s.
This is the only known photo of Browder in China.
(Courtesy of *People's Weekly World*. Used by permission.)

She may have been too immature for clandestine activities. Historians Klehr, Haynes, and Firsov have shown that she disregarded orders of Comintern superiors to vacate her residence, even though a local detective had begun watching it regularly and asking neighbors questions about Browder. Soon the Shanghai Municipal Police alerted the U.S. Office of Naval Intelligence about her. She returned to the United States in January 1929. When she tried to renew her travel papers in 1932, the Bureau of Immigration denied her application and eventually deported her to Canada, where she disappeared.[59]

Kuomintang agents made a similar report about Browder. The ONI told the FBI he had arrived from Manila on October 11, 1928, carrying a passport in the name of George Morris. As soon as the paperwork reached the FBI, J. Edgar Hoover ordered New York City agents to investigate. By midsummer 1929 the director was insisting that "no effort be spared," for the case was one of "greatest importance." On August 31 special agent H. Fink in Cleveland notified William Z. Foster about the bureau's search. Angrily he refused to aid the FBI in any way. Federal sleuths still had not tracked Browder down by the spring of 1930. At that point the assistant U.S. attorney in New York announced that he doubted he possessed jurisdiction to prosecute a passport case involving a journey from the Philippines to China. He added that he also lacked sufficient evidence to convict Browder of obtaining the spurious travel document in Gotham. Therefore, he closed the case. Not illogically, Browder believed the matter ended.[60]

The China years broadened his horizons enormously. For the first time he demonstrated clearly his greatest character strength: the ability to overcome challenges for which he possessed no previous training. His experience and subsequent writings increased his prestige exponentially and aided his rise in the Communist world. Klehr, Haynes, and Firsov have shown that the resourceful Browder even recruited his ex-brother-in-law Harrison George for covert activities. Indeed, unintentionally Browder laid the groundwork for greater things. China proved his dependability to the Soviets. As another future American Communist chief, Eugene Dennis, would do, Browder established himself internationally before becoming widely known at home. By contrast Foster, his most talented and popular rival after 1930, never did Comintern service overseas.[61] China also changed Browder's perspective. Here he began to shed his belief that a catastrophic capitalist system breakdown would inevitably lead the CPUSA to power. Certainly nowhere in the United States had he seen anything resembling East Asian desperation and suffering.

The American Communists, after their third-party debacles of 1923–1924, had turned their emphasis toward the labor field. Despite Moscow's antidual union policy, as historian Bert Cochran has noted, "for the next six to seven years" the CP "resembled the prewar IWW to the extent that it supplied leadership for workers abandoned or ignored by" the AFL. During the mid-1920s the TUEL captured some locals of the International Ladies Garment Workers Union in New York until a 1926 strike ended unfavorably. That same year the Communists, under dynamic twenty-five-year-old Harvard Law School graduate Albert Weisbord, also led a mass walkout by Passaic, New Jersey, textile workers, largely immigrants and 50 percent of whom were women. But that, too, met defeat. Also in 1926 the Communists won their only picket line victory. Behind Ben Gold they captured the Fur Workers Union despite the AFL's desperate opposition.[62]

Typifying the CPUSA's overall history, the crisis that brought Browder to high party rank concerned Soviet events. In December 1927 Russian

CP heads Stalin and Nikolai Bukharin expelled Leon Trotsky. He had championed the left wing as terms were then understood. At the Sixth Comintern Congress in the summer of 1928, Stalin stole Trotsky's thunder through a dramatic left turn, announcing the arrival of the international movement's "Third Period" (in the first, 1919–1921, Communist uprisings in Hungary and Bavaria were unsuccessful; in the second, 1922–1928, capitalist stabilization and Soviet diplomatic gestures toward the West occurred). For the Comintern, the Third Period signified a new round of wars and revolutions. In Russia the line change meant forced agricultural collectivization and industrial speedup. It created a human-made famine that cost millions of lives. It transformed the vague concept of "Socialism in one country" into the brutal reality of unrestrained personal despotism enforced by a police state. Abroad, it predicted a revolutionary upsurge and capitalism's final demise.

In addition, Stalin dusted off an old slogan of social fascism from 1924. He argued that the Social Democrats deliberately sought to betray the revolution, thereby becoming fascism's moderate wing or twin. Accordingly, Communists had to forsake the attempts at ties with Social Democrats (now the main enemy) and set up institutions capable of seizing power in the coming crisis. In the trade union field Communists had to abandon the policy of "boring from within" established labor organizations and form revolutionary or "dual" unions. Quickly the Americans responded by altering the TUEL, which became the Trade Union Unity League (TUUL), to compete with the AFL directly.[63]

Members of the TUUL included the National Miners Union under Pat Toohey, the National Textile Workers Union headed by Albert Weisbord and Ben Gold's Needle Trades Workers Industrial Union. In all the TUUL claimed to represent fifty thousand workers. Like the old IWW, it intervened in spontaneous protests against wage reductions and speedups.[64]

The CPUSA also reacted politically to the Kremlin's power struggle. Jay Lovestone, who had become general secretary when Ruthenberg died in 1927, joined the Foster faction in an anti-Trotsky heresy hunt. On October 27, 1928, they expelled Foster's factional allies James Cannon and Max Shachtman, who led a group that supported Trotsky's views.

Meanwhile in Moscow Stalin, clever and power-hungry, persuaded his ally Bukharin to declare that the greatest danger now lay in the Comintern's right wing. Then he identified Bukharin, who saw capitalism as growing stronger temporarily, as a right-wing Communist. His ouster followed quickly. Lovestone, a friend of Bukharin, found himself vulnerable as well. Though Lovestone is often associated with American exceptionalism, he never really ascribed to its tenets, as Harvey Klehr and John Haynes have shown. Lovestone did not believe America's lack of a feudal past, quick achievement of representative government, and wealth of national resources exempted it from Marxist historical principles. He did, however, criticize those who applied Leninist ideas mechanically to America's peculiar conditions. Clearly, his days and those of his closest associates Bertram Wolfe and Benjamin Gitlow were now numbered. Although Foster chaired the CPUSA's opposition faction, he would not replace Lovestone. Having spent most of his life opposing dual unionism, he accepted Stalin's new edict on labor policy but did not denounce his own earlier views. Though the Soviet struggle had no relation to American proletarian concerns, those involved considered it a life-and-death battle.[65]

Other Communists were in genuine mortal danger by April. Textile workers in Gastonia, North Carolina, walked off their jobs as part of a larger revolt that swept the Southern Piedmont company towns in 1928–1929. Historian Cochran has estimated that "it generally took three wage earners in a-family to piece together a subsistence wage." Nevertheless, company officials cut pay and required workers to operate more machines. The National Textile Workers Union sent in Communist reinforcements from the north, and they quickly "met the full fury of a semi-police state." Vigilante and National Guard violence culminated in a pitched armed battle with strikers, in which the police chief was killed. The strike was subsequently crushed, fifteen union leaders tried for murder, and lengthy sentences meted out. Did the specter of Red unionism prompt such violence? Cochran argues persuasively that "to the Gastonia elite [the] prime provocation was not the incidental mouthings of Communist hotheads, but their presence and intention to set up a union of textile workers." Certainly Gastonia proved that in some cases the CPUSA could play a leadership role, even among poor southern whites with conservative social views.[66]

That year Browder emerged as a dark horse candidate for party leadership. While overseas, he had begun to understand the Communist movement in global terms. Of significance, he had supported Stalin before Trotsky and Bukharin had been crushed. Isolated from American factional strife and provincialism, he had also come to view himself as an independent CPUSA force. Seeking to establish a political identity loyal to Stalin, Browder championed the new dual union policy, although it contradicted his previous sympathies. At the Sixth World Congress that

July, he joined other erstwhile followers in a vicious assault on Foster's foot dragging.

## PROMOTIONS AT HOME

Browder returned to the United States in January 1929, bringing Luganovskaya and Felix for their first visits. Like Stalin, Browder stood neither "right" nor "left," but could move in any direction circumstances dictated. Immediately he made himself an uncompromising enemy of everything associated with the CPUSA's right wing. On May 17 the Executive Committee of the Communist International (ECCI) ordered Lovestone's removal and the demotion of all unrepentant followers. This, plus the earlier purge of Trotskyists, depleted the party's top ranks. Stalin had become violently critical of American factional struggles, publicly denouncing Foster and several others. Now he sought to weld together a monolithic party loyal only to the Kremlin. The Comintern created a five-person secretariat to run the CPUSA. It included Foster, ECCI representative Boris Mikhailov (American party name G. Williams), William W. Weinstone, Robert Minor, and Max Bedacht. Weinstone was an acerbic young intellectual; Minor was a burly, pompous figure who boasted of his days as a YMCA boxer; and Bedacht was bland and unoffensive. Mikhailov named Bedacht "acting secretary" as a reward for betraying the Lovestone faction, to which he had belonged.[67]

That August Browder attended the Pan-Pacific Trade Union Secretariat's final congress at Vladivostok. In October, shortly after his return, the International reorganized the CPUSA leadership again. Now, for the first time, Moscow propelled Browder upward. Profintern head Lozovsky began telling Americans Browder would make the best general secretary, and Mikhailov offered to boost his candidacy. Foster, in Stalin's doghouse, supported the motion as his own prospects dimmed. Believing his former lieutenant could be easily dominated proved one of Foster's gravest political errors. Browder, however, declined the honor charily. Not feeling completely ready for the office, he sought time to grow and, most important, wanted to wait for the CPUSA's internal condition to stabilize.[68]

Lacking a consensus, the party's October plenum retained Bedacht and Minor as acting secretary and *Daily Worker* editor, respectively. It dropped Foster and Weinstone, designating the latter as Moscow-based

Comintern representative. The party quietly placed Browder on its new ruling triumvirate, heading agitprop. As such, he wrote most of the *Daily Worker*'s political articles and editorials. The turnover atop the CP, now reaching comic proportions, so embarrassed party chiefs that they hid it from the public and general membership.[69]

Stalin's new line gave Communists an optimism no other American leftist group possessed. They alone believed capitalism's collapse to be imminent. Liberals and Socialists displayed little vigor as the decade's prosperity continued. The Trotskyists, a small sect, quarreled over tactics. Publishing the *Militant*, they formed the Communist League of America, Left Opposition. Insisting they were still a CP faction, they sought to correct the party's views. Yet many members would soon leave to promote the struggle outside the CPUSA.

At decade's end Browder found himself among the CPUSA's top leaders, possessing flexibility, untapped executive skills, and boundless ambition. In his new post he was still an inconspicuous party functionary, virtually unknown to the rank and file. Although he stood on center stage, he remained unnoticed because he was an extra. Browder's confidence was growing, but how could he prove he was not just a colorless hack with friends overseas? Having spent so much time outside the United States, could he now deal effectively with intraparty rivals? If so, could he make any personal impact on the international Communist movement?

# TWO

■

# No More Tradition's Chain Shall Bind Us (1930–1933)

Barely days after Earl Browder reached the CPUSA's leadership troika, opportunity knocked for the entire movement. Capitalism's boom-and-bust cycle had worked against all leftists for nearly ten years. Then, in late October 1929, a decline of unprecedented magnitude hit the economy, bringing America's worst crisis since the Civil War.

The Great Depression had numerous causes, including a stock market crash; massive poverty pockets that included agriculture, textiles, coal, and the railroads; the nation's chronically unequal distribution of wealth; and a primitive banking system without federal insurance. When Congress enacted the Hawley-Smoot tariff in 1930 it set off a trade war that contributed to the economic crisis in Europe.

At home, factories cut hours, incomes plummeted, and unemployment grew daily. Because federal welfare programs did not exist, state and municipal relief agencies ran out of funds by early 1932. Hungry men and women filled the cities, and unemployed adolescents began roaming the countryside. Downward mobility increased, and for the first time large numbers of homemakers looked for work outside the family. Most Americans, products of Calvinist culture, internalized their distress rather than blaming the system.

For the left and for Browder, however, the depression seemed anything but depressing. Capitalism had stumbled, and liberals, Socialists, Trotskyist intellectuals, and Communists awaited its collapse with confidence and hope not seen since 1919. A number of liberals did not join a radical party but adopted a vaguely Marxist orientation as the system that had ignored their humanistic concerns teetered precariously. Others praised the USSR's economic achievements but rejected Communist ideology. Socialists enjoyed early election successes and membership growth in 1930 but began to divide into two quarreling factions the following year. A tradition-minded Old Guard, led by Morris Hillquit, Algernon Lee, and others, largely based in the New York needle trades, sought power through the ballot box. A younger group, the Militants, expressed sympathy for the Soviet Union and toyed with nonparliamentary routes to power. Perennial presidential nominee Norman Thomas tried to straddle the two tendencies, but increasingly identified with the Militants despite a generation's age difference. Trotskyist intellectuals, including James Burnham, advocated a nontheoretical type of Marxism in the *Modern Quarterly* and later in the *Partisan Review*. For them the depression vindicated youthful convictions that American culture had rejected during the 1920s.

## THIRD PERIOD MILITANCY

To Communists, a mere seven thousand members, the era proved Joseph Stalin's genius. In 1928 he had predicted the opportunity and identified social-fascist opponents. Accordingly, the CPUSA launched a two-pronged attack on America's political establishment and all likely seekers of proletarian support. It took dissent to the streets and shops through mass demonstrations and strikes. Simultaneously, members violently disrupted rival radicals' meetings.

In February 1930, when few others seemed ready to make unemployment an issue, Browder and the Communist party dramatized it boldly. In four consecutive weeks protesters converged on city halls in Cleveland, Philadelphia, Los Angeles, and New York. Except in Cleveland, police used brutal tactics to disperse them. Then on March 6 Communists held an International Unemployment Day, featuring demonstrations in industrialized nations. Sam Darcy recalled that demands in the United States included social security and weekly grocery bags for hungry families. Aided unwittingly by right-wing newspapers' alarmist accounts, the event drew thousands of peaceful demonstrators in Chicago and Philadelphia. Elsewhere club-swinging, mounted police broke up parades of 1,500 (Milwaukee), 4,000 (Boston), and 75,000 (Detroit). In New York's Union Square, William Foster, Sam Darcy, and Israel Amter told thirty-five thousand people seeking work to take their demands to Mayor Jimmy Walker en masse. The rabid anti-Communist police commissioner, Grover Whalen, nervously offered to escort Foster and a small delegation directly to Walker's office. When Foster and his followers rejected Whalen's proposal, Gotham experienced what historian Irving Bernstein has termed its "worst street riot in generations."[1]

Blood on the pavement made joblessness a front-page problem in urban America. There it remained as President Herbert Hoover's conservative economic dogmas precluded effective relief measures. On July 4 the Communists created a National Council for the Unemployed to demand such measures anyway. Local chapters led rent strikes and fought evictions, using idled workers to break locks and return belongings to victims' apartments. One such action in August 1931 proved fatal; Chicago police fired into a crowd, killing three black Communists. Within hours local party members organized protest demonstrations. A Comintern report claimed that sixty thousand marched at the funeral and that fifty thousand participated in subsequent gatherings.

Attempting to build stable, lasting influence, the party created a series of Unemployed Councils. Led first by the TUUL, these councils later would become organizationally independent under highly talented Herbert Benjamin. By August, the CPUSA offered a specific, generous plan to fight the depression. The program, known as the workers' Unemployment Insurance Bill, demanded direct government payments of not less than $25 per week plus $5 per dependent. A tax on high incomes and accumulated wealth would generate funds for the program. In a land that still had no social security system, the plan made excellent propaganda. A party-led National Campaign Committee for Unemployment Insurance gathered 1.4 million petition signatures, although Congressional leaders refused to receive them.

CPUSA efforts stimulated non-Communist imitators. A party hunger march behind Benjamin brought only fifteen hundred to Washington, D.C., on December 6, 1931. Members were permitted to parade past the Capitol and sing the "Internationale" before leaving. One month later, Father James R. Cox, a Pennsylvania priest, led twelve thousand jobless persons there. He blamed hunger on the nation's bankers and proposed raising $5 billion for public works through taxing the wealthy. Considering Cox a lesser evil, the Senate and a reluctant President Hoover accepted his petitions. Ten days later fifty-five thousand packed Pittsburgh's Forbes Field to hear Cox denounce the Rockefellers, Mellons, and both political parties. His activities prompted a lengthy report by an alarmed Comintern figure who had years of experience working within the American party, J. Peters.[2]

The Communists' labor activities between 1929 and 1932 proved no

James W. Ford, Angelo Herndon, and Earl Browder, 1930s,
unknown locale. (From the Syracuse University Library, Department
of Special Collections, 600 Bird Library. Used by permission.)

less dramatic. They led ten thousand native-born textile workers off their jobs in Lawrence, Massachusetts. Their National Miners Union, under William Z. Foster's personal supervision, directed a western Pennsylvania strike of forty thousand. Other organizers of the National Miners Union stirred up three thousand in Harlan County, Kentucky, one of the nation's poorest and most repressive areas. Indeed, the CPUSA told Moscow that it had led one-third of the stoppages in 1931. Massive police and national guard brutality helped the party politically, but the walkouts failed. Only the Needle Trades Workers Industrial Union enjoyed modest success, but it enrolled a mere fraction of the number of members enjoyed by competing unions.

A March 1932 Michigan auto workers' job action had the greatest impact. In downtown Detroit, the city with America's worst relief crisis, the CPUSA rallied three thousand Ford employees. Demands included rehiring those laid off, a seven-hour day, end of production-line speedup, equal opportunity for African Americans, and free medical care at the Ford hospital. The unarmed Marxists enjoyed a police escort to the city line. At adjoining Dearborn, however, Mayor Clyde M. Ford, a cousin of Henry Ford, denied parade permits. Demonstrators ignored the ban. Authorities fired tear gas and shot their handguns into the crowd. Shocked protesters retreated to an adjoining field, dragging their wounded; lawmen followed. Harry Bennett, company security boss, stepped from his automobile and approached the throng. A chunk of cement struck his head, knocking him unconscious. Thereupon police unloaded machine guns, killing four and wounding fifty others; most demonstrators were shot in the back. The shooting down of John Collins, a *New York Times* photographer, guaranteed maximum publicity.[3]

Far less spectacularly, the CPUSA set up a total of ten industrial unions between 1931 and 1933. Although most were minuscule, some, as historian Harvey A. Levenstein has noted, secured "footholds and organizational experience for Communist unionists who would play a major role in the future" when labor's opportunities improved. The diminutive Furniture Workers Industrial Union provided the foundation for the Congress of Industrial Organization's (CIO) United Furniture Workers. Veterans of the TUUL's Lumber Workers Industrial Union would build the left-wing International Woodworkers Association. New York City's Marine Workers Industrial Union provided cadres who later dominated the National Maritime Union.[4]

The Communists also addressed the nation's most painful issue, race. Three decades before the modern civil rights movement they christened themselves the "Negro party," nominating African American James W. Ford as their vice-presidential candidate in 1932. The CPUSA focused the world's attention on southern injustice. Members rallied behind Angelo Herndon, a black organizer sentenced to eighteen years' imprisonment under a Georgia antebellum insurrection law. He had organized an interracial demonstration of unemployed workers outside an Atlanta courthouse. The party also defended, with a candor that at least once embarrassed Moscow, nine young men sentenced to death for allegedly raping two white women near Scottsboro, Alabama. In addition, the CPUSA pro-

Browder and journalist Seymour Waldman with the "Scottsboro Boys,"
Alabama, 1930s. (From the Syracuse University Library, Department
of Special Collections, 600 Bird Library. Used by permission.)

tested deportations of Mexican laborers. Indeed, as Harvey Klehr and
John Haynes have noted, "Some Americans, looking for ways to protest
against the deepening misery, regarded the Communist party as the only
or the most effective weapon."[5]

Third Period dogma prevented the CPUSA from cooperating with
other radicals, who also sought to end unemployment. Clearly Stalin's
argument that Social Democrats constituted the main enemy had little
relevance to the United States, where no ideology hostile to capitalism
had made even marginal headway. There the industrial world's most conservative labor movement still could not enroll even half of the working class. Until a new direction emerged, the Communists would never
spread their influence much beyond the ranks of the most thoroughly
alienated.

Not satisfied with merely competing, the Communists launched a series of raids on their rivals, attempting to intimidate them and steal their

members. Almost any type of meeting sufficed. On March 2, 1930, the Lovestonites rented Manhattan's Tuxedo Hall to honor C. E. Ruthenberg, former Communist party leader and faction member. CPUSA regulars, considering his memory private property, broke in, smashing doors and windows. Fistfights erupted, and chairs and bricks flew. After police arrived a three-cornered battle ensued. The CP also took over a Union Square gathering of the moribund IWW and numerous Socialist party functions. That autumn they invited universal opprobrium by hailing a vandal who had painted "Vote Communist" on a Fifth Avenue church.[6]

The Comintern took great pains to tutor the New York–based domestic movement. The most direct supervision came through the Anglo-American Secretariat (AAS), a multinational committee that met in Moscow about six times a month to promote Communist activities in English-speaking lands. Not all of its members had mastered the language, but they displayed keen interest and a passion for detail. Israel Amter opened an address with the words "Workers and peasants of Brooklyn," and the International lectured on proper use of the term "farm laborers." It celebrated America's 1932 population decline (departures were outnumbering arrivals) as unprecedented in three hundred years. Patiently using a parade metaphor, the AAS gave instructions on avoiding dangers of left sectarianism and kvostism, which member Sergei Gusev defined as "tailism carried to the highest degree." The former occurred when only a vanguard broke ahead of "historically sleeping" masses, without their support. A comrade Bogdatev had displayed this when he had led a group of armored cars down Petrograd's main street, Nevsky Prospect, four months before 1917's Bolshevik revolution. Kvostism, by contrast, often typified the CPUSA's work. The party did not merely lag "behind the tail of the masses," but had "separated very far from it." Despite all the demonstrations and rapid spread of radicalism, Moscow feared that the Americans' emphasis had shifted from the shops and factories to the unemployed, farmers, and students. The party's contact with these "nonproletarian elements" had indeed grown over the past few years.[7] Jobless millions were not the kind of masses the International wanted most dearly.

## FIRST AMONG EQUALS

The Third Period also featured struggle within the CPUSA leadership. The Communists made a top-level change at their June 1930 convention. "Acting Secretary" Max Bedacht, installed one year earlier on Jay Lovestone's ouster, had proved a poor leader, party membership had stagnated, and the Comintern had indicated its displeasure. Therefore the party dropped him from the secretariat and handed him Browder's agitprop duties. Without informing the public, the convention appointed a new directory. This one, expected to last longer, featured Browder as administrative secretary and William W. Weinstone and William Z. Foster as organizational and trade union secretaries, respectively.

Browder enjoyed temporary command, however, assisted by a Polburo (also called Politburo and Political Committee) and larger Central Committee. Weinstone, courting Soviet favor, also became America's Moscow-based Comintern representative and remained there another thirteen months. Foster spent most of 1930 imprisoned for leading the March 6 unemployment demonstration riot. Factors favoring Browder included his early, unreserved support for Stalin, isolation from American disputes, and well-known dislike of the heretic Lovestone. Defending the old party leadership from foreign attack, Browder promised that the new one would engage in more self-criticism.[8] Despite Browder's impressive title, Moscow had not simply handed him control. The Comintern expected the three to abandon previous factionalism and reinforce one another's loyalty to it alone.

The years 1930 to 1934 were awkward ones for Browder, once again a family man. The era's militancy seemed hostile to his fundamental nature and maturing outlook. Although he advocated revolution publicly, he could not be found anywhere violence took place. Yet, despite his growing moderation, he still typified the kind of personality most successful in the Comintern apparatus. He had a history of following orders and a feel for power, understanding how it worked at every hierarchical level. He hid his emotions; few persons ever saw him display anger. His decision making usually radiated composure.

Browder trod a careful path, evincing more militancy than he really felt. In early 1930 he dismayed the American Civil Liberties Union's Roger Baldwin by defending disruptions of meetings addressed by Victor Chernov, a Russian Social Revolutionary party leader exiled for opposing the Bolsheviks. Baldwin felt particularly perplexed because arrested Communist intruders had requested legal aid. Browder, replying for the secretariat, called Chernov a terrorist, labeled the raids "decidedly healthy," and announced: "We are not in the slightest interested in preserving Mr. Chernov from the angry protests of the workers who attended his meetings." Afterward Baldwin likened the CPUSA to the Ku

Klux Klan; it also sought aid in holding peaceful meetings, despite its "long record of denying" others that right.[9]

Still, within the period's rigid confines, Browder managed subtly to reject militancy. Unlike Foster, he participated in no street battles and spent no time in jail. Physical violence was totally alien to his character. He produced necessary calls for revolt in future or conditional tenses. In high-level meetings extremists advocated direct confrontations to provoke police overreaction. Browder later insisted he had opposed the tactic behind closed doors. Publicly he urged protesters not to demand seizures of city halls.[10]

Some evidence supports Browder's contention. On January 6, 1930, police gunned down Steve Katovis, a union picket. When Katovis died, Sam Darcy, a Browder opponent, organized a funeral procession that stretched from Manhattan's Union Square to the Fifty-ninth Street bridge several miles away. Subsequently, Browder hauled Darcy before the Polburo, demanding to know if he planned to kick up such a fuss every time a worker was shot. In the economic crisis many people would die; it was adventurism for Darcy to be doing this.[11]

The troika members' dispositions virtually guaranteed strife. Browder's unexpected appointment quickly swelled his personal ambitions. The unassuming apparatchik of the 1920s began to display a lust for power and startling tactical skills. The forty-nine-year-old Foster considered his former lieutenant's appointment a grievous affront. He saw Browder as a good administrator who had no leadership qualities; he always had to be led and could be. Ever afterward Foster considered him an interloper. Browder felt intense bitterness toward his former boss, despised Foster's air of superiority, and determined to avenge old slights. Weinstone, upon his mid-1931 return from Moscow, found "an extreme, sharp situation" dividing the two.[12]

Both distrusted Weinstone. Whereas Foster and Browder were native born, Weinstone's parents had emigrated from Lithuania when Weinstone was a child. Foster possessed little formal education and displayed open anti-intellectualism. Weinstone, then only thirty-two, had attended New York's highly competitive City College (CCNY), where he had succeeded Jay Lovestone as Intercollegiate Socialist Society head. Nicknamed "Wobbly," he had switched sides in party factional battles three times in four years.

On an unarticulated level Browder had always felt comparative deprivation when he confronted the party's "City College boys." He knew he possessed as much intelligence as either. Yet he lacked their urbanity and polish; accurately he attributed the disparity to their formal education. With Foster and Browder closely watching each other's conduct, and Weinstone upholding orthodoxy in Russia, they eschewed Trotskyism, American exceptionalism, and other heresies. As Stalin had done in the USSR, they ended policy discussion among all but the party's highest echelons.

At most times in U.S. history it is difficult to understand why native radicals would join a foreign-oriented, undemocratic movement. Yet to disheartened, depression-era Americans an industrializing Soviet Union, with full employment and boundless confidence, had its appeal. Historian James Weinstein has observed, "It was difficult indeed in the nineteen thirties to think of oneself as a revolutionary without identifying with the living embodiment of socialism triumphant. And of course the Communist party had the franchise."[13]

Membership on the CPUSA's ruling triumvirate brought Browder little publicity before 1934, although when he delivered his party's 1930 convention keynote address, the *New York Times* termed him its "chief theoretician." To the public, however, he remained inconspicuous, a vague, gray blur.[14]

Browder anticipated the Comintern's shift from sensational public rallies to seeking tangible results. Organizational skills boosted him further. In November 1930, after months of mass protest had brought the CPUSA much publicity but few concrete gains, he urged the party to become practical. One important address, " 'Fewer High-Falutin' Phrases, More Simple Everyday Deeds,'—Lenin," typified his Third Period emphasis.

Browder told listeners to "get down to work" at the unspectacular yet vital task of organizing jobless Americans. He reminded members that the Soviet founder, on the eve of the Bolshevik coup, had "advanced the slogan of 'milk for the workers' children,' " along with "the seizure of power." By contrast since 1929, domestic Communists had talked too abstractly about revolution and not enough about relief. In fact, one sincere, misguided comrade had even declared publicly that no American capitalist government would ever enact unemployment compensation; benefits would begin after the revolution! Browder ridiculed this approach, terming it a major cause of the disappointing 1930 Communist Congressional election vote. He observed that although the CPUSA had penned an excellent unemployment insurance bill, it had not lobbied vigorously in Washington for its enactment.

In closing, the former accountant importuned the CPUSA to handle opportunities "in the most businesslike" manner. This would "bring Marxism down from the clouds" to everyday life. Employing such arguments, Browder brought intense seriousness and finite focus to national headquarters. Likewise, he possessed a better sense of public relations than most CP cadres. Clarence Hathaway and others usually treated Communist-dominated auxiliary organizations as cash cows. Browder, instead, solicited donations but tried to avoid the impression of "taxing" them.[15]

Browder had Luganovskaya's help at headquarters during part of this era. Darcy, CPUSA national education director late in 1930, reported that one day Raissa came into his office and seemed to be looking around by opening file drawers. He inquired what she wanted. Imperiously she asked if he knew who she was. Losing his temper, Darcy yelled at her to leave and not come back. He expected subsequent unpleasantness from Earl, but never heard a word.[16]

Meanwhile in Moscow, Comintern functionaries carefully scrutinized some foreign parties. The AAS, which supervised Communist organization in English-speaking lands, met in full three times monthly and held three smaller "Bureau" gatherings. In January 1931, after not receiving either British or CPUSA secretariat minutes for four months, the body ordered New York and London to send the notes weekly.[17] In addition, international observers usually witnessed proceedings.

Browder overtook his rivals in 1932. In Moscow and at home he displayed assertiveness and pragmatism. When criticized he defended himself ably and conceded points he could not sustain. By contrast, Weinstone's speeches revealed his leadership inadequacies while party presidential candidate William Foster spent the year crisscrossing the United States, isolated from Communist power corridors.

Browder's purposeful approach and dry wit played well in the USSR, to which he and other top figures journeyed by ship at least once every year. Before the AAS he cited his party's most egregious irregularities. Ranking comrades failed to read resolutions published in the monthly journal, *Communist*. Others brought their own authoritative pronouncements into delicate discussions without first checking relevant *Daily Worker* editorials. Numerous sympathizers had applied for membership. After eight months without an answer, they began asking whether the Communist party was a "completely closed corporation" requiring "certification from Moscow" to join. Browder wondered rhetorically what happened to the "thousands" unready "to fight to get into" the organization, which had grown only to nine thousand.[18]

Browder received severe reproach. The Comintern held him "mainly responsible" for collective CPUSA failures. He had articulated an East Asian position too close to Lovestone's. In September 1931 militaristic Japan had invaded Manchuria. The USSR, never having enjoyed capitalist allies, feared that the United States might support Japanese aggression on its maritime republics. Underestimating the danger, Browder had stressed historic U.S. enmity toward Japan and quoted uncritically a bourgeois press release calling the United States and USSR "natural allies." He had not cleared foreign policy pronouncements with the Polburo and neglected the fight against American imperialism. When attacked by an English comrade, he had rudely impugned the integrity of the entire British party leadership.[19]

Beyond failing to guard Soviet interests, Browder had overemphasized nonproletarian contacts. Certainly he had made a greater effort to attract intellectuals than any previous CPUSA leader. In May he recounted to historian Matthew Josephson his special overtures toward writers and artists, opining that previous radical movements had wrongly displayed contempt for them. A lesser Comintern indictment noted that he allowed secretariat meetings to end "without concluding anything."[20]

Contrite, he accepted "correction" and confessed his need to overcome impatience toward Weinstone. Shaking his head, Browder criticized his rival for hesitations producing "long debates, very long debates"; avoiding the Manchurian question altogether; and trying to remove the CPUSA from too many labor struggles. Meanwhile Foster had provided little time or attention to daily leadership, devoting himself to the political campaign. Browder also contended that CPUSA-led strikes had given pause to the wage-cutting movement. Efforts for veterans, farmers, students, and other nonproletarians only strengthened work among the masses, a more problematic assertion.[21]

All year Browder battled Weinstone. In February the Comintern handed the CPUSA a clearer Third-Period line. On the tenth Browder acknowledged that his party had not mastered collective leadership. Twelve days later the Comintern clarified troika assignments, giving Browder primary management responsibility and Weinstone agitprop duties plus the *Daily Worker*'s chief editorship. It reaffirmed Foster's trade union preeminence and told the three to collaborate on all important questions.[22]

In March the Comintern identified the ambitious Browder as the leading cause of discord and warned against factionalism, a most serious charge. By April he stood on even shakier ground. The AAS cited his high-profile efforts as an immediate right-wing danger.[23] He denied the charges, but at the CPUSA's plenum that month Weinstone, who had waited nine months for Browder to stumble, gave the Polburo's report. Predictably, it denounced the party's work during his own absence. That summer Weinstone used the Bonus March issue to challenge Browder openly.

Back in 1923 America's military lobby had persuaded Congress to give World War veterans a "bonus," payable with interest in 1945. Hard times depleted savings, and in May 1932, twenty thousand former doughboys descended on Washington demanding full payment early. They threw up tents and makeshift cardboard huts and eventually occupied abandoned government buildings. The Senate refused their demands, and in July President Hoover, calling the demonstrators criminals and Communists, sent troops under General Douglas MacArthur to drive the old soldiers into Maryland.

CPUSA figures had indeed advocated such a protest, and an auxiliary, the Workers' Ex-Servicemen's League had planned one. Yet a *Daily Worker* correspondent admitted that the movement had arisen spontaneously and that the party did not control it. Weinstone, attempting to direct efforts from his New York office, recalled Comintern criticism of Browder's flirting with bourgeois elements and persuaded the Polburo to create a special Bonus March subcommittee that excluded Browder. Weinstone argued that Marxists who associated with right-wingers leading the marchers thereby compromised themselves. Having received his fill of non-Communists as a CCNY student and ever ready to avoid difficult struggles, Weinstone used his rising CPUSA authority to offer a simplistic solution. If the Workers' Ex-Servicemen's League could not dominate the protest, the party should dissociate itself entirely. A more talented in-fighter might have elbowed Browder aside totally at this point.[24]

By contrast, Browder considered the demonstrators the "shock troop" of unemployed millions and the best radical manifestation in a generation. On June 23 he went to Washington, mingled with the protesters, and telephoned a series of slogans to Weinstone. The latter refused to discuss them at the Polburo meeting four days later. On returning to Manhattan an enraged Browder discovered them on an inconspicuous *Daily Worker* inner page.

That month Browder received more pounding in Moscow. Canada's Stewart Smith savagely accused him of trying to smuggle in a new party line—an offense that could bring expulsion. Americans "Randolph" (apparently J. Peters) and Harry Haywood rushed to Browder's corner, insisting he must not become a scapegoat for misguided policy.[25]

By July 7 the Weinstone-Browder brawl had become a full-blown crisis paralyzing party leadership. Jack Stachel tried to establish order, proposing semi-weekly secretariat and weekly Polburo meetings with no absentee voting. He or Clarence Hathaway would replace Foster until the election. The troika should submit all Comintern telegrams to the Central Committee. Browder welcomed the initiative, admitting that Stachel made a good intermediary. Browder found Weinstone's arguments "particularly unconvincing"; the latter considered his "the same." Browder energized his colleagues by urging them to "accept some responsibility and not just say 'Weinstone and Browder can't get along.' " On August 27 Herbert Newton reported that rank and filers knew personal differences existed and had begun choosing sides.[26]

That same day Browder, professing to minimize top-level conflicts, bragged about reorganizing the CPUSA's finances and launched a thinly disguised Polburo offensive. Under Weinstone's leadership the "entire party without exception" had failed to recognize the Bonus March's "mass character." Ecumenical efforts should not degenerate into a mere "united front with ourselves." Joseph Zack stated that cadres did not need inside information to realize that the central leadership simply did not work.[27]

Comintern observer "Allen" announced that the center needed "immediate and considerable improvement." Foster, in the field, made little impact on the secretariat. Browder and Weinstone did almost no collaborative work; most days they did not "even see each other." Their rift threatened to become a 1920s-style factional fight. Allen wanted to add Hathaway to replace the missing Foster, force the secretariat to hold regular meetings, and put decisions on paper. Quickly Browder seconded the motion and admitted that a "constant succession of differences on small questions" separated Weinstone and him but denied any political division.[28]

On August 29 Browder and Weinstone clashed over the timing of the next Washington hunger march. Browder wanted the march to occur in early December, as Congress reconvened, for maximum publicity. Weinstone, displaying characteristic indecision, urged the party to wait until grassroots organizations had chosen a date. Stachel and leftist ideologue Alexander Bittelman supported Weinstone, but remaining members backed Browder. On August 31 the Comintern representative wrote Moscow, seeking "some strong person" to stop the "squabbling."[29]

In Chicago on September 7, 1932, a dramatic development increased the purse for the Browder-Weinstone slugfest. A heavy, unremitting chest pain seized Foster and radiated down his left arm. Over the previous eight weeks he had complained of "attacks of oppression" near his heart and extreme weakness when giving speeches. His recent pace signaled grave danger. In three months he had traveled seventeen thousand land miles, spoken at seventy meetings from coast to coast, and addressed 200,000 listeners. He had compounded the strain by eating irregularly, getting minimal sleep, and taking no time to relax. Angina pectoris was diagnosed, and a specialist predicted tragedy unless Foster reduced his activity greatly. Foster had promised to comply, but had continued his tour nevertheless; at Zeigler, Illinois, fifty armed coal company goons had chased him from the town. After Foster's collapse his physician termed further campaigning "absolutely suicidal" and ordered complete bedrest, prohibiting Foster indefinitely from even giving dictation or receiving visitors. The symptoms were part of a total nervous collapse that left Foster "helpless as a child," according to biographer Edward P. Johanningsmeier. Subsequently Foster spent five months recovering at a sanitarium near the Black Sea and did not give another speech until 1935.[30]

Learning of Foster's disability, Weinstone and Browder took off the gloves and began gouging and biting. Victory now offered total party control. Within days Weinstone accused Browder of trying to revise the Comintern line and scheduled a September 23, 1932, Polburo discussion of the alleged heresy. "Allen," Weinstone's international friend, telegraphed charges to the AAS. A second communication insisted that Browder, as de facto leader, deserved blame for all recent party errors and shortcomings.[31]

Browder fought back viciously. Personal differences had existed for a year, but now Weinstone had politicized them. The latter had spoken and voted against every Bonus March preparation because the CPUSA was "not sufficiently prepared," a "totally wrong" approach. Openly Browder advocated sending Polburo stenograms, existing "records and any further statements" to Moscow so the ECCI could arbitrate "once and for all."[32]

When the Polburo met again the following week, Weinstone presented an omnibus indictment. Like a fractious schoolboy, he declared that Browder caused the 1931 strike failures in Harlan County, Kentucky, and

Lawrence, Massachusetts; Browder would not replace ineffective functionaries loyal to him; Browder resisted the secretariat's division of labor "definitely sealed in Moscow." Weinstone, who possessed a scholar's cautious temperament but only a middling mind, offered a lame answer to accusations of indecision: "Why not?" Browder had not convened the secretariat "for weeks at a time."[33]

The toughness and maturity of Browder's rebuttal speech presented a bold contrast. He claimed that trade union expert Foster had supported his strike positions. Weinstone's constant bickering undermined his work. Browder had "leaned over backwards" to avoid collisions. He acknowledged not always providing energetic secretariat leadership, but the worst criticism had come "from precisely those comrades" resisting action most stubbornly. Now some considered his restraint a weakness and had declared "open season on Browder." Never again would he "retreat from disagreements." The present "impossible relations" had to be changed "by whatever means necessary." He urged the ECCI to reassign one of them to overseas work. Feigning magnanimity, he suggested Weinstone should plead his case before the Comintern because he had not made a very coherent Polburo presentation.[34]

Having lost the debate, Weinstone nevertheless offered a prescient closing observation. After slamming his opponent's "bureaucratic, presumptuous" attitude, he predicted that nobody who did not "kowtow" would be able to work with Browder, because he cooperated only with "yes-men."[35]

In Moscow, from September 22 to October 5, the AAS discussed the CPUSA's fate. In New York rumors circulated that the Comintern would forcefully end the Americans' "stupid bickering." Finally Bill Gebert brought news of the verdict on November 13, although Browder had received an advance cable some time earlier.[36]

Recognizing only personal differences, the Soviet edict abolished the CPUSA's secretariat because of its total breakdown and because Weinstone had botched the Bonus March. Henceforth the American party leadership would be "built around Browder and Foster." Weinstone would become the new U.S. Comintern representative. Browder had to participate more frequently in "economic and political strikes" because of his isolation from the masses. The domestic Communists would bear greater responsibility for leading themselves. Some basis for appeal still existed because Weinstone, displaying an indolence ill-suiting a revolutionary, had submitted no statement presenting his side of the dispute.

Straining to seem modest, Browder accepted the reins, finally apologizing for attacking the British CP six months earlier.[37]

Thus the Comintern chose Browder in late 1932. Neither Foster's heart attack nor the resident international representative's input played a decisive role. Instead, Weinstone's bungling shifted responsibility to Browder and the disabled Foster, from whom the unduly optimistic Russians expected a rapid recovery. Moscow seems to have wanted Foster, chastened by his earlier rejection, and Browder to serve together. If the decision had any larger political significance at all, it probably represented the rejection of an indecisive element for eclectic, but action-oriented leaders. Ideology played no visible role.

No one ever accused the Communist movement of lightheartedness. Still, the incendiaries of 1932, buoyed by capitalism's crisis and their own growing optimism, had their humorous moments. At the August Central Committee meeting Browder berated party journalists for infrequently covering Foster's campaign talks. "And when we do get the reports what are they like? They are terrible, aren't they?" Suddenly Foster interjected, to much laughter, "Maybe they're terrible speeches." The same gathering heard Browder respond to a quick-witted heckler. He conceded Joseph Zack could "produce original ideas as fast as a sturgeon" could "produce eggs." Then Browder broke up the room by giving a downside. When criticized, Zack defended his proposals most desperately, like a "kulak holding on to his last potato."[38]

In October the CPUSA's national campaign committee upbraided a lethargic election worker facing steep legal hurdles in one of tiny Delaware's three counties: "That the clerk of the peace may demand 200 signatures of regular party members is hardly a Bolshevik reason for not making a serious effort to get on the ballot." In December Finland's Otto Kuusinen sardonically asked about a CPUSA oversight. Had it delegated denouncing American imperialism to the Communist party of Switzerland? Shortly after his victory over Weinstone, a whimsical Browder told the Polburo to reinvigorate its youth work: "Social life doesn't mean just holding dances. Dancing is one of the least valuable and least interesting forms, because I don't dance."[39]

That Browder could joke about victims of Moscow's agricultural policies is instructive. He was not merely insensitive and not simply telling listeners words they liked to hear. Although he decried the plight of virtually every American minority group before World War II, he displayed no curiosity about reports of mass murders in the Soviet countryside.

Where criticism of Stalin was concerned, Browder simply did not want to know. Of course, this never hurt him in the USSR, but it undermined his credibility in the United States.

## WE WANT NO CONDESCENDING SAVIORS

Nature and the Comintern had eliminated Browder's rivals at an auspicious moment. After 1929's stock market crash America's economy had continued an unabated slide. By late 1932 both industrial production and agricultural prices had declined by 50 percent. A quarter of the labor force received no income at all, and millions worked only part-time.

More significant to the Communists, capitalism's contradictions had become manifest even to those unschooled in Marx. Ten billion dollars sat in vaults on President Franklin D. Roosevelt's March 4, 1933, inauguration day, but thirty-eight states had closed all banks. In orchards and fields apples went unpicked and wheat unharvested; sheep cost more to transport than their sale would bring. Yet simultaneously hungry residents of urban "Hooverville" shantytowns established rules for fair turns at the municipal dump when a fresh garbage truck arrived.

Rumblings of revolt, predicted since 1848, now filled the air. Mobs of farmers blocked highways, dumped milk on roadsides, halted sheriffs' sales. Unemployed utility workers tapped gas and electric lines; jobless miners sunk their own shafts and stole company coal. Angry urban crowds raided grocery stores.

Yet the masses did not politicize their discontent. Roosevelt won election mouthing vague platitudes and promising a balanced federal budget. Despite the disaster, sixteen million people voted for Hoover. Socialist Norman Thomas received but 918,000 ballots and Foster a mere 103,000. CPUSA membership reached only fourteen thousand in 1932 and nineteen thousand in 1933.[40]

Worse yet in retrospect, a more virulent form of capitalism had arisen in Germany. Leading a campaign of ultranationalism, racism, and anti-Communism, Adolf Hitler took power legally in January 1933. Soon Communists made the first wave of concentration camp inmates. Still no repudiation of the social fascism doctrine ensued, although doubts about it grew. Boldly the Comintern welcomed capitalism's "final stage."

Indeed, the International considered the United States a greater danger to world peace than the ascending Hitler. As late as September 27, 1932, Moscow sent the CPUSA lengthy instructions declaring: "The American bourgeoisie is trying to find a way out of the crisis [through] further attack on the American working class; by a more intensive exploitation of colonial and semicolonial countries; by a war against its imperialist rivals; by war against the USSR." The Russians also explained how to advertise policies designed to serve the Soviet Union. They should "be organized by the Communist party primarily on the ground of protecting the interests of the working masses of its own country, because wars are fought by the masses and at their expense."[41]

As the CPUSA's sole pilot, Browder steered the party slowly toward more moderate positions. Indeed, the first Comintern observer's report in December decried his caution. It announced, "The bigger weakness in this work is . . . that one cannot find a single member of the center with whom it is possible to have a frank discussion." The same letter requested another Soviet tutor to help the party get on its feet.[42]

Browder had already begun marketing efforts. To a Polburo meeting on November 25 he reported that "eight to ten different groups of intellectuals" had offered themselves as "direct financial supporters." He promised to utilize them politically and began forming a well-educated group to demand unemployment insurance. The end result, the Inter-Professional Association, lobbied Congress during 1934 and 1935. Headed by noted social worker Mary Van Kleek, the eleven-hundred-member organization, filled with distinguished names, lent the concept academic-world respectability.[43]

In December 1932 at a hunger march on the U.S. Capitol Browder led the CPUSA to a major, bloodless triumph. Washington police chief Ernest Brown, determined to keep Communists away from Congress, herded twenty-five hundred protesters into a cul de sac. Enraged, the demonstrators demanded their freedom, but police threatened them with machine guns and tear gas. Despite the government's overwhelming display, some preferred violent consequences to compromise. Browder avoided a direct collision through Herbert Benjamin, an organizer whose eloquence could control any party crowd. Benjamin persuaded protesters to bed down under the open sky, and frantic negotiations began. Fortunately, Congressman Fiorello La Guardia presented a compromise with which the Communists could live. The plan featured having the demonstrators march to just outside the Capitol grounds and then sending a five-person delegation inside.[44]

When Browder pledged to honor the agreement, the police, on December 6, permitted the crowd to finish its trek. Political scientist Harvey Klehr described "the most rigid police supervision on record in Washington. . . . [Officers] were all about, three planes flew overhead and 4,000 regular army troops were on alert at nearby Fort Myers." Before nightfall La Guardia escorted demonstrators to the Maryland line, preventing further trouble. The next day on the House floor he denounced police for holding captive marchers who had broken no law. Immediately, the *Daily Worker* proclaimed a "splendid victory." Even the conservative Klehr has attested that the "Communists had reason to be pleased. They had garnered national publicity, forced the government to back down, and avoided violence."[45]

Browder still faced obstacles, however. That very day Allen, the Comintern representative, reminded the AAS that Browder had "been away from the factories" a "long time" and in a two-day November plenum had failed to mention the USSR even once. Soon he made a more costly mistake. Early in 1933 he denounced New York University philosopher Sidney Hook, perhaps America's most original Marxist thinker, for seeking a united front (alliance) with nonparty leftists. The Communists had courted him as an avenue toward his famous mentor, John Dewey. Hook declined suggestions that he write propaganda for the USSR. Alienating him cost the movement dearly. Quickly he became stridently anti-CP and led many established intellectuals away, although younger literati replaced them. Thus, according to historian John Patrick Diggins, the CPUSA, which had expelled theoreticians Jay Lovestone, Will Herberg, and Bertram Wolfe in 1929, remained "a Communist party without a leading Marxist philosopher." It had "lost the battle for cultural hegemony without knowing it."[46]

Browder took the defeat in stride but spoke out against raiding rivals. Before the Central Committee in January he discussed misuses of a recent slogan, "Not a single political meeting without Communists present." In his driest tones he reported that a few loyal comrades, willing even to die for the cause, had "interpreted this to mean to go in and break up" opponents' meetings and "they proceeded to carry out their Communist duty as they understood it [laughter]." But so doing they had hurt the CPUSA's public image "ten times more" than enemies' "slanders." The disruptions did not convert a single worker; they only created antagonism.[47]

Weinstone, sent to Moscow in disgrace the previous autumn, secured a rematch that spring. In a marathon AAS showdown, twelve meetings in twenty-nine days, he and Browder banged heads again while others hammered them with accusations. On March 28 Browder repeated all 1932's charges and deplored the need for ECCI intervention. Five days later others offered similar criticism. CPUSA expert on African Americans, B. D. Amis, accused Weinstone of "white chauvinism." Amis, Foster, and Harry Haywood had tried to link Scottsboro to the campaign to free imprisoned labor hero Tom Mooney. Weinstone had prohibited anyone from erecting Scottsboro banners. Aloof, he accepted only written communications. His removal had "improved considerably" party morale.[48]

Speaking on April 4, Weinstone admitted mistakes had occurred but tried to avoid responsibility for them. He blamed the divided leadership, reminding listeners that Browder and Foster had not got along either. He denounced the CPUSA's substituting spontaneity for careful strike planning and underestimating workers' radicalization. He denied opposing the African American liberation struggle and accused subordinate Robert Minor of misleading black comrades by putting secretariat orders "in his pocket or in a draw."[49]

When Weinstone sat down, Sergei Gusev, a veteran of numerous international Communist debates, stepped to the rostrum. Menacingly he issued solemn judgments in familiar tones, suggesting a higher authority. Browder's and Weinstone's speeches both bore the odor of factionalism, the latter's more strongly. Weinstone had expressed substantial self-criticism whereas Browder had sickened the audience with "unsurpassed bragging." Yet Weinstone had also talked too much about himself, implying that his chief sin was getting caught. Gusev expected success from the CPUSA's work. He pronounced Browder's optimism not well founded, but Weinstone's pessimism "of no use whatever."[50]

Thus Gusev halted the contest. Browder the bureaucrat had bested his party's intellectual. The AAS nevertheless handed him an ultimatum. Weinstone had charged that Comintern orders frequently arrived at CPUSA headquarters but reached rank and filers only in attenuated form. Gusev termed the practice intolerable. Americans must no longer come to Moscow to receive new resolutions that would "also not be carried out." Instead, they had to report on fulfillment of previous orders. The CPUSA had to reach the working masses; it was "a proletarian party, not a farmer-labor" organization. And, of course, it could "get along without bourgeois students." Clearly the Nazi takeover in Germany had not altered Third Period priorities. The ECCI would give "all possible aid" to Americans, but if necessary it would change the leadership again.[51]

Meekly Weinstone accepted defeat, kept quiet, and stayed in Moscow until 1934. Browder handled victory assertively, arranging to reply on April 8. On that day he apologized for his "provincial English and inexpert political methods." Then, in great detail, he reviewed his old speeches to suggest that Gusev had judged his actions out of context. He closed by proposing to organize America's homeless youth and asked for more ECCI guidance. In subsequent days Browder received additional criticism from old CPUSA rival Max Bedacht, Finland's Otto Kuusinen, and others.[52] Three more times Browder took the floor to defend himself.

On April 26 Kuusinen stated that the depression had proved a mixed blessing for the CPUSA. Unemployed, part-time, and endangered workers provided a weak financial base. The party's desperate revenue-raising activities had included selling alcohol at social functions. The practice, "perhaps for a good purpose," remained illegal in the Prohibition-era United States and created public relations problems. It conveyed the impression that "money collection" constituted the movement's "main mass work." Kuusinen also suggested that a detailed letter from Foster might help remedy Browder's lack of contact with factory workers.[53] Clearly, the Kremlin did not expect Foster's convalescence to require another two years.

While Communists battled in Moscow, the Roosevelt administration translated its undefined campaign promise of a New Deal into sweeping changes. During FDR's first one hundred days Congress enacted emergency relief for the unemployed and federal insurance for bank accounts. It refinanced 20 percent of the nation's home mortgages. It passed legislation to electrify the Tennessee Valley and build reforestation camps for unemployed young men. It legalized beer, attacked agricultural overproduction, and tried to initiate business recovery.

The vehicle for the latter, the National Industrial Recovery Act, fought the depression's downward price spiral through codes of fair competition. The codes suspended antitrust laws, established minimum wages and maximum hours, and outlawed child labor. Theoretically, public hearings allowed consumers and workers to help management create the regulations. In fact, trade associations dominated the process. The Communists condemned the measures as postponing capitalism's demise. Browder stressed the limitations of the act: it benefited primarily workers in easily organized industries, encouraged employer-dominated company unions, and divided the proletariat. He termed it a forerunner to American fascism.

Actually the National Industrial Recovery Act, which also established the right for employees to bargain collectively, helped kill the TUUL. It brought a tidal wave of recruits to non-Communist unions. Independent organizations bobbed up overnight; even the seemingly moribund AFL enjoyed a ripple. One great exception to the TUUL's relative submergence occurred on the West Coast. There the Cannery and Agricultural Workers Industrial Union survived fierce repression while organizing farm workers. It led a series of 1933 strikes among ten thousand migrant laborers who harvested melons, grapes, peas, lettuce, cherries, raspberries, and cotton. The struggle for better working conditions and higher wages, judged by historian Harvey A. Levenstein to be "the greatest agricultural strike in American history," was later depicted heroically by novelist John Steinbeck in the *Grapes of Wrath* and *In Dubious Battles*. Significantly, 75 percent of the strikers were Mexicans, long regarded by the AFL as unorganizable. Browder, however, chose to emphasize the union's Anglo component. Already campaigning to associate Communists in the public mind with indigenous radical traditions, he displayed his talent for hyperbole by contending that the party had now replaced the IWW as leading representative of America's "poor and middle farmers."[54]

The CPUSA, startled by Roosevelt's heightened popularity, called an Extraordinary National Conference to meet in New York that July. Its tasks included ratifying Browder's leadership and supposedly writing an "Open Letter" designed to "fight the New Deal's assault upon the toiling masses." In fact, the document, containing proletarian demands for the National Recovery Administration (which enforced the National Industrial Recovery Act), was very much an international product. As early as April 22, a special six-member Moscow commission, including Browder, Weinstone, and future Comintern representative to the United States Gerhart Eisler, were working diligently on the text. By April 27 either Gusev or Solomon Lozovsky had amended the draft. Subsequently a separate committee of five, also including Browder, Weinstone, and Eisler, reworked and shortened it after much discussion by the AAS. On May 11 the manifesto, along with a proposal to look into the *Daily Worker*'s editorial board composition, was taken to the Comintern's political secretariat for approval.[55]

At the summer ceremony in Manhattan, Browder offered heavy insincerity, hailing the day Foster could resume "playing his proper role" in party councils. The new leader helped create an illusion of spontaneity by disclosing candidly that for the textile industry's Washington hearings a few top comrades had compiled a list of proposals "a couple of hours before train time." CPUSA tasks included union building in basic industries (steel, auto, rail, marine, and mining), agitation for unemployment insurance, and continued struggle against social fascists. Near the end appeared a new charge: combating Nazism by demanding release of proletarian political prisoners, as Hitler had quickly silenced all German dissent.[56]

Almost from the day Browder achieved unquestioned control he began putting a domestic face on the movement. At party headquarters, his twelve-hour days brought new energy after four years of drift. His mania for organization, finally given free rein, produced dramatic results. Figures from the 1920s (Jack Stachel, Charles Krumbein, Robert Minor, Alexander Bittelman, and Clarence Hathaway) appeared in new places of authority. Historian Maurice Isserman has shown that shortly thereafter younger cadres, largely descendants of Jewish immigrants, moved into secondary leadership positions and held them for two decades. The party controlled the livelihoods of more than six hundred employees, and Browder, like Stalin, demanded personal loyalty.[57]

Opponents found the intraparty atmosphere inhospitable. Sam Darcy considered the national office a snake pit of petty bureaucrats vying for Browder's favor by gossiping each against the other. Browder loved hearing praise, especially for his modesty, and his clique provided it abundantly. Anti-Communist attacks by government and business made the best excuse to quell dissent, lest it break party ranks. Expulsions, ever a part of CP history, increased. Yet Browder also played the benevolent despot. For years he gave Darcy a birthday present. Once, for no apparent reason, he presented him with Vernon Parrington's three volumes on American history and culture.[58]

Inner-circle members, by contrast, had fonder memories. Gil Green recalled that Browder set a distinctly native tone for an organization heretofore dominated by East-European immigrants. Foster had titled one of his autobiographies *From Bryan to Stalin*. Green insists that Browder, "much more sensitive to America's special nature and psychology," never would have done anything that overt. Green considers Foster's linking of the nineteenth-century Populist-Democrat with the Soviet dictator "outrageous."[59]

Almost immediately Browder laid foundations for a personality cult by upgrading his title. The *Daily Worker*'s June 24, 1933, edition employed the rubric "National Secretary" for the first time. That August Stachel displayed his fealty by resurrecting "General Secretary."[60] The CPUSA formalized the appellation at its April 1934 convention. Browder began the fiction that he had taken the helm in 1930.

Students of American Communism may never know the veracity of Browder's subsequent claims that he developed qualms about Stalin's social fascism dogma. His Third Period behavior was ambiguous. Indeed, on February 16, 1934, five thousand CPUSA members invaded a Socialist Madison Square Garden rally of twenty thousand, prompting scores of fistfights. Browder stayed home but had urged his uninvited followers to crash the meeting. Years later he sheepishly tried to blame the violence on his close supporters Clarence Hathaway and Comintern representative Gerhard Eisler.[61]

The Socialists, still the American left's preeminent party, faced internal divisions and had increasing trouble resisting the Communists. The death of Old Guard leader Morris Hillquit in 1933 ignited an open power struggle. The following year the Militants offered the party's national convention a Declaration of Principles that supported the USSR, mass resistance to any international war, and revolutionary seizure of power if the opportunity arose. With its passage Old Guarders ceased offering radical programs and made anti-Communism an obsession. Difficulties only increased as youthful religious radicals who saw in Socialism the kingdom of God streamed into the party, founding the *Call* to oppose the right-wingers' *New Leader*. The Militants' actions cast doubt on social fascism's validity.

In 1933 more than 1.1 million workers engaged in strikes and lockouts, triple the number of 1932. The Communists launched a renewed effort to popularize the Workers Unemployment Insurance Bill. The Unemployed Councils lobbied municipal governments, labor unions, and fraternal organizations for endorsements. Yet sectarianism plagued the party's efforts. Browder displayed the problem dramatically when he addressed three thousand workers (including many women) who had struck Detroit's Briggs Company, an independent manufacturer of auto bodies for the Ford, Chrysler, Hudson, and Graham Paige corporations. Although workers and organizers represented nearly every shade of radical opinion, Browder boasted that the CPUSA deserved full credit for the walkout. Labor historian Roger Keeran has argued that such behavior "aided anti-Communism outside and inside the strikers' ranks and led to the removal of Communist leadership."[62]

From 1930 through 1933 the CPUSA, unwilling to work with reformers and torn by its leadership crisis, made little headway, although capitalism lay convulsing. Browder's consolidation of control raised questions, however. How could he take advantage of America's unprecedented economic difficulties? Could his leadership offer the CPUSA anything new? Or would he, like his predecessors Ruthenberg and Lovestone, remain a figure better known among the Soviets than among American leftists? As

Browder pondered these questions, events overseas were creating opportunities for his moderate brand of Communism. Yet political upheaval at home produced new challenges. In addition to competition from Socialists, Lovestonites, and Trotskyists, non-Marxist opponents left of Roosevelt had begun appearing all over the land. A violent outburst of working-class militancy signaled the opening of a new era in labor relations. Many proletarians began to feel that history's tide was turning.

# THREE

■

# *A Better Movement in Birth? (1934–1935)*

Although Third Period dogma energized the CPUSA and other Communist parties, the Comintern foundered between 1931 and 1934. Cataclysmic events buffeted the organization, but the most powerful Soviet figure, Joseph Stalin, played an indecisive role. Unprecedented famine stalked the USSR in collectivization's wake. He faced a severe leadership crisis at home and handled economic and political challenges himself. As historian E. H. Carr has shown, Comintern affairs were more complex, however, and Adolf Hitler's rise in Germany caused divisions within the organization. Stalin, who barely concealed his contempt for foreign Communist parties, did not bother to intervene. His spokesman, Vyacheslav Molotov, failed to attend ECCI sessions in 1931, 1932, and 1933.[1] Would the Comintern die, leaving the world movement totally in the hands of Stalin and his advisors? Could the organization affect his Third Period policies? If so, how could the head of the minuscule American party contribute to the dialogue?

## THE PARTY WE OF ALL WHO WORK

As early as autumn 1932, Georgi Dimitrov, an exiled Bulgarian National Assembly member who headed the Comintern's Western European bureau, pleaded for a working-class United Front without Communist domination. Few heeded his calls. Barely months later Hitler took power in Berlin and began sending Communists to concentration camps. His attacks created rank-and-file pressure in many countries for a more flexible policy.[2] Comintern heads, however, remained unswayed.

Soon Dimitrov gained widespread attention. Arrested by the Nazis and accused of torching the Reichstag building in early 1933, he went on trial in Leipzig that September. Here his courage and resourcefulness made him overnight the first hero to emerge from the Comintern's gray ranks. A fifty-one-year-old veteran Balkan revolutionary, Dimitrov was stockily built, heavy-jawed, and, as Sam Darcy noted, "not given to easy smiling." He had a thick head of hair that produced a shaggy appearance, at least by the standards of the 1930s. In court, dragging the chains the judge had forced him to wear all summer, Dimitrov forsook legal counsel and defended himself brilliantly against Hitler's best-known lieutenants, Herman Göring and Joseph Goebbels. A master of logic, Dimitrov spoke German fluently, and his formal courtesy and biting irony made him insufferable to the Nazis. Historian Fritz Tobias quotes him as remarking "Of course it's sheer bad luck for the prosecution" that many witnesses against him were "psychopaths, opium addicts, and thieves." Then in cross-examination, he posed a series of clever questions that rendered the usually articulate Goebbels speechless. Thereafter he provoked Göring into an angry outburst that ruined the prosecution's case. Dimitrov, though acquitted, languished in "protective custody" in Moabit Prison near Berlin until February 1934. Then the Germans put him on a flight to Moscow, after the USSR had granted him citizenship.[3]

Browder would come to consider Dimitrov his closest friend in the USSR. Nine years Dimitrov's junior, Browder admired the rugged Bulgarian's cleverness and gift for irony. They had first met in 1921 and worked together in the Profintern in 1926. Dimitrov and Browder possessed similar temperaments and, according to the latter, quickly became politically "intimate." Meanwhile the USSR and United States established diplomatic relations, encouraging East–West rapprochement. Shortly afterward Stalin told American reporter Walter Duranty that the League of Nations, now that Germany and Japan had departed, might play a positive international role.[4]

Stalin nevertheless displayed no desire to extend a new orientation to Communist International (CI) activities. His unwillingness created confusion; Comintern officials disagreed and issued vague, often conflicting, directives to different national parties. Yet external events drove them toward a united front. At a January 1934 Soviet party congress, Stalin remained silent on the concept but warned that Nazi Germany posed an enormous danger.

February 1934 stirred much of Europe. On the sixth, right-wing groups in Paris attempted a coup, which alarmed left and centrist parties. On the twelfth Austrian Chancellor Engelbert Dollfuss, with Italian dictator Benito Mussolini's support, used military force to crush Vienna's Social Democrats. That same day France's competing SP and CP joined spontaneously in a general strike, the first important working-class cooperation since 1920.

Dimitrov's arrival in Moscow on February 27 proved a crucial turning point. His trial had sparked what historian Carr has called a "world-wide wave of indignation and protest against a monstrous regime." Dimitrov's performance had made him an international antifascist symbol and brought him more influence than any other foreign Communist. For the next five years he projected a humanitarian image Stalin never could achieve.[5]

On April 7 he attended a Polburo session where he linked the Communists' failure to attract working masses to Third Period policies. Stalin, an unpredictable tyrant who, as historian Dimitri Volkogónov has shown, sometimes respected Communists who expressed bold ideas, was skeptical. He nevertheless suggested that Dimitrov head Comintern work and promised Polburo support.[6]

Although CP publications continued to denounce Social Democrats, Browder watched Dimitrov rise quickly to the top. There he received support from Finland's Otto Kuusinen, Russia's Dimitri Manuilsky, and Germany's M. Maddalena. Indeed, Manuilsky and Polish CP delegate B. Bronkowski urged the importance of wooing not only proletarians but also "petty-bourgeois and peasant parties." By contrast, Hungary's Bela Kun, the Soviet Union's V. Knorin and Solomon A. Lozovsky, and China's Wang Ming castigated liberalization attempts as a rightist deviation. This sharp division paralyzed the Comintern. In the United States Browder quietly hoped that Dimitrov's policies would win out.[7]

The ground began shifting in May. The Soviet Polburo appointed a commission headed by Stalin to prepare for the Seventh World Congress, the first since 1928. So encouraged, the ECCI's presidium named Dimitrov to report on the fascist offensive and working-class unity. This decision in itself constituted a program and revealed that his campaign had found approval in the highest quarters.[8]

International circumstances accelerated the process. That May fascist parties seized power in Latvia and Bulgaria. More ominously, on June 30 Hitler had several hundred potential rivals shot. The dead included Ernst Rohm, the Nazis' private army commander, Gregor Strasser, who had once sought party leadership, and Kurt von Schleicher, a former chancellor. The Communists concluded that Hitler had surrendered his forces to the Reichwehr, which had recognized his supreme authority, creating a steel dictatorship.

Onrushing events hastened the United Front. In Moscow resistance to change remained stubborn and vocal. Stalin still hedged. Yet in Western Europe French Communists and Socialists signed an antifascist common action agreement on July 27, 1934. Three weeks later Italian parties followed suit. United Front policies proved most popular in France, Austria, Czechoslovakia, and Britain. There democratic culture had bred familiarity with coalition building. Resistance to Hitlerism rallied the left more effectively than calls to overthrow capitalism.

Similar antifascist concern facilitated Soviet entry into the League of Nations that September. Two months later joint action was set back when the Socialist International's executive committee rejected by a narrow margin a proposal to negotiate directly with the Comintern. Meanwhile, the head of the French Communist party (PCF), Maurice Thorez, sought a full-fledged popular front that would include everyone except reactionaries and fascists. Browder played a minor role in the line change.

Traveling to attend the ECCI's Presidium meeting in December, Browder accidentally encountered Thorez on a Moscow-bound train in Warsaw, Poland. Browder spoke some French, and Thorez understood a little English. Together they attempted conversation. Browder explained that he had been trying to link the CPUSA to American revolutionary traditions, although he certainly was not courting New Deal liberals. This excited Thorez, who anticipated a harsh battle over the French Popular Front and wanted to test the waters before risking Stalin's wrath. He persuaded Browder to raise the tamer, less problematic American question first.[9]

In Moscow a ferocious ten-day Presidium battle ensued. A. Martynov, a functionary who hunted social fascists, attacked Browder for attempting to expropriate the Declaration of Independence. Youth leader V. T. Chemadonov and several German party (KPD) representatives joined the chorus. Despite the criticism, ultimately both Browder and Thorez received the majority's gentle encouragement. Even more significant, before year's end Stalin acquiesced. Thereafter progress toward the United Front accelerated. Nobody disagreed with the Soviet dictator very long. Quickly, Thorez celebrated his triumph by publishing a two-part article in the Comintern journal in January 1935.[10] Days later the last recalcitrant, the German party, fell in line.

World tensions contributed once again. On March 4 the British government published a defense study on the growing Nazi threat. The next day France extended her military service requirement. On March 16

Hitler issued a conscription decree, an open violation of the Versailles Treaty.

By May all remaining Comintern mystery on the issue was removed. France and the Soviet Union, whom Germany's growing aggressiveness threatened most, concluded a mutual defense pact. Browder was thrilled to learn that on May 16 Stalin, Molotov, and Litvinov had praised French national defense policy. Historian Carr has concluded that "world revolution became an article in a creed ritualistically recited on solemn public occasions but no longer an item of living faith," much less a summons to revolt.[11] Defense of the Soviet Union replaced it. Thus ended the Third Period. The Comintern victors became heroes, hailed for prescient awareness of the fascist threat. The defeated, including Knorin, Kun, and Russia's Ossip Piatnitsky, paid the ultimate price, perishing when Stalin purged the international Communist movement in the late 1930s.

## THE UNITED FRONT IN THE UNITED STATES

Even before the Comintern's dramatic policy change, domestic developments called into question Third Period sectarianism. President Franklin D. Roosevelt's early years brought little lasting reform except for banking and securities legislation. The administration concentrated instead on providing relief and on resuscitating a corpselike economy. If the depression stunned the public, the New Deal's arrival stimulated expectations of change. At the same time the rapid spread of destitution caused even comfortable Americans to identify with the downwardly mobile. Accordingly, a radical spirit rarely seen in U.S. politics arose.

This spirit produced movements widely perceived as leftist. Some of the movements' leaders, true demagogues, employed sharp but vague rhetoric; they encouraged followers to ventilate discontent but did not suggest much beyond listening to speeches, writing letters, and contributing pocket change. Other leaders, who had less clear motives, advocated overly generous legislative proposals based on unsound economics. A few, however, worked sincerely to push the president leftward by advocating reforms that could help democratize the economy. All demonstrated the growing popularity of radicalism. Cumulatively, they suggested that the New Deal had begun a social and political revolution that might devour its own early leaders. Although contemporaries and historians have likened some of the movements to the far right, such comparisons miss a salient point. To the Americans who supported (and opposed) them, these angry figures of the depression appeared to offer action while FDR still clung to diminishing business community support.

From Michigan, Father Charles Coughlin addressed the largest weekly radio audience in the world. His melodious voice thundered against Communists, bankers, and "Franklin Double-crossing Roosevelt." Coughlin offered frequently changing panaceas, including nationalization of banking and currency expansion. Although Browder and *New Masses* associate editor A. B. Magil considered him a fascist, not until 1936 did Coughlin display the overt anti-Semitism that has since likened him to Mussolini and Hitler in the public mind.

Huey Long of Louisiana did more to aid the underprivileged than any governor in his state's history. He lowered utility bills and launched a public works program that built new highways, bridges, schools, and hospitals. He gave Louisiana State University a medical school every qualified student could afford. Like many southern chief executives, he made a travesty of democracy. Yet, unlike the others, he displayed a nearly complete absence of racism. Elected to the U.S. Senate in 1930, he quickly began a national campaign that identified the most logical funding source for social programs: the wealthy. Likening the two major parties to snake-oil salespersons peddling the same elixirs under different brand names, Long proposed steep taxes on high incomes and an annual capital levy. His program wildly exaggerated the benefits progressive taxation would produce, however, offering every American family a guaranteed $5,000 annual income when 87 percent of them received less than $2,500. As a result by February 1935 his organization, Share Our Wealth, had twenty-seven thousand local clubs and a file of eight million names.

Californian Dr. Francis Townsend, an unemployed public health physician, sought pensions for the aged. His plan promised $200 a month to all citizens over age sixty who had never committed a crime. It offered easy requirements; recipients had to renounce other income, spend all the money every month, and not work. The scheme promised job vacancies and consumer demand. Although regressively financed, it proved enormously popular. Even Browder considered Townsend well intentioned. An unprecedented 20 percent of the nation's adult population signed his Congressional petitions.

Also on the West Coast, Socialist writer Upton Sinclair registered as a Democrat in 1933 and spent a year campaigning for governor. His program, End Poverty in California (EPIC), called for state appropriation of idle lands and factories, allowing the unemployed to produce for their own needs. In winning the July 1934 primary Sinclair received an absolute majority, although he was running in a nine-candidate field. That fall incumbent Republican Frank Merriam triumphed only after conducting a campaign that, according to historian Robert S. McElvaine, "set a standard for distortion and lies" not equaled until the 1972 presidential election. Hollywood studios produced bogus newsreels featuring carloads of unknown, unkempt actors posing as migrant laborers flooding into California. Even Sinclair's defeat confirmed the new radical spirit. The conservative Merriam felt a need to endorse the New Deal, Townsend's pension program, and a thirty-hour work week.[12]

In Minnesota Governor Floyd Olson, an avowed radical, led the nation's largest third party, the Farmer-Laborites. Wisconsin's Progressive party sent Robert La Follette, Jr., to the Senate and brother Philip to the state house. The latter was denouncing America's maldistribution of income.

The year 1934 also produced an explosion of labor unrest, unprecedented in its magnitude. It touched workers in every geographical area and virtually every trade and industry. The National Industrial Recovery Act's section 7A, supposed to guarantee the right to organize, sparked an upsurge in union membership. As historian Robert Zieger has observed, "Whole categories of workers with no previous record of activism" sought to unionize. "From Filipino fruit pickers to newspaper editorial employees, and from Hollywood actors to dry cell–battery workers, thousands signed up." Those "in auto plants, rubber factories, and electrical appliance shops joined despite their lack of previous laborite experience." At the heart of their militancy lay a desire for the union contract that offered an end to complex, ever-shifting systems of payment and arbitrary hiring practices that "forced workers to abase themselves for preference in employment and that discarded older workers in favor of presumably more vigorous younger ones."[13]

The TUUL unions claimed membership gains of 100,000, bringing their total to 125,000. Yet independent organizations quickly sprang up and surpassed them in size. A disappointed Browder admitted in April that the once-moribund AFL had benefited most of all, adding 500,000 to the two million on its rolls.[14] Its established conservative reputation, many workers believed, would make winning concessions from employers easier.

Historian Harvey A. Levenstein has shown that on the local level some CP members had already abandoned the TUUL for the AFL, especially in the auto, steel, and coal industries. Furthermore, despite the "TUUL's attempts to be comprehensive, in many industries its unions simply did not exist." Communists in those fields had therefore joined "whatever labor organizations existed at the time," including even "company-dominated employee representation groups."[15]

With a few notable exceptions, William Green's AFL hierarchy squandered a rare opportunity. Bert Cochran summarized the situation succinctly: "The unions that held the bulk of power in the AFL simply could not deal with recruits from the mass production industries, most of whom toiled in semiskilled or unskilled jobs." Would thousands lacking apprenticeship training or journeymen's cards "be enrolled as full members in the venerable International Brotherhood of Electrical Workers?" The AFL's auto industry efforts seemed to bespeak its fundamental attitude. There it acquiesced in the establishment of a National Recovery Administration (NRA) code emphasizing the merit concept and providing no pay increases for the majority of workers. In response to such timid leadership, flagrant management abuses, and governmental inability or unwillingness to enforce the law, workers turned increasingly to the strike weapon. Whereas a mere 324,210 had engaged in job actions as late as 1932, a dramatic series of industrial stoppages idled nearly 1.5 million in 1934. Although many proletarians remained fundamentally conservative in their values, they accepted the leadership of acknowledged radicals.[16]

Four major strikes spread a fear of class warfare across the land. In May members of A. J. Muste's American Workers party and competing CPUSA rank and filers defied a court injunction against striking AFL workers at the plants of three Toldeo, Ohio, auto parts companies. Violence, first between pickets and strikebreakers, and later featuring demonstrators battling National Guardsmen, led to a limited but highly symbolic union victory. Roger Keeran summed up the workers' accomplishments. They had defied the AFL's unstated policy against walkouts, secured "one of the few signed agreements in the industry," and established one of the federation's strongest auto locals. Later that summer striking San Francisco longshoremen and cargo handlers paralyzed the waterfront. Their leader, Australian-born Harry Bridges, was a CP member, and the party played a substantial role in the conflict. When police and strikebreakers arrived at the piers, a pitched battle broke out. Lawmen's bullets killed two pickets, prompting on July 9 a mass public funeral that idled the entire city. Two weeks later a Minneapolis Teamsters local led by Trotskyists closed down the trucking industry. Construction workers and taxi drivers walked out in sympathy, and commerce ground to a halt. Female family members played a crucial role in the job action. A Women's Auxiliary prepared food at strike headquarters around the clock, dishing out some ten thousand meals in one twenty-four-hour period. They also cared for dependent children in shifts, and a committee visited local landlords to lobby against evictions when rents fell due. Historian James R. Green recounts that "after a month of violence and nearly unbearable tension, the employers surrendered, opening the way for a Teamster organizing drive that would extend throughout the Midwest" to threaten the previously hallowed open shop. The summer's agony continued into September with what Gary Gerstle has described as the "single largest industrial action in the history of American labor." A textile strike idled 400,000 workers (40 percent of them women) from Maine to Alabama. The chief impetus was rank-and-file anger at employers' refusal to abide by the NRA cotton industry code.[17]

In such an atmosphere Browder made the type of balanced response that typified his CPUSA leadership style. On one hand, he brought Luganovskaya, who had recently received the best training on Soviet views of the United States, to live with him permanently. On the other, he strove to end the CP's isolation, giving greatest attention to achieving working-class unity, creating a labor party, and attracting liberal opinion molders beneath an antifascist banner. The increasingly obvious growth of the Nazi menace (which had destroyed the largest Communist party outside Russia and prompted increasingly apparent Soviet concern about it) helped push him in an ecumenical direction. It kindled an unarticulated, almost instinctual, desire to reach out for allies, even among the other leftists the CPUSA had previously attacked as social fascists.

Shortly after Browder's 1926 departure from Russia, Luganovskaya began a series of career moves that would cause controversy in the United States. The first was unspectacular; she left the Profintern to work on the central committee of the chemical workers' industrial union. She stayed there for three years. In 1930, however, she began serving in the trade union department of the Marxism-Leninism Institute. Located on Puskchinskaya Street in downtown Moscow, the institute was the Soviet Communist party's highest political training center. She had Browder's second son, Andrew, on June 10, 1931. Her party cell sent her to the Institute of Red Professors in 1932. The following year, back at the Marxism-Leninism Institute, she did graduate study on the United States.[18]

Later in 1933, at Earl's request, she took her expertise to the United States, entering illegally. She also began calling herself Raissa Berkmann

Browder, using the nicknames "Irene" and "Ria." Earl eventually came under government pressure and produced suspicious Russian-language certificates that attested to a 1926 divorce from his abandoned wife Gladys and remarriage to Luganovskaya. Federal officials and even his close friend Philip J. Jaffe doubted their authenticity. Browder usually became defensive when confronted with the subject. Once in 1936 Hubert Kelley, a hostile journalist who had done extensive research in Kansas, asked Earl point-blank if he and Raissa were married. Angrily the CP leader leaped from his chair, declared the question unkind, and terminated the interview. Raissa brought the couple's third son, William, into the world on January 6, 1934. Soon, she became a regular figure at the CPUSA's Manhattan headquarters. To camouflage her role, she later wrote a few articles on the party's foreign-language groups.[19]

Her presence elicited differing reactions from ranking cadres. Gil Green, who headed the Young Communist League (YCL) and sat on the CPUSA's Political Committee, considered Earl's actions courageous. Boldly he defied popular stereotypes by bringing to the United States a Russian wife and two children who spoke no English. By contrast, A. B. Magil was less impressed. He considered Raissa a loud, dogmatic, "very aggressive" woman who lacked charm and likability. He doubted that she had many female friends and resented how she seemed to assert the Soviet CP's authority without actually claiming to do so.[20] Raissa, used to holding important party and governmental positions in the USSR, must have had initial difficulty adjusting to the CPUSA's mundane atmosphere. She also probably missed the company of college graduates. Yet lacking any particular literary talents, she did not fit in with fellow-traveling writers either.

Shortly before the outbreak of World War II, ex-Communist Benjamin Gitlow contended that Stalin had assigned Raissa to give Browder companionship and to guide his steering of the CP. The story helped sell books, but Gitlow never proved it. A different scenario seems more probable. In a situation that reversed somewhat traditional male/female social roles, Earl was attracted to Raissa in part by his own inner craving for higher education. She, in turn, liked his good looks and curiosity. Certainly, with her long record as a Soviet apparatchik and doctoral student training, she provided a handy referent for likely Moscow views. Before 1936 she obviously had better credentials than he did. The personal affinity was real, however, as Felix's and Andrew's births suggest. Earl and Raissa's relationship, though politically beneficial to both, was nevertheless more than one of convenience. As he grew in confidence, her

Earl and Raissa Browder, New York, 1930s.
(From the Syracuse University Library, Department of
Special Collections, 600 Bird Library. Used by permission.)

role became less clear. Harvey Klehr, John Haynes, and Fridrikh Firsov
have shown that as late as 1939 she received a message from CPUSA Moscow representative Pat Toohey. It can be interpreted as a coded request for
her (and by inference Earl) to aid Comintern agents in the United States.[21]
By year's end, however, Raissa, besieged by U.S. government officials,
had settled into the unspectacular life of an American homemaker.
While battling deportation, she helped inspire her sons toward educational excellence, but her party contribution dwindled to insignificance.

In 1934 and 1935 Earl benefited from Raissa's Moscow orientation and worked closely with Gerhart Eisler, an exiled German Communist who represented the International in New York after mid-1933. The AAS kept Eisler, known in the United States as "E. Edwards" and "Ed," informed on "principal issues." One included a January 1934 preparation for "the illegality of the CPUSA." This, of course, did not mean resorting to terrorism or sabotage. Instead, Browder, Eisler, and "Randolph" (William Schneiderman) were ordered to begin planning the party's response to an anticipated federal government crackdown. At an AAS meeting attended by Otto Kuusinen and Ossip Piatnitsky the issue of sending a special Soviet plenipotentiary to oversee party readiness for the worst was discussed. Until that time Browder would direct the secret apparatus, ably described by historians Klehr, Haynes, and Firsov. That March the Comintern announced that it would send its specific proposals concerning the CPUSA's April convention through Eisler.[22]

At the same time the agile Browder also moved in the opposite direction, in part because of United Front successes in Western Europe. While performing his usual duties of supervising CPUSA activities and giving speeches, including several fiery ones to the striking Toledo auto workers, he began wooing the SP's leadership vigorously, reaching out to a broader section of intellectuals and trying to build an antifascist labor party. Results first appeared in mid-1934. Browder and his Central Committee pushed YCL leaders into an alliance with the Young People's Socialist League. Together, they captured control of the American Youth Congress's inaugural convention in August. That same month SP chief Norman Thomas hinted he might be willing to cooperate with the CPUSA on specific issues. Immediately Browder fired off a letter proposing a full-fledged United Front. Thomas could hardly accept the offer. The surging Communists had recently eclipsed the declining Socialists in membership to become the American left's paramount party. The SP had lost even the grassroots trade union support among brewery workers, machinists, and miners it had enjoyed since about 1880. The Old Guard blamed Thomas. Accordingly, he gave Browder an evasive reply and referred the matter to the SP's National Executive Committee. It rejected CP advances in early September. Discipline in the Socialist party was imperfect, however. In some small midwestern communities joint SP-CP "Workers' " tickets appeared.[23]

That same month Browder launched a vigorous effort to attract more intellectuals by having the CPUSA reexamine its John Reed clubs. Decentralized radical writers' guilds, the clubs took their name from the famous journalist and party founding father, one of only four Americans entombed beside the Kremlin wall. Although the groups had nurtured some talent, they had become hangouts for unemployed young men who talked of culture but wrote and painted little. Browder wanted to replace them with a broad organization that would welcome liberals and well-known fellow travelers. Here he made an important innovation for the CPUSA. Previous leaders, including the college-educated Jay Lovestone, had done nothing to entice the intelligentsia. William Z. Foster once told essayist V. F. Calverton contemptuously that mapping out revolutionary strategy was "a thousand times more important" than literary work. Browder did not deny that he valued writers more for their prestige than for "the purity of their Marxism or intrinsic literary merit," as historian Daniel Aaron put it. Browder, too, considered intellectuals undisciplined and unreliable, but he did not see them as ornaments. Rallying public opinion behind antifascist unity was serious business and required significant nonproletarian support.[24]

Accordingly, in September 1934 at the John Reed clubs' Chicago national convention, speakers attacked the organizations' sectarianism and their writers' sloganized verse. CPUSA cultural affairs director Alexander Trachtenberg proposed dissolving them altogether and organizing a much broader national congress of more established figures. A then-unknown African American poet and novelist, Richard Wright, was thunderstruck on learning of the decision. Not knowing that better things awaited him elsewhere, he protested the fate of the CP's many journeyman authors, who now found themselves ineligible for the new league of literati. Wright received a stony silence. Most intellectuals supported the party's abandonment of propaganda-laden "proletarian art."[25]

That November's off-year elections caused Browder to regret Third Period isolation all the more. Traditionally the party holding the presidency loses about twenty-five House of Representatives seats. This time, however, Roosevelt's Democrats gained thirteen House seats and picked up nine seats in the Senate, giving them the greatest upper chamber margin either party had ever held. Many new members stood left of the administration. Yet FDR, whom Browder still considered to be a near-fascist, hedged. Historian J. Joseph Huthmacher has noted that some observers believed that the New Deal was "running out of ideas or out of the will and momentum to press any one of them to a meaningful conclusion."[26]

Browder decided that the time for a new major party had come. Behind Third Period policies, the Communists could never attract large numbers. They could neither compete with the new demagogic movements nor steal their members. Reflecting on French and Italian Communists' recent good fortunes, Browder began to envision a labor party in America that would include the CP and SP.

Herein lay some of Browder's strengths. Socialist Robert J. Alexander, who came to know him casually, once cited willingness to follow Moscow's orders as the reason why Browder was leading the American movement. Many others also saw him only on this surface level, and certainly he never considered defying the Soviets. But loyalty alone did not make him valuable—Stalin had no shortage of errand boys. Browder enjoyed success because, within permissible parameters, he used initiative and sought his own solutions to problems. His keen bureaucratic intuition gave him the single most valuable Communist survival skill: the ability to anticipate change and end up on the emerging side.[27]

Ever since the Farmer-Labor fiasco eleven years earlier, Browder had ruminated over squandered opportunities. Now he moved cautiously. Shortly after midterm balloting he wrote an article for publication in February 1935. In it he envisioned four possible scenarios, three of them unattractive. He feared a "populist or progressive" party dominated by the La Follettes, Upton Sinclair, and their followers; an essentially similar grouping calling itself farmer-laborites; and an effort led by the "trade union bureaucracy" and SP, but excluding the Communists. Browder proposed a fourth alternative: creating a CPUSA-led antifascist labor party "boldly trampling the interests of capital." Communists should build it up in left-leaning states, adopting a practical position and suitable local tactics.[28]

Browder won Comintern approval, pleading his case in person, in December 1934. Returning to the United States, he promoted the idea dramatically. He chose the National Congress for Unemployment Insurance meeting in Washington as a forum. There, on January 6, 1935, he revealed his innovative platform publicly. In so doing he caught cadres by surprise. Over subsequent weeks he calmed their anger, but the labor party concept attracted few non-Communist adherents. Indeed, while Browder was in Moscow the SP's National Executive Committee prohibited direct cooperation with the CPUSA for eighteen months, exempting only a few local affiliates.[29]

Also in January Browder admitted that the international line on labor unions had changed as well. Actually four months earlier the flagging TUUL, following a Profintern ruling, had proposed a face-saving merger with the AFL. Historian Harvey A. Levenstein has observed that the smaller organization's weakness "as well as the obsessive anticommunism of William Green, Matthew Woll, John P. Frey and the 'old guard' clique which dominated the AFL, made the offer laughable." It brought "nothing but vituperation." By March 1935 the TUUL had simply collapsed. The only significant exceptions were a group of metal workers who entered the Machinists Union intact and Ben Gold's Fur Workers, larger numerically than their AFL counterparts. Although a failure, the TUUL left a heroic legacy. As historian James R. Green has noted, its "unions had fought on bravely for four years against the most brutal kind of anti-union violence, and they had kept the banner of militant industrial unionism waving."[30]

Still championing the labor party cause, Browder turned again toward the intellectuals. On January 22 the CPUSA's literary journal, *New Masses*, called an American Writers' Congress. It invited authors of "considerable achievement and standing" who could unite in a general antifascist defense of culture regardless of "aesthetic or political views." The gathering opened at New York's Mecca Temple on April 26, four weeks after the Socialists had rejected another CP United Front offer. Four hundred delegates attended, including Malcolm Cowley, Langston Hughes, and John Dos Passos. The chairperson read several papers of those who could not attend. Louis Aragon's "From Dada to the Red Front" traced many writers' intellectual pilgrimage from artistic protest to social activism. Browder, ever conscious that he was unlettered, was thrilled to give the opening address. Leading a workaholic lifestyle, especially since becoming CPUSA head, he had not had the time to read those artists' books. Still, he knew that their gifts had made them famous, and he envied them all. His speech praised those attending, characterizing artists as traditionally uninterested in politics. The depression, however, had forced them to recognize the class struggle. That decision rejuvenated and enriched their work. Browder alluded to Third Period programs and actions, coming as close as Communism permitted to acknowledging the party could make errors of substance. Instead of dwelling on an indefensible past, however, he indicated that a more positive outlook had now emerged. He assured his audience that the CPUSA did "not want to take good writers and make bad strike leaders" of them. He conceded that no political line could define works of art. Although dissident Communist intellectual Max Eastman had recently warned that the Stalin cult would put them "in uniform," Browder calmly assured listeners that the masses would constitute the final authority.[31]

Then he delivered the thrust of his message. The Communists sought to stimulate humanistic literature and promote cooperative relations among all antifascist cultural workers. Browder declared that the common enemy threatened "everything we hold dear" and spoke of strength through unity. "We are not alone. We have brothers in every land," he proclaimed, underscoring worldwide abhorrence of the Nazis. He closed by offering a carrot: associating with Communists could help the literati financially. He pledged that the new League of American Writers, which the party was now creating, would tackle economic problems by organizing a market and setting work standards. Intellectuals, no less than other citizens, suffered from the depression's economic blight. Moreover, they realized fully that people could forego books more easily than bread or clothing.[32]

This first American Writers' Congress marked an important early step in the CPUSA's United Front campaign. Communists clearly controlled it, packing its presiding committee. Yet at least half the members were nonparty figures. More significantly, according to Daniel Aaron, "no speaker" confused "political correctness with literary talent." In fact, many spent "as much time belaboring the inanity and sterility of would-be revolutionary writing as in praising or encouraging its producers." In later years a repentant former Communist Granville Hicks would dismiss the entire affair as a device for strengthening Soviet foreign policy. Nevertheless, historian Matthew Josephson, who spoke there, and many other liberals found the Communists' new words entirely reasonable. To them the idea of worldwide unity presented the most practical way to save civilization from fascist barbarism.[33]

Before most other groups, intellectuals appreciated the significance of the CPUSA's crusade. The intelligentsia's support in turn facilitated the CP's process of change. As scores lent their names to Communist-sponsored causes, they helped the party build an unprecedented degree of respectability.

While Browder enjoyed standing in ever-brighter spotlights, Bill Foster ached for a meaningful role in the movement. He believed that his breakdown had cost him the CPUSA leadership in 1932, and he had experienced an agonizingly slow recovery. Admirer Joseph North wrote that for three years Foster "dared not even make a ten-minute speech." Now back in New York and back at work, he found Browder's followers cruelly exploiting his fears, giving him the "genteel treatment." Constantly they admonished him to preserve his fragile health by avoiding overwork. Soon his role as CPUSA chairman became largely ceremonial. Although he provided caustic criticism every time Browder stumbled, Foster found himself dismissed as a relic of a bygone era. A mean-spirited rigidity set in. Associate David Ramsey later recalled that Foster "felt incomparably superior to everyone around him. He considered himself a mass leader against cockroaches and New York intellectuals."[34] He lived for the day when he could avenge slights suffered at Browder's hands.

The Communists and other depression-era radicals underestimated enormously Roosevelt's political acumen. That spring and summer, despite a major setback from the Supreme Court, the president pushed a series of sweeping reforms through the most liberal Congress Americans had ever elected. Collectively known as the Second New Deal, the legislation quickly won back for the Democrats eroding working-class support and stole the demagogues' thunder. FDR's 1935 actions proved him the greatest American politician of the twentieth century and removed any doubt the capitalist system would survive.

In March Congress created the Works Progress Administration (WPA), a gigantic federal employment program that in time reached one-third of the nation's jobless. On May 27, in the *Schechter* decision, the Court ruled the National Industrial Recovery Act unconstitutional, leaving workers unprotected in their organizing and collective bargaining activities. Seizing the offensive on June 19, Roosevelt sent a radical-sounding tax measure to Capitol Hill. Its provisions read as if Huey Long had written them: federal inheritance and gift taxes and higher personal rates on the upper income brackets. Congress, on learning that FDR would not fight an adjournment motion, quickly emasculated the bill without White House protest. The measure, though a cynical sham, brought the New Deal a political windfall.

In early July the Socialist party rejected yet another CPUSA United Front proposal. Browder and top cadres left for Moscow to attend the Communist International's Seventh World Congress. Public attention, however, focused on Washington. There, because of the labor militancy of 1933 and 1934, the president signed the National Labor Relations Act, which he had not originally supported. Sponsored by Senator Robert F. Wagner of New York, it placed the national government behind much of the proletariat in the struggle to organize. As historian James R. Green has noted, it "finally gave federal recognition to the rights workers had been asserting for more than a century": liberty to engage in collective bargaining, and free speech in advocating unionism and protesting unfair labor practices.[35]

In August a direct New Deal response to the Townsend movement occurred while the most important assemblage in Comintern history was taking place. The Roosevelt administration's Social Security Act provided pensions and unemployment insurance for most private-sector employees and mandated direct assistance to dependent children and disabled workers. Although other industrialized democracies offered national health insurance as well, Roosevelt instead established a commission to study and bury the issue.

Despite its shortcomings, the Second New Deal's legislation made Roosevelt the hero of the common man and woman. Union labor adopted the Democratic party as its own. Much of the SP's right wing, especially the Old Guard, mistakenly saw the administration's reforms as paving the way to socialism.

Browder despised FDR for stealing the working class from the workers' parties. As his steamship inched across the Atlantic, Browder pondered two questions. How would the International judge his innovations? How would it respond to Roosevelt's greatly enhanced political standing?

## DIMITROV AND THE NEW DIRECTION

The World Congress was theoretically the only body higher than the Comintern's Executive Committee. Originally expected to convene annually, it had lain dormant since 1928. By 1935 it had become totally ceremonial, showcasing policy changes. Browder, who had watched his friend Dimitrov's influence grow, knew the upcoming meeting would repudiate Third Period remnants and inaugurate a United Front policy with great fanfare. PCF leader Maurice Thorez and others who had anticipated the change would reap almost as much acclaim as Dimitrov. Confidently Browder expected a few accolades for his own labor party pioneering.

Back in April someone in Moscow had insisted that the CPUSA visa list include Sam Darcy. Darcy was a Political Committee member, but his name had been omitted because Browder considered him arrogant. Although not often rude, Darcy had frequently clashed with Browder over tactics; Darcy's proposal to support Upton Sinclair's California gubernatorial campaign covertly had led to an acrimonious exchange only months earlier. Browder's and the party's decision to reject the idea had proved a good example of Third Period lunacy. Browder wondered aloud to advisor Robert Minor why anyone would invite Darcy. Minor, whose

main function was to defend his boss at every turn, came to a quick conclusion. After obtaining Browder's permission, he sidled up to Darcy one
afternoon, gloating that the Comintern wanted to rub excrement in his
face to bring him to his senses.[36]

That summer in Moscow new delegations arrived daily, many in native
costume. The hospitable Russians greeted them with extra emotion because they came from underground movements. Profascist dictatorships
had convicted many in absentia on horrendous charges and put prices
on their heads. Some eight hundred deputies had arrived by the opening day of the Seventh World Congress. Darcy later observed that no one
could know that within just fifteen years almost half "would constitute
the core of government" controlling nations ruling "forty percent of the
world's population."[37] At the time combating Hitlerism was the only concern.

To ensure accurate reporting and forestall disputes, keynote speaker
Dimitrov first deliberated with representatives of every country his address would mention. Darcy, elected American delegation secretary, co-
ordinated the schedule with Dimitrov's assistant. On meeting day they
entered the conference room to find the walls decorated with scores of
CPUSA publications, more than half written by Browder. Their titles reviled the New Deal as Nazi-like and predisposed toward imperialist war
on the USSR. When the irascible Dimitrov arrived, battling stomach ulcer
discomfort, he called Darcy aside and showed him a paper written in
German. It asserted that "Roosevelt's policies are carrying the United
States in a fascist direction." Facing Darcy, who had learned German
from his wife Emma Blechschmidt, Dimitrov demanded, "Does this
fairly represent the propaganda line of your party?" Darcy answered yes
and was taken aback by the grim reply: "I've read a great deal of your
literature and I know it does. I just wanted to see if we needed to argue
about the facts."[38]

After about forty American comrades filed in, Dimitrov addressed
them, also in German. CPUSA members sat in small groups, each with a
translator. Somehow Darcy ended up between Browder and Foster, both
of whom spoke only English. Dimitrov previewed his report, summarizing the fascist monster's growth and the inadequate efforts to combat it.
Then, astonishing everyone, he praised President Roosevelt's policies.
According to Darcy, "as he spoke his bull neck" reddened visibly, and his
voice showed increasing ire. His anger reached its apex when he pulled
out his projected report and read: "One must indeed be a confirmed idiot

not to see that it is the most reactionary proNazi circles of American finance capital which are attacking Roosevelt . . . that the antiNazi forces must rally around Roosevelt."[39]

Dimitrov's words demanded a unity effort far broader than anything Browder had imagined. Attacking Sinclair, the moderate leftist, had been wrong, and now denouncing FDR, the centrist, was also incorrect. Clearly the Comintern had become more upset about fascism's spread than about Roosevelt's role in shortchanging the American working class. Dimitrov, wiping his brow, sat down. Looking at no one in particular, he requested comments. After a tomblike silence, he offered the floor to Darcy, who declined rather than lessen the effect. Next, Dimitrov sought a word from Foster. A sectarian even more critical of Roosevelt than Browder, he remained quiet, enjoying his enemy's pain. Finally, the Bulgarian told Darcy to ask Browder if he wished to speak. Barely containing his glee, Darcy translated the message. Browder, pale, stiff, and fearing his leadership days had ended, shook his head negatively.

Suddenly Dimitrov softened. "If your silence means assent then I'll reword this section of my report." Producing another paper, he read: "One must be very partial to hackneyed schemes not to see that the most reactionary circles of American finance capital, which are attacking Roosevelt, are above all the very force which is stimulating and organizing the fascist movement in the United States."[40]

Dimitrov then promised to put the criticism in his closing speech instead of his main report. The denunciation left a lasting impression on Browder. Deeply humiliated at receiving scathing public criticism from a friend he so admired, he vowed never again to appear left of the party line. Although he refused thereafter to acknowledge that the unpleasant confrontation had occurred, he swiftly changed his outlook on FDR and the New Deal.

When the Congress opened, Dimitrov gave two dramatic speeches, on August 2 and 13, designed to attract the entire world's attention. Detailing graphically the International's new orientation, he warned that fascism threatened civilization itself. Defined as the power of finance capital, it triumphed when the proletariat was divided and then employed terrorist vengeance against the working class, revolutionary peasantry, and intelligentsia. It marked chauvinism in its most brutal form, fomenting bestial hatred of other peoples. In Germany the Nazis had capitalized on existing xenophobia and appealed to outraged national sentiments that the Versailles Treaty had engendered. Everywhere fascism promised

"a broad highway to a brilliant future" but rapidly converted "the workers and unemployed into pariahs." It destroyed trade unions, the right to
strike, and freedom of the press. Although Dimitrov's message did not
constitute news, it revealed a fresh Communist approach. Since 1928
the Comintern had recognized no qualitative difference between fascists
and other capitalists. By contrast this Congress proclaimed: "Though up-
holders of Soviet democracy, *we shall defend every inch of the democratic gains
which the working class has wrested in the course of years of stubborn struggle
and shall resolutely fight to expand these gains*" (italics in original).[41]

Although Dimitrov blamed the reactionaries' rise on Social Democrats,
he admitted that Communist parties also had aided it. He listed numerous mistakes foreign comrades had made without mentioning that they
were following Stalin's policy at the time. Errors included underestimating the fascist danger and speaking in unintelligible terms. Dimitrov
also lambasted Marxist sectarians who had exaggerated mass radicalization and had refused to work in reformist trade unions. Extremism had
retarded CP growth. "The masses must be taken as they are and not
as we should like to have them."[42] Next, he outlined the new International policy, announcing two complementary programs: the proletarian
United Front and the antifascist Popular Front.

The former had only slight relevance to American conditions, but signified social fascism's repudiation. Dimitrov defined the United Front as
joint action by adherents of the two Internationals and intended it for
polities featuring large Social Democratic movements. Thus Communist
leaders sought alliance with the very Socialists whom, until recently, they
had considered the primary adversary. In fact, pan-leftist cooperation
had now become indispensable to progress.

Such a coalition would have a chance to win national elections in some
lands. It then could enact legislation to abolish capitalism. Unlike Euro-
communists of the 1970s, however, the CP leaders would not pledge
to preserve political democracy after gaining governmental control. Indeed, the Comintern called the United Front the "decisive link" to "the
forthcoming great battles" of revolution's "second round." Victory there
would bring proletarian dictatorship. Had Communists attained power,
they almost certainly would have banned political opponents, even those
also dedicated to socialism. The International contended, absurdly, that
because Marxism constituted a "science," its party line could never be
incorrect. Logically, therefore, the movement could not permit a loyal opposition. As historian Kermit McKenzie has noted, "Unused to genuine

democracy within their ranks, the Communists could hardly be expected to practice democracy outside their party."[43] Herein also lay one cause of the United Front's failure.

Although the United Front raised fascinating possibilities, it offered no significant impact on the United States, where only capitalists enjoyed mass followings. Accordingly, the Congress advanced a second unprecedented program: the antifascist Popular Front. Designed for nations lacking class-oriented workers, the Popular Front sought to attract to leftist programs the urban petty bourgeoisie, intelligentsia, and office workers.

The Communists thereby abandoned proletarian purity and courted the middle classes, lest reactionaries profit by exploiting the "red menace." Still, nowhere did Dimitrov sanction the ultimate revolutionary goal's repudiation. The Popular Front signaled the Communists' decision that defense against reactionaries had become paramount and that the offensive toward socialism had to be postponed indefinitely.

Dimitrov concluded by proclaiming "we want all this" in order to "sweep fascism off the face of the earth and together with it, capitalism."[44] He enunciated laudable goals. Yet, he neglected to mention that the Comintern also wanted to discard political democracy.

On August 11 Earl Browder stood before the gathering. An ECCI alternate since 1931, he had become a full member at this Congress. Chastened, he admitted to the packed auditorium past errors and echoed his friend Dimitrov. Browder announced that the American Communists would appeal thenceforth "to all opponents of fascism" yet not demand they support proletarian dictatorship. Dimitrov had congratulated the CPUSA for "taking the initiative" in trying to break away from the Democrats and Republicans, but criticized their failure to win mass support. He suggested that a Farmer-Labor party should constitute the "specific form of the mass People's Front in America." Such a coalition would be neither Socialist nor Communist. But it had to be antifascist and not anti-Marxist. Browder confessed that his own exclusion of farmers had been a mistake and supported the new line enthusiastically. In his speech, which appeared in the Soviet journal *Bolshevik* that very day, he demanded confiscation of idle factories; a capital levy to fund social insurance; proportional representation in Congress; and curbs on the Supreme Court's power to invalidate legislation.[45]

The Congress made a final, unprecedented contribution to the international movement. Its concluding report attempted to reduce the dogmatism many non-Russian Communist parties displayed. Previously they had copied Bolshevik forms so slavishly that they had diminished local

CP appeal. The document denounced "mechanical application of the experience of one country to another."[46]

Of course, the report ignored Stalin's repeated inference that Western CPs must prepare to seize power in the Soviet manner. It nevertheless gave individual parties increased responsibility to conduct "day to day leadership themselves" so they might exploit "sharp turns of events, independently and quickly." To add emphasis, the Congress "instructed" the ECCI to avoid interfering with Communist parties' internal affairs and instead to address mutual problems.[47]

The Comintern ordered followers everywhere to find links with native radical traditions. Supporting words with deeds, it recalled its representatives who had been supervising non-Russian parties. The changes lightened the burdens of Kremlin bureaucrats and, more significantly, allowed provincial CPs to employ the twentieth century's most potent political force, nationalism.

The increased autonomy created a historical antecedent for later reforms, including Titoism, polycentrism, Eurocommunism, perestroika, and other attempts to reconcile Communism with representative government. It also augmented Browder's power dramatically. Thereafter he advanced innovations with far less restraint. Although the World Congress had ordered CPs to softpedal insurrectionary rhetoric, Dimitrov's keynote address had alluded repeatedly to proletarian power seizures after United Front election victories. By contrast, Browder soon told a radio audience that the CPUSA "does not advocate force and violence. It is a legal party and defends its legality. Communists are not conspirators, not terrorists, not anarchists." He also revealed that his organization had begun expelling unrepentant revolutionaries in 1934.[48]

Browder, ever the history buff, recognized a characteristic of American violence that few scholars of his generation stressed. Force, though occasionally employed by radicals, has originated more often from the political right. He would soon declare that "machine guns are not strangers to American streets, but it has never been the Communists that have brought them out. It is usually the strike-breaking agencies employed by the capitalists which have." We "would like to stop all that."[49]

The SP's Old Guard, of course, considered the Comintern's new line a fraud. It emphasized the USSR's suppression of dissent and murderous elimination of the kulaks, agricultural collectivization's victims. It viewed Socialists who cooperated with Communists as dupes. For Old Guard members anti-Communism became an obsession, clouding all other vision.

Browder returned to New York in September 1935 to a press conference where he ballyhooed the Farmer-Labor party concept, which generated far less enthusiasm. How could Browder, a good Comintern soldier, make Dimitrov's idea work in the United States? The Communists, he announced, would provide all necessary support short of actually calling a convention, lest their enemies accuse them of bossing the effort. The new party could serve as a bulwark against reaction, avert fascism's development, and help prevent war. A reporter asked Browder about the New Deal's allegedly socialistic work relief programs. Scornfully, he denounced them, citing their separation from the rest of the economy. Only government operation of idle factories and paying workers union wages would end the depression. When the inevitable question regarding revolutionary violence came up, Browder reminded listeners that the greatest threat came from the far right and cited Nazi Germany as a recent example.[50]

Shortly thereafter third-party hopes crested. A fatally ill Minnesota Governor Floyd B. Olson, whose own Farmer-Labor party had captured the state house in 1930, invited Browder to visit and settle old differences. During the Third Period the CPUSA had reviled Olson as a social fascist. Browder made the initial contact. Olson responded by urging him to come to Minneapolis. Browder already had a speech scheduled for October 18, 1935, and secretly met Olson that afternoon. The governor sought to align his Farmer-Labor party with the left, but not let it degenerate into a sect. Browder considered the talk "very pleasant and productive." On parting, the two promised to maintain friendly relations even when they differed on policy questions. Olson subsequently discouraged those who wished to block Communist influx into his movement.[51]

Certainly Browder relished being the only CPUSA head ever to discuss political strategy with an incumbent American governor. He also took great pleasure as the Socialists' ban on cooperation began to unravel. Meta Berger, widow of the SP's first Congressman, Victor, defied it. She and forty-nine other prominent members worked for a complete United Front.[52]

Yet domestic events, however exciting, did not stop Browder from thinking globally. On September 2 he wrote to Dimitrov in Moscow concerning some items they had not enjoyed the time to discuss during Browder's recent visit. Having already conferred with top Comintern officials Otto Kuusinen, Dimitri Manuilsky, Wilhelm Pieck, and Palmiro Togliatti, Browder asked that Gerhart Eisler return to the United States at least until the CPUSA's 1936 convention. Eisler usually sided with Browder during intramural disputes. Browder also requested permission to create, and funds to sponsor, an anti-imperialist newspaper in Shanghai. The publisher, already in China, would be journalist Agnes Smedley. A radical American feminist and friend of birth control militant Margaret Sanger, Smedley was an intimate acquaintance of Soviet spy Richard Sorge. Shortly thereafter the AAS sent Eisler back to the United States. Smedley came up with money to establish the *Voice of China* and enjoyed the editorial assistance of Browder's secretary, Grace Granich, and her husband, Manny (also known as Max).[53]

Meanwhile the actions of a veteran anti-Communist were about to give the CPUSA a magnificent opportunity to spread its influence. United Mine Workers President John L. Lewis believed that the AFL was dissipating a golden chance to organize America's mass-production industries. Although the federation had adopted a high-toned resolution that advocated reaching out to steel, rubber, and auto workers, Lewis knew from long experience on the ruling Executive Council that traditionalists would block any genuine efforts. Yet as historian Robert H. Zieger has observed, the United Mine Workers had never recruited on a crafts basis, and "modern industry, in which the vast majority of workers toiled, had been making nonsense out of traditional definitions of skill." In October, when the AFL's convention defeated attempts to place the federation's resources behind an industrial unionism campaign, Lewis captured the entire labor movement's attention. After heated words on the floor with the carpenters' leader, burly "Big Bill" Hutcheson, Lewis planted a short, snapping right lead on his jaw, sending the dazed and bloodied crafts unionist sprawling against a table. Biographers Melvyn Dubofsky and Warren Van Tine insist that cool calculation, not anger, explained the outburst. The blow "was intended to symbolize publicly the UMW president's irrevocable rupture with labor's old guard." On November 9 Lewis, David Dubinsky, Sidney Hillman, and Charles Howard founded the Committee for Industrial Organization (CIO). Already assured a fighting image, the body announced publicly that it would operate through the AFL to promote industrial unionism.[54]

Although Browder had denounced Lewis as a reactionary a mere six months earlier, he was one of the first top Communists to grasp the CIO's significance. He had learned a lesson from the CPUSA's isolation during the 1920s. Now Browder was determined to create a significant Communist presence among the new labor organization. He knew it would require receiving as little personal recognition as his Minnesota Farmer-Labor party efforts had brought him.

Browder had good reason for making peace with his old enemy. Lewis, having decided to launch a frontal assault on the open shop, needed talented and dedicated organizers. The party had a wealth of them, whereas the bureaucrats of the United Mine Workers displayed no real abilities beyond defending the boss in every manner possible. In late October Lewis publicly offered an olive branch to the CP by giving *Daily Worker's* Marguerite Young an exclusive interview. Organizational director John Brophy visited Browder personally and requested the party's aid. Elated, Browder pledged full support in November. Indeed, in 1995 historians Harvey Klehr, John Haynes, and Fridrikh Firsov claimed to have found Comintern evidence that documented an explicit agreement between Lewis and Sidney Hillman of the CIO and Browder, Foster, and Clarence Hathaway of the CPUSA. The writers promised future publication of a list of Communist functionaries Lewis had agreed to hire.[55]

Browder, in a 1936 Moscow debate, defended the party's subordinate CIO role. He responded to a concern raised by Solomon Lozovsky that American comrades were being exploited by labor bosses. Browder declared boldly, "If Lewis is using us in this I wish [AFL president] William Green would use us in this way too." Such leaders might "ride this horse very high . . . but they are riding for a fall because it is our horse and they cannot steal it."[56]

The CPUSA's backdoor relationship with the CIO differed from its contacts with Governor Benson's followers in one important way. A role had to be found for rival William Z. Foster, who was recovering his health and reasserting his voice in the party just as the industrial unionism movement was gaining momentum. Rightly, Browder felt inferior to Foster in the labor field; he had never led a job action whereas Foster had organized the Great Steel Strike. Accordingly, Browder developed a dialectical approach to the problem. On one hand he tried to take advantage of Foster's experience for the greater good of the CPUSA. The latter's biographer, Edward P. Johanningsmeier, declares that "Foster remained the authoritative public spokesman for issues pertaining to the labor movement during the 1930s." At the same time, however, Browder appointed ex-seaman Roy Hudson to head formally the CP's trade union work. Clearly he wanted a yes-man with flawless proletarian credentials to counter any intraparty mischief Foster might stir up.[57]

Also in the autumn of 1935, a series of debates occurred between Browder and Norman Thomas. The most significant took place in Madison Square Garden on November 27 and drew twenty thousand spectators.

Browder allowed the SP to keep all gate receipts. The gathering featured communal singing of the "Internationale," "Red Flag," and "Solidarity Forever." Browder offered that the occasion heralded more united action, but Thomas expressed reservations. He cited the CPUSA's Third Period record and wanted the Communists to "prove sincerity and good faith." Browder announced that an "unbridgeable chasm" no longer existed. Thomas, willing to cooperate on specific issues, nevertheless underscored that the SP still supported democracy over dictatorship.[58]

Clumsily Browder praised Thomas's "advanced position" as wiser than the Old Guard's. Thomas snapped that Browder was not qualified to judge Socialist factional battles. Testily Thomas questioned how a Popular Front could ever emancipate the workers when it included Democrats and Republicans. The evening ended on a positive note, nonetheless, as he reiterated his desire for limited cooperation and called Browder "comrade."

Predictably, the Old Guard denounced the proceedings. New York City Chairman Algernon Lee termed the event a "love feast" that served only the CP. The *New York Times,* by contrast, considered a United Front a genuine possibility because Hitler had proved that "Communists are not predestined heirs of chaos." A younger generation found the squabbling passé, however. The Socialists' Student League for Industrial Democracy and the Communists' National Student League merged in December, forming the American Student Union. Both parties' unemployed organizations worked together openly. Thomas himself joined the Scottsboro and Herndon defense campaigns, both CPUSA causes célèbres during the 1930s. Subsequent unity efforts foundered but not because of Communist perfidy. Just as the CP was abandoning sectarianism, Thomas and his faction were approximating a traditional Leninist view.[59]

Despite Browder's frenetic efforts, by year's end his national Farmer-Labor party had clearly miscarried. The idea of directly following the Communists appealed to few. A cancer-ridden Governor Olson spent his final months building Farmer-Laborism but nevertheless endorsed President Roosevelt's 1936 reelection. He thereby forced Browder to face an unpleasant reality. The CPUSA had followed Dimitrov's advice dutifully, but it had produced no results. Browder now decided to use the increased latitude given national Communist leaders that summer. He would try to display the type of enterprise that had brought PCF leader Thorez international acclaim. Yet painful questions lay ahead. What more could the Communists do to show they sincerely sought to work with other groups? Had the left as an independent force spent itself? Should Browder help build a Popular Front behind the president? If so, how could the Communists bring him more votes than their endorsement would cost? Could radicals count on FDR to oppose capitalism's abuses in any fundamental way?

# FOUR

■

## Native Radicalism (1936)

In 1936 Earl Browder stumbled onto an approach that rapidly made him the greatest leader in CPUSA history. It brought the party out of the political wilderness and made it a recognized force in American life. Soon the Communists faced two questions they had never needed to contemplate before and to which Moscow could supply no answers. Why did they become so successful so quickly? Could they build on their achievements to reach full legitimacy in American life?

Although Georgi Dimitrov's proposed Farmer-Labor party idea generated no interest, the Popular Front developed widespread appeal among America's non-Communist liberals and radicals who had long advocated unity against fascism. It most inspired those who took up the monumental, often maddening task of pushing Franklin Roosevelt leftward. The Popular Front, by dropping calls for revolution and obscuring the distinction between progressivism and Marxism, allowed them to believe Communists had become reformers. Upton Sinclair chuckled, "I do not mean to be egotistical and imply that they have taken my advice, but it is a fact that they are now saying and doing what I urged them for many years to say and do."[1]

To some liberals Communists represented a valuable prize. Although few in number, they possessed energy and determination that had made them almost legendary. They were willing to spend icy mornings handing out leaflets at a factory gate or subway entrance. They knew how to pack meetings and delay crucial votes until late hours when opponents had gone to bed. In short, during the 1930s they were the left's organization people.

Why did the Popular Front succeed where the Farmer-Labor party had failed? Browder, without realizing fully how he was doing it, discovered a far more direct avenue to success in the United States. Like a modern, lost urban motorist accidentally turning on to an interstate ramp, in 1936

Browder unconsciously shifted his emphasis toward social and cultural factors rather than concentrating solely on the political. In the process he developed a significant insight. Whereas writer Max Eastman believed capitalism's collapse desirable but questioned its inevitability, Browder became convinced that the fall would certainly occur, but only in the distant future.

His new orientation led him to discover gifts he had not known he possessed. He had a flair for public relations befitting a Madison Avenue advertising executive. He stopped letting nonparty people see his Soviet traits and began marketing himself as a Kansas populist, complete with the boyhood twang he had never lost. The importance of this change transcends Browder's immediate career because it affected the whole Communist movement, and with it, the American left.

## AN ERA OF ELATION

The Seventh World Congress altered Western perceptions dramatically. Not since 1919 had Communism seemed less threatening. Friend Philip Jaffe termed the 1936 to 1939 era "years of euphoria" for Browder. Rapidly Browder became a public figure. Carrying his revised Marxist message, he addressed capacity crowds at Madison Square Garden. During the 1936 presidential campaign he toured the country, presenting the CPUSA's perspective in universities and black churches. Local radio stations sold him air time and even interviewed him. He won national visibility, although few recognized him on the street.[2] Not since Eugene Debs's day had an American leftist received such frequent favorable publicity.

No one considered Browder as proletarian as William Z. Foster, but he had a hundred times more impact. For more than a decade the domestic left acclaimed Browder almost as fervently as the Soviets hailed Stalin. Georgi Dimitrov labeled Browder the world's greatest English-speaking Marxist. He oversaw the Philippine Communist party and directly influenced Canada's. He reorganized Cuba's CP, mediated a Mexican party dispute in 1937, and maintained a running dialogue with refugees from Latin American dictatorships. New York City became a clearinghouse for the hemisphere's Marxist ideas.[3]

Browder publicized the CPUSA's new position well. His pleasant, bland nature and relaxed, confident manner offended no one. Quietly he copied Stalin's strategy of emphasizing his unspectacular straightforwardness as a character strength. Former YCL leader Gil Green recalled that Browder almost always pondered very carefully before reaching a decision. Afterward he could seem as stubborn as Foster, but he possessed broader vision that discriminating observers could not miss.[4] Indeed, Browder, more than any other individual, helped the party achieve respectability.

His easy-going demeanor surprised many. For the first time they could hear a Communist leader display wit. In 1936 he noted that the Great Depression had divided nearly all other political parties: "Even that old mummy, the Socialist Labor Party, revived sufficiently to suffer a major split that gave birth to a new baby mummy." Later he told a Congressional committee, "For the first time in my life, I am collecting sums of that much-talked-of 'Moscow gold.' I have received two checks from *Pravda* . . . paying me for articles." On another occasion Browder directed leftists who could not accept his innovations to turn to Norman Thomas and the Socialists, "who boast that their party is 'all-inclusive' and prove it" by taking in "every opinion under the sun."[5] Although Browder hardly rivaled comedian Will Rogers, neither did he seem the contentious, humorless zealot.

During the Popular Front era, Browder finally found his proper medium. Throughout the Third Period he had used rebellious rhetoric dutifully, but the bookkeeper in his soul had never fully adapted to the revolutionary climate. As his financial patron Philip Jaffe later reminisced, no longer did Browder "have to call FDR a fascist nor the NRA and the NLRB [National Labor Relations Board] enslavement programs." No more did he even have to dub Thomas a social fascist. In fact, Browder sought accord with nearly all past antagonists. He believed the new Comintern policy represented long-term strategy, not a temporary tactic.[6] These heady years gave Browder an opportunity to display a major character trait, his patience. During the depression many leftists underestimated the American public's conservatism and capacity to suffer. Passionate radicals, fired by the day's rhetoric, often developed unrealistic expectations. Yet the crisis never assumed a revolutionary character. As opportunity for fundamental change proved evanescent, bitter disillusionment frequently set in. Browder, by contrast, realized that the struggle for socialism would continue well beyond his lifetime. One may find countless examples of his overly optimistic predictions; indeed, his propagandist's role demanded them. Significantly, however, he never despaired after any of Marxism's defeats. Deep inside he knew his work would remain largely educational. Yet he clung to his conviction that economic injustice could not triumph forever.

The Popular Front affected CPUSA cadres profoundly. George Charney reminisced, "We were not only Communists, we were also Americans again. . . . And we were readily convinced that the two were not only compatible but inseparable." Dorothy Healey recalled, "We had a feeling that history was on our side and that we were making history every day."[7]

Browder and his followers attempted to break down social barriers between themselves and the public. Despite his playboy past, Browder dispelled notions that the CPUSA encouraged sexual perfidy. He rejected what he termed "all this bohemian pseudo-radicalism in relation to sex and the family." To Communists it proved only another example of capitalist society's decay. Asked to reconcile this statement with the USSR's easy divorce procedures, he produced one of his most intelligent defenses of Soviet policy: "We do not think that the home can be maintained, however, by making divorce more difficult. The proper way is to create conditions under which people won't want divorces. Permanent and healthy family life is built upon the secure possession by all people of the material basis of the family: that is adequate housing, plenty of food and clothing, and an assured income. It is still true very often that when poverty walks in the door love flies out the window."[8]

Occasionally Browder defended women's rights. He understood clearly that in almost every measurable way women workers, as a group, suffered more than their male counterparts during the Great Depression. At the time many people believed that working married women were responsible in part for unemployment, although only one-fifth of all U.S. women toiled outside the home. Historian Sharon Hartman Strom has observed that "because most women eventually married, the working woman was by default considered to be a young adult or 'working girl.' She was not a permanent member of the work world." Therefore, every "married working woman was an anomaly, present in the work force either through temporary financial necessity or personal selfishness. The implication for women was that work outside the home was a stage, not a right and that the mature woman belonged at home." Historian William Chafe has demonstrated that numerous state laws reinforced such an inference: often "a husband's consent was necessary for a wife to 'own' her earnings, [legislation] denied women the right to serve on juries or placed full responsibility on the mother for bringing up children born out of wedlock."[9]

The Economy Act of 1932 allowed the dismissal of one spouse if a couple worked for the federal government. Of the nearly fifteen hundred fired over the next twelve months, nearly all were women. Proposed state statutes sought to follow suit. Private industry repeated the practice. Virtually all banks and insurance firms refused to hire married women as clerical staff, forcing many workers to lie about their status. Browder denounced as fascist movements such efforts to drive women from the labor force.

The New Deal brought no fundamental reassessment of women's role in the economy. The codes of the National Industrial Recovery Act permitted lower pay rates for female employees. Federal protection did not extend to occupations where women appeared in disproportionate numbers: domestic and agricultural labor and clerical jobs. As Strom notes, "The NIRA [National Industrial Recovery Act] work relief section ignored women altogether and the Civilian Conservation Corps camps were originally for men only. When camps for females were set up, women received one half of what men were paid." Social Security taxed women workers the same as men but provided fewer benefits on retirement. The WPA provided jobs but only for one member of a family. Aid to Dependent Children often got women to stay home but paid far less than WPA rates.[10]

The labor movement, despite good intentions, did not always guarantee women succor. Ruth Milkman has shown that any successful efforts to organize women "had first to challenge the ideology of 'women's place'—a problem that did not arise in organizing men." By the 1930s many women worked in mass-production industries, but the AFL's policy of crafts exclusiveness hindered their organization. In addition, CIO unions perpetuated the AFL's tradition of contracting "women's jobs" at lower wages than men's.[11]

The Communists sent women a mixed message. Historian Robert Shaffer has demonstrated that the CPUSA, through its Women's Commission (a body with representatives around the country), independent committees, and auxiliaries of industrial unions at times raised feminist concerns. These concerns included legalizing and popularizing birth control (mostly before 1935), denouncing America's high infant mortality rate, and advocating child care and shared responsibility for housework. The party presented a Women's Charter to oppose the Equal Rights Amendment, which it deemed to be antiproletarian. Yet Shaffer concedes that the CP had a sexism problem; for example, it expected women to prepare food for strikers and often failed to push its organizations to go beyond gender-stereotyped roles. Party leadership "refused to admit any conceivable antagonism between working-class men and women."[12]

Elsa Dixler, however, has painted a far darker picture. She argues that during the Popular Front years the CPUSA "defaulted on its commitments to women" as it sought to ingratiate itself with the American people, most of whom "wanted to improve their standard of living, not alter their way of life." The Communists "undervalued women's work, denied them leadership and betrayed the theoretical Marxist commitment to human liberation." The party in the 1930s was "too thoroughly committed to a crude economic determinism to consider that culture can oppress as well as class." The organization appealed to women "in their roles as wives, housekeepers and mothers, rather than as people in their own right." Its "novelists made childbirth a symbol of struggle; they equated fertility with political change. Yet despite emotional appeals for the protection of mothers and children, the party only halfheartedly supported movements for day care centers and birth control."[13]

By the late 1930s the CPUSA's position came to reflect changes in the USSR. The Soviet Union, concerned about manpower needs in a hostile international climate and motivated by a desire to placate peasant men upset by earlier family reforms, launched a campaign against sexual promiscuity and irresponsibility. It declared homosexuality illegal in 1934 and banned abortions in 1936. American comrades reluctantly came to echo Russian views. More women held official positions in the Democratic party than in the Communist party. CPUSA women were underrepresented among candidates for public office and often given token posts in the peace movement and community organizations. Although Dixler's feminism degenerates into anti-Communism, the CP's priorities seemed clear to those willing to examine them closely: women's issues, though important, took a backseat to industrial unionism, African American rights, and the class struggle.[14]

Browder typified ranking cadres on this issue. In 1935 he announced that his party's concern for family values did not connote support for gender inequality, which he blamed on capitalism. He reprehended those who declared "that the oppression of women, their half-slave status . . . is the necessary foundation" for the home. Two years later he criticized the CPUSA for constantly postponing the question of women's total equality "to a more favorable moment which never comes." Yet he and other leaders, products of a decade when no mass-based autonomous women's movement relevant to the working class existed, used women for the greater good of the party. He ignored male supremacy and argued that the Communists' profamily orientation marked an improvement over earlier radical movements (such as the IWW) whose glorification of rootlessness had appealed more to men than to women. Browder saw his own renunciation of promiscuity for a well-connected Soviet wife whom he deeply loved as exemplary. By 1938 he was denouncing "sexual immorality" and "looseness" and blaming capitalism for them.[15]

Under Browder's leadership functionaries began to improve their public image. Business suits replaced leather jackets; Communist women began wearing high heels on formal occasions; bus travel yielded to Pullman. Party members began observing social customs. George Charney declared that the day Browder "stood up in a restaurant" to help Raissa "don her coat initiated a new standard of deportment." She tidied up his appearance; in freshly pressed shirts he now seemed to embody Popular Front successes. He added his own idiosyncratic twist to middle-class attire, however. During an era when men habitually wore hats, he constantly sported a proletarian cloth cap. Indeed A. B. Magil, a *New Masses* editor who saw Browder every week, could not remember Browder ever appearing in anything else. Magil believed Browder set the party's sartorial style during the 1930s.[16]

Popular Front innovations brought dividends. Throughout the rest of the decade Communism enjoyed an unprecedented following. Of course, the CPUSA never attracted the millions for which Browder longed. Indeed, no serious scholar could suggest that his political gifts approached, even remotely, those of genuinely popular leftists Eugene Debs or Norman Thomas. Under Browder's uncharismatic leadership the CP assumed preeminence on the left, nevertheless, surpassing the Socialists, while the populistic movements EPIC and Share Our Wealth collapsed entirely.

In May 1935 the Communist party claimed about thirty-four thousand members. Fifteen months later it numbered forty-three thousand. Comintern statistics revealed qualitative improvement in the members. Whereas 75 percent had been unemployed in 1932, in 1936 figures indicated that those without work totaled 25 percent "at most." Trade union membership, a mere 35 percent in 1932, had jumped to 80 percent. A full 75 percent of Communist members were blue- or white-collar workers (with or without jobs), and another 10 percent were housewives (mostly working-class). "Professionals, teachers and farmers" made up the re-

Browder in professional photograph, probably in New York between 1934 and 1945. (Courtesy of *People's Weekly World*. Used by permission.)

maining 15 percent. Significantly, as Nathan Glazer noted, under Browder the party passed an important demographic watershed. For the first time a majority was native-born.[17]

The CPUSA won a degree of influence that is surprising in retrospect. From 1936 until August 1939, it affected public opinion through fellow travelers in Hollywood, radio, magazines, publishing houses, and other mass media. Furthermore, Communists enjoyed an influential voice in the Agriculture Department and on the National Labor Relations Board. According to Gil Green, only the CP could fill Madison Square Garden on just five days' notice.[18] Indeed the party's popularity is difficult for people born after World War II to comprehend.

Concurrently the CPUSA reached others through political entities and auxiliary organizations, rallying support behind specific issues or among particular professions. The American League Against War and Fascism, the U.S. Congress Against War, and the Lawyers' Guild attracted persons who never would have joined the party. Polemicists have exaggerated the number who remained unaware of CP domination. A discerning individual could hardly fail to notice the number of Communists addressing such groups or holding high positions. During the McCarthy era many claimed a false innocence after such organizations had disbanded. Certainly in the late 1930s association with Communists did not carry the stigma it did after 1945. Still, auxiliaries could hardly broaden the CPUSA's influence if the general secretary played a significant role. Accordingly, Browder maintained a discreet distance. Behind the scenes, however, he encouraged the growth of a series of complex arrangements with Congresspersons, local officeholders, basketball coaches, musicians, youth leaders, and many others. In the end such efforts broke down. But the attempt to touch the lives of Americans of every stripe, in their own neighborhoods, constituted a remarkable anticipation of the late-twentieth-century's "multiculturalism."

Another area where Communists figured prominently but in which Browder kept a low profile was the labor movement. Embarrassed that he could never match William Foster's credentials as a mass strike leader, Browder strove to contribute where he felt he worked best, through backroom maneuvering. By 1936 a splendid opportunity for the CPUSA to benefit from such an approach had arrived. The CIO, formed the previous autumn, had elicited ringing denunciations from William Green and his AFL colleagues who considered it a dual union. Ostentatiously John L. Lewis resigned from the AFL's Executive Council; he and Sidney Hillman felt only contempt for the corrupt and ineffective federation. Yet they courted rank-and-file support by continuing to claim nominal attachment to it, even after its leaders orchestrated suspension proceedings in August and October 1936. Throughout that year the CIO made spectacular organizational and political gains. In June Lewis and his associates adopted a bold, innovative strategy. They would bring industrial unionism to America's half-million steel workers, bypassing established AFL unions having various jurisdictional claims. To do this they created a vehicle, the Steel Workers Organizing Committee, headed by Lewis's lieutenant Philip Murray.

The energetic, militant CIO captured the imagination and fired the hopes of the nation's Communists. Considering it a TUUL with teeth, they rushed into its ranks. They brought valuable talents: Browder estimated that about 25 to 35 percent of CPUSA members possessed union experience. Foster later wrote that sixty of the two hundred full-time organizers of the Steel Workers Organizing Committee belonged to the party. In many industries Communists put flesh on skeleton organizations and resurrected contacts originally developed during TUUL and Unemployed Council days.[19]

As historian Fraser Ottanelli has observed, the Communists, through their International Workers Order, proved especially adept at recruiting fraternal organizations of foreign-born workers. William Gebert, the CPUSA Pittsburgh district organizer, headed the efforts of the Steel Workers Organizing Committee in this endeavor. He chaired an October conference attended by 447 representatives from Russian, Ukrainian, Lithuanian, Polish, Slovenian, Serbian, and Croatian groups. A cheerful Murray addressed the gathering. Gerald Horne and other scholars have shown that Communists also worked diligently to rally African American support for the union movement. The previous February they had founded the National Negro Congress, which concentrated on spreading the idea in the black community.[20]

Like most astute political entities, the CPUSA hedged its bets as CIO and AFL leaders battled one another. While building the former the party sought to avoid a split with the latter, and for good reason. Having abandoned the TUUL's dual unionism, the Communists had built a presence in the AFL. By the summer of 1936 they numbered fifteen thousand. An official estimate declared that 39 percent of the party's members belonged to unions, ten thousand in New York State alone. Accordingly, before 1937 the CP kept the unions it controlled within the AFL. Browder's 1936 Labor Day network broadcast deplored the decision to suspend CIO unions and urged "a ringing cry for unity" to defeat all who sought "to weaken or destroy the labor movement."[21]

During the Popular Front years Browder believed that the political right contributed unwittingly to his expanded audience. He claimed its strategy of labeling opponents "reds" had won sympathy among civil libertarians. He chortled that no intelligent person believed the "arrogant lies that President Roosevelt or John L. Lewis" were Communists. Using inexact logic Browder argued that if mild progressives were so smeared "then the real Communists cannot be so bad after all."[22] Until 1945 most citizens agreed with him, considering fascism a greater danger.

## THE AMERICANIZATION CAMPAIGN

How did the CPUSA accomplish so much so rapidly? In part it rushed into a vacuum. The Second New Deal stole Dr. Townsend's thunder in 1935, Huey Long was assassinated in 1935, and Father Coughlin discredited himself by revealing increasing anti-Semitism after 1935. A Hollywood slander campaign destroyed Upton Sinclair's EPIC movement in a single election. Floyd Olson did not live to see his forty-fifth birthday. Yet a thinning field of competitors alone did not bring the Communists respectability.

Browder probably never contemplated Max Eastman's argument that nationalism represents an extension of individual egos, but he would not have rejected it. As party leader Browder certainly did not read Antonio Gramsci's prison notebooks, hidden in an Italian Fascist cell until his death in 1937. His widow smuggled them out, and they reached Marxist intellectuals only after World War II ended. Browder, however, would have agreed with Gramsci that overcoming capitalism's "hegemonic" domination of the masses' hearts and minds requires conscious identification with native traditions rather than cosmopolitanism. Had Browder possessed a musical voice, he would have sung folk songs to workers rather than the "Internationale."

He welcomed the Comintern's injunction to find links with domestic radicalism; the deliberate appeal to intellectuals was his own initiative. His midwestern childhood had bred a nationalist orientation he never lost. Thirty years before NeoMarxist historians began seeking a native leftist heritage, the innovative Browder tapped a promotional vein Socialists generally overlook, patriotism.[23] Not the first homebred Communist leader, he did more than anyone else to rid the movement of its "foreign" image.

Actually Browder had evoked an indigenous revolutionary tradition even during the extremist Third Period. In 1933, responding to a familiar taunt, he exclaimed: "We are not un-American!" When did it "become disloyal to advocate struggle to overthrow a tyrannical and destructive system? The United States was born in 'treason' against King George" and confiscation of the Tories' property.[24]

The Popular Front's arrival relieved Browder of the nearly impossible task of selling violent revolution to Americans. It also relegated uncompromising militants such as Foster to insignificant roles, and its outlook matched Browder's gentle temperament. He had always found insurrectionary posturing difficult. He made an astute observation when he noted that by default reactionaries had been permitted to monopolize nationalism. It was perhaps natural that the CPUSA, a party of immigrants' children, would seek to root itself deeply in U.S. soil. As historian Gary Gerstle has noted, Americanism had "emerged as a political language" before 1930 from a "medley of factors." These included the federal government's World War I crusade to enforce it on political radicals and cultural dissenters, large industry's adoption of the "American Plan" to secure high productivity through better wages and personnel management, and the emergence of a mass media that emphasized the English language and Anglo-Saxon cultural values through national magazines, radio, and motion pictures. Such a "patriotic" preoccupation forced "virtually every group seriously interested in political power—groups as diverse as capitalists, socialists, ghettoized ethnics and small-town fundamentalists—to couch their programs in the language of Americanism."[25]

Browder exploited this tendency in an unsophisticated yet vigorous manner. He draped party platforms with the stars and stripes. He also popularized the slogan, "Communism is Twentieth Century Americanism," which aroused widespread curiosity. With these words he launched his Americanization campaign, making an incredible series of speeches that soon reappeared as pamphlets.[26] Looking and sounding more like a midwestern college professor than a political activist, he argued that the United States did possess a viable revolutionary legacy that Democrats and Republicans deliberately minimized. He portrayed various national heroes as working-class champions; by inference they became forerunners to the Communist party. Lacking scholarly training and possessing a superficial understanding of U.S. history, Browder employed oversimplifications, half-truths, and selective samplings that colored his evidence. Writing as a radical, he used historical allusions for political analysis. The result was not scholarship (nor did he intend it to be), but it brought the CPUSA unprecedented attention.

External factors boosted Browder's efforts. During the early twentieth century a Progressive school of historians, reflecting its own generation's antimonopoly battles, had given the Revolutionary War a class-struggle slant and had convinced academia that the federal union represented the triumph of private property. Such writers influenced profoundly their era's thought. By the onset of the Great Depression, similar, less sophisticated arguments had sifted down to popularizers. In this atmosphere Browder's bold assertions found a wide audience.

Browder's radical tradition contained much hyperbole. Around a kernel of fact he constructed sweeping generalizations. Noting that European monarchs had considered American colonial rebels "the 'international incendiaries' of their day," he argued that the Declaration of Independence was a forerunner to the *Communist Manifesto* because it inspired French revolutionaries. Browder knew the eighteenth-century patriots had sequestered loyalist possessions, some of which had great value. Therefore he concluded that most Tories were "feudal landlords."[27]

Browder produced flat, colorless villains and heroes. General Benedict Arnold, the Revolution's most notorious traitor and Aaron Burr, who conspired against the early republic, merely foreshadowed Stalin's enemy Leon Trotsky. All Federalists were really Tories. Browder praised Thomas Jefferson's desire to water the liberty tree with tyrants' blood but ignored his ownership of human beings. Browder contended that Abraham Lincoln created the modern Republican party and "did not hesitate to confiscate the slaveholders' property and to arm the freed slaves." He implied wrongly that all Lincoln's doubts and vacillations occurred before secession, attributing them to "unstable class support" and the president's "abhorrence of war."[28]

Although Browder never sought scholarly balance, some distortions seem the result of the poor sources to which the self-educated can fall prey. His essays on America's early presidential administrations provide a striking example. Browder relied heavily on two books by Claude Bowers, a Democratic party politico. Although Browder labeled Bowers a "reactionary," nowhere did he seem to know that Bowers had penned a virulently racist account of the Reconstruction era. One may question whether the leader of the self-proclaimed "Negro Party" would knowingly call such an author a historical authority. Browder echoed Bowers's simplistic interpretations, showing President John Adams to be Alexander Hamilton's puppet and portraying Jefferson as a populistic chief executive who combated a power-hungry federal judiciary.[29]

Despite distortions and errors, Browder's arguments had some validity. He observed accurately that George Washington had favored a one-party political system. Browder reminded readers that Karl Marx "strongly influenced the British workers whose mass protests" helped prevent English intervention into the American Civil War. Browder even understated his case when he noted that Marx caused the first International Workingmen's Association to send President Lincoln a congratulatory letter on his 1864 reelection. In fact, Marx, a fervent union supporter, composed the message himself.[30]

Browder's most significant patriotic writings, however, concerned the U.S. Constitution. Leading one of the few predominantly white groups that demanded racial equality before the 1950s, Browder reminded his countrymen that the document had sanctioned human bondage. He echoed historian Charles Beard when he called the Constitution a compromise between conflicting regional influences, socioeconomic systems, and aristocratic and democratic principles. Yet he went beyond Beard to recall negative features Garrisonian abolitionists had stressed but subsequent writers had ignored. Browder declared, "The U.S. Constitution tolerated for generations the disenfranchisement of the great majority of the population; for 80 years it confirmed slavery for one-tenth of the population; its grant of suffrage to Negroes is still largely unrealized today; for over 130 years it excluded half of the population, the women, from suffrage; citizenship rights begin only at age 21."[31]

Browder also arraigned the Senate's "unproportional representation." Finally he criticized the Constitution for ignoring a twentieth-century concern: economic justice. Simply put, liberty is not enough for someone lacking home or livelihood. Unfortunately, Browder vitiated his denunciations of America's racism and widespread poverty by extolling Stalin's new Soviet constitution, a political fraud. Because he had visited the USSR frequently, he understood conditions there better than many American fellow travelers. Accordingly, his disingenuous arguments undermined his valid ones.

Still Browder, a homegrown, midwestern radical, probably took his nationalistic rhetoric seriously. His Americanization campaign helped transform the party's nature. During the Popular Front years it attracted thousands who lacked a proletarian background. Indeed, the CPUSA acquired a middle-class cast that separated it from other Western Communist parties.[32] Browder's flag waving helped change public perceptions. No longer did the organization seem a band of shabbily dressed immigrants with thick accents.

Browder helped bring American Communism greater legitimacy than it had ever known before or would enjoy again. The very qualities that made him less exciting than depression demagogues actually worked to his advantage. The CP no longer needed adventurers; instead it sought recruits on Main Street. To radio listeners Browder resembled a Great Plains clerk or shopkeeper. His unadorned speeches lacked theoretical acuity, contained little Marxist terminology, and rarely mentioned Soviet heroes. Yet the oversimplifications and patriotic rhetoric only increased his appeal in a land where white-collar workers considered themselves middle-class. Browder's disarming appearance furthered the effort. A middle-aged version of the all-American boy, he was a walking refutation of every Communist stereotype. By far not the movement's most profound ideologist, Browder proved beyond question its greatest salesperson.

## CLOSET NEW DEALER

Many voters considered the 1936 elections a referendum on Franklin D. Roosevelt, the first true test of his popularity. Almost any Democrat could have defeated Herbert Hoover in 1932, and the off-year contests had centered on radicalism's appeal. Like many successful politicians, however, the president overestimated his opposition's chances. Although 80 percent of the nation's newspapers opposed Roosevelt, his actions were unduly cautious. New Deal programs had assembled a coalition that would dominate national politics for the next thirty years. It included workers (organized and unorganized), ethnic whites, northern blacks, Jews, Catholics, women, intellectuals, progressive Republicans, and middle-class families concerned about security in old age. It also contained southern whites, whom FDR feared losing. Accordingly, he displayed no enthusiasm for civil rights legislation, although blacks and often Hispanics were segregated and disenfranchised below the Mason-Dixon line.

John L. Lewis and his CIO colleagues created Labor's Nonpartisan League to whip up unprecedented support for FDR and other Democrats. The United Mine Workers alone donated more than $500,000 to the campaign. Throughout industrial areas proletarians contributed their spare time and energy. As historian Bert Cochran has observed, they thereby transformed "the old Gompers policy of casual and largely symbolic endorsements of labor's friends," opening a "new chapter in unions' political involvement and rise to national influence."[33]

All of Roosevelt's opponents had problems. Hoover eagerly offered to run against New Deal "collectivism," but few Republicans thought he could win. The GOP had only seven incumbent governors, all east of the Mississippi, except Kansas's Alf Landon. The party wanted to refute its widespread identification with eastern bankers and thus nominated Landon, even though he had supported much of the New Deal. Rallying behind him was the Liberty League (an organization of millionaires and those aspiring to be), business, prosperous farmers, physicians, and other professionals whose relative status seemed threatened by the emergence of a large federal government.

The demagogues also sought to field a candidate, but Father Coughlin, born in Canada, was constitutionally ineligible. Huey Long's Share Our Wealth successor, Rev. Gerald L. K. Smith, proved only a pale imitation. Eventually, a North Dakota populist, Congressman William Lemke, won support from Coughlin, Smith, and Townsend. They called the new organization the Union Party, a rubric Abraham Lincoln had used for his reelection in 1864, but few voters remembered. The Socialist party tried to regroup behind Norman Thomas in 1936. It broadened its tent and admitted splinter-group Communist factions that followed Leon Trotsky, Jay Lovestone, and Benjamin Gitlow, thereby inviting more internal discord. Some Militant faction members worked with the newly formed American Labor party, a New York State group founded to support FDR but not on the Democratic ticket.

The Communists' year began with a campaign policy battle. Browder, lobbying in Washington, heard rumors from sources close to Soviet Foreign Minister Maxim Litvinov that the CPUSA would end up supporting Roosevelt's reelection that November. Meanwhile Sam Darcy, the Moscow-based Comintern representative, was demanding endorsement of FDR. Any Farmer-Labor party campaign, Darcy feared, might split the liberal/left vote and bring a Republican victory. This concerned the Soviets greatly because they believed that the Liberty League represented incipient American fascism. Darcy told ranking Comintern figure Dimitri Manuilsky, who had him explain his reasoning to Dimitrov. They thereupon summoned Browder and Foster to the USSR to present their views. Darcy, who believed both Manuilsky and Stalin agreed with him, began to savor success.[34]

When Browder reached the USSR in March, Dimitrov told him point-blank that a Comintern consensus backed FDR. Browder had misgivings and displayed reluctance. In a planning session Darcy developed his close-contest thesis fully, arguing that a lack of Communist support might defeat the president. Foster, Browder's perennial critic, rushed to Darcy's aid. Browder replied forcefully. Endorsing Roosevelt, he pointed out, would prove counterproductive; the media would then blast him as the "Communist candidate." CPUSA support would bring the president one million votes but cost him five million. The only way to support him effectively was to oppose him.[35]

For the next two weeks Comintern leaders huddled privately. Finally they accepted Browder's reasoning. The CPUSA would not support FDR directly. Browder received total responsibility for deciding exactly how the Communists could aid the president's campaign. After the announcement, Dimitrov told Browder in private that since his strategy had prevailed, he had to be the CPUSA's candidate. No one else could make the tactic work.[36] This was music to the ambitious Browder's ears.

The decision required the CPUSA to abandon its Farmer-Labor party efforts. For Browder the tactical change entailed no painful reassessment. On May 9 and 10 he addressed an enlarged Polburo meeting and announced that no Farmer-Labor candidate would seek the presidency that year. The task was now twofold: to build local and state parties and, more important, to defeat the GOP. Browder revealed the Communists' plans publicly and set the CPUSA's entire 1936 campaign tone at a Madison Square Garden rally on May 20, his forty-fifth birthday. He damned Roosevelt faintly as a lesser evil and excoriated the Republicans as representing the nation's most vicious reactionaries.

That same week, in an insincere effort, Browder made his final overture toward the Socialists. He knew they felt little enthusiasm for cooperation; in January their National Executive Council had rejected yet another CPUSA cooperation attempt. Just before the Socialist convention Browder announced a surprising offer. He told a press conference at his ninth-floor office that the Communists would propose a joint SP-CP presidential ticket headed by Thomas. Unlike a mass Farmer-Labor party, a Thomas–Browder slate could not endanger FDR's reelection. The Socialists had lost more than 80 percent of their 1932 following. Indeed, by now Browder enjoyed watching SP chiefs explode whenever he made a friendly gesture.[37]

Browder's proposal evoked more outbursts. Both Socialist factions rejected the bait immediately. Thomas and the Militant majority, influenced by the recently admitted Trotskyists, had become more radical than the Communists. They considered the election a single-issue campaign that pitted capitalism against socialism. The Old Guard, by now virtually a separate party, also spurned the offer. Louis Waldman, New York State chief, attacked the Militants. He termed Browder's idea "a natural consequence" of their actions and predicted subsequent defections to the Communists. Waldman denounced symbolic gestures already made and ridiculed Thomas for entering and leaving united fronts at will. If he could parade, sing, and cheer with CP members on May Day, he should work with them in November.[38]

Clearly enjoying the discord he was provoking, Browder made two final grandstanding gestures toward working-class unity. First, he sent the Socialist leadership a letter and a nine-page appeal, urging a common electoral slate to campaign on reformist issues. The proposal included supporting international action against fascist aggression. This ensured rejection because the Socialists believed that collective security increased the likelihood of a war. Second, Browder and several other Communists visited the Socialists' Cleveland convention to lobby for a United Front. They appeared on May 22, but their hosts ignored them.[39]

Browder's subsequent rhetoric should be considered within this context. The CPUSA, for eighteen months before 1936, sincerely sought to build a United Front. Although the Socialist left displayed some interest, party leadership refused repeatedly to cooperate on major projects. Thus Browder felt justified in castigating Thomas.

CPUSA passion for unity also had limits. Late in 1934 banished former General Secretary Jay Lovestone asked if he could bring his followers, the "Communist Party, USA (Opposition)" (CPO) into the united front. Browder responded with a *Daily Worker* open letter to CPO rank and filers, "barely a handful of individuals," telling how they could return to the fold. It reminded readers that only recently had the Socialists spurned the CPO.[40]

For nearly two years Lovestone made overtures toward the CPUSA and Comintern. His arguments might have convinced a democratic working-class organization. He noted that the Third Period line had brought only isolation. Now hesitantly, partially, and indirectly the Comintern was approaching CPO positions. Lovestone condemned Stalin's earlier formulation that termed social democracy fascism's moderate wing, and he recalled that the CPO had always considered Socialists to be reformist proletarians. He implored the CPUSA to abandon false pride and hollow pretense to infallibility and engage in self-criticism, not as a penitential rite but as a political responsibility. He urged mutual support of labor hero Tom Mooney for president in 1936. Finally, he entreated the Comintern to adopt internal democracy.[41]

Later, more circumspect communications merely advocated trade union collaboration, requested that two CPO observer delegates attend the CPUSA's 1936 national convention, and quoted Dimitrov at length on the United Front's imperative. The Communists spurned every offer

Lovestone made. He and Browder had despised one another throughout the 1920s, but the criticism of Stalin kept Lovestone anathema. In 1938, after the CPUSA had burglarized Lovestone's home, Browder gleefully offered to send the stolen political files to Georgi Dimitrov.[42] Antifascist concord did not extend to dissident Communists.

Browder's goodwill efforts nevertheless began to pay rewards by late May 1936. The Minnesota Farmer-Labor movement called a Chicago conference of organizations interested in eventually forming a national party after Roosevelt's reelection. Governor Olson insisted that Browder represent the Communists. Although the Wisconsin Progressives and some American Commonwealth Federation members immediately withdrew, not since 1923 had the CPUSA found itself in such respectable company. Browder proved a model of decorum. He acknowledged that most listeners would support FDR. He doubted that the New Deal could halt the growth of reactionary movements, advocated the creation of a third major party after the election, and, most significant, promised that the CP would not try to dominate.[43]

When the meeting ended, Browder, following the strategy worked out in Moscow, planned his own campaign. Indeed, as early as April 15 he and Eisler had written to the USSR, asking for advice on the party line. They also promised to cable a list of new Polburo nominees in time for the Soviets to veto any before the CP convention. About this time Browder ordered Agnes Smedley, an enthusiastic but ill-disciplined Comintern agent in China, to return to the United States. She had acted on her own authority, involved neutral friends in covert operations, displayed signs of emotional imbalance, and possibly caused a labor organizer to fall into enemy hands.[44]

Shortly thereafter the CPUSA staged its first public convention. Held in New York and commanding maximum media attention, it featured 750 young, mostly American-born farm and factory delegates. Generating hoopla befitting a major party, they filled the Manhattan Opera House's ballroom from June 24 through 27. Their final session on June 28 packed Madison Square Garden. Chairing was Ella Reeve "Mother" Bloor, the beloved seventy-three-year-old veteran of countless labor and farm struggles. Foster rapped the opening day's crowd to order with a gavel an aged former slave had carved from his wooden scythe. Foster accepted it, on behalf of the Communist party, which he proclaimed would free all the servants in the land.[45]

The *New Republic* reported a definitely native atmosphere, epitomized by a banner reading "For a Free, Happy, Prosperous America." The slogan "Communism Is Twentieth Century Americanism" appeared every-where, and bands played "Yankee Doodle." Browder, more anointed than chosen as presidential nominee, was introduced to twenty-five thousand rabid supporters as a mixture of the average citizen and "John Brown of Osawatomie." His personality never seemed so attractive. Receiving his first barrage of national attention, he responded with modesty, sincerity, and grace under pressure. Both NBC and CBS broadcasted his accep-tance speech live, prompting the *Daily Worker* to assert that Browder had spoken to millions. The festivities also spotlighted an African American running mate, James W. Ford, hailed as a modern abolitionist. Both Brow-der and Ford gave acceptance speeches that made no mention of Marx, Engels, Lenin, or Stalin.[46]

The CPUSA platform, clearly reformist, could have come from liberal Democrats a few decades later, except for its first plank: government em-ployment at union wages in idle factories, mines, and mills. Far less radi-cal were calls for universal social security, health insurance, WPA con-struction of public low-rent housing, schools, hospitals, and recreational facilities, free higher education, agrarian debt relief, total racial equality, Puerto Rican independence, and collective security against fascist ag-gression. The entire program depended on progressive taxation and in-come redistribution.[47] Consistent with democratic values, it did not seek to abolish voting, opposition political parties, or the right to dissent. Be-cause the Communists had no chance to win, they could promise too much to nearly everyone, as minor parties usually do. Actually, they ex-pected few votes.

Although he was a convicted felon, Browder could accept the nomina-tion. In 1933 President Roosevelt had issued a general amnesty restoring citizenship rights to peaceful violators of World War I's espionage, draft, and speech statutes who had served their sentences. The action benefited Browder and about five hundred others. He had two goals during the 1936 contest: to publicize that the Communists had not endorsed FDR and to pressure the New Deal leftward. The CP's Ohio campaign man-ager, Sandor Voros, called the first a lightning rod to draw off charges that Roosevelt was pro-Communist. Browder's candidacy produced a be-wildering slogan: "Defeat Landon at all costs; vote for Earl Browder." The phrase caused Voros to resign; he realized that Browder was not really seeking votes at all. Thomas and others also understood what Browder was doing.[48] While the Communists' campaign efforts did not fool many, they nevertheless prevented the GOP from smearing the president as the red nominee.

The energetic yet easy-going Browder proved unexpectedly adroit at publicizing his candidacy far and wide. Not physically powerful, he was nevertheless extremely courageous and eager to face audiences anywhere. Between June and November he traveled twenty-six thousand rail miles and addressed listeners in twenty-six states. He appeared before the National Press Club, the *New York Herald Tribune*'s Annual Forum, and the University of Virginia's Institute of Public Affairs.[49] He also spoke to radio listeners over a nationwide hookup. Never before had a Communist candidate received polite media attention. This was all the more remarkable because he lacked a mainstream politician's extroversion. One can hardly imagine his plunging into a crowd to shake hands; nothing seems more incongruous than a picture of Browder kissing a baby. Indeed, his campaign marked the triumph of willpower over inborn limitations.

Browder pursued his second objective, championing radical ideas, by delivering a stock speech all summer. Certainly he implied that Roosevelt represented the lesser of two evils. He denounced the administration's youth programs, advocating training and employment instead of Civilian Conservation Corps camps. Yet he ripped the Republicans for relying on deaths to create job openings. Roosevelt was unreliable, but Landon would perpetuate the sweatshop and promote international fascism. While FDR did not offer all that the people needed, some Landon backers might take away what little they had.[50]

The campaign proved one of the most challenging episodes in Browder's career, and he handled it superbly. Aware that newsprint of any sort advertised his candidacy, he deliberately made himself a magnet for controversy. Defying all dangers, he sought out scenes of recent labor strife, encountering extralegal discrimination, persecution by law and order forces, and even mass violence. Indeed, the treatment he received was reminiscent of that accorded the IWW two decades earlier.

Initially the First Amendment violations seemed inconsequential, especially when viewed out of context. They began on March 5, when Browder delivered a talk on CBS. This marked the CPUSA's first free nationwide air time. As he spoke, twenty-five National Americanization League members exercised their right to protest outside. But they also left a written demand that the network silence him. CBS answered that gagging Communists merely made them martyrs and gave conservative Republican Hamilton Fish, Jr., free equal time the following night. Yet, seven New England stations refused to broadcast Browder's speech, and four carried only Fish's. Similarly, on August 28 Pittsburgh station WCAE canceled a scheduled Browder talk at the last minute. The management later contended that it had a program of greater public interest but did not reveal its contents.

By now the CPUSA knew how to retaliate effectively. Campaign Chair William Z. Foster urged the Federal Communications Commission (FCC) to revoke the station's license. Shortly thereafter the American Civil Liberties Union (ACLU) entered the dispute, accusing Indianapolis station WIRE and Minneapolis's WTCN of similar misdeeds. The Communists complained that WTCN canceled a contract to carry several party speeches after they had spent $1,000 advertising them. Responding, the FCC ordered WCAE to "explain its actions."[51] Ten days later the station capitulated, granting Browder access on September 22 and October 23 and 30.

Other, more serious threats to free speech occurred. In numerous cities vigilantes, often including local officials, prevented Browder or his comrades from speaking publicly. One incident occurred on September 12 when Browder rode to an Atlanta, Georgia, campaign rally. As he left his railroad car four city detectives with arrest orders began shadowing him so closely that he simply ate at the station's restaurant and took the next Tampa-bound train. There he encountered not police officers but a fait accompli. He found the auditorium that the party had rented padlocked and chained, forcing cancellation of the second Communist gathering in two days. Feeling justifiable anger, he sent President Roosevelt a telegram making exaggerated charges. Quickly Attorney General Homer Cummings responded, noting that only state or local violations had occurred; the national government would not intervene. Browder's overreaction marked his personal low point in the campaign.[52]

Suppression also occurred outside the South. On September 19 the Board of Selectmen in Provincetown, Massachusetts, banned Communist meetings. About five weeks later Browder encountered resistance in Buffalo, New York. There the Fraternal Order of Eagles encouraged auditorium owners to deny halls to radicals.

These actions pale when contrasted with Browder's second Tampa reception. Earlier that year a jury had convicted five former policemen of kidnapping and flogging three organizers, one of whom died. Even the restrained Thomas believed that the Ku Klux Klan controlled the municipal government. On October 25 Browder prepared to address four hundred spectators on a vacant lot near the business section. He stood on the rostrum, an elevated wooden platform, as a sympathizer introduced him. Suddenly fifteen American Legionnaires rushed in behind, punching and pistol-whipping those in their way. Frantically the speaker implored spectators to offer no resistance. For a few moments a lull fell on the crowd.

Swallowing his fears and acting unruffled, Browder took the microphone and appealed to his audience to keep Tampa's name spotless by avoiding violence. Again scuffling broke out; some bystanders began to leave. Boldly he raised his voice: "I am not here to attack any individual and I hope no one else is here except to listen to an orderly discussion of political questions. There is one issue in this campaign. It is the defense of democracy."[53]

Just then the raiders struck again. Those behind the stand raised the back steadily skyward, causing everyone on it to slide off. The plucky Browder landed unhurt, and supporters hurried him into a waiting automobile. A nearby clinic treated four persons, including a woman, for facial blows from a gun barrel. Although the Communists had requested police protection, no officers had appeared. The mob included Fred Newberger, a local constable. Coincidentally, perhaps, that same week three hundred armed California vigilantes stormed an Imperial Valley radio studio and beat two leftists waiting to broadcast. Esco Richardson, the local CP Congressional candidate, and Bessie Kechler, its State Assembly nominee, had scheduled airtime on station KXO at El Centro. The thugs injured them and left the building in shambles.[54]

Despite these outrages, an earlier, preposterous series of events did even more to identify the Communists' campaign with civil liberties. On September 30 Browder journeyed to Terre Haute, Indiana, to lead a rally and make a radio broadcast. His entourage included novelist Waldo Frank, newspaperman Seymour Waldman, Indiana Communists Charles Stadtfeld and Andrew Remes, and attorney David J. Bentall. The moment Browder stepped from his train local police arrested him and four of his comrades for vagrancy, denying them counsel. Bentall, however, eluded authorities by hiding in a pullman car. All day he sought the group's release on a writ of habeas corpus, but failed because no judge would hear him.[55]

Local officials disrupted both CP functions. The president of Indiana State Teachers' College canceled a Browder speech scheduled at the campus auditorium, conducting a football pep rally there instead. Later, Police Chief James C. Yates deployed three patrolmen to station WBOW where Browder had a radio contract. They had orders to prevent any Communists from speaking there. Just before air time, attorney Bentall entered the building. Suddenly strategically placed Indiana Central Labor Union sympathizers, previously unnoticed, hustled him past the officers and into a small broadcasting booth. Immediately Bentall locked the door and began reading Browder's hour-long address. Soon Yates, ten lawmen, and about fifty townspeople arrived. Some wanted to halt the talk by force. The officers departed, however, rather than risk conflict with the FCC, and the crowd quickly dissolved.[56]

Yates and Mayor Samuel Beecher tried to justify the arrests. Earlier Yates had warned Browder against setting foot in the city. After the jailings, he proclaimed proudly: "Now these Communists know we mean business about staying out of town." Beecher invoked a curious sanction. He announced: "Both our Presidential candidates—Mr. Roosevelt and Mr. Landon—recognize Communism as a menace to this nation. Therefore Communistic speakers are not welcome in Terre Haute."[57] Although in June Congress had created a special committee headed by Senator Robert M. La Follette, Jr., to investigate the domination of local authorities by business and other antilabor forces, Terre Haute's officials displayed no fear of Washington.

The CPUSA protested to the president and Indiana Governor Paul V. McNutt. One day earlier the Communists' state leader had telegraphed the White House to report Yates's promise to arrest Browder. That evening Browder had wired Roosevelt from Gary contending that "such police and vigilante action violates the most elementary democratic principles." After the arrests on September 30 William Foster cabled FDR indignantly. A master of sarcasm, he quoted Beecher and asked whether the president countenanced use of his name to authorize imprisoning his political opponents. Sympathetic writer Granville Hicks's letter to McNutt seemed closer to the mark. It simply argued that the incident increased Browder's audience and convinced "more and more people that our form of government is unjust. To arrest such figures" as Browder and Waldo Frank for vagrancy was, "whatever one's opinion of their views, to make the law a farce."[58]

The Justice Department contended that it lacked authority because the controversy involved no federal statutes. McNutt's state administration noted that it could not free Browder because the powers of pardon and commutation required a prior trial and conviction. Privately the governor wondered what he could do about Beecher and Yates. Under Indiana law he possessed no power to discipline city officers, no matter how flagrant their conduct. He could displace a mayor or police chief only after a court conviction for a felony, misfeasance, or habitual drunkenness.[59] All seemed unlikely to occur in Terre Haute. Thus, McNutt could have done little to aid Browder even had he so desired. After twenty-five hours had passed, the police could no longer hold their prisoners without a hearing. Yates dropped all charges, freed the Communists, and ordered them to leave the city.

Townspeople seemed to welcome the arrests and the cancellation of the rally. The local Merchants' Association and right-wing groups hailed Yates and Beecher. City Hall claimed it received more than two hundred congratulatory cables, including one from Berlin, Germany. When taunted, Browder quipped, "Did it come from Hitler?" Smugly Beecher boasted almost unanimous national support.[60]

He could hardly have been more mistaken. Hundreds of protests streamed into Washington and Indianapolis. Many from auxiliary organizations sounded ludicrous. One decried the incarceration of "Communist President Elect Browder." Yet restrained objections from civil libertarians also appeared, including a few from businesspeople and even American Legionnaires. One pleaded for the right of CPUSA members to "express their crazy views." Scores demanded Yates's and Beecher's removal. Norman Thomas made the most cogent evaluation, terming the incident "an act of high-handed tyranny which advertises Communism and disgraces America."[61]

The national press caricatured Terre Haute's police. The *Indianapolis Times* felt that the lawmen had tried to imprison the Constitution. One wag wrote that they had given free speech "a swift kick in the pants." Some out-of-state newspapers lampooned the town and Indiana unfairly. One awarded Terre Haute "first prize for silliness in the campaign." A midwestern daily opined that Indiana had "never enjoyed any great reputation for tolerance or free thinking." An eastern editor denounced the pseudo-patriots who made the state "a happy hunting ground for the Ku Klux Klan." These judgments added to the snowballing controversy. Browder announced plans to return for another radio address three weeks later. Beecher replied by promising to jail him again. Shortly thereafter police arrested ten local sympathizers and confiscated ten thousand hand bills that contained critical editorials from every section of the nation.[62]

Between Browder's visits Thomas brought his own campaign to the city. He declared that "Browder was as much a vagrant" as Governor Alfred M. Landon, the Republican candidate, on his national tour. Both were "looking for jobs." Thomas "half-expected" to be incarcerated himself; two Chicago lawyers accompanied him. Meanwhile Browder sought redress in court. Acting in his behalf, attorneys Bentall and John H.

Kingsbury filed two $25,000 suits against Beecher and Yates for false imprisonment and malicious prosecution.[63]

Browder's return contrasted with his first visit. Determined to maximize publicity, he arrived on October 20, the tenth anniversary of the death of Terre Haute native Eugene V. Debs. Browder carried a copy of the Constitution and promised to read it to Yates if he were arrested again. To underscore that he was no vagrant, he also brought a certified $1,000 check. Pausing only to wave to supporters and the press, he hurried to Vigo County Superior Court as plaintiff.[64]

In court five ACLU lawyers sought a protective injunction. WBOW's station manager testified that Browder's radio contract was property endangered by official interference. Judge Albert B. Owens agreed that the jailing on September 30 was "uncalled for" but censured Browder for traveling "across the country" to seek the redress. Owens promised an immediate hearing if Browder were arrested before his broadcast, yet denied the petition. He contended that only twenty-five persons would listen "anyway." He also warned ominously that individual citizens "might stop him. He might break a leg."[65]

That night Owens's speculations almost became reality. Around 10:35 Browder's taxicab reached WBOW. Nearly three hundred vigilantes awaited him. As he courageously attempted to enter the station, the crowd pelted him with rotten eggs and tomatoes. Associated Press photographer Harold Harris began taking pictures, but the mob clubbed him and smashed his camera. Alertly, attendants capitalized on the diversion to rush Browder back into his waiting cab. Although he sped away unharmed, thugs injured local sympathizers Ester Ripple and Hartford Larrison and threatened two radical newspaper reporters. Employing a now-familiar tactic, a woman Communist used the confusion to slip into WBOW. She sought to read Browder's speech but was refused permission because it might endanger her life.[66]

Police appeared after Browder's departure; they made no arrests. Witnesses later identified as crowd members attorneys Ben Small and Charles Whitlock, who had represented Yates in court that afternoon.[67] At the riot Browder had called out to H. A. Collins, who headed Terre Haute's Law and Order League, standing amid a sea of American Legion badges.

Again the CPUSA demanded federal and state intervention; again Washington claimed no jurisdiction. Governor McNutt vacillated, terming the episode "a disgraceful performance on both sides." He refused to send troopers to protect Browder, because "it would be ridiculous to have two" groups of lawmen "working against each other." After further thought he ordered state police to provide a motorcycle escort, but Browder's train departed before the escort arrived. That evening McNutt, bowing to labor and civil libertarian pressure, finally denounced as illegal the September 30 arrest.[68]

Local circumstances help explain why Terre Haute's leaders reacted emotionally instead of simply ignoring Browder. First, strong passions lingered from a 1935 general strike that had brought martial law and a nine-month, thousand-man national guard occupation. Some residents, feeling that Beecher and Yates had not done enough for public safety, formed a pressure group, the Law and Order League. An ACLU figure linked its rise to five subsequent vigilante attacks on town radicals. Browder's 1936 visit prompted merchants who feared further unrest to demand that the administration silence him. Second, the mayor's own outlook precluded forbearance. Beecher, a man of dense ignorance and aggressive intolerance, insisted that the CPUSA still preached violence. He was also conducting a vendetta against town leftists, who had attempted to impeach him after the strike. Finally, election-year partisanship played a role. Beecher and Yates were Republicans. Although the former did not seek reelection, he supported the Vigo County GOP's campaign. Both men calculated that Browder's arrest would embarrass state and national Democratic administrations. They expected the publicity-loving Browder to appeal to Governor McNutt and President Roosevelt, forcing on each the dilemma of seeming partial to Communism or not protecting free speech.[69]

Jailed and chased by a mob, the resourceful Browder turned the difficulties to his benefit. While making his oppressors seem obtuse, even fascistic, he informed thousands that the Communists did not support the president directly. The incidents had a curious postscript. Civil actions against Beecher and Yates lingered for four years. The Communists enjoyed competent legal representation in Indiana, Bentall and Kingsbury. Yet postponements, a maneuver defendants often employ, occurred eight times for the false imprisonment charge and four times in the malicious prosecution case. Finally, on December 6, 1940, the court dismissed both lawsuits "for want of prosecution," ordering plaintiffs to pay all costs.[70]

The dramatically altered political climate in 1940 caused the Communists to abandon their litigation, which they had initiated primarily for publicity value. The 1939 Nazi–Soviet pact had brought down on the party the wrath of the Roosevelt administration. A massive government offensive left CP figures battling imprisonment, emptied party coffers, and rendered the Terre Haute suits an unaffordable luxury.[71]

The 1936 presidential election, despite Communist fears to the contrary, proved the greatest electoral rout since James Monroe ran unopposed in 1820. FDR beat Landon 523 to 8 and destroyed entirely Lemke's Union party. Riding into office on Roosevelt's coattails were hundreds of Democratic legislators, as well as mayors and governors in key industrial states. Norman Thomas's Socialist vote, a personal following, dropped to one-fourth of his 1932 total. In the German-American city of Reading, Pennsylvania, long an SP stronghold, two-thirds of the party members deserted for Roosevelt. The divided Socialists were on the road to insignificance in American life.[72]

The Democratic landslide obscured Browder's considerable achievements. He had unleashed a sudden display of imaginative, bold leadership seemingly beyond his earlier capabilities. In just twelve months the heretofore resourceful but mediocre bureaucratic infighter had accomplished more than former CPUSA general secretaries Charles Ruthenberg and Jay Lovestone had during their entire careers. Browder had brought his party more publicity for free than it could possibly have purchased.

Since winning the CP helm Browder had become increasingly vain. His 1936 triumphs confirmed his self-image dramatically. His career had already blossomed beyond his expectations, and now more than ever before he had reason to believe himself a person of destiny. The campaign also raised larger issues. How far would the CPUSA go in its support of FDR? Did Browder consider making the party's inner structure more democratic, or would he attempt to remain an authoritarian leader? The national media spotlight naturally called attention to less weighty personal questions. What was Browder the individual like? A curious (he would say intrusive) public wondered about his family life. Why was he so secretive? His wife's personal history was not the only reason.

# FIVE

■

# *Let Each Stand in His Place (1937–1938)*

At the Seventh World Congress Georgi Dimitrov had said nothing about sustaining capitalist politicians. Was Earl Browder ready to make support for President Franklin D. Roosevelt more than just an election-year tactic? If so, how could he reconcile it with orthodox Marxism-Leninism? If not, could a national Farmer-Labor party ever get off the ground? American Communism had reached a critical crossroad.

In late 1936 and early 1937, just as leftist political movements were going into eclipse, workers and unions seized the initiative in a burst of militancy reminiscent of 1934. They felt buoyed by a recent upturn in the economy (caused by federal spending programs) and, more important, by a sense that Roosevelt had become the greatest White House friend labor had ever known. Suddenly they were using the sit-down strike to challenge some of the world's most powerful corporations. The technique paralyzed daily operations, discouraged traditional kinds of strikebreaking, and raised the specter (though rarely the reality) of sabotage. As historian Daniel Nelson has observed, the work stoppages quickly overshadowed "more familiar contemporary events—the lingering depression, the New Deal, even the union organizing campaigns and the AFL-CIO split." The tactic was not new; workers under IWW leadership had taken over General Electric's Schenectady, New York, plant in 1906. Overseas, sit-downs had occurred in France, Italy, Yugoslavia, Hungary, Poland, England, and Wales. American auto body shop workers had conducted a few quick sit-downs between 1933 and 1935. Still, sit-downs did not receive widespread attention until rubber workers conducted forty of them in 1936 in Akron, Ohio, where two-thirds of the nation's tires were produced. Bert Cochran has noted that "Akron was a major CIO victory although the United Rubber Workers union was not yet formally an adherent. [The strike] was the crest of the gathering swell" that broke with a thunderous roar in 1937.[1]

Early that year CIO unions used sit-downs to win electrifying victories in two of the most obdurate open shop industries. Auto was first. Historian Roger Keeran relates that the executive board of the United Auto Workers (UAW), which included the energetic Communist Wyndham Mortimer, learned that the "key automobile dies" for the entire General Motors Corporation "were located in two plants—Cleveland Fisher Body [in Ohio] and Flint Fisher Body No 1 [in Michigan]. Since a shutdown at these two shops would cripple all GM production, Mortimer decided to make them his primary targets." The result was a six-week strike that Robert Zieger has called "one of the epic confrontations in American labor history." Although the La Follette Committee later revealed that General Motors had spent more than $800,000 to establish a private police network in its company towns, activists courageously built a UAW local in Flint. They relied on an existing Communist party apparatus and fraternal organizations of immigrants. Mortimer, a fifty-three-year-old veteran auto worker, huddled with new recruits in clandestine meetings, often in darkened basements or candlelit church buildings. Months of patient organizing yielded dramatic results. On December 29, 1936, a sit-down began in the Cleveland plant; it spread to Flint the following day. Soon photographs of strikers, lifting boxes of food through plant windows and lounging on rows of car seats, appeared in newspapers and magazines across the land.[2]

Bowing to Victorian mores of the time, union leaders sent women workers, many single and young, home. They feared the corporation might becloud the issue by accusing them of sexual promiscuity or by publicizing "unfit mother" court proceedings. A gender-segregated group of 200 women sewers sat down in a large room at the Fisher Body No. 1 plant, however, and soon 280 others joined them. After an early violent episode, some unionists' wives created a Women's Emergency Brigade. Sporting red berets and carrying ax handles, they bravely positioned themselves between strikers and mayhem-bent Flint police. Communist Dorothy Kraus chaired the food council, which, operating out of a restaurant across from Fisher 1, fed an estimated six thousand workers per day. Other women formed a "chiseling committee" to persuade sympathetic local grocers to maintain a continuous food flow.[3]

Browder, seeking to protect the CPUSA's labor movement gains, spared no effort to deflect Red-baiting charges. Not a single national party functionary spoke in Flint or visited union headquarters. The Communists closed down shop papers, dissolved caucuses ("fractions") within unions, and abandoned supervision of functionaries who did not endanger the left-center alliance. Browder announced that members and sympathizers could follow the party line by reading the *Daily Worker*, as their opponents did. William Z. Foster complained bitterly that the CP was "tailing" the CIO. Yet historians Harvey Klehr and Edward P. Johanningsmeier have shown that Foster had proved willing to pay such a price before Browder became leader.[4]

In February GM caved in, offering few concrete concessions but officially recognizing the UAW as bargaining agent for members in struck facilities. Beaming, bewhiskered employees who had sat down emerged from the plants in triumph on February 11; thousands of them endured freezing winter weather to celebrate all night. Historian Sidney Fine has contended that the strike was the "most significant American labor conflict in the twentieth century." It brought the entire CIO legitimacy and advanced industrial unionism's cause dramatically.[5]

The victory, plus the presence of New Deal Democratic governors in the key states of Illinois, Indiana, Ohio, and Pennsylvania, had an impact on the other legendary open shop stronghold. On March 2 the public learned that U.S. Steel's board chairman Myron Taylor had recognized Philip Murray's Steel Workers Organizing Committee without a strike. For a year local activists had been pressuring the corporation from different directions. While CIO members had built their own organization through bold demands, those within company unions had importuned in similar fashion. Fine has argued that Taylor and his colleagues had "undoubtedly concluded that a prolonged and costly steel strike was pointless" if in the end management would have to make concessions similar to those forced on General Motors. Thereupon the steel giant, despite an infamous antilabor hostility stretching back to the Homestead Strike of 1892, granted a 10-percent pay increase and a forty-hour week.[6]

Over the next seven months workers by the hundreds of thousands poured into the CIO, creating an apparatus larger than the AFL's. In April the Supreme Court upheld the Wagner Act's constitutionality, and Communist-influenced AFL unions in transport, maritime, fur, and other industries joined the torrent. Dramatic setbacks also brought proletarian sympathy and support. In May Henry Ford's private police viciously beat UAW pamphleteers near the Rouge plant. On Memorial Day Chicago bluecoats emptied their pistols into a crowd of strikers and their families outside a Republic Steel facility, killing ten and wounding fifty-eight. (So-called "Little Steel," Bethlehem, Youngstown, Inland, and Republic, spared almost no effort to prevent unionization.) *Life* magazine photographs of lawmen clubbing the wounded provoked outrage despite misleading captions.

Browder later claimed that his followers piloted "unions representing approximately one-third" of CIO membership and had "various degrees of minority" power in "another third." Certainly the labor movement marked one of the Communists' greatest success stories, despite Browder's exaggerations. The CPUSA controlled one big CIO union, the United Electrical, Radio, and Machine Workers. It was a dominant partner in heading seventeen smaller affiliates. By 1945 CIO unions with CP-aligned leaders represented about 1,370,000 workers, a quarter of total federation membership. Communists were junior partners in running the UAW, the CIO's largest single component. They also directed CIO councils in California, Minnesota, Wisconsin, Washington State, and New York City. John L. Lewis saluted party contributions by appointing member Lee Pressman as CIO general counsel and sympathizer Len DeCaux as publicity director. By year's end unions had called nearly five thousand job actions and secured favorable terms in 80 percent of them.[7]

The CIO's rise emphasized, more starkly than that of any other group, a transformation in proletarian thinking that had been taking place for a half century. Back in 1899 Thorstein Veblen, an alienated intellectual who did not join the political left, perceived that the United States would pass from being a society of producers and savers to one of buyers and spenders. Workers would take their individual identities not from their crafts, but from being consumers. Historian Stuart Ewen has enumerated the values and goals business deliberately sought to inculcate during the 1920s. They included aspiring to a larger share of the property produced by one's daily job, rather than "a larger share in the management of the enterprise which furnishes that job"; replacing concern over workplace satisfaction with a concern for one's personal appearance or "image of dedication"; abandoning all class thinking; forcing "Americanization" on immigrants; confusing purchasing power with political democracy; stressing "marginal utility" (fashion, taste); using the marketplace and peer pressure to control popular behavior; and blaming oneself for failure. Capitalism's triumph in the social realm was self-evident by the mid-1930s, as Veblen's predictions had become bleak reality for millions of Americans. Assembly-line technology, with its mind-numbing routine, had replaced the joy of the artisan's creativity. Labor, no longer central to workers' lives, had degenerated into an evil necessary to obtain an income. The concept of personal fulfillment had vanished from their consciousness. In its place appeared conspicuous consumption: clean, trendy clothing and, for some, a small home outside the working-class district. John Patrick Diggins has argued that American proletarians were mistaking the "abolition of scarcity for the abolition of capitalism" and accepting the "ruling class's power and values."[8]

Labor historians Bruce Nelson, David Brody, Melvyn Dubofsky, and Robert Zieger have found similar limitations on workers' proletarian consciousness. The latter may have expressed the point best in his study of battery workers in Madison, Wisconsin, during the 1930s. Although it strove to provide educational and recreational activities, Federal Labor Union 19587 "could never assume the dimensions of a full-fledged class subculture." Instead, members were attracted to popular mass diversions: radio, movies, and professional spectator sports. Zieger found that "both men and women invested enormous energy in the acquisition, refurbishment, and continual improvement of their homes. Well-trimmed lawns, carefully swept sidewalks, lovingly tended backyard gardens, and neat, though modest, internal appointments" characterized the residences of working-class Madison. Even in "the doleful thirties," battery workers resolved that their own difficult personal struggle "would provide educational and occupational opportunities for their offspring." In short the union filled an economic need and provided "a certain amount of camaraderie and cohesiveness" but could not compete with Hollywood, much less family, for "cultural and personal allegiance."[9] Although it frightened parsimonious employers, industrial unionism represented a call for inclusion—not revolution. That the CIO abandoned the AFL's practice of standing aloof from politics helps prove the point. Its Nonpartisan League became indispensable to New Deal election efforts. Thus organized labor became issue-oriented and reformist, at least until its own needs were met.

Browder, a Communist careerist, did not write discourses on job satisfaction, but his political instincts told him which way labor was moving in the late 1930s. He could never be a success if the CPUSA languished. Determined to build party influence in the CIO, he felt confident that, with effort, he could find some theoretical underpinning for his actions.

## REVISIONISM EMERGES

At age forty-six Browder decided to use his triumphs to push the CPUSA in a new domestic policy direction. Although Stalin's dictatorship was about to purge thousands of Communists on the vaguest suspicions of unorthodoxy, Browder believed that he could convince Moscow to let him adopt unique tactics for his party.

Despite their efforts on behalf of the president, the Marxists had always considered FDR a lesser evil. Just before the electoral college voted in December 1936, Browder termed him unreliable and likely to appease conservatives. After the campaign, Roosevelt did nothing to enlist leftist support, offering no radical new domestic programs and slashing WPA jobs for the needy. Ranking CPUSA figures still sought to obey Dimitrov's Farmer-Labor party edict; theoretician Alexander Bittelman even tried to argue that FDR had received no mandate.[10] Therefore the Communists faced a painful choice. They could continue advocating a third party, thereby risking isolation from other progressives, or rally behind a president whom members distrusted.

That month Browder revealed which of the dilemma's horns bothered him less and did some political soothsaying. He told his Central Committee that the recent contest signaled a momentous, permanent watershed. American politics, heretofore a struggle among northern, southern, and western bourgeoisie, had rarely permitted clear partisan expression of class antagonisms. Now FDR's landslide heralded the Republican party's collapse. The Democrats would split because their liberal and reactionary wings could not long continue under the same banner. Therefore, Browder urged the CPUSA to gauge public moods carefully before prematurely forming a third party. Not ready to discard farmer-laborism altogether, he sought to postpone it once again.[11]

The president opened his second term with a ringing address that decried the plight of "one third of a nation, ill-housed, ill-clad, ill-nourished" and suggested renewed activism. Eagerly, Browder entertained notions of a massive federal low-cost housing program built by a reinvigorated WPA. Instead, Roosevelt wanted institutional change. Since 1935 the Supreme Court had been striking down as unconstitutional major New Deal efforts to achieve business and agricultural recovery, even New York's minimum wage law. Roosevelt had every reason to believe that the National Labor Relations Act, Tennessee Valley Authority, and Social Security would fare no better. Accordingly, on February 15, 1937, he asked Congress for enabling legislation to appoint up to six new, liberal justices. Members of Congress, not notified in advance, offered angry resistance. FDR could not treat them like Huey Long's legislature. No one seemed to remember that Thomas Jefferson, Andrew Jackson, and Abraham Lincoln had successfully expanded the high tribunal, although not by six members. The president's request also set off a smaller controversy within the CPUSA. Although cadres welcomed FDR's actions, they retained misgivings about him. Bittelman publicly renewed calls for a Farmer-Labor party, and by May *Daily Worker* editor Clarence Hathaway was echoing him.[12]

Browder, by contrast, had moved the other way. Conservative Democrats' opposition to Roosevelt had convinced him to support the president wholeheartedly. Browder knew that this would meet stubborn intraparty resistance. The populist in him wanted to back FDR, but the follower of Stalin knew to get the USSR's permission first. Therefore, he took his case to the ECCI. He and ranking opponents visited Moscow in April.

On arrival Browder seized the offensive, appearing the model CP leader. He politely reminded his hosts that "just a year" earlier he had offered a "special application" of the Seventh World Congress's line for America, his own presidential candidacy, which they had accepted. Proudly he recounted its achievements. It had distanced the Communists from FDR, discrediting conservative propaganda. In the elections "every red-baiter" lost, "no matter to what group he belonged." Browder, using the dry wit Russian listeners enjoyed, conceded that the Republican defeat "was of course not entirely our work."[13]

He enumerated groups the CPUSA had cooperated with and around whom a national Farmer-Labor party might be built: liberal unions, labor's Nonpartisan League, remnants of California's EPIC movement, Washington State's Commonwealth Federation, Minnesota's Farmer-Labor party, Wisconsin's Progressives, New York's American Labor party, and incipient party efforts in Michigan, Iowa, and a few other states. Smoothly Browder turned to the controversy at point. These independent movements had spread their influence only by working with Roosevelt's campaign. Indeed, the president's following among them had grown even greater with the Supreme Court struggle. Now there was "no perspective at all" of their breaking with him. Thus People's Front forces were burgeoning while the third-party movement had stalled.[14]

Browder proposed to support the Roosevelt administration directly, working to make the Communists a small but vociferous part of the New Deal coalition. His plan met spirited resistance from Foster. He derided Browder for supposedly idealizing FDR, exaggerating the role of liberals in building the Popular Front, and underestimating the working masses' independent power. The Comintern noted Foster's objections but realized that Browder's plan more closely dovetailed with Soviet foreign policy needs. The USSR feared a war with Nazi Germany. If one occurred, allies would be essential. The United States was not yet a military power, but it possessed the strongest economy in the world. Any part Communists could play in the New Deal could help improve relations between Washington and Moscow. Accordingly, the international body criticized Browder mildly for inadequate recruiting and for allowing the *Daily Worker*'s circulation to stagnate. It agreed, however, with his assessment that sympathizers no longer considered the CPUSA a party exclusively of heroes and martyrs but, instead, one of advanced workers and their families. The Comintern approved his proposals.[15]

The decision constituted yet another victory for Browder. Stalin's silence showed at minimum his indifference. Browder chose to believe that he had contributed significantly to the international movement. That June he explained the change to his Central Committee. He now believed that two peculiarly American conditions doomed Farmer-Laborism anyhow. First, legal obstacles, "extreme and growing," impeded new political parties. In many states, simply securing a ballot position had become difficult. Second, primary elections allowed the masses, when aroused, to influence major party candidacies. Impressed with his victory abroad, Browder declared that Communists had given insufficient consideration to electoral features at home.[16]

The Farmer-Labor party idea died hard. Foster and Bittelman tried to revive it all summer. The latter denounced the "illusion" that Roosevelt constituted "the genuine class representative of labor" and held that support for Democrats must remain temporary.[17]

Most Communists considered foreign policy the final roadblock to endorsing the president. Historically they had opposed all American military expenditures. But on July 17, 1936, Spanish Moroccan army units had revolted, crossed Gibraltar, and levied war on Spain's Popular Front government. Led by Generalissimo Francisco Franco, these units soon received infusions of Italian and German troops. Fifteen months later, FDR finally delivered his famous "quarantine" speech, warning that continued, unchecked fascist expansion threatened the United States itself and that traditional isolationism offered no protection. Therefore, he proposed joining the world's peace-loving nations to isolate aggressors. Although subsequently he did nothing to turn his rhetoric into deeds, the Communists nevertheless hailed his perceived conversion to collective security.

On October 8, 1937, Browder, addressing a Canadian Communist convention in Toronto, praised the quarantine concept and Roosevelt. Acknowledging that the CPUSA had long included the president's "sharpest critics," Browder nevertheless promised "full and complete support." He now looked to FDR to prevent a second world war.[18] For Foster, this latest embrace came at the worst possible moment. The year 1937 brought a "recession" that crippled recovery efforts. The president had never liked large deficits or federal relief spending. Congress reduced WPA funding by 50 percent between January and August, laying off 1.5 million federal workers. At the same time the new Social Security system withheld $2 billion from employees' paychecks, reducing purchasing power further. No other set of circumstances hurt Roosevelt's standing among the left so greatly. Foster felt that Communists should denounce capitalism, not support a budget-conscious administration that many now likened to Herbert Hoover's.

Browder's response to the recession infuriated Foster. Browder announced that its causes were economic and political. He granted that cyclical downturns would always exist under capitalism but accused wealthy "economic royalists" of exacerbating the crisis deliberately to combat union growth and block progressive legislation. In short, monopoly capital had gone on a "sit-down strike." Browder urged stricter government regulation of finance and industry and greater unemployment relief and public works expenditures. Then he seconded John L. Lewis's proposal to guarantee every American worker a job. In December the Polburo officially endorsed FDR. Browder hailed him as the West's "most outstanding anti-fascist spokesman." Browder announced that Roosevelt's latest foreign policy direction, plus the CIO's legislative agenda, constituted "a rounded-out People's Front program of an advanced type."[19]

Thus Browder had revised his organization's domestic role. It had abandoned the Farmer-Labor party approach and endorsed the New Deal coalition as the Popular Front's specifically American form. Not incidentally, Browder believed he had also flexed some muscle internationally. Stalin, Dimitrov, and Thorez were not the only figures entitled to tinker with orthodox Marxism-Leninism.

Browder's heresy did not go unchallenged. At year's end, on the CPUSA's final group excursion to Moscow, the frustrated Foster appealed to the Comintern. He considered Browder's policies a dangerous surrender to reformism; the party had relinquished its vanguard function. En route, Foster attended the French Communists' congress near Paris. There he praised the PCF for entering the government. Attacking Browder's leadership publicly, he declared that the American CP deserved formal admission "as a party" into any coalition it joined. Foster squawked that Communists in all capitalist countries should learn from the Gallic example.[20]

Sparks flew before the Comintern's American Commission. Foster lambasted Browder's support of the president as uncritical and excessive. Browder's non-Marxist sit-down strike of capital concept resulted from his familiar fault of "tailing" Roosevelt. Browder was a dangerous revisionist and incidentally was misusing Foster's talents. Soviet economist Eugene Varga offered vigorous support in a two-hour speech. Although Bittelman and Sam Darcy remained silent, Browder considered them ready to pounce.

Assertively Browder noted that Foster's differences with the CPUSA's Polburo had over the previous nine months increased "in number and intensity." No one on the ruling body, and only William W. Weinstone on the larger Central Committee, agreed with him. Now Foster was presenting an indictment in "contemptuous" tones. If continued, Foster's actions "must inevitably result in a general opposition" to the organization's "whole course." The chief target of his criticism was the Polburo's practice of "issuing only general plans and directives," thereby allowing "district and local initiative to fill in the details." Yet "precisely this" represented the party's greatest recent improvement. Browder acknowledged that Foster played a special, irreplaceable role and found it the "most painful experience" of his life to launch in the USSR a major polemic against his former mentor. He had, however, "been learning from even greater teachers, from the greatest teacher of all, Comrade Stalin."[21]

Divided, the Comintern left the Americans in suspense for two weeks. For once Browder had time on his hands in Moscow. Heretofore he had always enjoyed the city. He loved its rugged beauty, especially in winter. Its centuries-old communal traditions and the residents' willingness to share what little they had with strangers had provided mighty contrasts to capitalist Manhattan where he worked. Russia and its people had reinforced his faith in Marxism-Leninism. For sixteen months, however, high-ranking Communists had been pleading guilty to monstrous crimes. Browder refused to let himself look critically at what was occurring almost daily. Instead, he submerged himself in games of chess and evenings at the city's renowned ballet.

Finally the Comintern announced its decision. In ecumenical tones Georgi Dimitrov thanked Varga for his analysis but declared that it contained "a certain amount of dogmatism and scientific schematicism." Issues dividing Foster and Browder were "not of a factional character," but instead "differences between comrades-in-arms who wish to equip themselves better for the struggle." Browder's approach to major political and tactical questions was correct and "with this Comrade Foster should also agree." The latter had expressed "remnants of sectarianism and showed fear of working with the petty bourgeois Democrats and Republicans. Browder, however, needed to display greater awareness of tailism's danger.[22]

Thenceforth Foster received a torrent of abuse. Varga delivered another speech, revising his previous analysis 180 degrees. Dimitri Manuilsky enumerated Foster's shortcomings. American Comintern representative Eugene Dennis, soon to return to the United States as party legislative director, taunted Foster. He emphasized that Browder's position enjoyed domestic and international support.

Victorious, Browder gave a talk on January 18, 1938, summarizing the strategy, which he now called the Democratic Front. He then left Moscow and returned home via the Spanish republic.[23] In Spain he visited American volunteers and contracted a severe case of influenza. Between February 18 and Washington's birthday, the domestic Communists conducted a mammoth conclave to ratify Farmer-Laborism's burial. The gathering brought hundreds of cadres to New York. Because of Browder's illness, which left him fevered and bedfast for a week, Hathaway presided.

At least three factors helped explain the new rubric. First, "Democratic Front" sounded less foreign. Indeed, Browder's Americanization campaign had assumed near-manic proportions. Second, a full-fledged People's Front on the French or Spanish model simply was not possible. Only dreamers could foresee Communists seated among the president's cabinet. Therefore, when applied to the United States, the term was semantically inaccurate. Finally, most leading cadres had resigned themselves to something far more modest.

Hathaway announced that the CP had to accept a junior, sometimes concealed role in its coalitions. Generally, progressives would not admit Communists without blushing. Party members should take heart nevertheless and show through diligent work that they comprised "a constructive force" entitled to open recognition in the future. Hathaway revealed publicly that the CPUSA would work with the groups Browder had listed in his April 1937 Moscow speech. Proletarian dictatorship lay relegated to the hypothetical. Browder would strive for it only if the president's "promise of a higher living standard were betrayed."[24] The party had a new ideological inspiration: not Lenin, or even Stalin, but Thomas Jefferson. Lesser indigenous forebears included Thoreau, Emerson, Walt Whitman, and Mark Twain.

By now Sam Darcy was a National Committee member working with the ninth district, which included the northern Great Plains states. He protested the policy of infiltrating the Minnesota Farmer-Labor party as giving Governor Elmer Benson's opponents unnecessary ammunition. Darcy wrote Browder a letter urging that the CPUSA run its own ticket; state clearly its differences with the Farmer-Labor party; withdraw sub rosa Communist candidates; and "engage in no activity" that could not "be reported on the front page of any newspaper," as Browder had done with the General Motors strike. The leader never responded directly but subsequently engineered Darcy's demotion to National Committee alternate and transfer to Pennsylvania. The actions added a deep personal animus to previous tactical disagreements.[25]

Browder's shabby treatment of Darcy helps shed light on the CPUSA's internal structure during the 1930s. The party of the Popular Front era manifested both an illusory image and a familiar reality. On one hand "Jimmy Higgins," the prototypal rank and filer, found the grass-roots organization open, candid, and filled with comrades evincing more day-to-day selflessness than did Christian fundamentalists. An atmosphere of friendly persuasion prevailed, and it sometimes exhibited a patient tolerance even of foot dragging on the ideological line. At the highest levels, however, General Secretary Browder always considered it a chore to display pleasantness toward anyone who frequently opposed him. He was going to get his way, and those who interfered were wasting everyone's time. Thus the local phantasm of internal democracy coexisted with the traditional power politics of national headquarters in Manhattan.[26]

Like members of the political mainstream, the Communists formalized the Democratic Front's adoption at a spectacular convention in May 1938. Browder had meticulously cleared the gala's "agenda, terms of representation, period of discussion," and similar details with Dimitrov in Moscow. The date chosen avoided "conflict with any international gathering." The ceremony filled Madison Square Garden and rated a live fifteen-minute early evening synopsis by CBS's Robert Trout. Browder addressed the fifteen hundred delegates before a gigantic blue U.S. outline map bearing red and white letters that read "Jobs, Security, Democracy, Peace." The atmosphere even made James W. Ford's boast that continued growth would bring future gatherings "in person" visits from New York's mayor seem conceivable. The throng sang the "Star Spangled Banner" and the original version of Eugene Pottier's "Internationale," which, significantly, did not contain the word "Soviet."[27]

After the pageantry, Browder got down to business on May 28. Confusing prolixity with profundity, he delivered a ninety-five-page formal report at Carnegie Hall. It included an admirable four-point program designed to coax the New Deal leftward. First, it advocated National Labor Relations Board–mandated better wages, hours, and working conditions. Second, it demanded full employment. Browder, who hated deficits, sought what modern liberals call "tax fairness." He entreated Congress to marshal unused resources through progressive taxation of wealth and high incomes. Third, he exhorted government to "reclaim for democracy an economic foundation" by nationalizing "banks, railways, and munitions," canceling farmers' debts, and enacting price controls. Under the same heading, Browder added a moral dimension, supporting the Wagner-Costigan antilynching bill, poll tax abolition, and voting rights for all Americans.

Finally, he implored that the nation assume international leadership by using its vast economic resources. Specifically he wanted to deny violators of the Kellogg-Briand Peace Pact access to American trade and, echoing FDR, supported quarantining expansionist states.[28]

As the convention closed, a jubilant Browder enjoyed greater renown than any American Communist leader had ever achieved. His loyalty to Stalin and new ideas had won from Moscow a special CPUSA role. No other major Communist party tendered the Democratic Front rationale to justify subservience to a capitalist government. At that very moment, Browder knew, Soviet Communists accused of unorthodoxy were being tried, sentenced, and executed en masse, but he believed he was reconciling the American reform tradition and world Marxism. As the spotlight of national publicity shone on him, his self-regard grew accordingly. Indeed, that May he became the only CPUSA chief ever to appear on *Time* magazine's cover, which occurred just as party membership and influence were peaking.[29] Although his ambition had taken him a long way, he believed still greater things awaited.

Socialist fortunes by contrast grew bleaker daily. In June 1936 Louis Waldman led an exit by the long-dissatisfied Old Guard, setting off a stampede. Large sections of SP organizations in New York, Pennsylvania, Connecticut, Indiana, and Oregon followed, along with influential Jewish groups. Many joined the Social Democratic Federation, supporting New Deal candidates. Norman Thomas and the Militants remained in a truncated organization of only twelve thousand, fast slipping toward total obscurity. In 1937 the SP expelled the Trotskyists for publishing their own journal and refusing to follow official policy. The Trotskyists formed the far smaller Socialist Workers party and concentrated on denouncing

Stalin's crimes while continuing to support the USSR's bold experiment.[30]

Browder's optimism, at least in the labor field, proved ill-founded. Growing public hostility and the recession of 1937–1938 curbed workers' activities and returned the initiative to capital. Historian Daniel Nelson has noted the insufficiencies of proletarian victories in the rubber industry: there "were few explicit challenges to the foreman's realm, no reports of shared power, no efforts to redefine the managerial role except in the personnel area . . . the sit-down was an act of censure rather than a step toward a new type of industrial management." Robert H. Zieger has stressed larger "sharp limitations in both the extent and character of the militant upsurge embodied in the early CIO." Little Steel remained an open shop bastion, as did Ford. While John L. Lewis and Sidney Hillman completed plans for a permanent federation separate from the AFL, David Dubinsky held back his 200,000-member International Ladies Garment Workers Union. The CIO put on a convention, adopted a constitution, and became the Congress of Industrial Organizations in November 1938. Yet by then the resurgent AFL had surpassed it in total membership.[31]

## SILENT EARL

Fifty-two years before 1988 Republican presidential nominee George Bush explained his own lack of allure, insisting he was a "quiet man" who listens, the Communists sang Earl Browder's praises in like fashion.[32] Indeed, the nation that has preferred charismatic chief executives such as John F. Kennedy and Ronald Reagan has often romanticized its radicals. Browder was not dashing and thereby disappointed friend and foe alike.

In this regard he was not alone. Many Communist cadres, such as Sam Darcy, Steve Nelson, and even William Z. Foster, possessed personalities that were 98 percent political. To understand this is to grasp an important aspect of the movement's nature. Those who became top Marxists did so in part because they gave so much of themselves. As a result their private lives were often less than exciting.[33] They were willing to pay that price, however. Browder personified a certain kind of bureaucratic method and organizational ethos; not all Communists were party yes-men with authoritarian personalities or remained in the movement because of their admiration for Joseph Stalin. Browder, unlike many rank and filers eulogized by historians, did, however. He enjoyed significant yet unprepossessing gifts: willpower and patience.

He also had a pathological fascination with, and attraction toward, fear. Danger energized him, dispelled his shyness, and gave him an advantage over every single adversary he faced. Under its influence Browder could out-debate more intelligent rivals, face down angry right-wing mobs, and peddle revisionist doctrines in Moscow at the very time Stalin was murdering tens of thousands of unorthodox (and orthodox) Communists. This is not to claim Browder had no inhibitions at all. The truly fearless often self-destruct early. Rather, Browder faced his external dreads as a way of avoiding the self-reproach any perceived cowardice might produce. Fiercely inner-motivated since childhood, his greatest nemesis was the critic within. He could and did confront danger more easily than face in the mirror someone who had turned and run. His courage, if that is the clinically precise word, in turn produced a sense of superiority most contemporaries noticed and many detested. Browder's unusual trait explains his rebelliousness, his boldness, his vanity, and (along with willingness to work hard and follow the Comintern) his triumphs over superior rivals. The reckless Browder did not carry guns and never ate a rat, but he would have understood Richard Nixon's covert operative G. Gordon Liddy.

Before 1934 Browder merely acted unassuming, but after he became general secretary a dichotomy appeared. To interviewers and the press he seemed outgoing, although his caustic replies to deeply probing questions silenced many reporters. To his comrades, however, Browder was ever-conscious of his rank and often aloof. CP veteran Steve Nelson acknowledged this but nevertheless characterized him as "a personable guy, tolerant of people and rarely sharp or nasty." Except for Foster and Darcy, Browder rarely antagonized colleagues, but he even less frequently radiated amiability. *New Masses* associate editor A. B. Magil described him as "very reserved, almost taciturn." He could be "gracious" but not "affectionate or emotional." Junius Irving Scales, a former CPUSA organizer, came to know Browder on a first-name basis during the late 1950s. In similar fashion Scales recalled him as a "decent, thoughtful" man, "quite forthcoming at times," but who always "tried to listen more than he spoke." Certainly Browder's only close friends were financial angels (wealthy Communist party patrons) late in life. As undisputed leader he had surrounded himself with sycophants such as Robert Minor and Eugene Dennis. Even they never called him warm. To most, his true nature remained an enigma.[34]

Because no serious observer could denounce the rational Browder as one of the depression demagogues, adversaries usually tried to dismiss him as dull, an impression he happily reinforced. In 1936 a *Current History* journalist complained that Browder seemed "more like a lyric poet than the leader of a revolutionary faction." He reminded others of a minister. So widespread was such disparagement that few paid attention when a more reliable source, philosopher Reinhold Niebuhr, termed Browder the "ablest spokesman of Communist policy and strategy" in the United States.[35]

Some onlookers fixated on his inaccessibility. In 1938 a *New Yorker* article declared darkly that Browder remained "as remote from the average Communist as Franklin Roosevelt" was from the average Democrat. No ordinary party member ever got to "see him at headquarters." Overdrawn, though factually accurate, such words distort Browder's complex nature because they could apply to any mass leader. Actually he oversaw the CPUSA much as a manager might run a large corporation, Marxist rhetoric notwithstanding.[36]

A mighty, carefully constructed wall separated Browder's party life from his family life. During his reign as YCL leader, Gil Green knew Browder well, had an office on the same floor, and enjoyed easy access. Yet he never saw Browder display closeness to anyone, was never invited to his apartment, and was not even formally introduced to Raissa. Dorothy Healey considered Browder's distance a deliberate tactic to compensate for political illegitimacy. She believed that because he owed his position to the Russians, he sought to create a leader's dignity through withdrawing. Magil affirmed that Browder's reticence did add to his aura. Like so many Communist careerists, he seemed to live in only one dimension, his work.[37] At home, by contrast, he made a warm, loving father who protected his family from publicity. His sons cherished him until the day he died.

Browder's aloofness stemmed in part from introversion and early suffering. He was the classic overachiever. A person of boundless ambition but provincial background, he had exaggerated his limitations before going to China. There, overcoming challenges previously unimagined, he surprised himself. Discovering that he possessed untapped potential intoxicated him. After 1927 every success fed his vanity. Sometimes doing well breeds complacency; for Browder it launched a vicious cycle of higher aspiration, gallant effort, mastery, and a new goal yet one step grander. The process worked, helping make him general secretary, the CPUSA's greatest leader and Democratic Front creator; yet never did success satiate his craving for advancement. Unsure how far he could rise, he stood always ready to employ his enterprise and fearlessness. In an authoritarian international movement such traits can prove both valuable and dangerous. In the United States Communism had fared poorly, but Browder was, in his own mind, a winner. The inadequacies he perceived in his followers made his own superiority all the more manifest. Foster's criticisms bothered him, but Browder knew that the world's greatest Marxists in Moscow would always recognize his own ascendant wisdom.

Vanity led to other character weaknesses. He distorted facts about his career. He always tried to read back his 1934 general secretaryship to 1930, when he only shared power. Worse yet, he constructed a cultlike following befitting a miniature imitator of Stalin. Browder never possessed governmental power, nor did he kill people. He did try to run the CPUSA like a dictator, however. He admired the tyrant in the Kremlin and longed for his own disciples to venerate him the way Soviet CP members worshipped their hero. A contemporaneous disparager exaggerated only slightly when he cracked: "There are more than sixty thousand people in the United States who are firmly convinced that Earl Browder is one of the greatest men in the world." Party hagiography praised him tirelessly while insisting on his modesty.[38] Before World War II he displayed no signs of believing this propaganda. Yet by savoring it, he armed his severest critics.

Browder camouflaged his personal life as too dull to bother with. Why? A need to protect his family gave him a compelling reason for distance and secrecy. Raissa's illegal entry into the United States meant that the first major disagreement with the administration would bring an Immigration and Naturalization Service (INS) officer to their door. Of course, nothing could conceal her nationality, but Browder was determined to hide her Russian civil war role. He remembered that the United States had aided the White Army. Because American and Bolshevik forces never actually met on the battlefield, Raissa could not have approved of, much less ordered, executions of Americans. Yet her past, if known, almost certainly would have barred legal residence.

Browder also spared no effort in concealing her Lenin Institute training, lest she be accused of espionage. One of his sister's activities could not bear public scrutiny either. Margaret Browder, a quiet woman who did not possess her brother's good looks, reminded those who met her of a rural Kansas schoolmarm. At various times she was married to American radicals Thomas R. Sullivan, Harrison George, and a mysterious Soviet operative in Germany who used the name James Meadows. An FBI agent who took surveillance photographs labeled her a "dowdy dresser" and guffawed that she was alert "but apparently not tail-conscious." A Communist party charter member, she had worked as Earl's secretary in Chicago and been permitted to transfer to the Russian organization. In Moscow she studied at a special school to become a code expert and radio operator. Posing as a language student named Jean Montgomery, she spent the 1930s doing clandestine work in Berlin and other Nazi cities for the foreign intelligence directorate of the Soviet secret police agency NKVD (later KGB). Her expert typing skills and unimpeachable reliability as Browder's sister made her a valuable, highly trusted agent. Her brother William told a U.S. government informer that she served as a humble courier escorting German Communists and Jews to the Russian border.[39]

Margaret was no starry-eyed antifascist romantic, however. She returned to the United States three times between 1931 and 1938 or 1939, though she denied conveying any documents. In the early 1930s she met Vasily Zubilin (alias Zarubin), chief Soviet intelligence officer assigned to Washington, D.C. Zubilin was one of the most important NKVD representatives ever to work in the United States, later supervising Soviet atomic espionage. He and his wife just happened to be visitors at the home of William and Rose Browder. When the hosts introduced the Russian couple simply as "Poppy" and "Mommy," Margaret knew not to ask questions. She saw them again in Germany where Vasily used the disguise of talent scout for an unnamed movie studio (possibly the one owned by Boris Moros, a courier for the Soviet apparatus later turned informer by the FBI).[40]

During the Cold War the FBI sought to persuade the Browders, living in retirement, to aid investigations of Soviet intelligence activities. A secondary goal included developing cases against family members. The 1950 Internal Security Act and related legislation required even inactive persons having knowledge of espionage, counterespionage, or sabotage tactics of a foreign government (or foreign political party) to register with the attorney general. The bureau opined that "should any one of the Browders talk," it would "undoubtedly" involve all deeply.[41]

By this time Margaret was calling herself Ann Meadows, claiming to have married a James Meadows in Germany before World War II. She told agents that she did not know from where he had come (though she believed him an American), his background, or relatives. Certain he was also helping refugees escape the Nazis, she lived with him for three years until "he disappeared one day." Prosecutors hauled her before a federal grand jury on November 3, 1952, but she said nothing incriminating.[42]

Nearly six years later a seeming break in the case occurred when Margaret agreed to a series of FBI interviews at her cramped Bronx apartment. On April 7, 1958, she identified photographs of Vasily and Elizabeth Zubilin as "Poppy" and "Mommy," but denied ever receiving instructions or money from them. In a subsequent meeting on April 23, however, she realized that agents were building a case against her. Becoming extremely nervous, she began to pace the floor exclaiming, "I must protect myself from self incrimination" and refused to say anything further. Over the next year and a half the Justice Department considered a proposal by the bureau's New York office to give immunity to one or all of the Browders in exchange for their information. Margaret, interviewed again on September 15, 1959, contended that she had never heard of the NKVD agents. When reminded of the pictures she had identified, she fell silent. On October 7 she faced another grand jury and was scheduled to return yet again seven days thereafter.[43]

On October 13, however, Earl told an unnamed lawyer that his sister might be "in serious trouble" and asked him or her to contact Assistant U.S. Attorney John S. Clark. The latter offered no deals because he did not believe that Margaret "had been entirely truthful." Yet he canceled her next appearance, claiming to have a full court schedule. Clark may have hoped to turn her or Earl. The bureau, moreover, was having difficulty compiling legally obtained evidence and finding witnesses with knowledge beyond hearsay. It never took seriously sensational charges that Margaret had helped kidnap Eugene Muller, head of the Federation of Czarist Army Veterans, and murder former Soviet operative Ignace Reiss. As other espionage cases unfolded, her name came up repeatedly. The Justice Department hoped at minimum for a perjury conviction, but her death in 1961 closed the case.[44]

Thus during the 1930s Earl Browder had a sister who worked for the NKVD in Europe and a brother and sister-in-law who hosted a top Russian spy in their New York home. For many thousands of American Communists, "Soviet espionage" was merely one more slander hurled by right-wingers to delegitimize their radical and labor activities. The USSR did enlist agents from the movement, but espionage was not the primary CPUSA activity. As Harvey Klehr and John Haynes have noted, to see the party as a sort of fifth column "misjudges its main purpose."[45]

Why then did Browder, a public figure, let the practice touch him so closely? Clandestine operations were not an important feature of his life but, rather, an occupational hazard. Again, he owed his position to the USSR and could not forget it. Without foreign intervention he would have been Foster's or another CPUSA figure's assistant or, worse yet in his own mind, an accountant for some capitalist. He and his relatives had delved into the CPUSA's covert work before anyone guessed that Earl would rise to general secretary. They would not quit, and now their actions and his high profile seemed destined to create a legal nightmare. Browder did not relish his position's hidden component, but neither did he shirk it. Klehr, Haynes, and Firsov have shown that before Browder became party chief he had recruited former brother-in-law Harrison George for underground work in 1929 and had expanded the duties three years later.[46]

As leader, Browder had more than a nodding acquaintance with the CPUSA's illegal wing, created by 1929. During the 1930s he knew members of the Ware group, part of a Communist underground inside various federal agencies in Washington. The open party's growth stimulated an increased determination to locate left-wing rivals and federal agents hiding among its ranks. Disciplinary commissions in the districts handled the problem, and Browder oversaw their work. Rudy Baker (Rudolf Blum), who replaced J. Peters as head of the secret apparatus in June 1938, reported to Browder. They maintained a personal and family friendship that extended well into the 1950s. During World War II Baker's organization participated in Soviet atomic espionage. After hostilities broke out in Europe, Browder used NKVD channels to send reports to Moscow and even to request Raissa's birth certificate. Before long he met with French politician Pierre Cot. A senior Soviet military intelligence officer in Europe who had defected to the West, Walter Krivitsky, had already identified Cot as a hidden source inside the French government. Recklessly, Browder continued to see Cot until at least 1943.[47]

Writer and former House Un-American Activities Committee (HUAC) investigator Herbert Romerstein has located a 1938 letter from Browder to Georgi Dimitrov that requests information about Raissa's sister Maria. She had worked in Moscow since 1921 for the newspaper *Za Industrializatsiu* and the Soviet news agency Tass. Maria, not a party member, had come under suspicion when her supervisor was purged (presumably in 1937) and because her father, seventy-six-year-old Boris Berkmann, lived in Berlin. Browder asked about any pending charges against Maria because such information "would be valuable in guiding our relations with her; if there is really nothing against her, as it appears to me, that is also important for me to know." In Maria's case at least, political correctness was more important to the Browders than the family tie.[48]

On sheer grounds of safety Browder could have tried to distance himself from clandestine operations. Yet the seemingly commonsense argument that no CPUSA leader should ever have been near these activities may represent a projection backward of American society's postwar nature. During the McCarthy era the FBI infiltrated the party well. Yet before World War II the agency had less manpower, and some of that was devoted to anti-Nazi investigations. Certainly Browder attracted less surveillance before 1939 than he received the rest of his life.[49]

That Browder did not act discreetly is instructive. He apparently never paused to consider whether Moscow cared about his vulnerability. Because his ambition impaired his judgment, he fatuously accepted Russian arguments that no one would get caught. Worse yet, he lacked moral qualms about cooperating with Soviet secret police actions that targeted not Hitler but the U.S. government. Browder saw no contradiction between his concept of patriotism—loyalty to America's working people—and support for the world's lone proletarian state. Where that countenance violated U.S. law, Browder reminded himself that capitalists had written the statutes.

Involvement in American Communism's secret world caused Browder to guard his family's privacy ever more jealously. "My office," he insisted, "is where I do my business. My home life is nobody's business but my own." Once Gil Green had an important message on a day Browder had off. Rather than invite him over, Browder took a special trip down to headquarters. He sometimes made exceptions of a sort. A. B. Magil reported that he and *New Masses* editor Joe North once enjoyed a pleasant working dinner at Browder's summer cottage. Afterward, without being asked, Browder played the flute.[50] In general, however, the household remained off limits to almost everyone.

Partly to divert attention from his family's clandestine activities, the chameleonlike Browder deliberately led a highly predictable public existence. Indeed, his daily whereabouts constituted no mystery at all. One could usually find him in his ninth-floor office at 35 East Twelfth Street, Manhattan. Like many cadres, Browder championed his cause indefatigably, working from early morning into the evening.

This routine left little spare time. Except when addressing an audience, he always seemed rushed. John McCarten, an unfriendly reporter interviewing him in 1936 beneath the portraits of Jefferson, Lincoln, and

Stalin, seemed surprised to learn that Browder's calendar was so crowded that he planned "half-hour interviews days in advance." When not in conference with functionaries, he was "busy reading reports from the district and state organizers, preparing his dispatches for the home office, going over the material" his assistants had gathered for his speeches, or simply thinking.[51]

Browder's faith in Stalin had its limits, however. Deep inside he knew the movement was a dangerous line of work; he insisted that his sons stay out of it. Whereas *Daily Worker* editor Clarence Hathaway sent his children to study in Moscow, the Browder boys attended public schools in Yonkers. In 1936 a bemused interviewer asked Earl if he let his sons salute Old Glory. "It's their flag," he growled, "Why shouldn't they?" Felix, Andrew, and William received pressure to avoid the cause. Earl announced the family's excuse: "No one should be politically conscious before age fourteen." Actually, like many working-class Americans (but not many heads of proletarian political parties), Earl and Raissa hoped that their children would rise to the middle class. They did not even let them join the YCL. This was extraordinary because CPUSA cadres lived in their own cloistered society. Socialist Robert J. Alexander noted that the Browders received significant criticism for their peculiar stance.[52] They encouraged the boys' interest in science, and all three eventually became university professors.

Browder defied the Communist boss stereotype by preferring to persuade and cajole rather than confront or command. Although he possessed an acid tongue and an administrator's skill at using the fait accompli, he sought to minimize intraparty conflict gently. A relaxed leader, confident of his superiority, he eschewed incivility. The CPUSA's most pragmatic chief, he lent the post a human touch, conducting "question meetings" four or five times a year. Here he candidly answered all queries rank and filers posed. The procedure horrified CP functionaries who considered it too dangerous. Browder, who excelled at unrehearsed discourse, profited handsomely from this public relations device. In fact, he later opined that such gatherings established openly his authority as head. Never before had America's top Communist displayed even an ersatz interest in ordinary members' needs.[53]

Modern radicals might have trouble identifying with the Browders beyond fealty to a foreign power. They were very much a product of the mid-twentieth century. Earl denounced racism at every turn and put a black on every dais, even the American Friends of the Chinese People.[54] Yet he had no close personal ties to any nonwhites. He criticized Western women's poor pay in the workplace and their robotic domestic duties. Yet he had no contact with feminists. Raissa, of course, played a nontraditional role before 1939. Indeed, A. B. Magil and Sam Darcy, who worked near her at CPUSA headquarters, considered her somewhat masculine. When not advising Earl, she channeled her efforts toward the party's foreign-language groups, which had fewer women than men. The couple remained silent in the mid-1930s when the Kremlin outlawed birth control and abortion, ordering the Soviet peoples to provide future soldiers for the state. Good at judging political winds, Earl, the former playboy, became an exemplar of marital fidelity. The Browders' Communism seemed more like a secular religious faith than a type of radicalism.

Although Neo-Marxists after 1960 addressed the question of alienated labor, few figures of the 1930s' "Old Left" did. Sidney Hook, one exception, argued that uncoerced, fulfilling work could overcome the estrangement that industrialization had brought.[55] Browder, however, reflecting prevailing depression-era sentiments, stressed the creation of jobs that paid a living wage. Except for denouncing the assembly-line speedup, he paid little attention to job-site ambience.

Browder affected fellow travelers more measurably. During the depression the party attracted an unprecedented number of sympathizers, and he helped convert good intentions into financial support. A few eccentric millionaires had long contributed money. In 1934, however, he recruited a sizable group that made substantial donations monthly, and soon more than one hundred backers gave an average of $400 to $500 yearly. Individual benefactions ranged between $100 and $5,000.[56]

Several nights a week Browder delivered public speeches, although he never developed theatrical qualities. Public speaking was one of his weightiest official duties, but he enjoyed it the most. Often he packed Madison Square Garden, Gotham's largest indoor arena. Usually his audience consisted of CP members, whom a hostile journalist conceded were arguably the auditorium's "most frequent and best-behaved customers." When Browder addressed them, he resembled international Communist chieftains of the Cold War era. His lengthy, detailed disquisitions attempted to place latest events within a Marxist perspective and relate them to current strategy. Although the CPUSA welcomed reporters, these gatherings remained essentially business meetings, not designed to convert or arouse. Unfriendly reporters enjoyed attending and ridiculing Browder's performances as "droning."[57]

By contrast non-Marxist audiences saw a cheerful, engaging, and satiric Browder. He contrasted with other 1930s radicals who used anger or buffoonery to gain publicity. Indeed, even when raising the Communist clenched-fist salute, Browder usually smiled. Avoiding excess emotion, he couched his arguments in logical, almost scholarly, terms. His speeches usually sounded good at the time, but listeners found their contents hard to recall.

No one could term Browder a great public speaker in the tradition of Franklin D. Roosevelt, although until Angela Davis came to the forefront he was easily the most dignified in CPUSA history. He carefully planned and orchestrated his public rallies, and they were never dull. Although he had long lived in New York, he still possessed a twang more Kansan than Alf Landon's. To eastern listeners Browder's voice seemed somewhat flat; indeed, though not a true monotone it lacked great variety in pitch. The era's stationary microphone did not bother him because he read his speeches. Their organization was not always crystal clear; introductions and conclusions seemed underdeveloped. Yet Browder knew how to hold the listeners' attention well. His talks deliberately polarized his audiences, vivified problem conditions, and presented bold, if generalized, solutions that related to spectators' needs. Indeed a professional rhetorician later judged him a "capable mass persuader,"[58] and he would have enjoyed far more popularity had he peddled down-home religion instead of an international movement led by Joseph Stalin.

Actually the folksy Browder possessed a style more suited to high-tech media than those of the 1930s. His low-pressure presentation, occasional dry quips, and irony would have served him better on television than they did before the distressed audiences of his day. No scholar could argue that modern electronic technologies would have given Browder a mass following, but certainly his tone of discourse more closely resembled Ross Perot's than that of demagogue Gerald L. K. Smith.

Some who heard Browder speak regularly had insightful observations. A. B. Magil noted that American Communists never produced spellbinders the way their rivals, the Socialists, did. Instead, CP leaders deemphasized oratory and, accordingly, stirred fewer listeners. Certainly Browder made a "thoughtful" speaker, who used pauses effectively and gave a "very logical" presentation. Gil Green recalled that Browder, who aroused his audiences more visibly than did William Z. Foster, liked to employ an oratorical trick. Often Browder curled his lips to seem to spit out key phrases.[59] Although he displayed wit, he always took himself too seriously. He had little willingness to employ Foster's self-deprecating humor.

As did millions of other working-class, depression-era citizens, Browder had little leisure time, and he hated to waste it. The CPUSA, like an extended family, continually celebrated leading cadres' birthdays, anniversaries, and other occasions. He considered the custom as unnecessary as a minister's preaching to the choir. Indeed, although Green knew Browder for years, he remembered seeing him at only one Communist party social function. Browder, who could not dance and disdained mingling, simply talked to those he knew and seemed ill at ease. Fellow traveler Philip J. Jaffe had better luck at helping Browder relax. Jaffe, a whimsical, charming conversationalist who did not mind even the company of FBI agents if they would agree not to pump for information, dragged Browder to a few gatherings. The CP leader and Raissa sat quietly in a corner and politely received those who chose to visit. Unlike Jaffe, Raissa had a negative effect on Earl's sociability. She overprotected him, much as she did her children. Although Jaffe enjoyed being around her, Sam Darcy called her a bureaucratic busybody, self-important because she was Browder's wife.[60]

Magil, who organized fund raisers for the *New Masses*, had greatest success at animating Browder. The chief considered these gatherings hours well spent, and they brought out the salesman in him. He appeared frequently, giving interesting, perceptive talks. The company of intellectuals and culture figures touched his innermost longings; he seemed happiest there, although proletarian colleagues raised eyebrows.[61]

On rare summer afternoons Browder abandoned the office for Yankee Stadium. Like many contemporaries, he admired baseball's greatest team. Babe Ruth, the game's most fabulous and celebrated hero, left after 1934, but legends Lou Gehrig and Tony Lazzeri remained. A youngster named Joe DiMaggio joined shortly thereafter. Browder's only activities that resembled hobbies were practicing the flute and playing chess. Other entertainment provided mere diversion: billiards, bowling, and a biweekly cinema.

His workdays ended on the Yonkers' commuter train. From the station he walked to the Mayflower Apartments, 7 Highland Place, a seven-story apartment building that housed approximately eighty families. Here he shared 3F, a five-room, book-filled flat with Raissa, their three sons, and an aged Russian housekeeper, Domenika Nikhonovna Nikolauk, whom everyone called "Nania." The family afforded only two extravagances: a telephone in Raissa's name and a steel front door that peeved FBI agents discovered while trying to arrest him in 1952. Although Browder seldom retired before midnight, he always rose early. He began his day by purchasing a paper from the corner newsboy at about 7:30. Browder read it over breakfast, then took a humble trolley and the train to party head-quarters.[62]

The Communists' quiet man was also an impecunious man. He lived the ascetic life of a revolutionary; indeed, few twentieth-century American political figures have endured so Spartan a living standard. Browder never owned a house or land. He lacked even an automobile, although he enjoyed limited use of a CPUSA vehicle. Before 1937, when the income tax was progressively financed, Browder never paid even the minimum. In 1938, a good year, his IRS form listed $4,270 gross income. He had access to a small residence in Monroe, New York, several summers. This aside, however, his position provided few worldly goods and only one perquisite: annual Moscow excursions. He paid Nania no compensation beyond her maintenance.[63]

Browder's existence was not as austere as figures suggest, even when adjusted for inflation. Part of his personal success stemmed from an ability to avoid costly vices that victimized many other mid-twentieth-century working people. While hardly a modern fitness buff, Browder did not overeat or drink alcohol, except socially. He eschewed habitual use of cigarettes, the public health curse of his era, although he enjoyed an occasional cigar and affected a scholarly pipe. He did not gamble, and more than most talented, ambitious Americans he renounced conspicuous consumption. Browder never doubted that capitalist society conditioned the poor to chain themselves needlessly.

## A SMALL DARK CLOUD

During an otherwise joyous era a seemingly insignificant augury surfaced on the horizon: Foster's opposition. It posed no immediate threat, but foretold trouble. His discontent became audible within top CPUSA committees by 1936. Starting as pique at being overtaken by his underling, it grew into rancor at Browder's patronizing treatment. No lightweight, Foster had been a working-class hero for an entire generation. Edward P. Johanningsmeier has shown that Foster's long career as a street fighter, hobo, and union organizer endeared him to the down-and-out in a way Browder could never match.[64] Had CPUSA members elected their general secretary democratically, they certainly would have chosen Foster. More ideological than Browder, he was determined to see his brand of Marxism triumph. With patience rivaling that of his foe, Foster waited to catch him in a slip and avenge indignities suffered. He liked to remind listeners of his fame before becoming a Communist and, by inference, of Browder's insignificance at the time.

Beneath the palpable tension and bitterness lay substantive differences. Rightly or wrongly, Foster represented a coherent, principled opposition. Because of party loyalty and discipline, however, he could seldom display it openly. Accordingly, most observers saw only that he disliked Browder personally. Yet Foster consistently maintained his left-wing perspective. And by 1939, if not earlier, he had to worry about the danger of expulsion, which Browder had threatened not-so-subtly. The threat must have meant a great deal; to most Communists there was no meaningful life outside the party.

Browder loathed Foster's cult of toughness, and the feeling signified more than mere jealousy. Browder, though small and, during his twenties, good-looking almost to the point of femininity, believed that he was now hardier than his adversary. Who had succumbed to his inner demons and suffered a nervous breakdown while competing for leadership? Who had to fear a coronary every time he lost his temper? And who got angry frequently? By contrast, whom had the Soviets, the world's greatest revolutionaries, invariably favored in head-to-head disputes? Regarding rivals, both ideological and personal, Browder could be a vicious infighter. He had helped destroy William W. Weinstone's career with no visible pangs of guilt.

Cruelly, Browder repaid with compound interest the slights he had endured a decade earlier. Philip Jaffe noted that Foster, surrounded by Browder loyalists, "increasingly became a figurehead even as Chairman." Browder "never gave him any important responsibility"[65] but exploited his reputation constantly. At CPUSA rallies Foster would take his seat on stage, ten minutes after everyone else, to triumphant music. Browder's Moscow victories in 1937 and 1938 only increased tensions because Foster refused to consider his reduced status permanent. His bitterness and principled dissent rapidly hardened into implacable opposition. Yet Browder, a lenient Stalin-era party leader seeking to look magnanimous, took no disciplinary action.

Nor was Browder abashed when the USSR denounced a portion of his handiwork. During the summer of 1938 Boris Panamarov, a Comintern official who would head the Soviet party's international department for many years, summoned visiting CPUSA member Sidney Bloomfield to his office. The latter reported being told to "inform the comrades back home" that Moscow did not approve of the party's greatest slogan, "Communism Is Twentieth Century Americanism." Bloomfield complained of never receiving an "adequate explanation for the position"; cadre Joseph Starobin eventually concluded that the phrase offended overseas Marxists.[66]

Indeed, during this era Browder began to believe he might be destined for fame. He had made his mark in Moscow. The CPUSA press constantly reminded members that he was a minor deity. A growing portion of the non-Communist public had come to know him. Browder's success, however, had been mostly an individual victory. Why had party growth slowed? Could Browder's increasingly personal leadership get it moving dramatically once more? Why was the New Deal able to consume ever-larger segments of the American left without providing any radical new programs? Between 1934 and 1938 Browder had handled good fortune with ever-increasing self-confidence. Would his pathological fascination with danger continue to serve him well? If not, how could he handle adversity?

# SIX

■

# Crisis Days (1936–1939)

The Communist party claimed to be truly indigenous, and certainly most of its members considered themselves patriots. In this spirit former cadre Joseph Starobin has argued that the CPUSA's foreign ties constituted an Achilles heel.[1] Even for Earl Browder they proved a mixed blessing. Although installed by the Comintern, he was always on firmest ground as a domestic leader. He possessed no international expertise despite his China service and annual Moscow excursions. Indeed, between 1936 and 1939 events overseas endangered his leadership. Did CPUSA foreign policy differ from Soviet policy in any important way? If so, how? If not, could Browder legitimately attribute the congruence to a mutual antifascist urgency?

## BLOODSHED IN IBERIA

Revulsion toward Hitler's and Mussolini's aggression in the Spanish civil war united American liberals and radicals as had no issue since the Bolshevik Revolution. It inspired writers and intellectuals, not normally a truculent group, as had no crusade since the one against slavery. To them the conflict pitted workers, peasants, and poets on the Loyalist (or Republican) side against estate owners, bishops, generals, and foreign troops who supported the rebels. In short the American literati saw a rare, clear-cut struggle between right and wrong. As historian Milton Cantor has noted, "That fascism could eliminate the left in Europe was final proof that the left in the United States must organize against it."[2] The Socialist party pressed the government to save the Spanish republic, but instead Washington heeded prevailing isolationist sentiment. Throughout 1936 it refused to intervene. Early in 1937 Congress passed a joint resolution forbidding arms exports to Spain. On January 11 the State Department attempted to prevent Americans from joining the con-

flict, ruling U.S. passports invalid for travel there. That spring's Neutrality Act barred aid to foreign governments facing civil wars, thereby according Generalissimo Francisco Franco's rebels de facto belligerent
status. Browder, carefully avoiding criticizing President Roosevelt,
termed the new law an "act of war" against Spanish democracy.[3] The
frenzy to prevent American involvement assumed ludicrous proportions:
the State Department even refused to permit medical personnel to go to
Spain.

The world's Communists aided the Loyalists directly, however, recruiting volunteer fighters known as the International Brigades. Prodded by
Georgi Dimitrov, Joseph Stalin contributed Soviet troops. Yet within the
republic the real forces of the left were the anarchists, who experimented
with workers' councils and collective farms. The Soviet leader, ever the
cynical power politician, feared that a revolutionary Spain would an-
tagonize Western nations whose aid he might someday need. Therefore,
he eschewed a true Popular Front and, of course, never considered allying
with indigenous Trotskyists. When all was said and done, avoiding war
with Germany remained his highest priority. He therefore exacted a high
price and took few risks. He demanded the republic's entire gold reserve
before providing supplies. In all the International Brigades sent forty
thousand fighters to the Iberian conflict from fifty-two countries, but
never more than eighteen thousand at any time. Of these barely two thousand came from the USSR. The Soviets always maintained high positions
far from the front.[4]

Unlike Stalin, Browder felt free to display boundless enthusiasm. His
goal was to win the war, and he had no fear Hitler would attack the
United States. Accordingly, he glorified CPUSA contributions, and no
party cause ever enjoyed as much popularity. Historian Eric Hobsbawm
called the Spanish civil war the generation's Iliad. Auxiliary committees
raised large sums, and more than three thousand Americans, four-fifths
of them party or YCL members known generically as the "Abraham Lincoln Brigade," joined the combat. The Socialists contributed a smaller
force named after Eugene V. Debs. Volunteers were young, and a large
proportion were school teachers and college professors. Many were Jewish, alarmed by the Nazis' infectious anti-Semitism. One hundred blacks
joined in anger at Benito Mussolini's earlier bombing of Ethiopia. Typically U.S. fighters circumvented the State Department ban by journeying
to France before enlisting. Loyalist agents made most surrender their
passports so that deserters could not return home, and all had to accept
the Spanish Communist party's political and military leadership.[5]

Historian Robert A. Rosenstone has compared the Lincolns to 1960s freedom riders or southern voter registrars, and Peter N. Carroll calls some of them inspired by populism, labor protests, and the IWW. They displayed great courage, as most had no previous military experience. Their side lacked proper air support, possessed little artillery, and had few heavy tanks. They endured medical deficiencies and ammunition shortages. The Lincolns participated in three of the war's four major offensives: Brunete, Aragon, and the Ebro. For nearly three years they helped the republic withstand Franco's militarily superior forces. Between nine hundred and sixteen hundred Americans died in Spain, including Ring Lardner's son James. Many others received at least one battle wound.[6] In even so noble a cause however, intolerance raised its head. The International Brigades put down a popular uprising in Barcelona and murdered anarchist and independent Marxist (POUM) figures whose doctrines resembled Trotskyism. Yet in the United States only a handful of writers publicized the repressions before 1938.

Browder played a personal role in the conflict. Considering himself a courageous Communist party leader during an epic struggle against fascism, he visited the battlefront twice. With the State Department's winking approval he skirted the travel restrictions; *Daily Worker* editor Clarence Hathaway petitioned successfully to have Browder "replace" the newspaper's correspondent in Spain.[7] He sought to rally the troops and take some credit for victory.

The nonviolent Browder proved an unlikely warrior. He had never donned a uniform, much less faced enemy fire. He had not even participated in Third Period street riots. He made a disastrous showing on an unpublicized February 1938 trip, arriving from Moscow at the worst possible moment. Americans had just suffered their first defeat at Teruel. Many had entered the battle embittered on learning that their units had extended their six months' enlistments for the duration. Location proved as unfortunate as timing. Philip Jaffe noted that Browder spoke "in an open, snow-patched field" against a "background of icy winds and the distant roar of guns." Here he recounted recent American labor victories and Roosevelt's Quarantine Speech. He expressed hope FDR soon would permit arms shipments.[8]

Poorly briefed and displaying abysmal judgment, Browder then forgot his public relations skills. Unable to empathize, he criticized "unhealthy attitudes" and announced that the Lincolns would remain in Spain until Franco was expelled. Then he made the curious threat, "If some of you don't straighten out, you just *may* be sent home." His remarks met loud

Browder and Abraham Lincoln Brigade members in
Spain, 1937. (From the Syracuse University Library, Department
of Special Collections, 600 Bird Library. Used by permission.)

boos and hooting; subsequently, a number inquired when the next ship
was leaving. Only when he promised prompt replacements did he receive
even mild applause. The incident proved one of the most embarrassing
of his career.[9]

As Franco's inevitable victory neared, the volunteers faced two major
problems: financing their homeward journey and recovering their passports. Fund-raising help came from a Popular Front group organized
in 1937, the Friends of the Abraham Lincoln Brigade. Led by David
McKelvy White, son of a former Ohio governor, it sponsored nationwide
speaking tours by early returnees, employed mass propaganda tech-
niques, and raised more than $400,000.[10] Under international pressure,
the Loyalist government eventually also contributed.

Meanwhile Washington prodded the CPUSA directly. Many Lincolns
had arrived in France destitute and in need of medical treatment. The
State Department refused to issue replacement passports, forcing the

CPUSA to maintain the troops while awaiting their original papers. Many languished in French detention centers with little protection from the elements. Recovering original passports proved more difficult than raising money. Both International Brigade headquarters and the Spanish government denied knowledge of their whereabouts. In June 1938 the CPUSA's David Amariglio tried to persuade Loyalist officials to return the documents.[11]

When this effort failed, the State Department, fearing passports might be used for espionage, allowed Browder to return to Spain for the same purpose. Determined to atone for earlier blunders, he arrived in October and retrieved some documents. Mainly, however, he received excuses from the International Brigades' sadistic Albacete base commander, André Marty. Marty contended that some volunteers came to Europe lacking identification. Others allegedly lost their documents during battles.[12]

Shortly before Browder reached Spain, the Lincolns' role came to a sudden end. On September 21 Spanish Prime Minister Juan Negrin announced a desperate unilateral decision. The Loyalists, determined to eliminate every doubt about their cause's national character, had ordered the International Brigades' withdrawal. This effort failed to secure Italian or German reciprocity or to save the republic. It nevertheless allowed remaining Lincolns to return home before Franco's triumph. American diplomats made a final attempt to recover the veterans' passports, and they secured large numbers. For volunteers still lacking papers, consular officials issued temporary identification cards. Browder allowed himself to think his minimal role had been decisive.

The following year a former Soviet intelligence officer charged that many missing documents had appeared in the USSR; they helped establish false identities for Russian espionage agents who prized them most highly. In 1941 another writer made a similar claim. Yet no one accused Browder of clandestine activities on the Iberian peninsula or of insincerity in seeking the Lincolns' documents.[13] The most serious indictment is that he apologized for a reign of terror that the International Brigades inflicted on political opponents. For Browder, who thought in neat logical formulas, Joseph Stalin led the only legitimate Marxist struggle; disagreement meant disloyalty; disloyalty in wartime was treason. Therefore, those hastening the republic's collapse deserved their fate.

Browder garnered no glory in Spain, although the CPUSA could view its contributions proudly. It did more to aid Loyalist forces than anyone could have anticipated. The subsequent conquests by Hitler and Mussolini proved that the volunteers, not Allied leaders, best understood the fascist menace. The party's flouting of State Department policy and circumvention of federal law, however, left a sour legacy in Washington.

## THE MOSCOW TRIALS AND MUNICH

If aiding the Spanish republic earned the CPUSA acclaim but embarrassed Browder, supporting the Moscow show trials proved disgraceful for both. Between August 1936 and mid-1938 the Soviet government indicted, tried, and ruthlessly shot virtually every living Old Bolshevik. Veteran revolutionaries found themselves branded Trotskyite conspirators, terrorists, would-be assassins, and fascist agents. Confessions came from Lenin's coworkers, some of them heroes to the American left: L. B. Kamenev and Gregory Zinoviev, Stalin's former ally Nikolai Bukharin, ex-premier Alexi Rykov, and publicist Karl Radek. Others executed included famous Marshal Mikhail Tukachevsky and most of the army's general staff. Soviet courts convicted the officers, Jews and gentiles alike, of plotting with the Nazis and Leon Trotsky. Beyond the show trials lay a broader purge that killed thousands, including Comintern figures Ossip Piatnitsky and Bela Kun, hundreds of Moscow's Yugoslavs and Italians, and the entire Polish Communist party leadership.

The trials created a crisis of conscience for American radicals. Some leftist intellectuals decried the proceedings. V. F. Calverton, editor of the *Modern Monthly,* argued that they betrayed the October Revolution. The trials killed Edmund Wilson's last flickering sympathy for the USSR. For many, Trotsky held a special, valiant place. He symbolized revolutionary purity, untainted by Stalin's bureaucratic mind-set and unspeakable crimes. He represented the only hope of salvaging something from 1917. An inquiry commission headed by philosopher John Dewey heard him, in Mexican exile, answer Stalin's allegations and published the findings under the title *Not Guilty.*[14] Even writers such as Max Eastman, who blamed Trotsky for failing to use Lenin's Last Testament to seize power from Stalin, admired him.

Such views, though forcefully articulated, hardly represented the left intelligentsia. In March 1937 eighty-eight of them signed an open letter denouncing the Dewey Commission findings. Fourteen months later 150 artists, novelists, actors, critics, and academics lauded the Bukharin trial verdict. Granville Hicks articulated their sentiments. They neither understood nor cared about the fine points of doctrine. It was enough that

"Marxism was in general right and the Communist party was in general Marxist." For people who derived their primary identity from radicalism, the idea that Stalin had besmirched the revolution (and duped them) proved difficult to accept. Now they would have to question the moral distinction between Communism and fascism. Even Jay Lovestone, driven from the CPUSA by Stalin himself, justified the purges as carrying the revolution forward.

The trials extinguished the Socialist party's final romantic feelings for the USSR. Norman Thomas considered the trials an unspeakable tragedy. He noted that at no point did the confessions dovetail with available evidence regarding time and place. He believed that the defendants had deliberately given erroneous details "so their confessions could be refuted." Other SP figures formed a defense committee.[15]

Although not vicious by nature, Browder stood behind Stalin uncritically. He tried first to minimize, then later to justify the Soviet tyrant's crimes. He had to know his idol was a murderer because on annual Moscow visits he discovered that leading figures had mysteriously disappeared. Yet he displayed the moral indifference on which authoritarians thrive. Browder even rejected the pragmatic consideration that Stalin had killed more Communists than anyone but Hitler. The only twinge of conscience Browder revealed was his preservation of Thomas's most cogent criticisms among his personal papers. A good Comintern soldier, Browder defended the trials during a 1938 national speaking tour. His talks left audiences cold; even many party members remained unmoved. Therefore, he published only two of these speeches, labeling Trotsky an egomaniac firebrand who sought a new world war to realize "his hopes of glory and power." Browder likened Trotskyism to "cholera germs" and called the purge "a signal service to the cause of progressive humanity." The Old Bolsheviks, he contended, had always opposed Lenin, though Browder had no way of knowing this. Attempting to give his argument an American idiom, he compared the defendants to domestic traitors Benedict Arnold, Aaron Burr, disloyal War of 1812 Federalists, and Confederate secessionists. His labored analogies likened persons who "smeared" Stalin's name to those who had slandered Abraham Lincoln and Franklin Roosevelt.[16]

Despite his extravagant rhetoric, Browder must have found justifying the Moscow trials difficult. The embarrassment that his weak speeches suggested may indeed be the first small evidence of internal conflict. It was becoming less easy to ignore the disparity between faith in Stalin and the American left's humanistic, democratic values. Browder preferred instead to crusade for causes more defensible. His collective security advocacy made far greater sense than his apologetics. After President Roosevelt's Quarantine Speech on October 5, 1937, the Communists proved intervention's most vociferous backers. Every week Browder implored the democracies to join the Soviet Union in an antifascist alliance.

Since 1933 Adolf Hitler's shadow had lengthened across central Europe. Like a medieval ghoul he seemed the thorough personification of evil. Posing as a German patriot and the anti-Bolshevik champion who would save the West, he had steadily chipped away at much of the 1919 Versailles Treaty on which peace had been built after World War I. He began secret rearmament and pulled Germany out of the League of Nations. Open violations (creation of an air force and a conscription law) started in 1935 and 1936. Although article 44 of the Versailles Treaty had demilitarized the Rhine River's left bank permanently, Hitler sent troops across the Hohenzollern Bridge at Cologne; others traversed at Dusseldorf and Mainz. An alliance with Mussolini's Italy in 1936 and annexation of Austria in March 1938 had destabilized the continent. Allegedly to complete unification of German-speaking peoples, Hitler demanded Czechoslovakia's Sudetenland. For two weeks in September Europe seemed on the brink of war. Finally at Munich on September 29 Britain and France preserved "peace" by signing over the territory to him. Suddenly the previously innocuous verb "to appease," which had meant "to lessen friction and conflict" took on a sinister new meaning. The USSR, Czechoslovakia's only defender, now began to doubt the West's sincerity and to suspect that the capitalist democracies sought to turn Hitler's aggression eastward. By contrast, the American Communists' solidarity calls now became more desperate. To Browder, Britain's Prime Minister Neville Chamberlain was Hitler's accomplice in history's "blackest treason." Munich aided anti-Semitism's growth everywhere.[17]

Why did Browder fail to see that Munich made some Russo-German understanding inevitable? With a passion that seemed almost irrational, he dismissed as reactionaries those who speculated the Soviets might "try to beat Chamberlain at his own game by joining hands" with the Nazis.[18] The crisis led to Browder's final Moscow visit as CPUSA head. On his second trip to Spain he received a French CP cable inviting him to Paris. There in October he attended the National Assembly's Munich Pact ratification vote; almost alone the Communists opposed the sellout. Browder drafted the CPUSA response and flew to Moscow for Comintern approval.

His text compared the Western democracies to nineteenth-century

Europe's Holy Alliance against revolutionary and Napoleonic France. Dimitri Manuilsky, possibly aware of Soviet planning, told Browder to delete the reference. The Holy Alliance had lasted for a generation. The Munich agreement would not endure two years. Why did Browder ask no questions? Why did he meekly expunge the passage instead? The trip brought a more telling portent of forthcoming change. Georgi Dimitrov revealed that Browder would not see Moscow again for a long time. He then told him to acquire a particular shortwave receiver with an attached recorder and to listen for coded messages during prearranged night hours. Eager to please and considering rapport with Berlin unthinkable, Browder obliged quietly.[19]

After leaving the USSR he stopped in Paris again to publish his essay. It appeared in the October 29 edition of the Comintern's journal, *World News and Views*. He warned that "two oceans alone" could no longer protect the United States because Munich had strengthened reaction everywhere, energized Germany and Japan, and whetted Franco's appetite for Latin America. Thus the fascist menace, previously considered a European problem, now threatened U.S. interests directly.[20]

In Moscow Browder also had discussed reversing the CPUSA's traditional opposition to American defense spending. Once home, he told party leaders that the United States and the USSR had "common problems, common interests and common enemies." They needed to collaborate because Munich had shattered any likelihood that a "relatively unarmed" United States could halt fascism's advance; even Belgium had a larger infantry. In January 1939 the CP endorsed a U.S. military appropriation for the first time. Specifically, it supported President Roosevelt's request to boost the defense budget by $300 million and to form an Atlantic naval squadron. Not coincidentally in May the Communists began a quiet campaign to secure for FDR a third term.[21]

These coalitionist policies rankled William Z. Foster. He had long been bitter, in part because the CIO's rise had left him something of a relic in the labor field. The new year emboldened him to resume his anti-Browder vituperations. When the Spanish republic fell in February, Foster tried to unseat Browder by arguing that everything was going wrong and that time for a change had come. His proposal caused displeasure in Moscow. Dimitrov suggested finding Foster a Comintern assignment overseas.[22]

Now Browder made a severe misjudgment. He could have eliminated a talented, determined rival without a messy expulsion. A few years earlier he had not hesitated to transfer William W. Weinstone to Michigan and relative obscurity. Now, however, he rejected Dimitrov's sound advice. Displaying a petty meanness, Browder sought to keep Foster around and inflict humiliations almost daily. He considered Foster a helpless old man he could beat on at will. Stalin, by contrast, knew to dispose of his enemies rapidly. Here, as elsewhere, Browder did not make the most effective Communist leader.

The conflict had become so disruptive that on March 23 it consumed an entire Political Committee meeting. Browder, in complete control throughout, opened the discussion by giving his rival the floor. Foster displayed frustration and rancor and launched a lengthy, acrid harangue. He declared that Browder had neglected his talents ever since he had returned from his illness. As he "began to limp back into the movement," nearly all his proposals had been voted down or disregarded.[23]

Foster's resentment transcended the personal. He had proposed breaking into Congressional anti-Communist hearings and demanding a voice, an action that would have brought the worst publicity possible. Browder, who personified the Popular and Democratic Front outlooks, would have spurned such a scheme from anyone. Aspersions of disloyalty and diminished competence tormented Foster most, but he also groused about abusive actions. When the CP had demoted Darcy from National Committee membership to mere candidacy, Foster had called the move unjustified. The following day, as he arrived at work, five district organizers waylaid and hectored him. Later Browder had told Foster that his complaining hurt the party more than all enemy attacks combined and threatened to put the charges into writing if Foster did not desist. With exasperation approaching rage, Foster avowed his party loyalty, termed his criticisms constructive, and demanded Browder remove the "padlock" from his hands.[24]

Once Foster yielded the floor an orgy of vilification ensued. As Browder sat back quietly, relaxed and contented, every speaker pounded his rival. Eugene Dennis, a rising Polburo star, labeled Foster's remarks "irresponsible" and "unprincipled." Unless he showed Browder more respect, "serious difficulties" awaited. Jack Stachel, the party's organizational secretary, ridiculed the notion that anyone writing as much as Foster, who published more than Browder, could experience difficulty spreading his views. Bill Gebert, Pittsburgh district organizer, observed that nearly everyone who opposed Browder's leadership huddled with Foster. Rose Wortis, a New York labor figure, decried his impatience and demanded a healthier attitude. Roy Hudson, CPUSA national trade union secretary, told Foster he had a persecution complex. Robert Minor reduced tensions slightly by blaming some problems on Foster's health. Browder, who spoke only briefly, remained calm but displayed no magnanimity. He declared that Foster had not learned how to criticize constructively. Their differences were political, not personal.[25]

After this protracted bashing Browder felt even more overconfident. Four days later he displayed his increased poise at a HUAC executive session. The members of Congress questioned him in an inept manner; blithely Browder fielded all queries and suffered no damage. Indeed, a reckless element had crept in. The session made him proud he could handle government inquisitors, who lacked the mental discipline that Marxist dialectics imparted. Would he always enjoy such success?[26]

Meanwhile the Western press had begun reporting rumors of a possible treaty between the USSR and Germany. Although most reports emanated from right-wing sources, some progressive journalists, including Anna Louise Strong and Vincent Sheean, made similar speculations. Within the CPUSA, Foster and Alexander Bittelman had become convinced an accord was inevitable. With a wave Browder still dismissed the possibility. Instead he allowed wishful thinking to cloud his judgment, persuaded himself nothing substantive could transpire between Stalin's government and fascists, and scoffed at all alliance talk. On July 5, in words soon to become infamous, he told a Charlottesville, Virginia, audience there was as much likelihood of Russo-German agreement as of Earl Browder being elected Chamber of Commerce president.[27]

## STRUGGLES WITHOUT, TORMENT WITHIN

August's events struck CPUSA members as so many body blows. On the twenty-first the USSR and the Third Reich signed a long-term trade agreement. The *Daily Worker* and the *Freiheit*, the party's Yiddish-language newspaper, minimized its significance. The following morning the Soviet news agency Tass announced that German Foreign Minister Joachim von Ribbentrop would fly to Moscow to sign a nonaggression treaty. American Communist rank and filers went into pandemonium, but an embarrassed hush fell on the party building. Functionaries avoided each other. Switchboard operators suffered most, swamped by incredulous calls. Groups kept asking the two papers, "Is it possible?"[28]

The crisis found leaders as unprepared as ordinary members. Browder was vacationing in the country; Foster and Bittelman were also out of town. The emergency summoned them. Opponents believed the

CPUSA's collapse imminent, and the pact certainly dumbfounded Browder. The Comintern had given no warning of its first major line change since 1935. Learning of the treaty through the media proved a rude and degrading shock. Browder and most followers clutched remnants of the Democratic Front with manic determination. Many fellow travelers disappeared, although the American Labor party and its most important figure, Congressman Vito Marcantonio, remained. Of more significance, so did cadres. Loyalty vied with emotion. One member, Al Richmond, recalled that they hated the Nazis "as the supreme embodiment of political criminality and moral malignancy."[29]

Browder returned to party headquarters on August 23 and reluctantly granted a 3 PM interview. Reporters, curious and mordant, jammed his ninth-floor office. They saw an unfamiliar Marxist leader. Trying to affect confidence, he rocked back and forth uneasily in his swivel chair. His scholarly looking pipe had vanished. Now he smoked cigarette after cigarette.[30]

Snidely they hurled old *Daily Worker* quotations. Defensively Browder termed charges of a policy change "nonsense." The Soviets and fascist Italy had had a comparable treaty for years. The Russo-German concordat would strengthen Popular Fronts everywhere and weaken Hitler at home. It constituted "a wonderful contribution to peace." Western democracies and the USSR should "sign similar agreements." Asked if he had received advance notice from Moscow, the visibly irritated Browder snapped: "I have exactly the same information which all you gentlemen have." He then pledged another interview if hostilities broke out and abruptly closed the session.[31]

The next day brought further embarrassment. Newspapers carried photographs of Ribbentrop and Soviet Foreign Minister Vyacheslav Molotov signing the pact, the most consequential diplomatic document since the Versailles Treaty, while Stalin looked on benevolently. Again, scores of Communists descended on party offices, begging for explanation. A bewildered Political Committee met that day but made no decisions.[32]

Thenceforth Browder became more cautious. On September 1 he addressed a Chicago party rally commemorating twenty years of American Communism. Stalling, he ignored the week's breathtaking events and discussed instead a recent Supreme Soviet speech by Molotov. Although Germany had attacked Poland that day, Browder broke his promise to meet the press again.[33]

The invasion familiarized the public with a terrifying new concept and some ugly words. The Nazis used a tactic of *blitzkrieg*, lightning war, the massive accumulation of armaments and supplies to win in a single decisive strike against an unsuspecting enemy. Designed to overcome Germany's strategic disadvantage—lack of resources for an extended war—the tactic offered not only immediate victories but also the capture of enough materiel to more than compensate for losses. It even spared the Reich's civilians a war economy's sacrifices. As the hapless Polish cavalry prepared to defend, six Panzer divisions swept into the country. They featured three hundred fast tanks each, plus support forces carrying supplies at equal speed. From above, Stuka dive bombers equipped with sirens destroyed a demoralized opposition below.

The CPUSA's efforts to avoid splitting with the Roosevelt administration revealed how out of step with Comintern wishes it had become. Although Browder eschewed the spotlight after Chicago, befuddled party leaders confounded their friends and kept their critics howling. The CPUSA could hardly shut down until the Comintern deigned to clarify the situation. Forced to continue talking, functionaries did so mindlessly.

Finding a proper attitude toward Poland provided the most painful example. For a fortnight the CPUSA championed her cause, although early in the conflict Browder urged joint U.S.–Soviet intervention to halt the bloodshed. The party praised Polish determination and held rallies for the besieged population. The *Daily Worker* published photographs of refugee women and children, and it reviled American isolationists. The CP continued to campaign for the repeal of the Neutrality Act. As late as September 11 its paper considered Poland "heroic." Yet the same issue contained an ominous contrasting viewpoint. Harry Gannes, a columnist inspired by *Pravda*'s most recent editorial, decried the Polish government's alleged "pro-Nazi" policies for failing to fortify adequately the nation's western frontier.[34]

The conflict's fundamental nature also puzzled CPUSA heads. Two contrasting views coexisted uneasily amid top party circles. One saw the hostilities as imperialist because the Western powers had refused to ally with the USSR. The other welcomed a major war against Germany, while denouncing Britain and France as insufficiently antifascist. Browder embraced the latter but strove for balance publicly. On September 11 he told a Madison Square Garden crowd that Hitler's followers were the war's "immediate instigators" but termed Britain and France "so-called democratic governments" that would not protect Poland. Still he concentrated his main fire on Berlin. Earlier he and Foster had penned a public letter to Roosevelt, pledging Communist support for recent pronouncements against American entanglement.[35] Browder, struggling to preserve the Democratic Front, had avoided any substantive CP policy alteration—no small achievement.

About eighteen hours later the CPUSA received a blunt directive from Moscow, denouncing the Polish government and calling the war an imperialist conflict.[36] The message labeled both sides equally guilty and ordered domestic Communists to support neither. Its timing caused added distress. The orders arrived in the afternoon. Browder's speech was already set in type to run in the *Daily Worker*'s September 13 edition. Time did not permit revision, twenty thousand people had heard it live, and the capitalist press had commented on its contents.

The Communists employed an awkward device to extricate themselves. They buried the démodé address inside the paper. The front page carried an exclusive interview Browder granted Gannes, delineating Moscow's new line but not acknowledging anything had changed. The newsman asked Browder to amplify points from his recent speech; the CP head responded with a shocking new interpretation the public had not heard before. The struggle was not being waged to eradicate fascism. Instead, it resembled World War I, offering common folk only "death and destruction, further miseries and burdens."[37]

The Soviet edict, though decisive on the fighting's nature, contained few details and much ambiguity. It brought Browder something unfamiliar and difficult to handle. Previously his life, though rough, had been remarkably free of inner conflict. Abandoning Gladys, a loyal wife, had not torn him emotionally. Transmogrifying his Leninism into loyalty to Stalin had involved no agonizing. Only Browder's distaste for Third Period militancy had troubled him, and that not greatly. Now for the first time he suffered indecision. His commitment to the Popular Front had been genuine, the Democratic Front his claim to distinction. Already he had become too vain to accept loss of his individual importance. He could not abandon FDR and return to being a faceless bureaucratic party leader.

Private torment was not the only problem Browder experienced. A few days after the communiqué's arrival the Political Committee, unsure of what Moscow wanted precisely, called a meeting to reevaluate a host of CPUSA positions. Foster, after years of humiliation, now saw his opportunity to undermine Browder's authority. Between September 14 and 16 the CPUSA's top leaders bickered almost continuously. Foster and Alexander Bittelman, the party's expert at interpreting Soviet twists and turns, sought to bury the Democratic Front and revert to a militant Third Period position. By contrast, Browder tried to salvage a pro-Roosevelt perspective and argued that socialism lay in the distant future.[38]

For the first time since becoming general secretary, Browder found himself on the defensive, increasing his distress. Animosity toward Foster, and now his henchman Bittelman, made backing down difficult. Yet painfully Browder understood that their approach fit the USSR's new needs better than his did. Willing to move leftward, he doggedly maintained his support for the president. Usually reliable Political Committee supporters Roy Hudson, Gil Green, and Eugene Dennis straddled the issues. In an ominous move the group allowed Bittelman to make the opening report, a sign it expected his position to prevail.

Bittelman pronounced the Popular Front against fascism a failure. It had produced neither a progressive government in England or France nor collective security with the USSR. In the United States the administration's vacillations had helped defeat the Spanish republic.[39] He argued the struggle no longer lay between the progressive coalition and reaction. Instead it had become support for the war versus opposition to it.

Bittelman anticipated the Comintern's order to cease supporting a third presidential term. Although he favored a more combative CPUSA approach, he considered "premature" any call to defeat one's own government. Yet he did seek to make a motto then in use, "For Jobs, Security, Democracy and Peace," more militant by changing the final word to "Socialism." Proposed Neutrality Act revisions also caused problems. The administration sought to call a special session of Congress to secure the munitions embargo's repeal and begin rearming Britain and France. Although Moscow now considered these nations no better than Nazi Germany, Browder supported FDR's proposal. Bittelman disagreed but offered an unconvincing program, opposing both the president's recommended changes and the existing law's retention.

Foster, backed by Browder's normal ally Dennis, longed to shift strongly leftward but proposed the impossible: retaining the peace slogan, adding socialism, supporting the existing Neutrality Act, yet avoiding any split with the president. Foster's illogic undermined the position of all those opposing Browder. Still Browder's leadership was in trouble. Enemies felt emboldened to attack while sympathizers had deserted. Certainly Browder believed that any dramatic swing away from the New Deal would cost the party support built in liberal circles so painstakingly since 1934.

Shrewdly Browder stole the initiative. He praised Bittelman's report and declared its general conclusions the only ones possible. Then he did everything he could to preserve the existing party line, telling his comrades that "continuity" was essential. The greatest danger lay in suggesting that the CPUSA made its policy changes "disconnectedly." Over Foster's objection Browder argued that any arms embargo flip-flop would reinforce slanders that the nonaggression pact was an alliance with Hitler. Browder proposed giving Roosevelt's promise to keep America out of the war the benefit of any doubts. For three confused days the Political Committee convulsed. Some members came full circle on issues. Finally they compromised, publishing a stirring manifesto titled "Keep America out of the Imperialist War." It retained the peace slogan but declared that the working class would soon advance toward socialism. The document dismissed the Neutrality Act as no longer important. It mentioned FDR just once, favorably.[40]

Browder emerged a subdued yet genuine victor. Although challenged, he had diverted his enemies' thrust and retained his authority. Russia's new line had not ended support for Roosevelt. The following May, when the CPUSA responded to governmental persecution by streamlining its structure, Browder remembered the episode and dropped Bittelman from the National and Political committees. Foster, however, could not be dismissed so easily and remained a thorn in Browder's side. Gil Green later reported that constant tension and competition marked the relationship. Other sources told Moscow that Browder did not make a serious effort to improve the situation.

From September through late October 1939 an agonized Browder took his followers down a unique, schizophrenic path. The British, French, and German parties, all originally war supporters, abandoned their antifascist crusades, demanded peace, and denounced Allied governments.[41] Browder feared that a direct rupture with the president would be a political disaster, yet he could not bring himself to defy Moscow openly.

A leader possessing greater vision and moral courage (as distinguished from physical courage) might have chosen an alternative path. It would have required recognizing that Stalin and Socialist humanism were incompatible and that an eventual break was inevitable. Browder knew a Bulgarian proverb that declared that sometimes it is necessary to walk with the devil until one has crossed the bridge. In Russia Stalin's megalomania had consumed Trotsky, Bukharin, Kirov, and others more brilliant and talented than Browder. The CPUSA chief had reached the other shore in 1939 but nevertheless continued traveling in Stalin's shadow. Someone less enamored of the Soviet dictator might have asserted independence, resigned his party post, and attempted to forge a truly indigenous leftist movement. Even conservative journalists conceded that Browder had the ability to run a depression-era corporation; he should have tried organizing remnants of the disintegrating SP, dissatisfied Townsendites, former EPIC members, and possibly some of the followers of the assassinated Huey Long. By so doing he might have perpetuated his antifascist crusade, Democratic Front, and support for Franklin D. Roosevelt. Why did he not even attempt it?

Instead, Browder abandoned the first, risked the second, and clung fervently to the third. He tried to find a compromise position, regrettably turning a blind eye to Nazi depravity. Browder sought to separate CP domestic policy from the USSR's new international requirements. Dutifully he labeled the war imperialist and reprehended British Prime Minister Neville Chamberlain and French leader Edouard Daladier. Yet Browder refused to allow direct attacks on Roosevelt, fearing that abandoning the Democratic Front would devastate American Communism. Beset by exceptional pressure, he responded with dubious logic. Hoping against reason that he could go on supporting FDR, Browder constructed an inordinate, irrational faith in the president's pledge to keep the United States out of the war. Not even FDR's request that Congress scrap the Neutrality Act for a cash-and-carry concept, the idea that offered munitions sales but no credit to nations with their own shipping, could shake Browder. Until October 28 the CPUSA blamed presidential advisors for administration policies it did not like.

The Polish issue continued to underscore the CP's compliance with Soviet directives. On September 15 the party, theretofore Poland's stoutest defender, published an article translated from Russian that anathematized the Polish forces for putting up "not the slightest serious resistance" to German aggression. Two days later the Red Army overran the country from the east, fulfilling an unpublished section of the Ribbentrop-Molotov agreement. Buried deep inside the *Daily Worker* lay a boast that the USSR made "no secret treaties." Over the next six weeks the Soviet Union forced Estonia, Latvia, and Lithuania to sign mutual assistance pacts, a precursor to complete annexation. After a suspicious border incident, and ostensibly because its second city, Leningrad, lay just twenty miles from the frontier, the USSR invaded Finland on November 30. The

Red Army's poor performance against a toothless foe confirmed Western suspicions about the massive nature of Stalin's purges. The CPUSA, considering Russian security sufficient justification, supported the actions.[42]

Into October Browder maintained his pro-FDR stand. Adamantly he clung to the notion that he could do so indefinitely. So dogged was his determination to salvage the tattered Democratic Front that he even resisted explicit Soviet orders. Since the autumn of 1938, when Dimitrov had directed Browder to obtain a prescribed shortwave radio receiver/recorder, a CP functionary had awaited clandestine directives nightly. Finally in late September 1939, an initial six-hundred-word message broke the year-old silence. A second communication arrived two weeks later, and Browder decoded the transcripts.[43] Together they summarized a Dimitrov article awaiting Comintern publication. On foreign affairs the edicts offered nothing new. Both, however, ordered Browder to alter his party's view of the president.

The first decree declared that the new international situation had undermined the People's and Democratic fronts. Browder still remained a "prisoner of the notions which were true before the war but are now incorrect." He had to cease trailing in FDR's wake. The CPUSA needed to oppose the war without echoing the American bourgeoisie's neutrality, which demonstrated "rapacious strivings" to profit from European suffering. The second decree, received in early October, warned that a "big job" faced the American CP. It could expect relentless opposition and needed to "take every step" to protect its legal existence. Although as yet the United States had not entered the conflict, the ukase apprised Browder that FDR might "want to help Chamberlain and Daladier."[44]

Each communication increased Browder's angst, which had grown to an almost unbearable level. Still, summoning all his toughness, he refused to yield. He ignored those Dimitrov commands that affected the president and observed the remainder. Indeed, Browder even hid the messages' existence from other CPUSA leaders. For several weeks FDR received no direct criticism. Desperately Browder tried to link his party's opposition to the war to Roosevelt's neutrality promises. On October 22 an article by Foster decried American foreign policy, but Browder permitted no direct attack on the president. In a rambling, unconvincing manner the article instead blamed the "reactionary" Undersecretary of State Sumner Welles.[45] Ignoring Soviet orders and resisting pressure from domestic cadres, Browder could not have continued much longer without foreign retaliation. Yet he showed no signs of backing down. He hoped that his stubbornness would prompt the Russians to reconsider the radio orders. Moscow, however, had no intention of changing Comintern policy for an American client.

Why did Browder not break with the USSR? He possessed better name recognition than did previous renegades James Cannon, Benjamin Gitlow, and Jay Lovestone. Browder's politically oriented mind may have considered such action, but he remained immobilized for at least four reasons.

First, despite recent events, he retained a lingering belief that he could continue to harmonize domestic leftist interests with Soviet foreign policy needs. The world movement was the path of human progress. Browder clung to his faith that America's radical tradition could someday mature into Communism.

Second, Browder knew that any true independence on his part could expose Raissa's personal history. Without causing any harm to Soviet intelligence, Moscow could have released her autobiographical Lenin Institute file. Such a move would have destroyed Browder's family by giving a vindictive U.S. government a powerful pretext to deport her. Now the Comintern's cynical logic of 1929 at last became fully clear to Browder. By choosing him over Foster to lead the CPUSA, the Soviets had guaranteed that they would face no repeat of Lovestone's American exceptionalism. As Edward P. Johanningsmeier has shown, the Russians had nothing incriminating on Foster and indeed did not fully trust him as late as 1938.[46]

Raissa's vulnerability also helps explain why Browder had refused even to consider the possibility of a Nazi–Soviet pact and why he had neglected to ask Manuilsky and Dimitov crucial questions. Intelligence agencies have a way of implicating their operatives; the Soviets had made Browder dependent a decade earlier. As long as he loved his wife, he would also remain married to Mother Russia. Until 1939 he had never fully thought this through.

A third reason for not seeking autonomy lay in Browder's growing ego. He was still the hard worker he had been in the 1920s, but he was no longer willing to play anything less than a leadership role. Certainly he lacked Norman Thomas's moral stature; a truly indigenous leftist movement would not necessarily consider Browder the person to follow.

Fourth and most important, Browder remained, as he claimed to be, a Stalinist. As such he could not bring himself to defy the man he idolized. He would continue to praise the Soviet dictator even after the latter's death. Yet Browder hated the Nazi–Soviet pact. What could he do? He felt that his only recourse was to bluff. The Soviets, however, showed no signs of taking such behavior seriously. They treated Browder like a sickly, temperamental child, displaying patience because he could not make good any implied threats to run away.

On October 23 the U.S. government spared the Communists an emergency. A deputy marshal seized Browder on passport fraud charges stemming from the 1920s. Never before had the national government jailed a Communist party general secretary. Many bewildered cadres believed that the indictment constituted an initial step toward outlawing the organization. Immediately the CPUSA began attacking Roosevelt in the wildest terms and did so for the next twenty-two months. It spread the slogans "The Yanks Are Not Coming" and "Hands Off." It set up a "perpetual peace vigil" across the street from the White House. Browder announced that FDR, head of the "war party of the American bourgeoisie," was no better than J. Edgar Hoover. When critics charged Browder with hypocrisy and opportunism, he made the lame announcement that "it is not we who have changed but rather the present administration."[47] So ended Browder's psychic agony over the Nazi–Soviet pact. No spineless Russian puppet, he had nevertheless lacked sufficient courage to challenge the Comintern directly because of the costs entailed.

After October 23 Browder backed the USSR's unprincipled alliance instead of addressing progressive needs at home. Indeed, the CPUSA even dropped its boycott of Nazi goods. From late August on, the party's words and deeds alienated a crucial segment of its members and friends: writers, artists, and persons in the mass media. These groups, perhaps more than any others, had given the Communists influence far beyond their numbers and had brought unprecedented respectability. The intelligentsia and other liberals had expected the USSR, the world's first anticapitalist state, to rise above realpolitik. Thenceforth, many of the same intellectuals would join the chorus of denunciation.

Munich had enhanced the Soviet Union's credibility, but the compromise with fascism was unforgivable. The American Labor party abandoned the CPUSA as did many fellow-traveling Jewish trade unionists. The party itself lost nearly half its members. Walter Reuther and other CIO figures supported the president's program of aiding Hitler's enemies.

In the autumn of 1939 Browder remained the greatest leader in CPUSA history. His inability to take an independent stand on the Nazi–Soviet pact, however, had alienated a significant portion of his following. The Democratic Front, his unique contribution to world Communism, lay in ashes. Indicted and awaiting trial, he faced a new set of problems more

Browder with October 24, 1939, *Daily Worker* in New
York City. (From the Syracuse University Library, Department
of Special Collections, 600 Bird Library. Used by permission.)

serious than any he had known before, including threats to his personal
freedom, family security, and party leadership. How could the government prosecute him after so long on a passport charge that carried a
three-year statute of limitations? Had federal officials learned any of the
Browder family secrets? Could Browder keep Foster and his newly found
Political Committee allies at bay while he fought his legal battles?

# SEVEN

■

# *Agitator in the Hands of an Angry Government (1939–1941)*

The CPUSA's defense of the Nazi–Soviet pact in September 1939, after five years of strident antifascism, convinced many that Communism's Americanization had been mere rhetoric. Liberal intellectuals distanced themselves in disgust, and conservatives began demanding the suppression of the party as Stalin's "fifth column" in America. A Red scare swept the nation. Twenty-two years earlier wartime hysteria had ended the Socialist party's dream of becoming a major force in national politics. Would the latest panic destroy the CPUSA altogether? Would the public's anti-Communist feeling tar the entire American left? Why was Earl Browder certain he could beat the charges against him? Did his confidence make adequate provision for public passions?

The Red scare signified something more profound than simple anger at the CPUSA's perceived duplicity. It represented a response to a bewildering international situation. An overwhelming majority of Americans hoped that the Allied democracies would defeat the Nazis. Yet most did not want Yankee boys to die in the process. A whole generation interpreted World War I's experience as proof that only isolationism could guarantee American safety. The appeal was especially strong for midwestern German-Americans, Irish trade unionists, racial minorities, and others who saw little reason to die for the English or French. By contrast, President Franklin D. Roosevelt believed that saving Western Europe— and the British fleet—could best protect the United States. In November 1939 he persuaded Congress to allow the Allies to buy American weapons on a "cash-and-carry" basis. The action provided aid but precluded two perceived causes of the previous war: loans to belligerents and transporting munitions in U.S. bottoms.

Poland's collapse in September 1939 led to a misleading calm. Subsequent months of inaction, quickly dubbed the "phony war," gave Americans the false hope that merely supplying the Allies could defeat Germany. By spring that notion was dispelled, however, as the Nazi blitzkrieg subdued Denmark, Norway, the Netherlands, Belgium, and Luxembourg in just days. France, which had held off the Germans for four years during World War I, fell in only six weeks. Hitler's forces occupied the nation's northern half and set up in the south the technically neutralist Vichy government composed of French fascists. As the Luftwaffe rained bombs on Britain during the summer and autumn of 1940, U.S. isolationism found new strength. A belief that the Nazis were invincible plus the hope that the United States could trade with Hitler's Europe prompted the far right to create the America First Committee. Rapidly, it received support from famed aviator Charles Lindbergh, former NRA administrator Hugh Johnson, and the Hearst newspaper syndicate.

Long before the first bomb had fallen, Congress had created HUAC. In 1938 anti-Roosevelt members had beguiled an impassioned Representative Samuel Dickstein, a liberal New York Jew seeking to investigate pro-Nazi elements, into leading a campaign to hunt subversives. Chief victor was new chairman Martin Dies, a young, gangly east Texas Democrat who, according to historian Walter Goodman, "epitomized an entrenched, embattled suspicion of big cities, big capital, big labor and big government as well as of foreigners big and small."[1] From its inception the Dies Committee, whose seven members never included Dickstein, targeted the New Deal. Almost immediately it set on the WPA's Writers Project and Federal Theatre, both of which it smeared for promoting radicalism and dirty language.

Earl Browder did not believe Congress could touch him but worried about his sister Margaret. In January 1938 he wrote to Georgi Dimitrov, mentioning her seven years' faithful service to the NKVD in Europe. Immodestly Browder cited his own "increasing involvement in national political affairs and growing connections in Washington political circles" to request her release from intelligence work and "return to America." Margaret would have to stop working for the Soviet secret police before Browder achieved mainstream acceptance and attracted mainstream media scrutiny. Dimitrov approved. Despite its anticapitalist mission, the Comintern gave Margaret, who had neglected her health and was by now a nervous wreck and in need of massive dental work, several thousand dollars to start her own small business.[2]

In early August 1939 Browder wrote again, desperately seeking visas to go to the USSR before mid-October. He had decided he could not "properly protect" Raissa and his children from "mounting political tension" whipped up by the Dies Committee and other right-wingers. Rashly, Browder felt no fear of hayseed lawmakers or former Communists they might bribe into testifying. Yet he wanted to sequester his family in Moscow "until after the 1940 elections." He even offered to bring Foster along, although no difficulties separated the two momentarily. Dimitrov's reply is unknown, but events surrounding the Nazi–Soviet pact derailed Browder's travel plans.[3]

## BESIEGED

Browder's indictment in October occurred while he was still trying to ride Comintern winds without jeopardizing the Democratic Front. Because the Nazi–Soviet line aroused unprecedented curiosity on college campuses, he launched a national speaking tour. Quickly the Dies Committee invited him to testify publicly. To avoid a subpoena Browder complied. Proudly he recalled his success before HUAC's executive session that spring. Too bold by half, he welcomed awaiting risks with the eager anticipation that danger had always brought him. Appearing in early September, the confident Browder made a congenial witness. Hearings in August had featured a shouting match between German-American Bund führer Fritz Kuhn and Alabama Representative Joe Starnes. It ended with two Capitol police officers restraining the Congressman physically. By contrast, Browder offered calm answers, subtle equivocations, and clever evasions that impressed even a hostile *New York Times* reporter. The newsman noted that Browder explained Communist aims and practices "so suavely and dialectically" that he often appeared to have the "Committee members' heads swimming."[4]

The minds of Dies and his colleagues seemed especially buoyant anyhow. Several exchanges reinforced liberal notions that the Committee was a band of yahoos. Ten months before Browder had appeared, Hallie Flanagan of the Federal Theatre Project had quoted playwright Christopher Marlowe, William Shakespeare's contemporary. The same Congressman Starnes, a former schoolteacher, had demanded to know if Marlowe was a Communist. When Browder hailed Marx, Engels, Lenin, and Stalin, Starnes interjected, "Who was the second?" Later Browder reminded his audience that the American Revolution had featured violence, but Starnes insisted that "there was nobody in the United States slain."[5]

The national spotlight fed Browder's appetite for publicity, and he displayed his celebrated dry wit. At one point Starnes taunted him about radicals who hid their politics to protect their livelihoods. "Don't you think a man who is a professor in a college and a Communist," Starnes inquired, "ought to have the courage to say so?" Browder brought snickers with his reply: "Sometimes he may be forced to adopt the morality of those who run the college."[6]

The proceedings were not all jovial banter, however. Browder advocated nationalization of "trustified industries," stressing that "a small fraction of the population" owned America's productive capital. He warned that this elite might resist unfavorable election results. He opined that collective ownership could "never be brought about in the United States" without a permanent consensus. Shifting back and forth between socialism and capitalism would bring "nothing but chaos." This was the closest he came to the Neo-Marxist concept of the historical compromise, a peaceful transition to Socialism arriving through overwhelming electoral support, not a plurality or slender, easily reversible majority. Browder also told a number of lies, fooling nobody and underscoring his foreign allegiance. Asked if the CPUSA received instructions or suggestions from Moscow directly or indirectly, he responded, "It does not." Similarly, he maintained that the USSR did not control or even contribute financially to the Communist International.[7]

A true statement, however, hurt Browder gravely. Halfway through, as he sat basking in his afternoon as a celebrity, committee counsel Rhea Whitley suddenly inquired if he had ever traveled on a counterfeit passport. Browder had visited Moscow every year since 1926. He had used various aliases, but he now had proper papers. Incognito journeys had been an occupational hazard; until the New Deal, the government had refused to issue travel documents to known Communists. Certain that the three-year statute of limitations protected him, Browder responded carelessly, "I have." After frantic whispering from his attorney, he invoked the Fifth Amendment to dodge all other incriminating questions. Leftists hauled before Congressional inquisitors would soon make the tactic standard procedure.

Two days after Browder's appearance, ex-Communist Benjamin Gitlow, an intense, somewhat bitter individual, raised Committee tempers to their August pitch once more. A follower of Jay Lovestone who had sat among the highest party circles until his 1929 expulsion, Gitlow had the unusual distinction of having once been denounced publicly in Russia by Joseph Stalin himself. Bringing with him reams of CPUSA documents, Gitlow grabbed headlines by detailing old but spectacular

Comintern activities, including counterfeiting, passport fraud, and jewel smuggling. He accused Browder of lying to Congress and declared that "Moscow pays the bills and Moscow controls the party." He went on to lump Communists and Nazis together as the nation's common enemies and argued that the CPUSA should lose all its rights. It was not a legitimate political party but rather a "corroding, corrupting, sinister activity within our body public."[8]

Shortly thereafter calls for Browder's indictment flooded federal agencies. Although few complainants recognized the statute of limitations problem, one resourceful correspondent advocated placing Browder before a grand jury to discuss passport fraud more broadly. "In an inquiry concerning others," he "could not very well refuse to testify on the grounds that he might incriminate himself."[9]

The Roosevelt administration, like Herbert Hoover's before it, had long known of the ancient charges. Until the Nazi–Soviet pact it displayed no zeal to prosecute one of the president's most vocal left-wing supporters, but the evidence remained in federal files nonetheless. For alleged inaction, the Justice Department now received enormous criticism, including some from within the government itself. Assistant Secretary of State George S. Messersmith provided the most trenchant reproach. On October 21, 1939, he reminded Attorney General Frank Murphy that the matter had been referred to his office ten years earlier with a recommendation to prosecute. Messersmith felt "at a loss to know what reply" would answer the furious telegrams arriving at the Passport Division. For at least a decade the State Department had considered Browder's file likely to contain irregularities. A month before the Soviet–German accord the department sent Browder forms for registering as a foreign agent. To no one's surprise, he refused to sign.[10] By the time Messersmith wrote Murphy, Justice had already moved. Browder's public testimony caused the department to throw him to the wolves, a politically expedient way to end embarrassment to the president.

On Sunday, October 22, the day before Manhattan grand jury testimony concerning Browder, the Republican National Committee's publicity division issued a vitriolic press release. In it New Jersey Congressman J. Parnell Thomas accused the Justice Department of being "strangely indifferent and listless" in Browder's case. Thus eleven years before Wisconsin Senator Joseph McCarthy made the practice commonplace, the GOP's right wing was implying that the New Deal coddled Communists. Thomas, a Dies Committee member and future HUAC chairman, feigned toward Browder and began hitting Attorney General Murphy.

Seizing on Browder's well-publicized university appearances, Thomas portrayed him as "swaggering [and] apparently untouchable," arrogantly spreading subversive doctrines. Stalin's "number one stooge in this country" was mocking the U.S. government's "might, power and majesty." The spectacle was "nauseating the American people," who wondered whether Murphy was "really an intrepid Galahad in shining armor or a complacent Don Quixote tilting at windmills." Thomas's demand for law-and-order would one day seem ironic. Caught embezzling federal funds, by 1950 he held a position that fellow convict Ring Lardner, Jr., titled, "custodian of the chicken yard at the Federal Correctional Institution, Danbury, Connecticut." The public had no reason to question Thomas's integrity in 1939, however, although at least one informer had lodged a complaint.[11]

A few hours after Thomas's jabs, the Justice Department parried. Finished readying its case against Browder, it promised decisive action and suggested that the GOP's National Committee had learned of the proceedings in some devious way. Thereafter the government struck Browder and his family mightily, raising issues that would haunt them for nearly two decades. The attack's intensity and scope showed that the Roosevelt administration sought to prove itself as vigorously anti-Communist as anyone, an eerie preview of the Cold War. The Browders were not the only targets. FBI surveillance of the CPUSA increased. Arrests of ranking cadres followed, and some members of Congress considered outlawing the party totally. State and local authorities emulated Washington's example. Extralegal persecution rose also; mobs stormed Communist meetings in at least three cities.[12]

Even before Thomas's denunciations, officials had moved on Browder. At 5 PM on Saturday, October 21, he received a summons to appear forthwith as a grand jury witness. He refused to respond, declaring he would call at the U.S. attorney's office Monday. Shortly after 11 AM on October 23, Browder entered Manhattan's federal building. While waiting in an anteroom in expectation of testifying, he learned he had been indicted. A bailiff led him to arraignment, although his attorney had received no notification. Browder faced complex charges, which accused him of entering the United States after Moscow visits on a passport bearing his name but secured originally through a false statement. The indictment noted that he had obtained documents illegally as Nicholas Dozenberg (1921), George Morris (1927), and Albert Henry Richards (1931). Then, applying for a passport in his own name in 1934, he had falsely sworn he had never possessed one before. A three-year statute of limitations protected all these actions, so the grand jury indicted him for having renewed the travel papers in 1937.[13]

The dazed Browder pleaded not guilty, and his judge set bail at $10,000. Authorities handcuffed him to a seedy drug peddler and drove him to a federal holding center. That afternoon Hester G. Huntington, a wealthy socialite, posted bond, but suspicious legal foot dragging forced Browder to spend the night in jail. The same grand jury summoned Huntington the next day. Decrying political persecution, Browder noted that celebrities traveled under assumed names regularly.[14] Yet he deliberately eschewed the crucial legal distinction between surreptitious touring and carrying a spurious passport; deceiving the press differs from deceiving the State Department. Denouncing the ongoing Red scare put him on firmer ground, but Browder had obviously committed repeated crimes. That he could not claim innocence did not aid his case in the public mind.

Far from acting "listless" as Thomas had charged, the government proceeded vigorously. The Justice Department, uncertain it could evade the statute of limitations successfully, began searching for other violations. Late that year Assistant Attorney General O. John Rogge received permission to audit Earl Browder's and William Browder's tax returns. The investigation merely documented that they were financially incorruptible, a marked contrast to Thomas and some other right-wingers. The administration's ardor did have limits. Democratic Representative John D. Dingle termed a Browder call for a "quick transition to socialism" a seditious threat that deserved "a long sojourn at Leavenworth Penitentiary," but his protest did not receive any serious consideration.[15]

The INS joined the fray, accusing Raissa Browder of having entered the United States illegally. Its investigation began a week after the Nazi–Soviet treaty. On October 30 Raissa surprised everyone by requesting to meet an INS agent in her attorney's office. There she admitted slipping into the country furtively from Canada by train nearly six years earlier. Accordingly, he recommended her arrest as an illegal alien. The following day the district director at Ellis Island, New York, commenced deportation proceedings. Ranking State Department figures and the attorney general's office doubted her confession but did not mind using it against her. They suspected her of traveling on illegal passports; they may have known of rumors that she had received espionage training. Indeed, the INS found no evidence to verify any "landing" at Rouses Point, New York, where she claimed to have entered. A similar search by Canadian officials did not locate any records either.[16]

Shortly thereafter Raissa's motives became more clear. Earl submitted a petition on November 15 seeking a nonquota immigration visa on her behalf. The INS at the time operated under the National Origins Act of 1924, which limited immigration from outside the Western Hemisphere to 157,000 persons annually. In a blatantly racist attempt to make America a whiter society, the law prohibited immigration from Asia and Africa totally and assigned annual numerical quotas to each European country. Nations in the north and west, where residents had light complexions, received generous allotments; the United Kingdom never filled its share. Lands in the south and east, however, where many populations had swarthy skin tones, got absurdly low shares. Often, applicants from Italy and Greece waited years or even decades for admission. Browder's request, if granted, would have allowed Raissa to leave the United States at her own expense, request readmission at an American consulate abroad, and return a legal resident. The unusual procedure required approval by the U.S. attorney general, secretary of state, and INS Commissioner James L. Houghteling. All the applicant's supporting information had to be factual. Browder presented financial affidavits and Russian-language papers documenting his purported 1926 divorce from Gladys Groves in Moscow and alleged remarriage to Luganovskaya.[17]

Houghteling, however, suspected single-party foreign divorces and wondered whether a new wife qualified for a nonquota visa. Subsequently his deputy studied the matter and prepared a brief citing the leniency and informality of Soviet matrimonial statutes during the early Bolshevik years and the general U.S. policy of honoring other nations' civil proceedings. On January 13, 1940, nevertheless, Houghteling asked Browder to prove that the documents he had submitted referred to him. The commissioner also noted that the State Department considered Browder's presence in the USSR impossible in 1926 because he had possessed no valid passport. To this Browder never replied.[18]

For the next five months the case lay dormant. Officially, Justice postponed Raissa's arrest lest it prejudice the proceedings against Earl. Yet a ranking department official admitted privately that the administration shelved the matter for public relations purposes: the government did not want to seem overzealous.[19]

Actions against the Browders prompted numerous protests. To nobody's surprise letters from CPUSA members and sympathizers deluged government agencies. Simultaneously, however, complaints arrived from anti-Communist civil libertarians. Some saw the technical charges against Earl in October 1939 as threatening free expression. Their arguments ranged from the plebeian to the eloquent. A Brooklynite wrote to Attorney General Murphy, "I am not a Communist, but the case against Browder smells like a frame up." Present methods created more "reds every day." That same week the *New York Herald Tribune*'s city cable editor cautioned: "The lights are going out all over Europe. Please, Mr. Murphy, do not begin turning them out in our country." The haste by the authorities to prosecute bothered some. One attorney, who labeled himself a New Dealer, sent an objection cogent enough to reach Eleanor Roosevelt's desk. It denounced the circumstances surrounding Earl's detention as a flagrant violation of the right to counsel between arrest and arraignment.[20]

John T. Cahill, U.S. Attorney in Manhattan, came under special fire. His office had served a federal grand jury subpoena on Browder's bailor. Lawyers inveighed mightily against this. Some termed it "not a common custom"; "obviously nothing less than an attempt at intimidation"; and "indefensible from any point of view." The ACLU, which had recently denounced Browder for calling the group a Democratic Front "transmission belt," also entered the dispute, asking Murphy for the "legal authority for such action" and for a history of its use.[21]

The Justice Department refused to budge. It considered the complaints serious enough to request a written explanation from Cahill. Yet, it accepted his reply that Huntington's status as sister-in-law of Browder lieutenant Robert Minor justified the action and that the New York office sought to learn whether foreign money had supplied bail. In early 1940 Rogge, responding to what he termed "bitter criticism," defended the department's actions. Addressing a civil libertarians' convention in Boston, he denied charges that his agency was oppressing "unpopular political groups" through technical indictments. "Major criminals," he declared, "had no license to commit minor crimes, and no right to yell persecution when they are caught." Most effectively he claimed that the government did not pursue "these small-scale cases for their political content" but that it was "obvious strategy for the defendants to exploit that content."[22]

The Socialist party escaped government repression but not its own internal contradictions. Its position on the war resembled the CPUSA's latest twist, minus the concern for the USSR. Norman Thomas's confused views seemed to typify those of his comrades. Militantly antifascist, he had criticized Roosevelt's policy toward Spain. Yet memory of the persecution of Socialists during World War I had scarred Thomas deeply, and he believed a new global conflict might well destroy all dissent at home. He denounced the Nazi–Soviet pact but, when Germany invaded Poland, insisted that the Allies were fighting for imperialism, not democracy. The United States should not aid them, lest it be drawn into the war. Thomas offered no answer to the question of how to halt the cancer of Hitlerism, however. Instead, he simply sought to ignore foreign policy. Not surprisingly, the net effect of the Russo-German treaty was to accelerate the SP's decline by rallying liberals and radicals of many stripes behind the president.

## THE LAW OPPRESSES US AND TRICKS US

Browder's trial opened January 17, 1940, in New York's federal district court. Selection of the eleven-man, one-woman jury took all morning. That afternoon his attorney, white-haired G. Gordon Battle, introduced seven motions for dismissal or modification of the charges. Some would have prevented discussion of violations on which the statute of limitations had expired. Judge Albert C. Coxe rejected all motions.

Next, Cahill explained to the jurors the two-count indictment, which carried a maximum sentence of a ten-year incarceration and a $4,000 fine. It charged that Browder had returned from Europe on April 30, 1937, and February 15, 1938. Each time he had shown New York authorities a passport bearing his own name but "secured on an application containing a false statement." Cahill declared Browder had committed a felony in 1934 when applying for this document. He had written "none" after the "all-important" question, "my last passport was obtained from. . . ." Because a statute of limitations prevented direct prosecution after 1937, the government could only attack Browder's use of the passport that year and in 1938.[23]

Battle, opening for the defense, argued that Cahill had quoted the form selectively, changing its meaning. Battle read the remainder aloud. After the word "from" and a blank space for answering came the phrase "and is submitted herewith for cancellation." This, he insisted, did not constitute a question at all. The "flimsy, uncertain, vague and meaningless" language made it merely an "administrative regulation," demanding the previous document's surrender. Of course, he ignored Browder's failure to tender any old papers, legitimate or forged. Battle reminded jurors that the government had not charged Browder with impersonating anyone; extraneous details must not confuse them.[24]

The prosecution summoned a parade of federal officials to the stand. A State Department employee identified Browder's 1934 passport. Incorrectly he testified that Browder had never filed an application in his own name. Actually he had done so at least four times. State listed the refusal reason as the fact that he was a "Communist."[25] Over Battle's protest, an FBI graphologist avowed that one single hand had made applications as Nicholas Dozenberg, George Morris, Albert Henry Richards, and Earl Browder in 1921, 1927, 1931, and 1934, respectively. All four matched the penmanship on Browder's 1937 and 1938 customs declarations. The defense tried to concede these points, but the government insisted on demonstrating handwriting similarities on forty-by-sixty-inch photostatic charts. Minor officers, including immigration and customs inspectors, related Browder's use of passports and swearing of oaths. Adroitly, Cahill subpoenaed Communists to strengthen his case; perjury statutes compelled their cooperation. He called former CPUSA Secretariat rival Max Bedacht, who admitted seeing Browder in Moscow during 1921 and 1933, when Browder held no legal passport. Bedacht also identified Browder's photographs on the Dozenberg and Richards papers. George E. Powers, an erstwhile associate, recounted witnessing Browder's application as Morris in 1927.[26]

With much drama, Cahill put convicted Soviet spy Nicholas Dozenberg on the stand. A Lettish immigrant who had reached the United States in 1904, Dozenberg had become a citizen in 1911 and later joined the Soviet military intelligence. In 1939 federal agents had arrested him. In return for a 366-day prison sentence, Dozenberg pleaded guilty, aided the FBI, detailed his espionage career before the Dies Committee, and testified against Browder. Dozenberg identified his naturalization papers and Browder's photograph on the document issued. Finally he denied having applied for or receiving permission to travel abroad and claimed that he misplaced the citizenship forms in 1924.[27]

Browder made a poor initial impression. For some reason he had trimmed his mustache; now it covered only the area immediately below his nose. Indeed, a *New York Times* reporter observed that "Browder's lips were a tight, unsmiling line," which, "with his slicked-down hair and intent expression, gave him a slightly Hitleresque look." Battle presented a weak defense. He told jurors his client had to travel secretly to avoid personal danger in Europe. He requested dozens of exceptions for the appeals process, yet challenged testimony infrequently. His best efforts merely underscored the graphologist's Justice Department employee status and forced Dozenberg to admit that his own sentencing had been postponed until after the trial. Battle called no witnesses but made twenty-one motions to suppress exhibits and dismiss the indictments.[28]

When the court denied the motions, Browder moved boldly. Feeling the surge of adrenalin that danger had always brought him, he brushed Battle aside. The overconfident Browder possessed an undue faith in the American legal system and exaggerated his own command of it. Using knowledge gained from a correspondence-school law course taken twenty-five years earlier, he seized control of his case. This unusual maneuver enabled him to advance his points without facing cross-examination, invoking the Fifth Amendment, or risking perjury, though it did nothing to enhance his credibility. Like Battle, he called no witnesses, but instead summarized defense arguments for seventy-five minutes, occasionally reading from a thick manuscript.

Browder presented a surprisingly competent argument for someone lacking formal training and courtroom experience, although he of course could hardly match the U.S. attorney. Browder reminded jurors that his trial did not concern false names in the dim past. The prosecution had buried the real issues under trivial, irrelevant details and a "web of technicalities" that forced him to reply in kind. Displaying his passport did not constitute "use" or the type of use the statutes prohibited. The government, he noted, could not legally prevent U.S. citizens from entering the country even if they "suffered from the bubonic plague." Fishermen and pleasure boaters crossed the three-mile limit every day without documents. Border officials dealt only with aliens. Browder noted solemnly, "I received nothing from the inspector of Immigration except the recognition that if he interfered with me he would be violating the law." Browder then addressed the statute of limitations issue directly. The 1934 passport's expiration, his new application, and the new fee had created a new document, breaking the prosecution's chain of evidence. Immediately Cahill bombarded the court with objections, but Judge Coxe, mindful of the appeals process, patiently let Browder continue.[29]

Browder pushed the court's leniency to the limit. He also taxed the jurors' credulity, stating that the word "none" meant "I do not have any passport to present because I have destroyed it." Witnesses had shown that the government knew of previous documents, yet issued him papers anyhow. Division head Ruth B. Shipley had even given Browder special permission to visit war-torn Spain before political winds had shifted. The statute of limitations treated old crimes as an "unconditional pardon." Allowing charges to accumulate over "five, ten, fifteen years" invited selective enforcement. Had he dropped his passport "overboard from the ship" and "merely informed the inspector 'I am Earl Browder,'" no question of crime would have existed.[30]

Charges against him, he insisted, represented merely the opening gun in a broad attack on American civil liberties and workers' rights. Warned against speech making, Browder closed with the ringing affirmation, "I am a Communist, the Secretary of the Communist party. . . . I am proud of it and have nothing to apologize for because of it." He asked for a verdict "consistent with the best American traditions."[31]

Cahill's emotional summation featured massive rhetorical overkill and demonstrated that a competent legal professional can usually defeat the most determined layperson. Few cases, he thundered, displayed so much "willful intent." Clever criminals cover all the big "angles" but usually get caught on small slips. He likened passport integrity to protecting the currency from counterfeiting. Browder's selfish, fraudulent misuse of "sacred documents" through deep schemes made "a mockery of everything we hold dear." Browder was a "disgrace" to his country. More calmly Cahill observed that Browder had submitted no old passports because they bore the names Dozenberg, Morris, and Richards. And, of course, in addressing the jury he had at no time spoken under oath.[32]

Jury members deliberated for less than one hour. They found Browder guilty, according to Judge Coxe the only verdict possible. The judge issued a sentence of four years' imprisonment and levied a $2,000 fine. Although it was not the maximum allowable, the penalty exceeded those given most similar offenders. The court did permit Browder to remain free on his previous bond after he agreed to file his judicial review papers promptly.[33]

Browder fared no better before the circuit court of appeals. Considering only the question of what constituted a passport's "use," it upheld his conviction unanimously on June 24. Actually, prosecutors took Browder's contentions more seriously than the decision suggests. At least one Justice Department lawyer accepted his reasoning on a passport's exercise. Others feared that the Supreme Court might reverse the conviction on a technicality. Therefore, they obtained, secretly, another indictment that charged Browder with twelve more illegal uses.[34]

Browder had misjudged the temper of the times. He seemed to have forgotten the hysteria that had sent him to Leavenworth during World War I. Now he placed all his faith in the Supreme Court. Certainly its members would not allow such blatant political persecution. Indeed, on this issue Browder proved more Kansan than a follower of Stalin. His midwestern sense of fair play eclipsed his mistrust of capitalist institutions. He was surprised that no great cry of indignation had swept the land. Indeed, before June 1941 few non-Communists protested at all. The liberal journal *Nation* proved a significant exception. A February 3 editorial decried Browder's punishment and the larger Red scare as "fantastically excessive" and "grotesque." Jurists "from Justice [Louis] Brandeis down" had frowned on "imposing consecutive rather than concurrent sentences." It noted that the passport laws were originally designed to curb the influx of suspect aliens in wartime. Now the government had made them instruments for "purge by technicality."[35]

Browder never learned that the penalty deeply disturbed Justice Felix Frankfurter, who considered it "outrageous." The justice cited Cahill's stress on offenses protected by the statute of limitations as possibly confusing Coxe. Although Frankfurter thought that the Supreme Court should not interfere with the sentencing discretion of the trial court, he proposed remanding the case to Coxe to "leave no doubt." The other justices dissuaded Frankfurter, however, and on February 17, 1941, the tribunal upheld Browder's conviction. Seven voted affirmatively, Hugo Black abstained, and the recent appointee, former Attorney General Murphy, did not participate. Stanley Reed, who wrote the decision, insisted that the Supreme Court heard the case to clarify passport law administration. One angry antiwar protester told him, "I am sure sufficient technicalities can be found to send us all to concentration camps."[36]

## TWICE SCORNED BY THE VOTERS

Edward P. Johanningsmeier has argued that preparations for the legal case consumed three quarters of Browder's time during this period, causing him to forfeit de facto CPUSA leadership. Actually, although William Z. Foster's influence did increase, Browder retained vigorous control. Indeed, between 1939 and 1941 he engaged in more public activity than at any time since 1936. Working ever harder helped take his mind off his trial, appeals, and eventual imprisonment. Just weeks after the Nazi–Soviet pact, Browder took his party's message to prestigious American university campuses. Six provided unexpected aid. Harvard, Princeton, Cornell, Dartmouth, CCNY, and Brooklyn College banned his appearance or rescinded speaking invitations. By raising issues of civil liberties and academic freedom, they inadvertently created sympathy for the Communists. Indeed, Browder's speeches at Yale, Columbia, and the Massachusetts Institute of Technology brought him

Browder addressing Yale University students, November 28, 1939.
(Courtesy of National Republic Collection, Hoover Institution
Archives, Stanford University. Used by permission of Corbis
Bettmann, L.L.C., 902 Broadway, New York, New York, 10010.)

more newspaper ink than he had received in years. At New Haven that
November he exploited his opportunity, proclaiming that his presence
stemmed from the Bill of Rights, not CP influence on campus.[37]

The *New York Times,* which smugly had ridiculed as rustics the Terre
Haute officials who had gagged Browder three years earlier, now straddled the First Amendment issue. An editorial denounced Browder as having an "undergraduate sense of humor" and advocated permitting his
followers to "write and talk themselves to death." Yet it also made disingenuous complaints. It contended that Browder "as a representative of a
small and unpopular minority group" had "a right to be heard" but not
"in a particular place at a particular time of his own choosing." Certainly, however, the *Times* knew he had received invitations. It maintained that "people who don't care to listen to Mr. Browder ought not to
have to do so," although no one could compel nonparty members to at-

tend his speeches.[38] Attacking such straw men, the press did little to dampen enthusiasm for hearing him.

That fall Eleanor Roosevelt, who did not seek to silence Browder, made more cogent criticisms of CPUSA cadres. Commenting on YCL leader Gil Green, she wrote: "He is one individual, as Earl Browder is, who seems to feel that his first allegiance is to another country." She added, "The sooner they are discredited the better."[39]

Browder entered two political contests in 1940. To the nation, his candidacies had only curiosity value. Because of his impending prison sentence, however, they constituted his final efforts toward public office. They illustrated the depths to which he could sink in promoting Moscow's interests. For both elections the Communists produced openly isolationist platforms. They did not, however, return to Third Period rebellious rhetoric, enforce rigid doctrinal purity, or resurrect the theory of social fascism. Instead, they tried to build an antiwar coalition by methods of the late-1930s. Browder urged "a mass Farmer-Labor party of peace" to "oppose the establishment of a war economy" and prevent loss of "vital appropriations for social welfare."[40]

Certainly the Communists had turned 180 degrees on FDR. Yet Popular Front–like rhetoric survived, and Browder still dressed his organization in red, white, and blue. He argued that the president's role had become as pernicious as the popular motion picture *Gone with the Wind*, which idealized slave society and ignored John Brown's heroism. Indeed, Roosevelt had negated the "traditional American spirit" much as U.S. imperialism sought to repudiate "everything represented by Washington, Jefferson, Jackson, and Lincoln." Other important CPUSA continuities existed. Browder did not allow the party press to encourage proletarian uprisings, and fellow travelers took their cue. Socialist Robert J. Alexander noted that Browder resisted the drift toward "an all-out Nazi-Communist alliance." Alexander Bittelman and William Z. Foster saw the Soviet-German pact "as the beginning of a long-term rapprochement without a fundamental change in the German regime." Browder, by contrast, considered the treaty a temporary expedient. At one point he scolded CPUSA writer John Gates furiously for speculating that Stalin might seek a full military alliance with Hitler.[41]

These significant moderating influences could not obscure the reprehensible nature of CPUSA policies in at least two areas. First, shortly after his arrest, Browder began contending with anger-inspired hyperbole that "no essential difference" separated the Allies and the Axis. During the "phony war" period in early 1940, no major fighting occurred on the

Western front. The Communists concentrated their criticism on Britain and France. By April the *Daily Worker*'s line seemed not so much antiwar as simply pro-German. A CPUSA communication to Mexican Communists stated nakedly the party's chief concern: "The infallible test of all persons, policies, groups and parties" lay in their "attitude toward the Soviet Union."[42]

Second, American Communism's basic direction was even more disgraceful when it addressed Jews. By 1940 one could see early evidence of what would become the Nazis' "final solution." In an egregious pamphlet, Browder nevertheless announced that the Jewish people had "nothing to gain from" a victory by either side. Britain and France were "taking cynical advantage of the Jewish people's profound hatred for Nazi barbarism" to serve Allied imperialism, which he called "equally destructive." Reaching his moral nadir, Browder did not display even the slight embarrassment he had shown in defending the Moscow trials. Strangely, no mass departure of Jewish members (as opposed to fellow travelers) occurred. Historian Nathan Glazer averred that when the Soviet–German "pact was signed the party was shaken, but the Jewish part of [it] seemed hardly more shaken than the others. No important leaders left." Philip Jaffe considered Browder's statements "for a Jewish Communist more meaningful than whether Hitler was anti-Semitic."[43]

Supporting such blameworthy positions, Browder entered the 1940 elections. Circumstance allowed him to campaign twice. His first effort took place in January and February, after U.S. Representative William I. Sirovich's death had vacated New York's fourteenth Congressional District seat. Its Lower East Side, predominantly Jewish constituents, had sent Socialist Meyer London to Washington in 1914, 1916, and 1920. Now a Communist stronghold, the area contained nearly three thousand party members. The CPUSA tried to liken Browder's plight to that of World War I resister Eugene Debs, America's greatest leftist. Browder pledged to help keep the United States out of the "Second Imperialist War" and to preserve civil and political rights. His party passed out thousands of handbills in Yiddish, Russian, Polish, Italian, and English. The literature attempted to relate the Comintern line to lower Manhattan. One pamphlet demanded three million new WPA jobs (instead of armaments), federal housing (not "loans to Finland"), and government assistance to young and old (rather than "aid to Chamberlain and Daladier"). The CP also sought to enact national health care, prevent Communist registration laws, and protect, not militarize, labor.[44]

Browder's conviction on January 22 complicated matters. Two former politicians sought to strike his name from the ballot because of his Marxist beliefs and federal sentence. The New York Supreme Court ruled that he met all requirements for office, however. The first objection illegally imposed a philosophical test. Chance helped Browder beat the second complaint. The penal code barred only those ordered to state prisons, not federal penitentiaries. The jurists opined that any attempt to extend its scope might contravene the Fourteenth Amendment.[45]

Browder's campaign climaxed on January 30 when his years of trying to legitimize his party yielded a surprising dividend: a debate featuring Democratic, Republican, and CPUSA Congressional candidates. At an East Side auditorium Browder appeared with Tammany Hall's M. Michael Edelstein and the GOP's Louis J. Lefkowitz. All sang the "Star Spangled Banner." Then each spoke for one-half hour. After lots were drawn, Browder went first.

On this night at least he felt like a mainstream politician. Merrily he told his "future constituents" they could make themselves "heard around the world" by electing Congress's first avowed Communist. The Republican, a former state assemblyman, introduced himself as "just plain Louis Lefkowitz." This was a dig at Edelstein, who began his name with an initial, a practice more common on Park Avenue than in Greenwich Village. Edelstein defended the New Deal and denounced Communism, eliciting a torrent of abuse from Browder's cohorts who came early, got good seats, and roared at every opportunity. They continued heckling the pugnacious Edelstein until his own followers pulled him down into his chair.[46] Such CPUSA actions did little to attract uncommitted voters or encourage future debates.

Despite the Communists' ardor and favorable locale, a Manhattan area stretching from Fourteenth south to Franklin streets and including Washington Square, Browder marshaled only 3,080 votes to Lefkowitz's 6,665 and Edelstein's 12,962. Although orderly, the election produced some unexpected excitement. The Alcohol Control Board's closing of district liquor establishments brought barrooms on Fourteenth Street's north side a land office business. Browder's total represented 13.6 percent of all ballots cast, not impressive for the national center of CP strength and activity. One newspaper concluded that the results proved the district "Left-Bank" but "only mildly left wing."[47] Actually the party, by endorsing the Nazi–Soviet pact, had alienated thousands of non-Communist Jewish radicals.

After Browder's trial, federal authorities focused on Raissa again. They pursued her with vigor, although her husband's case remained on appeal.

In June Assistant Attorney General Rogge asked the FBI to investigate the couple's relationship. Accordingly, on July 12, J. Edgar Hoover ordered the bureau's New York office to concentrate entirely on the question of the marriage's legality. Later, a Justice Department official noted that Earl still had not answered the INS commissioner's request on January 13 to prove his presence in the USSR fourteen years earlier. Therefore, on August 6 he directed the Certifications Division to deny Raissa's nonquota visa petition.[48]

If Washington persecuted her, she facilitated the task. To qualify for voluntary departure at her own expense, she needed to prove she belonged to no group advocating violent revolution and possessed "good moral character." At the time, however, federal court decisions still considered the CPUSA a violent organization. On August 11 she attended a Board of Immigration Appeals hearing accompanied by her attorney. Raissa, who had repeatedly lied about her age to Marxism-Leninism Institute officials in Moscow, flatly denied ever belonging to the CP "either in Russia or this country" and claimed not to know the American party's aims.[49]

Not surprisingly, the board recommended that her relief request be denied. A special study by the attorney general concluded that if Raissa's deportation were suspended or voluntary departure permitted, critics would note "with fine irony that the Department of Justice cannot even prove that Earl Browder's wife is a Communist." On October 30 Attorney General Robert H. Jackson, appointed after Murphy took his Supreme Court seat, ordered her expulsion, citing her dubious eligibility and evasive testimony.[50] The CPUSA sought to portray Raissa as a victim of a double standard in mid-twentieth-century American law. As an immigrant she faced possible deportation for her beliefs and associations, whereas her native-born husband could make a career preaching Leninism to anyone willing to listen.

Shortly after France's June 1940 surrender, public opinion polls indicated for the first time that a majority of Americans believed a German victory would threaten national security. To promote a bipartisan foreign policy, President Roosevelt appointed two lifelong Republicans, Henry Stimson and Frank Knox, to become secretary of war and secretary of the navy, respectively. Later that summer FDR circumvented 1939's cash-and-carry neutrality legislation. He used an executive order to trade fifty aging destroyers for the right to build U.S. bases on British Atlantic colonies.

On August 20 an NKVD agent named Ramon del Rio Mercader drove an ice pick through Leon Trotsky's skull as the Soviet exile sat studying a manuscript in his private Mexican fortress. After twenty-four hours of agony, Stalin's most brilliant, resourceful, and tenacious opponent died. The news upset Browder even less than had the Moscow trials. To him the world now contained one less villain. He perpetuated Moscow's fiction that the killer, who had been dating one of Trotsky's secretaries, was a disillusioned follower.

In October Congress approved the first peacetime conscription bill in American history and hiked the defense budget dramatically. Roosevelt, who had not designated a successor in case the European war threatened the United States, allowed the Democratic National Committee to "draft" him for an unprecedented third White House term. The Republicans passed over isolationist senators Robert Taft and Arthur Vandenberg and New York's youthful District Attorney Thomas Dewey. Instead, they nominated a dark horse internationalist businessman, Wendell Willkie, who had voted for FDR in 1932 and had only recently registered as a Republican.

The CPUSA also ran a campaign that autumn, although top cadres really wanted to enlist in a larger antiwar coalition under labor leader John L. Lewis. His CIO had welcomed the cadres during the 1930s, and Lewis resented FDR's unspoken determination to join the wartime allies. Between February 10, 1940, and early summer Lewis considered launching an independent presidential campaign. Browder offered support on the seventeenth, calling a third party more appealing than a third term. Shortly thereafter, Lewis abandoned his brief White House quest, and the Communists renominated their 1936 ticket of Browder and James W. Ford. The former labeled Roosevelt and Willkie "Tweedledum and Tweedledee," called himself the peace candidate, and urged even Taft followers to vote Communist. The far right, of course, saw no reason to support CP plans for federally financed pensions, public works, education, national health care, rural electrification, and a modern, large-scale public housing program.[51]

Browder had no opportunity to proselytize nationally. Federal Judge John C. Knox ordered him to remain within the southern district of New York. Government agents watched closely, eager for a violation. At one point Browder's crowded itinerary put State Department sleuths in near panic. Hearing that he had led a recent Boston rally, they dashed off eight frenzied telegrams in two days. Ultimately, they learned that his "speech" had consisted of a recording played over a loudspeaker. Yet not all laughs were on the G-men. One discovered Browder booked at three separate Gotham meetings in one evening, "all scheduled to begin at 8 PM." The agent snorted, "Earl will have a busy night."[52]

The Communists faced other hurdles. In mid-June Congress passed the Smith Act, which required aliens to register and submit to finger-printing. Of most significance, it established the first federal peacetime sedition statute since 1798. It gave prosecutors sweeping power to punish dissenters: not for burning city halls, not for spreading the idea, but simply for joining an organization deemed to favor such advocacy. Although intimidating, the statute was never used against Browder's CP, which, despite the Nazi–Soviet pact, still did not encourage insurrection. Also in 1940, CPUSA canvassers materialized across the land. Even before Lewis decided not to run, scores of petition carriers, seeking signatures to put the party on the ballot, met arrest. Others fell victim to unwarranted police raids and mob attacks. Sympathizers refusing to repudiate their signatures often lost their jobs. Courts joined the frenzy. They ruled Marxists off the ballot in fifteen states, including strongholds New York, Ohio, and Illinois. Browder decried the persecution but handled it stoically: "It has always been difficult to get Communist votes cast and even more difficult to get them counted."[53]

Threat of confrontation affected Browder directly. On October 11, John J. Bennett, Jr., New York's attorney general, who gave formal opinions only to government agencies, expressed his "informal" belief that Browder's federal felony conviction had voided his state citizenship. When the CP head attempted to register, a Republican election board member protested. Browder insisted that he had broken no New York law and could cast a ballot because his appeal still awaited U.S. Supreme Court review. He registered successfully, but his adversary vowed to challenge any voting attempt. On election day the mild-mannered Browder drove past the polls, saw the official, and did not stop.[54]

Franklin Roosevelt received twenty-seven million ballots to Willkie's twenty-two million. Working-class Americans still considered the President their spokesman. Browder's performance proved especially anemic. Final tabulations showed he had garnered only 46,471 votes. Norman Thomas, whose party had disintegrated, amassed 99,557 votes. Even Roger Babson, the prohibitionist candidate, outtallied Browder, receiving 57,812 votes. Browder's total had declined 40 percent from 1936 when he had conducted a thinly disguised effort to reelect the president. Federal and state repression had devastated the CPUSA's campaign so badly that no true figure could assess support lost by the Soviet–German accord. Like a superstitious person whistling past the graveyard, the party conceded a 15-percent membership decline since 1939. Recruitment, a more meaningful measure, dropped to one-fourth of 1938's monthly average:[55]

In October 1940 an event far more significant to Browder than the national election occurred. Congress passed the Voorhis Act, to take effect the following January. The act sought to regulate organizations that had international ties by forcing them to register with the Justice Department and to provide information concerning meeting places, activities, propaganda, officers, and contributors. The statute threatened to dissolve those extrinsic bodies the attorney general considered national security threats.[56]

Browder contended that the law, if enforced impartially, would cover even the AFL, YMCA, Rotary, Masonry, and Kiwanis. Before the Senate Judiciary Subcommittee in early July he had denounced its concept as inherently discriminatory, citing the enormous discretion it would give the attorney general. Browder termed it a "blacklist," likened it to the 1790s' Alien and Sedition laws, and insisted that it menaced all dissent. Under the measure's "smooth camouflage" lay fascism's "sharp claws." This hyperbole concealed a cogent insight. The bill's sponsor was liberal Democrat Jerry Voorhis. Browder insisted that once the open CP was abolished, "every known progressive" would come under suspicion as a surreptitious leftist. He predicted that some day Congress would purge " 'Comrade' Voorhis as a secret Communist."[57] Six years later Browder was not surprised when the lawmaker did lose his seat to a challenger who smeared him as soft on Reds. The victor, young and destined to use more of the same campaign tactics, was Richard M. Nixon.

On November 16, 1940, Browder told a special CPUSA convention, "We are not foreign agents" and canceled the party's Comintern affiliation specifically to avoid the new statute's penalties. This tactical departure from orthodoxy, more dramatic than the Democratic Front, set a precedent for later initiatives yet bolder. He justified the action by contending that reactionaries would otherwise exploit the international bonds to weaken labor. At the same time the Communists proclaimed their fealty to proletarian internationalism. In Moscow Georgi Dimitrov personally approved the action.[58]

Hearing that the Supreme Court had upheld his conviction depressed Browder greatly. After February 17, 1941, his confidence declined precipitously, and a gripping tension set in. Although a Leavenworth veteran, he proved a most reluctant prisoner as he neared age fifty, a married man with three dependent children. He felt betrayed by the president and oppressed by the justice system. He also distrusted William Z. Foster.

He had good reason to worry. His impending absence provided a window of opportunity. According to Gil Green, Foster proposed an unusual solution to the party's leadership problem. At some point Browder had agreed to discuss the situation with Foster. The latter persuaded Green, whose loyalty to Browder had wavered after the Nazi–Soviet pact, to attend the meeting and then nominated him as acting general secretary. The proposal surprised Green, who had received no advance notice and was wondering why he had been invited. Believing that "no one could replace Browder," he considered Foster's proposal "ridiculous." He declined immediately rather than knife his chief. Browder listened silently. Finally, he announced: "Seeing that Gil himself does not think it should be he, then I propose it be Bob Minor."[59] The latter, a blundering, slow-speaking old war-horse from the 1920s, somewhat deaf, was a sycophant. Possessing neither leadership qualities nor entourage, he would follow any orders Browder could smuggle past prison censors.

On March 25 Browder surrendered to U.S. marshals who transported him by rail to Atlanta Penitentiary. Again the CPUSA press compared him with Eugene Debs, who also had served there. The lawmen, a Sam Swartz and a man identified only as "Marty," had no respect for Browder and did all they could to humiliate him. When the train reached its final station, they held him, shackled to two other prisoners, until all paying passengers had departed. Soon about forty reporters and photographers gathered outside. Marty pulled a large handkerchief from his pocket and cut two eye holes in it. Then, chuckling, he placed it over Browder's face, creating a mask. Swartz quipped, "You'll fool them now." Meekly Browder, who never defied authority while in custody, mumbled "This is not my suggestion; it's your suggestion."[60]

As the five left the train, Marty shook his blackjack theatrically, swore at the reporters, and threatened to crack their skulls. This produced smiles, laughter, and a dozen flashbulbs popping. Once Browder and the others were securely inside a waiting automobile, Browder complained that he looked like a "Lone Ranger" and asked submissively if he could remove the cover. In silence the car pulled away. After about a block, Marty replied, "The show is over now." Jubilantly he grabbed the handkerchief mask and threw it out an open window with the words "We'll not need this any more."[61]

That same month the United States virtually entered the war. Britain,

Surrender at Foley Square Courthouse, March 25, 1941, to begin sentence at Atlanta Penitentiary (William Browder, Earl Browder, and Robert Minor). (Courtesy of *People's Weekly World*. Used by permission.)

having fought for a year and a half and having endured nightly bombing of her cities, could no longer afford to pay cash for arms. The president told a "fireside chat" radio audience he would hand, not sell, his garden hose to a neighbor whose house was ablaze. Congress enacted a bill empowering Roosevelt to "lease, lend or otherwise dispose of" weapons to any nation whose defense was vital to American security. The ruse that the hardware would still exist at war's end and be returned to the United

States helped overcome public reluctance. The legislation did not surprise Browder, but it increased his gloom. Full belligerency and massive repression, he feared, lay just around the corner. Trotskyists, Socialists, and many civil libertarians shared his concern.

More than twenty years earlier Leavenworth Penitentiary had altered Browder's personality. How would Atlanta affect him? How could the weak, obtuse Robert Minor hope to hold the party for Browder when the Nazi–Soviet pact had pushed other nations' Communists strongly leftward? A larger question also loomed. The Moscow-oriented CP and the pacifistic SP had declined to near insignificance. Most workers and intellectuals had rallied behind the president. How could the left resuscitate itself? Or was it already doomed to extinction in the early 1940s?

# EIGHT

■

# To Free the Spirit from Its Cell (1941–1944)

On June 22, 1941, without warning Nazi Germany invaded the Soviet Union. The immediate cause appeared to be disagreements over Rumania, Finland, Bulgaria, and Yugoslavia. Hitler's anti-Communism, however, which was exceeded only by his racism, had probably made bloodshed inevitable. American and British intelligence tipped off Joseph Stalin in advance, but he ignored all warnings. Not trusting the West and determined to give Hitler no pretext whatever, the Soviet dictator continued delivering grain and oil until the shooting started. Overnight World War II ceased to be an imperialist conflict for America's Communists, and the White House peace vigil disappeared. Would old allies on the left ever trust them again? More important to Earl Browder, how could he and his followers put forth enough patriotic effort to rebuild some relationship with the Roosevelt administration? Could the party's new position end the Red scare or at least win protection from it?

Hitler's aggression threw the unprepared Soviet troops into confusion, and they retreated in disarray. Civilians, particularly in the Ukraine, welcomed the Germans as liberators, unaware that the Nazis considered all Slavs subhuman. By November the enemy had conquered more of Russia than Napoleon had: to the gates of Leningrad in the north, Moscow's outskirts in the center, and the Don River in the south. Most CPUSA members wanted to forget the previous twenty-two months.

The U.S. government had already aided the process. Hoping to get lend-lease supplies to the United Kingdom, not the ocean floor, the United States had extended its Atlantic "security zone" one thousand miles east of New York. This made war with Germany only a matter of time. Soon the U.S. Navy would begin escorting supply ships all the way to Iceland. On June 24 President Roosevelt pledged aid to the Soviet Union, and on July 12 Britain did the same. The domestic Communists began demanding a second front in Europe, and the *Daily Worker* denounced John L. Lewis's isolationism. That fall the party set up Russian War Relief, a respectable front to channel supplies to the USSR.

Not all on the left agreed that Moscow was worth saving, however. Max Shachtman and James Burnham led a secessionist Socialist Workers party faction that established the Workers party. Its members argued that Stalin's crimes had eliminated any moral responsibility to defend the "bureaucratic collectivist" USSR and that the war remained an imperialist struggle. By contrast, the Trotskyist majority, led by James Cannon, summoned followers to defend the Soviet Union despite the tyranny. That previous spring the federal government had seized the headquarters of the Socialist Workers party in Minneapolis and indicted twenty-nine members for allegedly violating the Smith Act. The new international situation halted the CPUSA's leftward drift, cut the ground from beneath William Z. Foster, and protected Browder's leadership even as he languished in prison. What sort of condition would he be in by April 1944, his earliest possible good-behavior parole date?

## COMMUNIST LEADER ON ICE

The German invasion appalled an already depressed Browder. Now federal prisoner 60140, he found Atlanta Penitentiary far more painful than Leavenworth. No longer an anonymous midwestern radical, he could not finagle special privileges. Officials did not permit him to play the flute in the prison band or read and write about political matters. Serving as a humble storeroom clerk proved a difficult adjustment for a proud workaholic used to speaking before thousands and piloting a large organization. He compounded his misery by shunning recreation, isolating himself from the other convicts. Brooding alone, he pondered Soviet defeat after Soviet defeat. He also puzzled over domestic affairs. He had been correct after all on the need to avoid breaking with FDR after the Nazi–Soviet pact. Browder always believed he could have worked with the administration despite the Comintern's requirement that he criticize Britain and France. Ever vain, he wondered what sort of important role in the nation's affairs he might have played had the treaty never come about. Yet at the same time he harbored anger toward Roosevelt for jailing him on an outdated charge. He felt special frustration because the new patriotic line fit his personality and leadership style so well, yet he remained (in his own mind at least) a political prisoner.

Remorse over Nazi–Soviet pact policies welled up inside him. He wrote Raissa that he felt "burdened to the point of sleeplessness" by fears that recent flirtations with the extreme right might throw fellow travelers toward isolationists such as aviator Charles A. Lindbergh. American security began to bother Browder. He urged Robert Minor to emphasize U.S. "national interests at all times." Soon CP officials began attacking antiwar newspapers as the "Copperhead press." By August they contended that the United States had "never since the battle of Gettysburg been in so great a danger."[1] Daily Browder sunk into an ever-deepening gloom that made these years of incarceration the worst of his life. Soon he faced a horror unlike anything he had ever experienced before.

In some ways Browder's plight resembled that of Eugene Debs, who also had gone to Atlanta Penitentiary during a period of national hysteria. As historian Nick Salvatore has noted, Debs too had become disconsolate during his 1919–1921 confinement. His brother Theodore considered the institution a "Southern hell-hole," and believed that the sentence was designed to shatter Debs's health completely. Certainly the climate, confinement, and regimentation took their toll. Debs lost weight, suffered anxiety-induced insomnia, and, according to Salvatore, faced a "nearly daily struggle for emotional survival" while persistent self-doubt "stalked his soul." He read that outside the walls factionalism was ripping American socialism apart and that the federal government had launched a "furious purging of dissidents and radicals of all persuasions."[2]

Debs, then in his mid-sixties, served in a prison even harsher than the youthful Browder's Leavenworth. Atlanta had become frightfully overcrowded, swelling from 893 inmates in 1915 to nearly 2,200 in 1921. Complaining about institutional cuisine is an honored inmate pastime. In 1919, however, warden Fred G. Zerbst reported to the attorney general that his prisoners lacked milk, vegetables, and fruit, although a year later their new prison farm had begun to address this "much-needed want." For an incredible six years the penitentiary had lacked adequate water. City plumbing difficulties cut off the supply frequently, and, in the best of times, pressure was so low as to create health hazards. A 1917 hailstorm had damaged the roof of the dining room–chapel building, and every time it rained water leaked through the ceiling and down the east wall. Despite repeated pleas to Washington, insufficient appropriations prevented effective repair until mid-1921.[3]

Indeed, conditions threatened the convicts' very survival. The prison possessed no isolation building, and inmates with contagious diseases simply joined the normal population on arrival. Debs had not been there in 1918 when an influx of military prisoners brought epidemics of measles, smallpox, chicken pox, and mumps. He arrived in time to face part of the influenza pandemic that killed more persons than all of the battles of World War I. In 1920, no less than 44 percent of the inmates were treated in the prison hospital for tuberculosis. Those the disease rendered bedfast lived in outdoor tents, even during the winter. Guards, who were political appointees, received no training whatever. Petty graft abounded, and narcotics appeared. Famous German saboteur Robert Fay escaped and evidently reached his homeland. One inmate murdered a deputy warden with an iron bar, and two others stabbed an employee. Before 1920 prisoners were confined to their cells with no work to do and received no exercise and little entertainment, although champion boxers Jack Dempsey and Georges Carpentier made visits.[4]

Before Browder arrived in 1941 a revolution in corrections had occurred. James V. Bennett, a minister's son working in the Bureau of Efficiency (later the Office of Management and Budget), issued a scathing report on prison conditions. He noted that Western penology "had progressed from" the Middle Ages but argued that it "had not progressed very far." Boiling in oil, disemboweling, and limb severance no longer existed. Instead American law provided terms "of savage length." Men were routinely "strung up by the thumbs, handcuffed to high bars, [and] kept for weeks in solitary confinement on bread and water." Bennett's work led to the creation of the Federal Bureau of Prisons in 1930. Under Sanford Bates and later Bennett himself, penitentiaries became more sanitary and spacious. A therapeutic environment appeared, built around factories that produced products for other government agencies rather than simple make-work. Expanded recreational programs included baseball, football, and volleyball leagues. Joseph W. Sanford, Atlanta's warden from 1938 to 1948, was a less vigorous reformer. He nevertheless created a "Town Hall Forum," copied from a popular radio program. It allowed inmates to elect discussion leaders who, after a week's preparation, gave three-minute papers on controversial issues and fielded audience questions, moderated by the prison's education supervisor.[5]

Thus Browder entered an environment far less cruel than the one he had experienced at Leavenworth. He was fifteen years younger than Debs had been in Atlanta. Although Browder feared loss of his leadership position, his party was not disintegrating as Debs's had. Why then did Browder not fare better? Certainly he resented the fascination officials displayed toward him. In addition to giving him the now-familiar prison physical, they administered intelligence tests and even probed his psyche. They deemed him "a man of very superior intellectual capacity"; on a particular examination he achieved "one of the highest scores observed in this institution." Of course, the era's culturally biased testing procedures equated literacy with intelligence. Browder, who wrote nine books and nearly one hundred pamphlets in his lifetime, stood heads above a prison population that had recently improved its reading to the fifth-grade level.[6]

When the psychiatrist, a Dr. Zbranek, and the psychologist examined Browder, they did not get to see his abnormal fascination with fear. For the only time in his life it deserted him. Undergoing psychotherapy, Browder reacted poorly. A brave, even heroic individual may harbor a phobia; a professional boxer may be unwilling to board an airplane. Browder could not face the subject of mental illness. To his generation even routine examinations were far less familiar and far more threatening than they are today. Mid-twentieth-century America had few community-based mental health centers. Only the very rich and the very sick ever saw a psychiatrist, and Browder was neither.

He found the experience the one true terror he had ever known, and it seems to have left psychological damage from which he never fully recovered. In truth, Browder faced a daunting specter virtually unknown in the modern United States: involuntary commitment to a mental institution. Although the procedure brought a term of unspecified, possibly lifelong duration, it was considered a reasonable and routine way to treat the abnormal at the time. That it rarely punished American political dissenters did not reduce Browder's angst. He knew unpopular views could be equated with pathology, a phenomenon that would later become tragically common in Stalin's Russia. Accordingly, Browder saw Zbranek and the psychologist as vindictive authority figures employed by the same repressive state that had conducted the recent Red scare. Predictably, he greeted their friendly gestures with utmost suspicion. When they made pointed comments, he responded defensively. Their procedures so vexed him that he still complained about them a decade later.[7]

The diagnoses told almost as much about the analysts as they did about the patient. Interviewing and testing took place in April 1941, when Communists were considered Hitler's allies. Few fields of inquiry are as imprecise and subjective as psychiatry and psychology, and Browder, not a patient, did not want help. Understandably, he loathed the inquiries into his private life as unnecessary. Compensating, he feigned utter indifference.[8]

Zbranek found Browder "pleasant, alert, and cooperative" but recognized his real feelings remained submerged. He categorized Browder as having a "cyclothymic" personality, which can range anywhere from healthy extroversion to manic-depressive psychosis. Zbranek considered him a true believer, classifying him with "reformers, prophets and litigious people." Certainly Browder lived for his career and cause. Yet Zbranek did not report pathology. Instead he noted that Browder's attitude was "not martyrlike, but certain of ultimate vindication." He concluded there was "no evidence of psychosis or fixed delusional ideas" and deemed Browder's outlook "very good."[9]

The psychologist painted a similar portrait in darker hues. Browder's replies in the "Rorschach experiment" connoted a "psychoneurotic background." His "original elaboration of popular responses" with the suppression of color suggested "strongly compulsive components." Professionals attach the label "compulsive" to numerous personalities, from those who simply take their labors seriously to those who exist for nothing else. It is usually employed pejoratively, however; perhaps the psychologist detected Browder's workaholism. He wrote that Browder appeared "very rigid," although trying to be forthright. He possessed a "very broad" thought content but displayed an "extreme tendency" to integrate new stimuli into the context of his own experiences and value system, rather than simply observing details. Suggesting fanaticism, the diagnosis continued in gloomy terms: "From the psychological tests it would appear that this man [has a] strong drive to gain his goal by any manner possible. His original elaborations of the common responses differ from others in that they present more of the bizarre elements frequently seen in the psychoneurotics and latent psychotics."[10] Thus the psychologist accused Browder of extremism and strangeness.

A "Release Progress Report" by the Bureau of Prisons, prepared the day before Browder left, offered a pessimistic assessment. It lamented that he had "made no contact with the Psychiatric Department" during his incarceration and asserted that "prognosis for this man's adjustment in civilian life is guarded because he is one who reveals compulsive traits, bolstered by a superior intelligence and who reacts to his environment by an intellectual aggressiveness as defense. Because of his suggestible nature and inadequate cyclothymic personality, he will need general supervision upon release."[11]

These judgments ignored the political and technical nature of Browder's prosecution and the major reinforcing factors in his life. He possessed an abiding faith in Marxism's eventual triumph and relished his role as idol to an entire nation's Communists. He also had a happy family life that provided a healthy diversion. In addition, his knowledge about Soviet espionage, however shallow or deep, added a vicarious excitement to his daily existence that few persons ever knew about. Strangely, however, none of the prison evaluations identified Browder's most obvious psychological problems: clinical depression and loneliness.

Browder's incarceration prompted great concern for his condition. When he entered the penitentiary, his wife petitioned officials to give him "milk in his daily diet" because he had experienced digestive troubles in recent years. Raissa and CP figures Jack Johnstone and Robert Minor urged Browder adamantly to guard his health.[12] In April 1942 Browder's brother William told a protest meeting that the rigors of penitentiary life were wearing on Earl and that if he was not released soon, he would become quite sick. Josephine Truslow Adams, an eccentric fellow traveler and acquaintance of Eleanor Roosevelt, persuaded one of the First Lady's friends to write the White House urging a pardon because Browder "might die in his cell."[13]

Actually the CPUSA exaggerated Browder's physical problems. During his first five months he did not make the sick line even once nor did he ask to see a physician. When Congressman Vito Marcantonio visited him on April 11, 1942, Browder claimed to be "getting along well." According to the warden, Marcantonio left "highly pleased" with the prisoner's appearance. The party paid Browder's salary to Raissa, which prevented financial hardship, but publicity hurt the family greatly. A social worker reported that Andrew, the middle son, suffered a "severe psychological reaction" from the ordeal. Schoolmates hurled painful taunts at all three boys. The family felt disappointed that the Soviet government, which had tried to win Eugene Debs's release in exchange for an American saboteur, made no effort to secure Browder's freedom.[14]

The Atlanta sojourn made directing the movement difficult. The Bureau of Prisons scrutinized all incoming and outgoing letters. When Browder wrote anything resembling specific policy directives, the administration returned it unmailed. He tried a camouflage technique in communications with Minor. Using what the latter termed "Aesop" language, Browder inserted his own words into lengthy literary quotations and disguised orders as chess problems or anecdotes. Minor distributed Browder's correspondence to Political Committee members for study and interpretation. Even this primitive system brought difficulties.[15] The Warden's office eyed the long passages suspiciously and eventually objected.

202 ■ TO FREE THE SPIRIT FROM ITS CELL

Minor visited Browder several times. Harsh restrictions hindered their colloquies. Warden Sanford or an assistant always interviewed each man separately. Verbally and in writing, both had to agree to regulations beforehand. They then enjoyed only about forty-five minutes of conversation time. Although Marcantonio had spoken with Browder privately, Sanford or his deputy monitored every conversation with Minor. Immediately thereafter the observer sent J. Edgar Hoover a lengthy summary.[16]

Two decades earlier an unknown Browder had experienced no overt cruelty at Leavenworth, but now he faced some during one of Raissa's visits. Early on, emotion overcame them. They sat staring in teary-eyed silence, each simply clutching the other's hand. Suddenly the guard broke in: "Damn it, you can't just sit there saying nothing" and terminated their rendezvous early.[17]

Although Browder and the Communists concentrated their international attention on Europe, events elsewhere also threatened U.S. security. During the 1930s Japan's military dictatorship had begun building a colony in China as a stepping stone toward hegemony over East Asia. Since the turn of the century the State Department's Open Door policy had sought to maintain American trading rights there. Of more significance, much of the public felt a strong sympathy for the Chinese people. In December 1938 Japan announced plans to build a "Greater East Asia Coprosperity Sphere," or empire, in much of the Pacific, including European colonial possessions. Then in September 1940 Japan moved troops into north Indochina and signed the Tripartite Pact with Germany and Italy. The treaty provided for mutual assistance if any of the signatories became involved in war with the United States. In retaliation the administration ordered the Pacific fleet, then at Hawaii on maneuvers, to remain at Pearl Harbor indefinitely.

Franklin D. Roosevelt considered this a deterrent. His main foreign policy concern was to function as the "arsenal of democracy" to aid Britain's struggle against fascism. A conflict with Japan would only dilute that effort. Even if war with the Axis proved inevitable, civilian and military leaders considered Japan a secondary concern. Nazi Germany was the greater ideological and military threat to human freedom. Japan's inability to attack the U.S. mainland settled the issue. British Prime Minister Winston Churchill wanted an American commitment to defend his endangered colony of Malaya and the Dutch East Indies. The president refused, doubting that many Americans would fight to protect European imperialism in Asia. Much of the public believed that economic pressure alone would cause Japan to yield, for it possessed neither oil nor other essential raw materials. By contrast, the Japanese saw China as the minimum compromise: a source of strategic supplies and potential markets. Free and united, China would hinder the Japanese Empire's growth.

In the summer of 1941 Japanese army units occupied south Indochina, a move that menaced the Dutch East Indies and the Philippine Islands, the latter an American possession. In response the United States, Britain, and the Netherlands impounded Japanese assets and embargoed oil shipments, forcing Japan to spend dwindling reserves. After fruitless negotiations, Japan attacked the American fleet on December 7. A Congressional war declaration followed immediately. Just days later Hitler and Mussolini joined the struggle against the United States. Suddenly a Grand Alliance with Britain and the USSR became possible. In November a Soviet counteroffensive had taken the city of Rostov-on-Don, the first conspicuous defeat the Nazis had ever suffered. A similar move after Pearl Harbor relieved pressure on Moscow.

Browder saw U.S. entry as a dream come true. Now one could fight for Communism and Americanism simultaneously. Immediately he asked Warden Sanford to inform Washington that he would help the war effort in any way possible. Outside prison fifteen thousand CP members rushed into the armed forces. Others joined the merchant marine or entered war-related industries.

The Western Allies strove for a common strategy. In a January 1942 Washington summit meeting British Prime Minister Winston Churchill and President Roosevelt agreed to demand unconditional surrender and plan an assault on Hitler's Europe. Churchill envisioned a tightening ring around the periphery because a frontal attack, employed during World War I, had cost his nation casualties unimagined. Most of all he wanted to protect his empire's supply line to India through the Mediterranean and Suez Canal. Roosevelt favored a direct invasion launched from the British Isles but deferred initially to his more experienced partner.

The Grand Alliance increased the Communists' acceptance at home. It also made Browder appear the victim of a previous era's passions. He had gone to prison demanding a full pardon; he felt that seeking parole would imply that the verdict had been just. A few months' incarceration changed his mind, however. On August 25, 1941, he applied for executive clemency, stressing the government's earlier concession that his crime did not involve moral turpitude. He noted that he had already served longer than those convicted in more than 90 percent of passport law cases. He argued that his sentence's length stemmed from the trial's hysterical atmosphere. The prosecution had cited his 1917 felony conviction but not his full pardon thereof. He claimed to have a good reputation in his community that contrasted with his "newspaper reputation." Because he enjoyed support in "not inconsiderable circles," his release would further national unity. In early November 1941 Robert Minor believed freedom imminent. Browder expressed less optimism. By the following April Congressman Marcantonio felt that no prospect of clemency existed and that parole remained Browder's only hope.[18]

The White House did not always take pleas for Browder's release seriously. Eleanor Roosevelt marked an early petition to the president, "For your amusement." FDR responded, "I think I will send Browder as ambassador to Berlin. The place is vacant!" The First Lady wrote back, "Please do!"[19]

In truth the CPUSA had a strong argument. Between 1918 and November 1941, New York agents had arrested 131 passport case suspects. Justice Department figures showed that Browder's sentence exceeded the average greatly:

19 defendants were nolle prossed (had charges dropped)
28 had suspended sentences
17 were sentenced to fine
12 were sentenced to 30 days or less
 8 were sentenced to 60 days or less
 9 were sentenced to 90 days or less
13 were sentenced to 6 months or less
14 were sentenced to a year and a day
 5 were sentenced to 18 months or less
 2 were sentenced to 2 years
 1 was sentenced to 3 years
 2 were sentenced to 4 years (including Browder)
 1 was sentenced to 5 years[20]

Of all defendants convicted on multiple counts, moreover, only Browder received consecutive sentences. A songwriter arrested immediately after Browder on a substantially similar charge escaped with a $500 fine.

In the best Popular Front tradition, Communists created a Citizens' Committee to Free Earl Browder. Its publications likened him to followers of Thomas Jefferson arrested during America's undeclared war with France in 1798. Chaired by IWW hero Tom Mooney, it rained petitions on federal officials. The FBI and Military Intelligence Service monitored its actions closely, expecting "a million signatures" by September 25, 1941. On May 20, 1942, alone, the Committee planned to send the White House twenty-five thousand telegrams.[21] Suppliants included eminent men and women from all walks of life: clergy, union leaders, law school deans, a state supreme court justice, and Elbert Thomas of Utah, the Senate's Foreign Relations Committee chairman. The ACLU termed Browder's punishment "excessive," and 1940 Republican presidential nominee Wendell Willkie questioned its propriety in the *New Republic*.

Because Mooney suffered poor health, day-to-day leadership of the Free Browder campaign fell to Elizabeth Gurley Flynn, another IWW veteran who was now a ranking CPUSA figure. According to biographer Helen C. Camp, Flynn was temperamentally "quite close to" Browder: "impatient with theory," deeply "concerned with demystifying the party and with making it respectable and acceptable to the American working class." She spent much of the 1941–1942 winter "on a nationwide speaking tour, trying to arouse public indignation at the politically motivated nature of his imprisonment."[22]

Accumulated protests finally paid off. On May 16, 1942, four days before Browder's fifty-first birthday and just prior to a diplomatic visit by Soviet Foreign Minister Vyacheslav Molotov to Washington, President Roosevelt commuted the sentence. His action constituted a gesture toward the USSR far more easily delivered than a second European front. Browder, passing through the prison gate, handed reporters a typed statement that thanked backers and pledged to support the war effort. Minor, who had traveled to Atlanta, accompanied him on the long New York–bound train ride. Browder, aware his release would enrage veterans' groups, halted celebratory gatherings. The two men got off in Newark, New Jersey, where brother William awaited them. They thereby avoided four thousand sympathizers at Manhattan's Pennsylvania Station.[23]

Quickly the party canceled rallies around the country that had been scheduled for Browder's May 20 birthday. The Citizens Committee commended FDR for his "act of simple justice," closed down, and donated its $20,000 treasury to the military. Thereafter the Justice Department dropped a two-year-old secret indictment, secured in case a technicality freed Browder. His release confounded the FBI, which had scrutinized his activities for years. Agents bewailed the administration's failure to notify the bureau in advance. They continued to tap Browder's telephone, follow his footsteps, monitor his bank accounts, and read his incoming and outgoing cables.[24]

## SERVING CAUSE AND COUNTRY

Browder found the world outside prison a source for optimism. Although Nazi armies remained deep inside the USSR, they had not fulfilled Hitler's strategic objective of a quick 1941 knockout victory. Once the eastern front settled into a war of attrition, the enormous Soviet Union had long-term advantages. On the home front Congress, seeking to put twelve million soldiers in uniform, had enacted a new draft law just after the Japanese attack. It covered all men between ages eighteen and sixty-five, with those over forty-four liable for possible labor service. Those already in the armed forces would remain for the duration plus six months.

As Browder boarded his New York–bound train, the military was preparing for its first women personnel; some 200,000 would soon serve in clerical, communications, and administrative fields. The civilian labor force was in the process of adding fifteen million new workers, eliminating the Great Depression's final traces. Ultimately three million of them would be women, some breaking out of the pink-collar ghetto and taking relatively well-paying assembly-line positions heretofore reserved for men. To coordinate the growth, Congress created the War Manpower Commission under Indiana's former governor Paul V. McNutt.

Labor historians have placed the innovations within a larger context. Nelson Lichtenstein has called World War II "a watershed in the history of women's work." Previously the typical female toiling outside the home had been young, single, or both. By contrast in the early 1940s well-paying employment attracted "large numbers of older married women" not theretofore part of the labor force. Their entry, however, did not constitute a "general feminist advance," but rather an opportunity to aid society's industrial mobilization at a financial gain to the family. Their appearance "led to a shift in the location of the boundaries between men's and women's work," not the elimination of job-site gender segregation. Aircraft riveting and wiring, for example, became "predominately female occupations" below the level of foreman. Women paid a price. "When they were considered an alien intrusion into formerly all-male departments," they "suffered a good deal of petty harassment." Outside the factory, shortages in housing, transportation, and child care facilities often made "the traditional responsibilities of women at home even more difficult." To James R. Green World War II previewed critical issues that working women would make a permanent part of the nation's social agenda by the late 1960s: "equal pay for equal work, government-subsidized daycare for working mothers, an end to sex discrimination in employers' job classifications and in unions' seniority systems, and the Equal Rights Amendment," first proposed during the 1920s and revived during the 1940s. Earl Browder, shortly after his release, announced his party's position. "It is a pressing necessity to abolish all existing remnants of inequality between men and women." Communists, as historian Roger Keeran has noted, "became particularly active in the pursuit of better conditions for women."[25]

Liberty rejuvenated Browder mentally and physically. Swiftly he resumed active CPUSA leadership. The party profited handsomely from growing public admiration for the courageous Soviet armed forces. For the first time since the Democratic Front's death he could express his nationalism openly. Cadres and rank and filers continued to press for a second front in Europe and demanded the Axis powers' unconditional surrender. Browder argued that Hitlerism threatened to throw humanity backward tens of centuries and destroy civilization's most fundamental values. No other domestic leftist organization aided the Allied effort so tirelessly. Callously Browder impugned the patriotism of Socialists and Trotskyists.

He began to display a reckless exuberance and an unnatural craving for status and adulation. That craving, in turn, impaired his judgment, leaving him unduly susceptible to the flattery a mid-twentieth-century Communist leader customarily received. Browder had always enjoyed, but probably never taken seriously, his cult of personality before going to prison. After Atlanta he showed every sign of believing party propaganda that lauded his brilliance, wisdom, and originality of thought. So buoyed, he strove passionately to make the Communists not merely the left's largest party, but a fully legitimate component of the Roosevelt coalition.

Browder spent the summer of 1942 writing *Victory and After*. In an unprecedented move he published it without showing it to Political Committee colleagues. For the war's duration the CPUSA would make no proposals for socialism that might "disrupt national unity." Furthermore, he announced that toiling men and women would make the major sacrifices necessary for victory. By contrast, Browder declared that the "owning classes," accustomed to "luxury and idleness," had to be indulged lest they "become disaffected and sabotage the war." Believing that he had learned from Abraham Lincoln's experience with the slaveholding planter class, Browder argued that suppressing their resistance would cost more than buying their allegiance. Going one step further, he

Felix, Earl, and William Browder with unidentified friend,
early to mid-1940s. (From the Syracuse University Library, Department
of Special Collections, 600 Bird Library. Used by permission.)

elevated placating the wealthy to a "United Nations" goal lasting beyond
Axis surrender. Triumph and continued harmony would make possible
peaceful reconstruction in Europe. Clearly he considered saving the Soviet Union more urgent than raising workers' living standards at home.[26]

Browder also supported organized labor's no-strike pledge, issued by
the CIO and AFL after Pearl Harbor. The Communists stuck by it even
as profiteering became widespread. Years later Browder blamed rank-
and-file party members for the mistake, arguing they had adopted it
while he was in prison. He contended that he had favored a more flexible
no-strike "policy" that left room for walkouts or sit-downs where conditions warranted them. Historian Harvey A. Levenstein has attested that
Browder's "actions and statements during the war" lent "little credence
to this claim," however. Instead, he pursued labor peace without restraint. James R. Green has added that "the CP's reputation declined fur-

ther when Communist-inclined leaders" such as Joe Curran of the National Maritime Union called for the pledge's extension into the postwar era.[27]

Marxists were not the only persons seeking a second front. In August Winston Churchill flew to Moscow to solicit Stalin's support for operation TORCH. Over a Kremlin dinner, Churchill drew a crocodile on the tablecloth, pointed to its soft underbelly and explained that the Western Allies would relieve pressure on Russia by attacking Vichy France's North African colonies. They then planned to save Suez and march up the Italian peninsula. None of this impressed the Soviet leader, but he understood that Roosevelt needed casualties at German hands in 1942 to keep the American public committed to beating Hitler first. This version of a second front became reality in November when U.S. forces hit beaches in Morocco and Algeria.

Browder, in what Levenstein has termed "Stalinesque delusions of omniscience," quickly "metamorphosed into a self-styled expert on all phases of production, from the level of national planning down to the shop floor." He conducted lengthy correspondence with union and business leaders regarding bottlenecks hindering the war effort. By December he was the proud author of a Communist variation of incentive pay. Knowing that American workers considered the concept anathema, he nevertheless argued that the idea was not inherently unfair. Instead, capitalists made it so. Once productivity began increasing dramatically, owners usually downgraded piece rates, dropping workers' earnings to previous levels. Herein lay the exploitation. Browder insisted that incentive pay could work fairly if rates remained frozen until war's end. Accordingly he called on the national government to adopt the policy, promising that labor would then make heroic sacrifices. In return he hinted that the CP would not oppose the forced savings measures others might advocate. The party reprinted Browder's speech as a pamphlet titled *Production for Victory* and circulated 100,000 copies widely. Cadres hailed it as answering all home front problems. To Browder's chagrin, neither capital nor labor found the program appealing. Employers had no interest in greater governmental supervision. Proletarians, of course, feared any type of speedup, knowing that war's end would bring slashed rates and layoffs. According to Nelson Lichtenstein, UAW Vice-President Walter Reuther hammered the Communists with the slogan "Down with Earl Browder's piecework."[28]

When Browder put forth his controversial suggestion the war's most important battle was taking place almost half a world away. In November the German sixth army of 500,000 men swept into Stalingrad, gateway to the USSR's oil-rich Caucasus region. Soviet troops held on in house-by-house fighting while the military command ordered encircling counterattacks in winter weather. Adamantly Hitler refused to permit any tactical retreats. On February 2, 1943, Field Marshal Friedrich Paulus surrendered the eighty thousand who had survived the fighting. It marked the first time in history that a German officer of his rank had been captured. To the north the Red Army broke a 506-day siege of Leningrad, opening a precarious supply route.

At home the CPUSA enjoyed a surge of popularity, especially among ethnic Americans. Communists of Greek, Hungarian, Polish, and Armenian extraction felt close to their native parties and freedom fighters. The CP's antifascist propaganda, from Hollywood to the neighborhoods, was unsurpassed; it never failed to stress that the Soviet Union was taking the blows and winning the struggle.

Vigor to champion the war effort seemed to know no bounds. The CPUSA did not even protest when the federal government, in March 1942, began putting 100,000 West Coast Japanese Americans in internment camps. Indeed, according to Karl Yoneda, the party suspended "all members of Japanese ancestry and their non-Japanese spouses" for the war's duration to further "national unity." Browder argued that "the best place for any Japanese fifth columnist to hide is within the Communist party." Therefore racially based expulsions were in order.[29]

The CP's record among African Americans, not associated with an Axis power, was far better. Indeed, according to historian Maurice Isserman, although the party "limited its struggle for black rights to those areas that it believed benefited the war effort," the Communists were the most outspoken group pushing the CIO to fight for equal employment. The party denounced white supremacists and a "pro-Nazi conspiracy" in June 1943 after one of the century's worst race riots broke out in Detroit. When Harlem erupted five weeks later, the *Daily Worker* blamed inadequate housing, unemployment, and discrimination. Browder announced that African Americans had made the transition from oppressed nation deserving self-determination to a national minority that had chosen integration.[30]

There was one concern more immediate than winning World War II, however: protecting Communist parties from government infiltration. William Donovan, director of the Office of Strategic Services (OSS, the ancestor to the Central Intelligence Agency) offered to place reliable veterans of the Spanish civil war at the disposal of British intelligence for diversionary work behind enemy lines. Although the CPUSA agreed to the proposal, from Moscow Georgi Dimitrov vetoed the idea. He considered it a "political mistake" that would "give the services a chance to penetrate the American and other Communist parties." Eugene Dennis notified Dimitrov that Browder and other top cadres accepted his decision.[31]

The party's public efforts did not hurt the CPUSA among the working class and, in fact, brought prodigious gains. Although many liberals and intellectuals continued to regard the party contemptuously, enrollment began climbing. Even Wendell Willkie aided the Communists. The government had stripped California organizer William Schneiderman, an immigrant, of his citizenship. Willkie successfully argued his Supreme Court appeal in 1943. Influence within New York's American Labor party grew. Its Vito Marcantonio became the CP's strongest Congressional supporter.

Browder received gestures of unprecedented acceptance during 1942 and 1943. Three times he visited Under Secretary of State Sumner Welles in Washington to discuss foreign policy. The two corresponded frequently. The exchanges began when Browder attacked what he understood to be America's priorities in China. During World War II the USSR sought mediation in the long civil war between Communists and nationalists so both armies could resist Japanese invaders. Accordingly, Browder pressed for an American commitment to a truce. In an October 4, 1942, *Daily Worker* article he accused unnamed State Department reactionaries of urging nationalist Generalissimo Chiang Kai-shek to withhold one million troops from the Japanese front to battle the Communists. This freed Japanese units to attack Americans in the South Pacific.

Two days later Welles denied the allegations and invited Browder to his Washington office to receive the facts. Certain that no American Communist had ever attained such an audience, Browder barely contained his delight in dashing to the capital. On October 12 he and Minor conferred with Welles and Roosevelt's administrative assistant Lauchlin Currie, who had just come back from China. Welles convinced Browder that his fears were groundless; the United States sought to merge all Chinese forces. Welles gave him a prepared memorandum to quote in correcting his misstatements. It declared that Washington had discouraged strife as China struggled against the armed invader. No indigenous armies could engage the Japanese immediately because of supply problems, but it promised action soon. It also denied Browder's accusation of anti-Marxist crusading. It concluded by urging solidarity in Asia and America. World War II ended a State Department policy of nonintervention in Chinese affairs. Browder would later tell a Congressional committee that "from 1942 to 1946 there was no occasion for the Communists to press for a change of relations with that nation."[32]

After leaving Welles's office, Browder, more than satisfied, respectfully withdrew his earlier charges. On the *Daily Worker*'s front page he announced, "What I had thought of as a heavy door that needed pushing open proved to be but a curtain of lack of information." The Communists ballyhooed the meeting, believing that it provided previously undreamed of recognition and respect. An FBI informer reported Browder's saying the conference would lead eventually to CPUSA representation among governmental circles. Over the next six months Browder and Welles exchanged letters. On April 2 and May 21, 1943, Browder visited him again. They discussed French Communists who were still being held in North Africa, Puerto Rico's problems, and Browder's unsuccessful bid to obtain permission to visit Latin Marxists in Mexico.[33]

The talks did more to enhance Browder's already abundant self-esteem than any events since 1933. He felt vindicated by history. Freed by the president himself, he now believed that he had become a recognized national figure. Although the CP considered the conferences spectacular and expected the government to seek its continued advice on important issues, Roosevelt regarded them as a sop that repaid wartime debts. The meetings cost even less than anticipated because the mainstream press ignored them.[34] The following year Secretary of State Cordell Hull replaced Welles, and his successor made no attempt to reestablish contact.

Browder found his unprecedented success intoxicating. Gil Green later noted that the General Secretary now felt he could state his own feelings more openly and disagree with other Communists more freely. His escalating sense of self-importance permitted credulity to creep in also, with predictable results. Shortly after he left prison, mutual friends introduced him to Josephine Truslow Adams. A pudgy middle-aged artist, Adams belonged to the Daughters of the American Revolution and possessed a famous family name. She had championed Communist causes from the Spanish civil war through the Citizens Committee to Free Earl Browder. Historian Joseph Lash described her as having a pleasant, vivid personality "with flashes of imaginative brilliance that sometimes shaded into hallucination." In an engaging manner she told colorful tales punctuated by digressions and generous laughter at her own wit.[35]

Back in 1941 Adams had become a minor CP cause célèbre. Testifying before the House Judiciary Committee, she spoke against a bill that would legalize wiretapping. She also contended that her defense of Communists' civil liberties had prompted someone to bug her office and residential telephones. Two weeks later Swarthmore College, where she had been teaching art since 1934, refused to renew her contract. As she struggled unsuccessfully to keep her position, Esther Lape, a friend who also knew Eleanor Roosevelt, hired her to do a flower painting. Lape gave it to the First Lady. Adams met Mrs. Roosevelt in April when she visited Swarthmore.[36]

Soon Adams shipped another painting and began deluging Mrs. Roosevelt with lengthy letters. A largely one-sided correspondence continued throughout the war years. In December 1941 Adams, now a fixture on the Free Browder Committee, made a plea for a presidential pardon. She received a short, noncommittal reply. In April 1942 she wrote again, attempting to arrange an audience for organization head Elizabeth Gurley Flynn. Roosevelt replied that Flynn carried "no weight" because she was a Communist. Adams, however, would not drop the issue. She penned yet another missive, now requesting that a non-Marxist discuss the Browder issue with the First Lady. Adams's note promised not to raise the question again. Roosevelt did not respond, but in May her husband commuted Browder's sentence.[37]

Adams suffered from severe psychiatric problems. An FBI agent described her "emotional and intellectual state of unbalance." Significantly, however, the bureau ignored the agent's judgment and accepted information from her until March 1954. Adams began claiming presidential audiences during 1942 or 1943, but her only White House visit had occurred in 1939, with a lobbying organization. Beyond doubt she made a convincing fraud. She astounded Lape at the verisimilitude of one yarn. Adams had told her how "Franklin" had greeted her from his desk when she entered the room. The expression was exactly what he might have said to someone who knew him. Lape wondered how Adams had learned enough to fabricate such a characteristic greeting.[38] The erratic Adams was not patently psychotic during World War II, although she would spend her final years in a mental hospital.

On July 4, 1942, Adams met Browder at a CPUSA Independence Day shindig. She contended that she had helped negotiate his release. He made no judgment, but allowed her to become a "frequent family visitor." Her next adventure hooked him. Late that autumn anti–New Deal columnist Westbrook Pegler published a letter from a Philadelphia area army tank worker blaming slow production on alleged featherbedding and other union practices. On December 4 Adams wrote an alarmist account to Eleanor Roosevelt charging that Pegler's source was an open Nazi. Adams asked her to facilitate an investigation. The president contacted FBI Director J. Edgar Hoover, who found no evidence and so informed Mrs. Roosevelt on January 6, 1943. Hoping to close the matter, she sent Adams a copy two days later. Using it, over time Adams convinced Browder that she enjoyed an intimate White House relationship.[39]

By summer Browder, still ecstatic over the Welles conferences, had come to consider himself a State Department advisor. He felt that a controversial figure of his stature might want more discreet communications avenues. Indeed, he had once told Welles that he could not think of anyone better suited to inform the president of his concerns.[40] Now however, he believed he had found a direct Oval Office pipeline.

Meanwhile in Europe events were making the USSR look ever more heroic. In March 1943 alone German submarines sank more than one million tons of U.S. shipping, double the rate shipyards could produce in a similar period. Building manpower and materiel in Britain had become far more difficult than imagined. The Western Allies decided to postpone the cross-channel invasion for another year. Instead, in July they attacked Sicily, a move Stalin considered a duplicitous diversion. Italian Fascists, fearing invasion, overthrew Mussolini and sued for peace. Immediately the German army rushed in, rescuing the imprisoned dictator and setting up a puppet state. Instead of an easy avenue, the Italian campaign brought protracted war. By contrast on the eastern front a crucial turning point occurred. Heretofore Nazi troops had won the important summer battles, and the Soviets had taken the winter ones. In July 1943, however, the Russians defeated the invaders at Kursk-Orel and begin a slow but relentless drive to the Polish border. Without a true western front, the USSR had nevertheless started down the road to victory.

Josephine Adams filled her letters to Eleanor Roosevelt with Browder's views, activities, and newspaper clippings. She also provided savory political gossip. She repeated his contention that Red-baiting Republican presidential nominee Thomas Dewey had earlier cut deals for tacit CPUSA support when he ran for district attorney and governor in New York. Furthermore, one of Dewey's campaign advisors, Carl Byoir, had reportedly written Axis propaganda. By early 1944 the First Lady recognized that Adams obviously intended the missives for her husband. At least three times she revealed that they went to FDR's desk. The president had "some secretary" cull them for information because Browder knew left-wing circles intimately and the CPUSA obviously served the war effort by cooling the ghettos and preventing strikes.[41]

From the beginning Adams brandished the First Lady's letters. Browder, aware that Communist ministers had sat in prewar European cabinets, in time became convinced. Then Adams raised the stakes, contending that she visited the president in Washington and at Hyde Park. She asked whether Browder wanted to "transmit" his views through her. Foolishly, he began meeting her regularly, providing information he believed the White House should have. As Harvey Klehr has shown, periodically Adams would "reappear with Roosevelt's supposed answers, comments and requests." Somehow Adams made the ludicrous charade seem convincing. Browder displayed unprecedented gullibility. He refused to believe she possessed enough political sophistication to hold "up her end" by inventing FDR's responses.[42] Two minor coincidences concerning his wife's legal case "proved" Adams's veracity to Browder.

Indeed, he clung to his illusion tenaciously. Gil Green reported that Browder thought he was "definitely influencing national policy." Using the idiom of the day, Browder later gloated: "One of the reasons why I was able to keep such a steady course" during 1943 and the early part of 1944 was "because I had this girl visiting me every week [proud chuckle]. I knew what was in Roosevelt's mind!"[43] Browder's fatuous acceptance of an imposter's lies demonstrated a major judgmental weakness. It called into question his fitness to continue leading the CPUSA. Yet surprisingly, the whole shabby episode had little effect on his decision making. Only once, in 1943, did it influence a specific action. Adams told him the president wanted to reduce the role of minor parties in the following year's national elections. Browder promised that the CPUSA would support the planned merger of Minnesota's Democrats and Farmer-Laborites. Unification occurred smoothly in early 1944 without Communist obstruction.

Adams's greatest impact concerned self-deception. Illusion inflated Browder's ego further and fed his growing sense of personal destiny. Certainly her intrigues made a less profound impact than meeting with Welles. Adams appeared, however, at a crucial point in Browder's life, offering matchless confirmation of his import just as he had begun to believe himself capable of greatness. Browder became convinced that he could deliver Communism from its ideological wilderness by reconciling it with American political and cultural realities. He did not deem a moderate Communist party an oxymoron; he sought the type of success Italy's CP would achieve after World War II. Adams, not unlike a flim-flam artist, could hoodwink Browder because he wanted desperately to believe her claims.

His final wartime endeavor concerned armed forces' treatment of party members, now eager volunteers. By January 1943 thousands had joined the military. Despite their zeal, the party members received frosty welcomes. Since 1940 official army policy had assigned fascists, Communists, and enemy aliens to locations far from any battle front. By design or accident the services permitted unit commanders flexibility for a time. In 1942, however, the War Department ordered heads of outfits scheduled for overseas duty to identify such potentially subversive elements for transfer to remote stateside labor battalions. Military authorities kept Communist GIs under careful scrutiny. That July one suggested a rationale for such actions publicly. Army Air Corps Lieutenant Colonel G. E. Strong told a Detroit area union meeting not to trust Communists because Russia had "deserted the Allies in the last war" and might do so again.[44]

In a long letter to the president, Browder called Strong's remarks discriminatory and objected vigorously to segregating CPUSA members among the nation's adversaries. In February 1943 he labeled the detention centers "polite substitutes for concentration camps" and predicted a Red-baiting United States would have great trouble building realistic alliances with the far more powerful European and Asian Communist movements. Soon Browder ventilated his continued discontent in the *New York Herald Tribune:* strictly speaking it was illegal for a CP member to draw his army pay. Practically all appropriations required that "none of the money" could compensate Communists for their services. To civil libertarians Browder also complained of other military mistreatment: isolating Russian immigrants, mandating surveillance of National Maritime Union members, censoring literature, and "busting" transferred men to the rank of private. A national petition protest drive realized scant success, however.[45]

Browder's complaints attracted the mainstream media. Columnist Drew Pearson and *PM* magazine presented human interest stories, and several liberal Congress members asked the War Department to investigate. The publicity and growing manpower needs brought a de facto policy reversal in February 1944. By December the military finally issued an explicit prohibition against anti-Communist discrimination.[46]

Browder's post-prison successes, real and imagined, had given him enormous aplomb. Now he approached the crossroads of his career. The Allies were going to win World War II, and the CPUSA would share victory's fruits. How exactly could he finally legitimatize domestic Communism fully? Could he do for his party what Samuel Gompers had done for crafts unionism?

## BROWDERISM GERMINATING

On May 15, 1943, without warning, the Comintern voted to disband. A Moscow press release recalled specifically and favorably the CPUSA's 1940 withdrawal to avoid Voorhis Act penalties. Two weeks later Stalin, desperate for a genuine second front and eager to remove obstacles to East–West harmony, applauded the Comintern decision, as if he had not ordered it. The move took Browder and other Americans by surprise. It should not have. Stalin's 1937 and 1938 purges had decimated the organization and its affiliates, the Communist Youth International, Trade Union International, and International Labor Relief Committee. Exiled Communists from many Eastern European countries had perished for allegedly being too friendly to fascism. Their replacement with puppet regimes had reduced the national CPs' popularity, and of course the Nazi–Soviet pact had discredited them all the more.

The Comintern's death fed Browder's swollen self-image. In practice the war already afforded him a measure of autonomy; he had not seen Moscow since 1938. Now he began to consider himself a sovereign national Communist leader. Certainly self-interest pushed his independence claims. Yet a close friend insisted that Browder "never ceased to believe" that dissolution truly allowed local Communist parties to "work out their own destinies" freely.[47] The USSR did nothing to discourage Browder's notion.

In late November 1943 Roosevelt, Churchill, and Stalin first met in the Soviet embassy's large walled garden in Teheran, Iran. Talking harmoniously over state dinners for seventy-two hours, they set a May 1, 1944, date for invading Western Europe and agreed to execute Nazi leaders. They guaranteed accord by postponing divisive issues and published an optimistic but deliberately vague declaration, pledging cooperation during the forthcoming peace that would banish war for many generations.

Browder took the communiqué literally, and it emboldened him dramatically. In fact, the following weeks constituted a critical juncture in his thinking. Now, he concluded, his role resembled that of Communist partisan leaders in occupied Europe's underground. As an independent Marxist chief, he felt duty-bound to apply the forthcoming East–West détente to domestic politics. Henceforth he lost all sense of proportion, abandoning even the pretense of modesty. Before 1944 careful circumspection had always tempered his personal ambition. Now, however, ego raged beyond control. Believing himself freed from Moscow's tutelage, he expounded what he considered his greatest contribution to the

CPUSA's ideology, the Teheran Thesis, although he possessed neither philosophical insight nor economics training. In the process he was determined to show Foster and any other intraparty critics that they were trifling with a Marxist of world stature. They would have to pay him even greater obeisance in the future.

Between December 1943 and April 1944 a sweeping sense of elation engulfed Browder. Displaying more energy than perception, he wrote three major documents concerning Teheran: a speech delivered at Bridgeport, Connecticut, on December 12; a protracted opening report given to the CPUSA's National Committee meeting on January 7; and a book-length elaboration that the party published in late April.[48] The usually ruminative Browder did little actual reasoning on the matter. His only real thought was based on two assumptions, one valid and the other fallacious. Accurately he termed Teheran a military guarantee for Hitlerism's elimination. Then he inferred, erroneously, that it signified an overall agreement by the Big Three on the postwar world's shape. His logical mind assumed that Stalin, Roosevelt, and Churchill simply must have agreed on long-term goals. The untidy reality was that they had not.

In December at Bridgeport Browder began hailing Teheran extravagantly, calling it the "greatest, most important turning point in all history." At last the capitalist democracies had accepted the USSR "as a permanent member of the family of nations." Now the Allies could banish the scourge of war for decades to come. Indeed, postwar unity had become "the only hope" for continuing "civilization in our time." Offering positions unusual for a Communist, Browder announced that the American people were so "ill-prepared for socialism" that to propose it would only weaken the progressive camp and benefit reactionaries. Therefore, the CPUSA would not challenge the existing economic system.[49]

Displaying his proclivity for overstatement, he declared that "class divisions or political groupings have no significance now." He even sanctioned using the term "free enterprise," although he noted that it merely meant "freedom of capital to concentrate and centralize itself in ever larger units." He insisted that the CPUSA wanted to make capitalism work, placing the fewest possible burdens on the people. This required removing fears of a postwar Socialist revolution. To reassure plutocrats, Browder took his rhetoric to a silly extreme, offering to clasp J. P. Morgan's hand if he would "go down the line" for "this coalition." Recklessly Browder predicted that anyone standing against it would "be driven out of American public life."[50]

Having obtained business's attention, he appealed to its more enlightened leaders, asking them to accept government regulation of its antisocial tendencies. Placing undue faith in their vision and selflessness, Browder warned that radicals' "undifferentiated hostility" drove "intelligent capitalists back into the arms of their most reactionary fellows" and united them against all progress. Such remarks left him sounding like the most conservative New Dealers.[51]

Browder realized that national unity required prosperity. Therefore, to him Teheran also meant a new economic program. Mobilization had created "a special market," expanding the U.S. economy to twice that of 1932. He cited a national income figure of $188 billion for 1943. Then he focused on the "$85 to 90 billion" of military orders therein. Society's greatest task was to find a peacetime substitute. To complicate matters further, the war had multiplied capital investment instead of destroying it, as in other lands. His solution lay in expanding foreign markets geometrically and doubling the domestic wage earner's purchasing power. He insisted that his blueprint represented the only possible alternative to another Great Depression. Immediately he became a prisoner of his own logic.[52]

Browder envisioned creating American heavy industry markets through massive foreign aid. Other observers shared his concern. Their proposals, however, ranged between $4 billion and $6 billion per year. By contrast he sought a 1,000-percent foreign market increase to $40 billion for highway building and agricultural and industrial development. He noted that financing would require nothing more than that spent during the war and, instead of bringing destruction, would "start great new streams of wealth flowing." Self-liquidating in a generation, the projects would be "the best investments the capitalist class ever made."[53]

Specifically Browder proposed creating "great semigovernmental development corporations" to send $6 billion of British and American capital annually to Latin America, Africa, and Europe; $20 billion to Asia; and $2 billion to the USSR. Anticipating conservatives' objections, he called laissez-faire dogma the greatest obstacle to foreign markets. He insisted the federal government find them if private capital failed to do so. He admitted that conventional economic wisdom considered his program impossible, thereby proving all hope for full employment an illusion. That, he argued, doomed the United States to a "catastrophic economic crisis." If an explosion of class conflict occurred, he did not want Communists blamed. The responsibility would lie instead with people who "did not know how to use their power in the national interest and yielded instead to greed."[54] Clearly he never foresaw the possibility of Cold War prosperity.

The grand design also pictured vastly expanded internal consumption. Workers' buying power limited the domestic market. Yet the wealthy owned $77 billion more than they could spend. No longer did traditional investment avenues provide a likely remedy because the war had expanded plant capacity exponentially. Browder insisted that the nation invest in production's human factor, "through large-scale government policies of educational, health and general environmental improvement." He sought to double the annual purchasing power of those who spent their entire income on life's necessities. Even this would not suffice for long because the United States "would receive imports to pay for expanded exports."[55] Here too, he eschewed systematic argumentation and contended hurriedly that without his program the economic system would collapse.

Beyond doubt Browder's Teheran projections represented delirious wishful thinking. A. B. Magil characterized accurately the hope that capital and labor, "the lion and the lamb," would cooperate cheerfully after the war as Browder's "most utopian contribution."[56] Browder's proposal to elevate working-class living standards had relevance to postwar domestic needs, but in 1944 leaders everywhere ignored it. Browder's problem went beyond ideological flabbiness. The Teheran program shows that after Atlanta Penitentiary Browder could no longer be content as an American imitator of Stalin. He had to become a respected international Marxist theoretician in his own right, though of course he would never defy the Soviet dictator.

Teheran created a severe crisis within the CPUSA's highest circles. Foster resisted vehemently and made a counterproposal at a Political Committee meeting. He considered voicing his unhappiness publicly, but several colleagues dissuaded him. Sam Darcy, now district organizer for eastern Pennsylvania, shared Foster's misgivings. Rank and filers did not learn of the strife for another fifteen months, however. The leadership's outward harmony inspired election-year efforts.

Veteran George Charney recalled that members felt "a sense of traversing the frontiers of 'creative Marxism.' " Foreign Communists had long considered Americans "incapable of abstract theoretical work." Labeling the accusation "rubbish," he retorted, "One of the aspects that endeared Browder to us was that he made some effort to stimulate speculative thinking in the party."[57] Charney made a good point. Indeed, weaknesses in the Teheran Thesis did not obscure totally the significance and positive character of what Browder was attempting. He was offering a flexibility that provided a refreshing contrast to the mechanical quality of much of earlier Marxism-Leninism. In 1944 Browder shepherded his comrades to one final leap away from orthodoxy.

Everywhere since the Nazi–Soviet pact the CPUSA had encountered mistrust. Thoughtful political observers expected the Communists to perform new somersaults at war's end. For months Browder had sought a dramatic gesture to relieve liberals' suspicions. Recent events suggested a precedent. In October 1943, YCL delegates had voted to disband and form a broader organization without party ties. Previously auxiliary organizations had come and gone, but Communists had considered the YCL family. With the Comintern dissolved, however, a new sense of adventure filled the air.[58]

Browder delivered his greatest bombshell at the party's National Committee meeting of January 7 to 9, 1944, putting his personal stamp upon the Communist movement as no American had done before or would do again. The group usually held closed sessions, but Browder packed it with a claque of two hundred to stifle Foster and Darcy's dissent. Party discipline required the illusion of monolithic unity to outsiders. Browder addressed the gathering twice, presenting a startling, if somewhat rambling, message. Communist "classics" offered no solutions for the day's problems. To justify his own innovations, he contended that Marxism had a fertile nature that did not tie followers' hands when new situations arose. It constituted a theory of deeds, not of "don'ts."[59]

Then came the shocker. Browder expected the CPUSA to remain in long-term alliance with larger forces, and Leninism had not foreseen peaceful coexistence. Therefore, organizational adaptation had become necessary. Americans regarded minor parties as sects, withdrawn from practical politics. The Democrats and Republicans, who stood for "nothing in particular," were really coalitions of regional interests, sheltering diverse political tendencies. Buttressed by the primary system, they formed a stone wall that had bruised even Theodore Roosevelt and Robert La Follette's heads.[60]

Consequently Communists could have greater effect as a nonpartisan left-wing pressure group. Browder suggested the rubric "Communist Political Association" (CPA). Thenceforth members would sail uncharted waters, advancing programs through the existing party structure. Exultantly, he proclaimed that the movement was "standing on its own feet for the first time." Without seeking the USSR's prior approval, he steamrolled his colleagues into accepting the most fundamental transmutation in American Communism's history.[61]

Browder marketed his new arrangement masterfully. Needing a spokesperson on January 9 to advertise over a nationwide radio hookup, he ruthlessly chose Foster. Most members learned of it on the tenth in the *Daily Worker.* That night nearly twenty thousand dazed Communists somnambulated into Madison Square Garden for the annual Lenin memorial meeting. Browder, explaining his coexistence plan, received only polite applause instead of his accustomed thunderous ovations. Worse yet, halfway through his address spectators began a steady trickle toward the exits. Prepared for the tepid response, Browder had National Committee members fan out across the city to endorse his proposals at branch conclaves the next evening. He also laid the groundwork for a massive partywide reeducation program that spring.

Browder's proposals led his followers yet another tactical step away from the vanguard party concept. Critics later damned his actions as dissolving the movement, a gross slander. He himself had denounced any liquidation in an earlier radio address. The Communists remained a coherent force near the peak of their strength. Joseph Starobin has noted that the CPUSA was "already penetrating and influencing a wide variety of existing institutions." Browder wanted to give it greater legitimacy and flexibility "to do more of the same." When capitalist newspapers across the land denounced the transformation, he cited their words as proof of its soundness.[62]

The Communist leader made a convincing salesman. A. B. Magil recalled that no one within the CPUSA had suggested such a change publicly or privately. Yet once Browder announced it, only Foster and Darcy objected. Early 1944 proved a thrilling time, not unlike the Popular Front's pristine days a decade earlier. Now "Browder could work with impunity," as Bella Dodd put it, to make Communism acceptable. Steve Nelson likened the approach to "a breath of fresh air." Joyously, workers modernized the dingy Twelfth Street Manhattan headquarters. That May the organization formally changed its name and adopted American terminology. "Brother" and "sister" replaced "comrade" as the form of address, making Communists sound like Quakers or members of a Roman Catholic religious order. Although Browder considered the Teheran Thesis his greatest contribution, in reality the CPA could have marked Browderism at its best. Whereas Teheran was unduly optimistic, the association seemed eminently reasonable. It embodied his understanding that Communists always had played primarily an educational role where capitalist values reigned most triumphantly. Browder faced the reality that Marxists could merely enlighten for decades to come. To Junius Scales and other cadres, the revolution now seemed "perhaps a lifetime or two away." The CPA's creation showed Browder eager to make his followers a legitimized part of U.S. political dialogue.[63]

By January 1944 Browder felt a great sense of self-regard. He believed that his CPA, despite retaining the CPUSA's authoritarian structure, could lead to greater influence on the two-party system. Always a fourth-rate Marxist, he would have brought American Communism to its single, most sensible point had he received anything significant in return from the administration. Because the government did not value Communist contributions enough to offer any concessions, however, Browder's policies in practice represented a capitulation. Beyond doubt his innovations anticipated Titoism, polycentrism, Eurocommunism, perestroika, and other attempts to accommodate Marxism to democracy. Yet parallels are easily overdrawn. Like Yugoslavia's Marshal Tito, Browder considered himself independent of Moscow. Yet he commanded neither troops nor a national police force. Browderism resembled polycentrism and Eurocommunism but never defied the Soviet Union or advanced any blueprint for the transition to socialism. Instead, it simply postponed the entire question to the distant future. Browderism sought to reform Communism, as did perestroika and subsequent Soviet permutations before the USSR's collapse. All failed. Actually such comparisons have limitations because Browderism represented an idiosyncratic adjustment to American conditions before the Cold War's outbreak.

January 1944 brought Browder's happiest year but raised fundamental questions. Why did he not foresee the Cold War? One did not require sagacity to notice that the United States and USSR did not share strategic interests beyond Hitler's defeat. Why did Foster, who rarely prognosticated (as Edward Johanningsmeier has shown), put forth a more accurate assessment of the postwar international situation? How would Foster's dissent affect party leadership?

# NINE

■

## *Browderism in Full Bloom (1944–1945)*

Dimitri Volkogónóv has written that Joseph Stalin began to believe in his own infallibility as early as 1920, at age forty.[1] Earl Browder, who fancied himself a miniature copy, did not reach this point until the first months of 1944, when he was fifty-two. Like Stalin, he had once deliberately cultivated the myth of his own modesty. Now, however, he began courting openly the most obsequious praise. Why did Browder's conceit shade into egomania? How would his personal creation, the CPA, differ from the CPUSA? How would non-Soviet CPs view the transformation? Did the new organizational form help or hurt the American left during 1944 and 1945?

The year 1944 began auspiciously for the Allies and for liberals at home. Since the breakthrough at Kursk-Orel in July 1943, Soviet forces had marched steadily westward. During the winter they recaptured land that approximated their 1939 borders. The United States and Great Britain continued stockpiling for the invasion of Western Europe. Franklin D. Roosevelt awaited its arrival more anxiously than perhaps anyone outside Russia, aware that earlier postponements had strained the Grand Alliance severely. The president was also planning for a 1944 election victory. Trying to energize labor, African Americans, and youth without alienating the segregationist South, he came up with two broad programs: an economic bill of rights and a GI bill. He did not expect to achieve the former immediately, but it made a good campaign platform and could set the postwar domestic policy agenda. It included employment remunerative enough to provide workers adequate food, clothing, and shelter; decent family housing; and improved social security and educational programs. A "normal" economy would be something closer to World War II's full employment than to the previous decade's Great Depression. Veterans could expect benefits sooner because even anti–New Deal Congress members were eager to express the nation's gratitude. Ex-military personnel would receive generous monthly allowances while they looked for work, preferred hiring status, and loans for purchasing small businesses, farms, and homes. Education got an enormous boost through programs that paid veterans full tuition plus cash for study at any level from elementary through professional schools.

Not all signs called for optimism, however. FDR seemed a very old sixty. Plagued by chronic illnesses, he often felt fatigued and had difficulty walking with the heavy braces he had used for twenty years. In late 1943 he contracted influenza and still had not recovered by the following March. A general physical examination at Bethesda Naval Hospital near Washington revealed that he suffered from hypertension and a serious coronary condition, although one not unusual for a sedentary, overweight male his age. Following physicians' orders the president shed some pounds, began sleeping more, and generally looked well until after the November 1944 elections.

## ATTACKED IN NEW YORK

Earl Browder spent 1944 idolized by his followers. His party was, for the moment, largely Jewish and female. He had always enjoyed disproportionate support among such Communists. As Joseph Starobin has noted, by late 1944 half the CPA's branch officers were women, most new to the position. The party had once looked askance at nonproletarian females. Indeed, as late as March 1936 writer Irene Leslie had, in the pages of the *Communist*, denounced the wives of the very wealthy as "parasites upon parasites" and directed efforts toward women toilers and working-class wives. During the Popular Front years, however, the CPUSA had generally appealed to organizations that did not challenge women's traditional role in mid-twentieth-century society. Indeed, Elsa Dixler has observed the irony that Communists who had once "faulted the feminists for their middle class orientation and lack of class analysis" now reached out more to bourgeois than proletarian women.[2] The party was also in favor of creating an Israeli state after the war.

Although Browder's vanity had become too conspicuous to ignore, his triumphs had boosted American Communism incomparably and had brought greater accommodation to hard-working cadres. No other left-wing party could rival the CP in size. The Socialists' splits had trivialized them, and the Smith Act had criminalized the Trotskyists. Except for intellectuals, most Americans had forgiven or chosen to forget the Nazi-

Soviet pact. Within the CIO Communists retained disproportionate power, and they had penetrated the Democratic party's left wing. Accordingly few members dared to question Browder's right to display smugness.[3]

William Z. Foster and Samuel Darcy, however, had no emotional commitment to the Teheran Thesis and saw it as their opportunity to wound Browder gravely. Darcy likened its foreign markets proposal to Kaiser William II's promise to raise German living standards by acquiring an overseas empire before World War I. In the week following Browder's National Committee meeting speeches on January 7–9, Darcy drove the primitive, congested roads from his Philadelphia home to Foster's cluttered Bronx apartment several times. There they discussed theoretical weaknesses in the Browder program and prepared a palaverous seven-thousand-word letter over Foster's signature alone, so neither could be accused of factionalism. According to Darcy, Foster suffered grave doubts and could not sleep "even with pills" because he feared another breakdown and, of course, expulsion. Courageously, however, he faced the danger and addressed the document to all twenty-eight National Committee members, although Browder allowed only his closest associates to read it. It did not question the CPUSA's uncritical support for the Roosevelt administration, its anti-strike policy, or even the scheduled transformation to the CPA. Instead, it ripped Browder's Teheran Thesis. Under it American imperialism had virtually disappeared, "hardly a trace of the class struggle" remained, and socialism played "practically no role whatever." Foster predicted that reconstruction problems, especially in Europe, would "be gigantic and, in the long run, insoluble under capitalism." He augured an economic collapse "worse than that of 1929."[4]

Foster ridiculed Browder's sanguine view of big business. The concept of enlightened capitalism was a "dangerous illusion." Entrepreneurs would not support the Teheran decisions, much less lead the nation in carrying them out. Finance capital remained "strong, greedy and aggressive," and only social democrats believed it otherwise. Browder's understanding of domestic politics, Foster charged, was equally muddled. Unfairly he accused Browder of giving FDR inadequate support; then he denounced the consequences thereof. Foster cautioned that a 1944 Republican victory would give "monopoly capital a much freer hand"; encourage reaction everywhere; weaken the United Nations' foundations and "sow the seeds for a World War III." Domestically, the GOP would respond to a new economic crisis with "fragmentary, skinflint programs of government work relief."[5]

Foster also accused Browder of lacking vision. Browder implied that the no-strike policy would continue after the Axis surrender. His curt dismissal of socialism was reprehensible. Although it would not be an immediate postwar issue, it comprised "the only final solution" for America's problems.[6] Foster's letter hardly constituted the ringing defense of orthodox Marxism-Leninism he would later insist it did. It nevertheless posed a stark alternative to Browder's optimistic prognostications. Equally significant, the message questioned Browder's leadership. Now for the first time since the 1939 Nazi–Soviet pact, Foster believed that his rival was vulnerable.

Browder considered Foster's missive the rankest insubordination. Determined to crush the opposition quickly, on February 8 he called a special, confidential conclave. Members included the entire Political Committee plus prominent figures sympathetic to Browder: the transport workers' Mike Quill, maritime union leader Blackie Myers, Ben Gold of the fur workers, and California CP head William Schneiderman. Aged CPUSA heroine "Mother" Bloor completed the group. Foster attempted to have his message read and debated. In a carefully orchestrated response, members rejected the motion. Then Browder magnanimously gave the choleric Foster the floor to add anything he wished to his communication. Pledging to keep his remarks brief, he launched a ten-thousand-word onslaught. Browder's national unity excluded "only the most outspoken, fascist-minded elements." His approach meant entering quicksand because it ignored American imperialism's role in sabotaging the Teheran agreement. Foster charged that domestic entrepreneurs would eschew cooperative planning and attempt to devour world markets while "German, Japanese and even French capital" lay prostrate. Not inaccurately he implied that the upbeat Browder was naive to expect employers to understand the wisdom of doubling workers' wages. Foster insisted that labor courted disaster when it assumed capitalists were farsighted.[7]

Political Committee members reacted swiftly and harshly. Morris Childs termed Foster's words "an insult" to every Communist. Robert Minor sought unqualified rejection of Foster's opinions. Gene Dennis accused him of factionalism. If Foster raised his viewpoints in public sessions, he might provide ammunition to the Trotskyists, New Republic, and the New York Times. To do so would destroy his prestige and usefulness to the party. Of the two score present, only Darcy supported Foster. Speaking from notes after difficulty getting the floor, he reminded listeners that the U.S. economy had never maintained full employment during peacetime and asked rhetorically what use the Communist party could have once it abandoned the working class.[8]

In the long run Foster proved a better prognosticator. His early career as a labor organizer gave him a more concrete appreciation of capitalism's coarser nature. Browder, a wishful thinker who had never led a strike, was more willing to believe that the government's wartime intervention into the workplace would remain benign and become permanent.

In 1944, however, most signs, foreign and domestic, seemed to reinforce Browder's quixotic views. At long last his opportunity to crush intraparty opposition had arrived. Figuratively seizing his antagonists by their throats, he wrung both men viciously. Darcy, not a hero to left-wing labor, could be treated especially roughly. His views, Browder intoned, had to be combatted, defeated, and eliminated. To attack Foster, however, required greater finesse. Up to the task, Browder described him as a rueful case. He was "terribly confused, tragically confused"; the world had "become too complex for him." Yet his name carried weight far beyond the CP's confines. His mistakes, if broadcast, would imply "a very serious split in the Communist movement" with opposition led by the party chairman. His opinions endangered the war effort, the working class, and the Teheran program. The CPUSA, Browder stressed ominously, was neither an amicable "debating society nor a friendly club." Rather, it constituted a political army struggling to conquer the world, and now Foster stood "between the troops and their objectives." Finally Browder, heretofore a lenient Stalin-era chief, issued an ultimatum. The party had no "wet nurses" for weak leaders. If Foster raised the question again he would become "merely one more unfortunate casualty" of a war that had had many.[9]

Facing annihilation, Foster retreated as he had done for more than nine years. He pledged to keep his dissent within the top committee. Quickly he received an opportunity to promote unity's facade publicly. On March 9 a short, precise *New York World Telegram* article revealed Foster and Browder's "bitter clash." The FBI, which had bugged CPUSA headquarters earlier, listened to the entire February 8 battle and briefed President Roosevelt. Along the way someone leaked the story to reporter Nelson Frank. Swallowing his pride, Foster ridiculed Frank's "florid imagination" and reaffirmed publicly his loyalty to Browder.[10]

Over the next two months Foster changed only his tactics. In early March he handed Browder a suspicious letter postmarked Rochester, New York. Dated February 29 and addressed to "Comrade Foster" from "a soldier on furlough," it echoed his rhetoric. Browder, infuriated, labeled the letter "Trotskyite" and reminded him that "anyone capable of writing it" deserved no place among party ranks.[11] About the same time Foster presented a single-page synopsis of his views and asked Browder to transmit it to Georgi Dimitrov, director of the now-defunct Comintern. Foster's message concluded with a promise to accept his "advice." Browder cabled it, in code, to the USSR. By more secure avenues he also sent the complete Foster letter and transcripts of the January and February proceedings. The action followed a longtime Comintern practice of documenting divisions voluminously. Years later, when asked point-blank why he had forsaken his prized autonomy, Browder sheepishly blamed "habit." In truth he cared more about self-interest than independence. Browder always took all the foreign help he could get.[12]

In fact Browder's pioneering did not impress Moscow. In a letter to V. M. Molotov, Dimitrov proposed sending Browder a cipher saying:

I have received Foster's telegram. I ask that you let me know who among the leading Party comrades supports his views. I am somewhat troubled by the new theoretical, political, and tactical positions being developed by you. Are you not going too far in accommodating the changing international situation, even going as far as the denial of the theory and practice of the class struggle and the necessity for the working class to have its own independent political party? I ask you to think again about all this and communicate your thoughts. Confirm receipt of this communication.[13]

Indeed, there is as yet no direct evidence that Molotov or Dimitrov ever approved Browder's innovations, although the latter's secretary, Maria Aerova, personally endorsed the actions in written reports dated September 2 and November 9.[14] Boldly Browder had ventured where no CP leader had ever gone before, and he had presented the Soviets with a fait accompli. Now he told Foster that he had Dimitrov's support and not to press his differences. Foster, knowing not to disagree with Dimitrov— Comintern or no Comintern—backed down, thoroughly cowed.

Earlier the CPUSA had released Darcy, at his own request, from his duties as Pennsylvania district organizer. Browder made at least three attempts to buy him off. He sent Johnny Williamson, a friend from the youth movement, and offered six months' paid vacation in Florida if Darcy would rethink his views. Through Williamson Darcy sent back an obscene reply. Then Joe Starobin, an acquaintance, brought a similar message. Finally coworker Herb Benjamin simply stated that Browder wanted to talk. Darcy felt a deep contempt for what he regarded as Browder's lack of principle. To him Eugene Debs had been an eagle; "Browder was a road bird."[15] In April the chief's patience finally expired, and he ordered Darcy expelled. At his meanest, he chose Foster to preside over the ostracism. That the latter did not protest showed that he and Browder were cut from similar cloth.

## A CORONATION, NOT A DISSOLUTION

Browder's contributions appeared against a backdrop of wartime optimism. Earlier the beat-Germany-first strategy had allowed widespread Japanese conquests in Asia and the Pacific. In 1942 those conquests stretched from Burma in the west to the Aleutian Islands of Attu and Kiska in the east. They extended southwest to the Netherlands' East Indies; Japanese aircraft bombed points as distant as Dutch Harbor, Alaska, and Port Darwin, Australia. In May the expansion had been checked in the Coral Sea, and the battle of Midway in June had brought Japan's first naval defeat since the late nineteenth century. Thereafter the Allies had made offensives in the Pacific ahead of schedule. Japanese planning had envisioned enemy attacks on every single island taken and a fierce defense that would prolong the war for years. Eventually the American public would tire of the sacrifice necessary and negotiate a compromise peace, leaving Asian conquests untouched. Instead, the Allies had adopted the unexpected policy of island hopping, seizing certain strategic outposts through the Central Pacific to the Philippines. From there they prepared an invasion of Japan itself. The process left more than 100,000 Japanese troops stranded, dug in to protect points totally bypassed. By late 1943 American forces began the drive to take bases from which to bomb the home islands. In mid-June U.S. forces hit Saipan, only fifteen hundred miles from the Philippines. That same month the Western Allies opened the long-delayed second European front, invading the French coast at Normandy on the sixth. Simultaneously the Russians marched toward Warsaw, Poland, preventing Hitler from shifting his troops westward.

Browder's creativity occurred within a larger atmosphere of intellectual deradicalization, a reaction to Soviet Communism. America's wartime economy, providing virtually full employment, seemed anything but irrational. Some ex-leftist economists turned away from redistributionist schemes and the goal of equality. Instead, they became fascinated with Keynesianism, increased production, and industrial growth. Unconsciously, they helped sow the seeds of manic postwar consumption, a new popular opiate. Sociologists began to redefine the concept of class to reflect the worker's self-image. Anxieties about status helped explain the conservatism of a growing middle class and why the downwardly mobile would not bring themselves to identify with the proletariat, as Marx had expected. The nation was on its way toward the 1950s society Seymour Martin Lipset and Max Lerner would describe as dominated by economic individualism and social conformity—and suspicious of mass movements. Trotskyist James Burnham was already predicting a new ruling elite of technicians and administrators, whose skills would control the means of production. Thus in 1944 Browder was not the only thinker on the left impressed with America's seemingly exceptional nature.[16]

Many rank-and-file workers, however, were moving in the opposite direction. Historian Nelson Lichtenstein has noted that as military victory approached, home front inequities became less bearable. Increasing numbers of proletarians, though not disloyal, began to "ignore the no-strike pledge and lay down their tools. In 1944 and 1945 more strikes took place and more workers stopped work than in any similar period since 1919, and well over half the wildcat strikers were CIO union members." Their job actions did not hinder the overall war effort but had "explosive social implications." They threatened the "myth of a common national interest and undivided purpose." Many CIO unionists considered stopping them to be imperative, as part of their commitment to the Roosevelt government. Communists used their considerable labor movement influence to press for cross-class unity, still believing it necessary for total victory over fascism.[17]

Browder's initiatives found foreign, non-Soviet support in 1944. French Communist figure André Marty, who represented his party in Charles de Gaulle's Algiers-based exile government, hailed Browder's actions. A former Comintern executive who had spent much of the war as a refugee in Moscow, presumably Marty knew Kremlin wishes. He called the Teheran Thesis speech beautiful and promised to publish it in the PCF's theoretical journal. Italian CP chief Palmiro Togliatti also saluted the policies.[18] Browder now prepared the greatest spectacle in American Communism's history, a meticulously orchestrated convention to formalize the CPUSA's transformation and celebrate his own political sagaciousness.

Supporters and detractors alike called the new structure a liquidation of the party. Indeed, Browder employed the misleading term himself. At May's extravaganza he proclaimed the CPUSA "dissolved."[19] Actually this declaration did more to display his penchant for overstatement than to describe the CPA's nature. Browder's rhetoric shows that he remained a public relations person who never lost his abiding passion for melodramatic ceremony. In truth the change spotlighted a process of altering the CP's tactics and reflected his individual priorities noticeably.

The CPA comprised a public recognition of his movement's evolving role since the mid-1930s. World War II had permitted, indeed required, renewed creativity. Lacking regular Russian contact forced the CPUSA to find its own path. The Comintern's dissolution had in Browder's mind made the absence of Soviet guidance permanent, except when he needed support against a domestic leadership rival. Now he considered the CPUSA a maturing member of the world family of Communist parties. Sensing grandiose destiny, he proclaimed his organization ready to stand without its foreign crutch.[20]

The new arrangement met a second exigency for Browder. It culminated the lengthy Americanization process. He considered the CPA's creation a logical redefinition of Communism's role for decades to come. With the vanguard party concept passé and the Comintern liquidated, Browder felt free to adapt his movement to American conditions. He knew that the single-member district system for choosing Congresspersons and the winner-take-all nature of most local balloting marginalized minor parties. Indeed, the Communists' only important electoral successes had occurred in New York City, which possessed proportional representation, an American political rarity. Browder envisioned the CPA making a significant educational contribution to the national legislative dialogue. He knew that small, vigorous, politically astute coteries enjoy success every day in city halls, state houses, and on Capitol Hill. They thrive not as parties, but as pressure groups seeking specific, limited objectives. A lobbying organization seemed a reasonable extension of Browder's favorite Democratic Front tactic: conspiring behind the scenes with leaders of the Minnesota Farmer-Labor party and other reformist groups. He believed that such machinations yielded quicker results than proselytizing. That the new organizational apparatus, created by edict, underscored the CPUSA's lack of inner democracy did not bother him at all. Special interest groups are often run in a top-down manner; Browder's business and apparatchik backgrounds taught him to prize tight organizational control above rank-and-file discussion. Nor was the CPA concept inherently flawed. Using similar methods, the National Rifle Association and American Medical Association would soon exert power in public life far beyond their numbers. Years later Browder likened the CPA's role to that of the Americans for Democratic Action.[21]

The conversion also fulfilled needs more personal. An adjustment to U.S. society as much as to the nation's politics, it mirrored Browder's salesmanship skills. He discarded the old party packaging, with its wrinkled Russian paper, for a shiny new red, white, and blue container. His egotism also showed. Believing himself a covert presidential advisor, he sought to take his skills to the halls of Congress. The reorganization guaranteed his rightful place in history. Already he imagined that his Teheran Thesis had made him a world-class Marxist theoretician. Now he had finally perfected the correct blend of innovation and continuity. A coronation ceremony would formalize his role as Communism's American redeemer. The personal metamorphosis had become complete: the modest Popular Front innovator of 1936 had by 1944 become drunk with success.

In a larger sense, however, the CPA was not as unique as Browder tried to make it seem. Parties across Central America, the Caribbean, and down South America's west coast became Browderite, many dropping "Communist" from their official titles. The Colombian, Jamaican, Puerto Rican, Cuban—even the Greek—parties reorganized under his influence. Soon Cuban Marxist chief Blas Roca would announce that his followers, heretofore Yankee imperialism's militant opponents, would begin cooperating with U.S. and British investors. He would cite Browder as inspiring the line change. All this manifested the tendency of most of the world's Communist movements to follow policies and tactics similar to Browder's. They participated in extremely broad popular fronts during World War II, seeming to melt into the political woodwork of their respective countries. Georgi Dimitrov told Soviet foreign minister Molotov that Communist parties in all occupied countries "must immediately begin organizing a united national front" to "establish contacts with all the forces opposed to Germany, not taking into consideration their political orientation." Outside Nazi Europe national fronts needed to emphasize democracy and "independence from Hitler's oppression."[22] Even in the USSR Stalin began to resurrect the memory of czars who were great nationalists. Browder excelled at taking other people's ideas to unprecedented extremes. Despite all his innovation, he observed international trends more than he cared to admit. His greatest mistake lay not in "dissolving" the party but in allowing his zeal for respectability to prompt him into making all the concessions to the Roosevelt administration early, obtaining nothing in return.

In 1944 and 1945 Browder lacked time to develop the CPA further. It might have taken on a muckraking nature as Ralph Nader's groups would do several decades later. That the American left's largest organization had a foreign, undemocratic orientation and a careerist leader did not help domestic radicalism. Still, Browder's CPA offered a reasonable avenue to influence when it could deliver votes at election time.

Browder considered the Manhattan convention that formalized his proposed changes the greatest in American Communism's history. At every turn it stressed harmony with the CPUSA's progressive past. The four-day spectacle opened at the ballroom of the Riverside Plaza Hotel on May 20, not coincidentally Browder's birthday. At his insistence Foster called the gathering to order on a large dais flanked by U.S. flags. Behind him stood an immense blown-up photograph of Stalin, Roosevelt, and Churchill seated together at Teheran. A red-bordered service banner with a blue star and another of gold covered the speaker's stand. These symbols denoted a relative on military duty and one killed in action, respectively. Also displayed prominently was the figure 9,250. It represented the number of Communists on armed forces' leave. Foster told the 402 delegates and alternates that over a quarter century's existence the party had made numerous structural modifications but always led "every fight for freedom." Thereupon he urged his audience to support forthcoming proposals.[23]

Then Browder ascended to the stage. All rose to sing "Happy Birthday to You" and the old labor tune "We Shall Not Be Moved," which for some time had included the refrain "Browder is our leader." Next he offered his resolution converting the CPUSA into the CPA and a ninety-minute keynote address emphasizing patriotic and cautionary themes. He boasted of eighty thousand followers, a figure that approached 1939's numbers. The Communists were making up for their Nazi–Soviet pact losses. Then at great length Browder explained how recent international events guaranteed the inevitable Allied victory and supported his Teheran Thesis. Finally he warned that the United States possessed "tremendous productive powers" but would "surely choke to death" on surplus goods unless the "national gullet of consumption" grew dramatically. If capitalism could not accomplish this, the people would find "another system."[24]

Two days of pageantry followed. Four Communist government and labor officials from Chile, Colombia, and Peru brought messages of antifascist solidarity. Also appearing were domestic trade union leaders who had never admitted publicly to CPUSA membership. They included CIO figures "Blackie" Myers, a seaman; the auto workers' Nat Ganley; William Sentner of the electricians; the furniture workers' Max Perlow;

and furrier Ben Gold. Louis Weinstock of the AFL's painters' union also attended.

Browder placed on stage twenty-five of the movement's eldest veterans, including the august "Mother" Bloor, to represent American Communism's two and one-half decades. He greeted the throng as "Ladies and Gentlemen," which immediately replaced "Comrades" as the standard salutation. He insisted that the new association supported socialism's ultimate goal, but would fight lesser short-term battles. The CPA's constitution defined it as a nonparty working-class organization advancing the traditions of "Washington, Jefferson, Paine, Jackson, and Lincoln" under modern society's conditions. It welcomed all citizens at least eighteen years old, but rejected anyone seeking to subvert American democratic institutions.

Hierarchical alterations, cosmetic and substantive, appeared. Browder's title went from general secretary to president, and the Political Committee became the National Board. The Communists expanded their twenty-eight-person National Committee to forty. They retained all previous members and added trade unionists Ganley, Weinstock, the municipal employees' Bella Dodd, and Dave Davis of the electrical workers. Not accidentally, the CPA's creation dealt Foster yet another humiliation. The new constitution abolished his chairman's position, replacing it with eleven vice-presidents. Although Foster headed the group, clearly Browder had begun easing him toward triviality.

The convention's final rally took place on May 23 in Madison Square Garden and marked the most jubilant evening of Browder's career. His speech detailed again plans for expanding postwar markets and linked Americans prejudiced against Jews, Catholics, African Americans, and Marxists to "agents of Hitler," history's most vicious racist.[25] Browder's reception contrasted vividly to the lukewarm response given to his January 10 proposals. Now his words elicited repeated waves of applause and audience demonstrations. Afterward he summarized the week's highlights to a nationwide NBC radio audience. Never had he felt so much like a mainstream figure.

Although the CPA inherited the CPUSA's authoritarian structure and fealty to Moscow, members proved eager to follow Browder in 1944. Some irresolution existed, and a few grumblings were voiced, but after Darcy's expulsion no one raised any challenges. Only Foster attempted to alter Browder's path in any way. Early in 1945 he sought to publish an article that tried to reconcile his and Browder's positions. Browder killed the manuscript, however, covering it with spiteful comments.[26] The highest ranking CPA cadres, who knew of Foster's agony, followed Browder compliantly. His innovations brought dividends in 1944. That spring's recruiting drive attracted twenty-four thousand new members, many of whom were workers in basic industries. Communists began to play more visible roles in communities outside New York City.

## BACKING FDR OPENLY

The publicity-loving Browder featured prominently in 1944's national elections, a campaign Franklin D. Roosevelt characterized as the dirtiest he had ever experienced. The CPA supported him and backed liberal candidates. Republicans whispered about FDR's health, vilified his advisors, complained about the federal bureaucracy's growth, and charged that Communists would dominate in a fourth term.

Since 1942 the administration had been in retreat. That year's midterm elections, the Roosevelt era's low point, had seen dramatic Republican successes. The war had displaced large numbers of soldiers and defense industry workers. Resulting poor turnout allowed conservatives to capitalize on shortages, rationing, and inflation. The GOP won forty-seven new House seats, added nine Senators, and elected Thomas E. Dewey governor of New York. Southern Democrats joined Republicans to battle FDR over tax policy and his plan to give soldiers federal ballots in 1944. In June 1943 they enacted the Smith-Connolly bill, which attempted to restrict the right to strike and limit union financial support to political campaigns. In this atmosphere HUAC breathed new life, sniffing the ground for radicals.[27]

The Communists would have supported Roosevelt against any Republican. They sought, however, a rerun of 1940's contest with Wendell Willkie, who had since written a best-selling pro-Soviet book, *One World*, and who as an attorney had won the Supreme Court denaturalization case for William Schneiderman. Dewey's nomination fed Communist fears that GOP leaders would seek a compromise peace with Germany. CPA members resolved to surpass all previous campaign efforts; forty thousand of them lived in crucial New York. They did not press for Vice-President Henry A. Wallace's renomination, however. The most outspoken liberal in the administration, he advocated an end to European colonialism and supported international economic policies that he half-seriously characterized as ensuring "everybody in the world" the "privilege of drinking a quart of milk a day."[28] The clear choice of the CIO leadership and of Eleanor Roosevelt, Wallace had made all the right enemies: the segregationist South, big city Democratic machine bosses, and the oil industry. In a demonstration of shallow thinking, Browder feared a Republican victory so much that he championed conservative alternatives to Wallace. After Missouri Senator Harry S. Truman became FDR's new running mate, Browder helped lead forces selling him to the left. The Communist leader paid no heed to Roosevelt's mortality, dismissing rumors as pro-Nazi propaganda. Browder and his followers could not have prevented the switch. By helping put Truman a heartbeat away from the presidency, however, they inadvertently hastened the Cold War.

The 1944 election saw organized labor come of age politically. Although the Smith-Connolly Act prohibited union contributions to federal campaigns, CIO leaders Sidney Hillman and Philip Murray knew that wartime enrollment gains had increased workers' potential influence vastly. They also understood that the government's newly acquired authority to regulate wages, prices, and working conditions could constitute a boon or a disaster. Accordingly, they learned how to circumvent the 1943 statute and put together the CIO's Political Action Committee (PAC) to support prolabor candidates. PAC solicited $1 contributions from union members and channeled the money into a special political fund. Hillman and Murray also created a National Citizens Political Action Committee (NCPAC) to rally sympathizers outside the movement.

Hillman possessed great ability and abundant energy. He also knew where to look for help. As CIO organizer John L. Lewis had once done, he turned to the Communists for skilled, committed organizers to staff national and regional offices. They provided tireless, fervent cadres. PAC made a monumental effort in 1944. It urged union members to attend Democratic rallies, distributed eighty-five million pieces of campaign literature, and taught canvassers gentle persuasion. It conducted mammoth registration drives and urged southern workers to pay the poll tax. On election day PAC volunteers telephoned union members, provided baby-sitters, and transported voters to the polls. Its $7 million provided 20 percent of the Democrats' total campaign fund. PAC's efforts proved especially effective in Michigan.

Despite the campaign's meanness, the president exercised his legendary humanitarianism in a manner directly affecting the Browder family. He told Attorney General Francis Biddle that continued efforts to deport Raissa were "getting into the silly stage." Quickly, she received a new Immigration Appeals Board hearing. The body permitted her voluntary departure to Canada. There she applied for an American visa and reentered legally, to the FBI's chagrin.[29]

Long before voters cast their November ballots, the actions of HUAC Chairman Martin Dies foreshadowed the Republican campaign. Outraged that organized labor had targeted HUAC members for defeat, he accused PAC of violating the Smith-Connolly Act. Dies also contended that government officials who cooperated with labor were transgressing the Hatch Act, which banned activism by federal employees. With a straight face he even warned the full House, "Sidney Hillman will soon succeed Earl Browder as head of the Communists in the United States." Fearing a crushing primary election defeat that spring, Dies took his brand of patriotism back to his Jasper, Texas, ranch and retired.[30]

Roosevelt began serious campaigning in September, two months after American forces had conquered Saipan in the Mariana Islands, bringing down the cabinet of Japanese Premier Hideki Tojo. The president's effervescent opening speech twitted Republicans for resisting New Deal legislation and soldier voting. He attacked the Smith-Connolly Act and sardonically denied GOP charges that he had spent tax dollars on his pet dog Fala. The Fala speech energized the campaign and swelled Democratic registration lists. More significant, it goaded Dewey and the Republicans into making wild accusations, which in turn stimulated voter interest even further.

Heretofore the Republicans had floundered about, searching for issues. They could not deny that the president was leading the nation to military victory. Their sudden support for Social Security and the National Labor Relations Act had brought accusations that they were running a "me-too" campaign. They had even tried mudslinging, spreading outrageous stories about Harry Hopkins's private life and defaming Jewish Americans who held high governmental office. Yet nothing had stirred much public enthusiasm. Immediately after the Fala speech, leading GOP figures began exaggerating ties between the president, PAC and the Communists. Roosevelt, a master politician, immediately repudiated all CPA support but, as historian Leon Friedman has noted, "made no effort to have the Communists ousted from the various PAC operations they controlled." Becoming desperate, Dewey contended that Browder had been pardoned in time to organize FDR's fourth campaign.[31]

In such a contentious atmosphere Browder could hardly have maintained a low profile for long. Just before Dewey's attack, the conservative-dominated House Special Committee on Campaign Expenditures invited Browder to answer questions. He responded readily, although his 1939 Dies Committee appearance had sent him to prison. Actually, the summons exhilarated him. Knowing the full extent of Communist influence, he welcomed an opportunity to minimize it publicly. Deep within he had always craved Washington's spotlight despite attendant risks. His fascination with danger had returned after he left prison. Indeed, as a secret presidential advisor, he felt practically invincible; this time no one would dare attempt to indict him. Fearlessly he presented himself and, in his most reassuring tones, attempted to placate the legislators. "No one," he insisted, who was not first and last "a good American" could be "a good Communist in this country." The party's transmutation merely signified its pragmatic response to a changing world. Browder envisioned no resurrection of the CPUSA because it would signify that "the present policy had been defeated." He announced that the CPA's National Committee had decided against raising campaign funds in 1944.[32]

After an hour, two Republican solons began demanding that Browder name CPA members in other organizations, a practice Senator Joseph McCarthy would make infamous six years later. Representative Clarence J. Brown of Ohio, a newspaper publisher and gentleman farmer, sought high-ranking Communists among NCPAC. Illinois Congressman Ralph E. Church, a viscerally anti-Marxist financial expert who saw subversives in every New Deal agency, pressed Browder even more vigorously.

When Browder refused to identify anyone, the proceedings turned ugly. Brown and Church bombarded him with quotations from his 1940 book, the *Second Imperialist War*. Browder's words of the Nazi–Soviet pact era embarrassed him, but he responded with pro-administration passages from later writings. Church, an emotional right-wing mainstay until his dramatic sudden death during a Committee session on March 21, 1950, quickly adopted an ad hominem tone. He grilled Browder over his sentence commutation. When Church inquired tauntingly whether he had done his patriotic duty during World War I, Browder answered calmly, "I served in prison."[33]

Visibly ruffled, Church began demanding that Browder list all the aliases he had used two decades earlier. Browder's casual suggestion to check the public record only incensed his tormenter more. Vehemently Church kept enjoining him to supply names. At one point Browder mildly threw up his hands, responding, "Mr. Congressman, I feel myself as only a spectator and not a witness." Then Pennsylvania Democrat John W. Murphy reminded his colleagues that "as a matter of law" they could only impeach Browder's credibility by proving "guilt of moral turpitude." Finally, Chairman Clinton P. Anderson, a New Mexico Democrat, ruled that Church was merely trying to stigmatize Browder, and the hearing soon ended. Browder departed galvanized, having displayed confidence and composure while his inquisitors behaved churlishly.[34]

Roosevelt defeated Dewey by 432 electoral votes to 99. Although *Newsweek*, the *New York Times*, and the president himself in a pool with his aides had predicted a significantly closer contest, the results nonetheless constituted FDR's smallest winning margin. The major industrial states of Michigan and New York keyed the victory, and in both, according to historian Maurice Isserman, "PAC probably had made the difference." By aiding the president's reelection the Communists convinced themselves that they were, as Joseph Starobin noted, "sophisticated and desirable political allies," but they received no tangible compensation.[35]

One day after the president's victory, Browder proclaimed the impending United Nations triumph over fascism. Until the spring of 1945 the Communists gave the Roosevelt administration unnecessarily strong support. When radical unionist Harry Bridges offered a postwar no-strike pledge, the CPA leadership seemed to second it. The association even endorsed the national service concept, although left-wing labor leaders opposed it vehemently. Basking in respectability's arresting glow, Browder believed that the Communists would long remain a "small, if important sector of the great patriotic coalition."[36] The CPA seemed vindicated by history. Now Browder's cult of personality reached its apex, buoyed by the added name recognition the Republicans' irresponsible charges had brought. Browder allowed his ego to grow even more.

GOP politicians were not the only source of spectacular charges. A few years later Elizabeth Bentley, an ex-NKVD agent, claimed that she and her lover Yasha had discussed espionage with Browder over lunch at his home once during this era. Although he had severed his sister's ties with the secret police in 1938 for safety reasons, Browder received diplomatic intelligence from Soviet agent Pierre Cot until the war ended. According to Bentley, Browder, looking weary and flabby but acting "so nice," agreed to help establish Washington contacts Yasha could not have found otherwise. In return Browder allegedly wanted to review all the nonmilitary data collected. He needed it to protect his precarious position from power-hungry rivals and had to convince Moscow he knew how to anticipate policy twists and turns. Obviously an advance look at intelligence going to the USSR would improve his calculations. Bentley contended that at this time the Russians did not know of the activity and disapproved when they found out. "They were against building up the personal power and prestige of any of their puppets like Earl, because this meant that sooner or later they might have difficulty controlling them." For the same reason they also "distinctly resented" his meetings with Sumner Welles.[37]

Before the USSR's collapse most historians ignored Bentley's charges. Her purported verbatim recollection of conversations, unaided by stenographic skills or recording devices, helped discredit her. Misjudgments in her account abounded; she believed the right-wing myth that Moscow had forced marriage to Raissa on Earl to keep him "in line." In addition, her unwarranted use of names led to successful litigation against her. Bentley's charges no longer seem totally ludicrous, however. The accusations about Browder have a ring of veracity where they concern his post-Atlanta personality: egocentric, curious, crafty, and reckless. Even his best friend, Philip Jaffe, acknowledged that Browder knew where to point people interested in Soviet espionage work.[38] The burden, of course, rests with Bentley, who even the FBI noted could not document her accusations. Until more Soviet archival material is released, the only possible conclusion lies in one of Browder's favorite devices: the Scottish verdict, "Not proven."

While yearning for still greater public influence, such as European CP heads enjoyed, Browder received his most flattering invitation. Shortly before former Republican presidential nominee Wendell Willkie's death on October 8, 1944, he asked Browder to visit his New York area home. A union leader, whose organization was one of Willkie's law clients, arranged the meeting. Browder leaped at the opportunity. He found his host cordial, "curious and friendly." Willkie voiced interest in Teheran and sought primarily to listen. The quickened Browder obliged, talking most of the evening.[39] He returned to his Yonkers apartment convinced he would soon be a celebrity.

## ASSAILED ABROAD

Lost in 1944's euphoria were signs that not all influential Communists overseas welcomed the innovations. An American liaison officer stationed in Yenan, China, sent *Amerasia* magazine publisher Jaffe a letter indicating that trouble awaited. Soon after Browder's Teheran book arrived there, Chinese Communist party members living at the U.S. Army Observer Section translated it. According to the correspondent, Mao Tse-tung told his Central Committee associates that it expressed a capitulation policy. Sanzo Nosaka, head of the Japanese CP who spent the war years in Yenan, agreed. Jaffe did not receive the communication until after more dramatic events had transpired, however.[40]

Browder expected the Chinese Communists' support, unaware that their conception of anticolonialism was far more militant than his. He wanted the United States to back China's "teeming millions" in their national liberation struggle. He asserted that Chiang's "antidemocratic, authoritarian" government was "based upon economic policies which cultivate landlordism, speculation, market monopoly, usury and all sorts of profit seeking not through expanding the economy but by parasitically preying upon" it.[41] Because the ever-logical Browder had excoriated Chiang's regime, he felt he deserved an endorsement from Mao.

Browder's swelling vanity also distorted his reasoning on China. Late in 1944 Communists in the United States published the first English translation of Mao's booklet, *China's New Democracy*. It contained a glowing introduction, which Browder had written, complete with added vituperations against Chiang. Browder, considering himself equal to other national Communist party leaders, presumed that Mao would return the favor by praising his Teheran Thesis.[42]

Mao did send a courteous acknowledgment, dated April 3, 1945. It congratulated him and stated that East Asian revolutionaries knew his work well. Although the message concluded on a unity note, it nevertheless avoided any mention of Teheran. Despite the letter's perfunctory nature and careful wording, Browder believed that he enjoyed Mao's backing. Although Browder considered his grandiose Teheran scheme a practical avenue for reaching anticolonial goals, it never appealed to Mao. Although he would not gain control of China until 1949, Mao already expected victory. When a delegation from the Chinese Communist party visited New York in early 1945 Browder offered uninspiring words. He told members if they wanted help, they must allow American capitalists to make a profit.[43]

If Mao's politeness fooled Browder, no one could have mistaken the open opposition the English and Australian Communists gave him. British CP leader Harry Pollitt privately decried Browder's views and refused to publish his book in the United Kingdom. Pollitt did not inform the rank and filers, however, to preserve wartime unity. The Australians' general secretary, L. L. Sharkey, displayed less concern over appearances and none about Browder's vulnerability. He printed an article contrasting the British party's programs and those of the CPA. It attacked American innovations, declaring that enemies misrepresented Browder's statements to imply that Communists everywhere were renouncing socialism. Browder responded immodestly in a letter in March 1945. It professed "intense interest" in all foreign Communists' progress then criticized the Australians' program as "insufficiently based on Teheran."[44] Browder expected comrades overseas to study his contributions and master his teachings. He had always considered himself capable of handling any challenge. Now, at last, his ambition had eclipsed his abilities, and he began to display an ugly hubris. Believing he had earned personal greatness, he was determined to achieve it and receive worldwide recognition.

Browder's postwar projections also angered two prominent Italian refugees living in the United States, Giuseppe Berti and Ambrogio Donini. The former had been second in command to Italian Communist party (PCI) leader Palmiro Togliatti during their prewar exile in France. He published the theoretical journal *Stato Operaio* first in Paris, then in New York. American Communists paid him a small subsidy for his work. Donini, destined to become one of Italy's Communist senators in the postwar years and an ambassador to Poland, edited New York's Italian-language newspaper *L'Unita Del Popolo*. The two men represented themselves as PCI leaders, built a separate organization, and refused to subordinate themselves to the CPUSA. Shortly after 1944's transformation they and other exiled countrymen wrote Browder, seeking to present their views to the CPA leadership. He ignored their letter. By October they decided to acquaint the PCI's Central Committee with the American program and their objections.[45]

Had Browder been less obsessed with his personal role in the international Communist movement and domestic politics, he might have anticipated the Grand Alliance's collapse. Germany's defeat approached, but Browder devoted neither time nor attention to the sandy soil on which he had constructed his Teheran Thesis. East–West collaboration had been, from its inception, unnatural. Fascism's singular threat provided unity's only common ground. In the United States, reactionaries had accepted wartime cooperation grudgingly, praising Russian armies but maintaining a virulent domestic anti-Communism. Once victory had removed the incubus of a Hitler-dominated world, prolonged accord became unlikely at best. Browder failed to anticipate the Cold War because he refused to engage in contingency planning. So immersed in persuading himself and others that Teheran could work, he never set an alternate strategy in case it did not. Heavy emotional investment had produced intellectual sloth.

In December 1944 the slaughter of Communist-led Greek resistance forces by British troops surprised and upset Browder. He, of course, did not know that Churchill and Stalin had already divided southeastern Europe that October. The British prime minister, who sought Eastern Mediterranean naval facilities and investment opportunities, reestablished Greece's old monarchy and ruling classes. In return, the Soviets set up Communist states in Hungary, Rumania, and Bulgaria.[46]

Browder would have had difficulty accepting the agreement even if he had known of it. The history buff in him understood that spheres of influence had a long, inglorious record. His Teheran program provided a splendid opportunity to chart a different course. Having convinced himself that humankind's salvation depended on it, he thought that world leaders should also understand.

CPA cadres, however, quickly noticed the Soviet press's silence on the Greek events. Puzzled, Browder offered a measured response. Through public speeches and *Daily Worker* articles, he criticized Churchill for making a "first serious departure" from Teheran. Browder urged new U.S. Secretary of State Edward Stettinius, Jr., to tell Churchill to forsake all imperial dreams on the Continent. At the same time, however, he cautioned Americans that distrust of Britain would only hinder postwar unity.[47]

As the New Year opened, Browder looked for signs that supported his projections. He found them overseas and at home. In February 1945 British and Soviet labor leaders created the World Federation of Trade Unions, seemingly a benchmark in international proletarian solidarity. That same month at the Black Sea resort of Yalta the Big Three met to celebrate Allied harmony. Anglo-American troops stood west of the Rhine, while Russian armies, which had occupied Balkan territory in November, paused a mere one hundred miles east of Berlin. Postwar occupation zones would be built on wartime conquests of the respective forces. American military leaders, fearing a million added casualties, wanted Russian help against Japan. In return, Roosevelt agreed to Soviet expansion in East Asia: possession of the Kurile Islands and Sakhalin, postwar influence in Korea, and warm-water ports from the Chinese in Manchuria. Establishment of the United Nations as a permanent organization and the disarmament and occupation of Germany completed the accord. Latent conflicts over the governments of Poland and other Eastern European nations were ignored in celebration of impending victory.

That month at home heads of the AFL, CIO, and U.S. Chamber of Commerce signed a charter pledging mutual recognition and respect. As a new era unfolded, Browder pondered. What greater glories awaited him in the postwar world of détente? Would the president give him a more public role in the New Deal coalition?

# TEN

■

## *Browderism Uprooted (1945–1973)*

The events of April 1945 altered the course of world politics. On the twelfth a cerebral hemorrhage killed Franklin D. Roosevelt. An unprepared but pugnacious Harry S. Truman ascended tó the presidency. On April 26 American and Soviet troops met at the Elbe River, rendering the forthcoming German surrender a formality. Adolf Hitler committed suicide on the thirtieth. Would these earthshaking occurrences disrupt the Grand Alliance? Earl Browder's shortwave radio picked up only static. Why did the Russians not send instructions to the greatest Marxist in the English-speaking world? He could only conclude that the silence signified no strategic changes. Germany's collapse, however, brought a plethora of contentious issues that divided the United States and the Soviet Union. The United States wanted a permanent international peacekeeping organization and markets in Eastern Europe and feared that the Red Army, the world's largest military force, might march to the Atlantic. The Russians sought their own sphere of influence, buffer states to help stall future invasions, and Western financial assistance.

### A SIGNAL FROM STALIN?

Browder found himself totally unprepared when a separate tremor struck. The April edition of the theoretical organ of the PCF, *Cahiers du Communisme*, published an article under the name of Jacques Duclos, its second highest figure, ripping Browder viciously. Of significance, the PCF was championing accommodationist tactics at the time. Its vituperation thereby placed Browderism outside even the era's most relaxed Communism.

The PCF would not have criticized another party publicly without Moscow's approval. More than half the tract quoted American documents. Some had circulated far and wide: Browder's Bridgeport speech;

his paperback *Teheran and America;* and the CPA's constitutional preamble and resolutions. Ominously, however, Duclos also cited *Communist* and *Daily Worker* articles from early 1944, published when he was hiding in a Paris suburb, the Communist press was illegal, and the Nazis still ruled France.

Only one organization could have provided such material: the Soviet news agency Tass. Most sinister, Duclos quoted Foster's January 20, 1944, National Committee letter and subsequent Political Committee debates, airing the Americans' intraparty division. The Soviets must have given Duclos these materials if in fact he wrote the article at all. Indeed, Philip Jaffe has argued that the inexact rendering indicated that the PCF had not used the original sources but instead "a re-translation from another language."[1] Browder believed it could only be Russian.

The article breached Communist discipline, and its references to Foster's objections revealed an unmistakable intent: to humiliate Browder before the entire world. He had tried to grow beyond Soviet puppet status, something Joseph Stalin did not welcome. The dictator could have sent precisely the same communication via private messenger, cable, or shortwave radio. The article portrayed Foster as Leninism's heroic American defender and Sam Darcy as its martyr, thereby wounding Browder's leadership critically. At minimum, the piece demanded a policy reversal. Unsubtly it suggested Browder's complete removal, calling him the CPA's "former secretary." To retain his position, he would have to grovel and abandon forever his illusions of international stature. Possibly, the writer envisioned a divided leadership resembling early Third Period arrangements.

Duclos's text issued sweeping judgments that attacked Browder directly. He had deformed the Teheran Declaration, a purely diplomatic document, into a postbellum blueprint for international labor–management cooperation. So doing constituted a "notorious revision of Marxism." Browder suppressed the class struggle and sowed "dangerous opportunist illusions" among workers. Duclos denied that capitalism and socialism had entered a period of coexistence and contended most Communist parties had rejected Browder's views.

The writer used problematic statements and incomplete evidence to denigrate Browder further. He excused intervening into CPA affairs by insisting that *Cahiers du Communisme* readers had asked for clarification of recent American events. This was an obvious lie; members of the PCF, France's largest single party, had little interest in the minuscule U.S. movement. He offered misleading figures to suggest that Browder's policies had cost the American Communists thirty-five thousand of their eighty thousand civilian members. Ignoring what Joseph Starobin has termed "important gains, particularly among industrial workers," Duclos astonished CPA leaders.[2]

He also employed a misleading analogy. He applauded former Vice-President Henry Wallace's antimonopoly statements and then declared that the PCF also sought national unity but would never ally with "the men of trusts." When Duclos penned these lines French business's collaboration with Hitler remained fresh in readers' memories. Certainly Browder's program offered little to combat corporate greed, but no one could argue that American capitalists as a class had betrayed the nation.[3] Dishonestly Duclos lambasted Browder for allegedly believing that the nationalization of monopolies could constitute a peaceful transition to socialism. Duclos then insisted in orthodox Marxist-Leninist fashion that socialism's achievement was "impossible without preliminary conquest of power."[4] That the PCF in its daily politics actually was behaving in an entirely nonrevolutionary manner while brandishing leftist rhetoric is significant. More crucial, however, is that Browder's Teheran projections had neither stressed nationalization nor discussed any ultimate socialist transformation. To Duclos, destroying Browderism had become more important than merely exposing its fallacies.

Browder's myopic view of the postwar era was not unique, however. Communists in many lands had offered similar estimates, making the Duclos denunciation all the more striking. If Browder were such a revisionist, then he was in good company. Rather, his greatest sin lay in "dissolving" the CPUSA. Indeed, the article even upbraided Foster for not resisting the change. Ranking cadre John Gates later wrote that Browder "had violated the one thing so sacred" no one else would touch: Lenin's concept of the Communist party as laid down in 1903.[5] Browder found this reproach especially painful. It decreed the renunciation of his most original and perceptive adaptation to U.S. conditions. Ultimately the ukase proved more than he could swallow. He had propounded and reiterated his new dogma so forcefully and frequently because it established his claim to international status. He had made too great an emotional investment to drop the phantasm completely. Circumstances, however, allowed him to use a psychological defense—denial. In 1939 he had received clarification of the last major line change directly. Now he concluded that the Duclos piece did not reflect Stalin's wishes. Uncertain exactly what it did connote, Browder determined to fight it.

In retrospect, the meaning seems self-evident. Philosophically, it argued that cooperation with liberals such as Henry Wallace was not the same as uncritical alliances with capitalists. Duclos sent a personal message as well. Moscow, speaking through the moderate PCF, declared that Browder had exaggerated enormously his independence and importance. He would never play a major role in the international movement. He would have to scrap his CPA, renounce his rosy Teheran projections, engage in self-criticism, and accept a reduced status at home. Former National Board member Gil Green later concluded that Browder was not the USSR's real target. Instead, the article was meant to chasten the Italian and French CPs. In 1945 each possessed "tremendous" prestige from fighting fascism, and each commanded more than one million followers. Green also contended that PCI chief Palmiro Togliatti opposed "Moscow's meddling" in CPA affairs as a "dangerous precedent."[6]

Duclos did not call specifically for Browder's excommunication, although many domestic cadres leaped to that conclusion. No denunciations of him appeared in the Soviet press. The PCF's subsequent cooperation with France's postwar government shows unmistakably that the edict, despite its strident rhetoric, did not denote a worldwide Communist return to revolutionary tactics.

The U.S. State Department, however, considered the tract a declaration of Cold War. Diplomatic historians echoed the interpretation, and Browder himself eventually came to share it.[7] The essay had been written while FDR was still alive and the USSR was creating Eastern European puppet governments. Stalin may have intended it as a signal of the damage he could do in the West if the United States interfered with his plans.

The feisty new U.S. president, Harry S. Truman, however, possessed neither Roosevelt's insight nor patience with Stalin's diplomatic intrigues. He and his tough-minded confidants believed that any Russian stubbornness meant that the Soviet tyrant was bent on conquest. The Duclos article appeared just as East–West relations had reached a new low point. Washington believed that it ordered Western Communist parties to adopt militant tactics, a not-illogical conclusion shared by William Z. Foster.

## THE FINAL CONFLICT

The Duclos piece encouraged Foster to release long-repressed anger, making any amicable settlement unlikely. Meanwhile, Browder clung to his fundamental belief that the Comintern's 1943 liquidation allowed national Communist party leaders to enjoy autonomy. He first realized that he faced a problem in April 1945 when the United Nations's founding convention met in San Francisco. Two PCF Political Committee members, labor leader Benoît Frachon and health minister François Billoux, belonged to the French delegation. They neglected to pay the protocol-conscious Browder a courtesy visit. Worse yet, Frachon, journeying through New York, met with a half-dozen left-wing figures, including the voluble Robert Thompson, an American Communist war hero who felt no need to quell controversy. Frachon then stopped in Washington and saw discontented Italian exiles Giuseppe Berti and Ambrogio Donini. Frachon revealed Foster's February 1944 dissent, enraging the two further. Immediately, they began plotting to destroy Browder.

The CPA chief remained euphoric even as the anti-Nazi coalition disintegrated. President Truman cut off lend-lease aid abruptly; ships already bound for the USSR turned around in mid-ocean. He hinted that the Soviets would receive no loans until they set up democratic governments in Eastern Europe. Browder, still touting his Teheran panacea, refused to believe that anything resembling a cold war could be possible. At worst the Grand Alliance might be disrupted temporarily. The threat of world chaos and a return to depression conditions in the United States, however, would reweld the partnership. Deeply concerned about disruptive foreign Communists in his land, nevertheless, Browder demanded to meet Frachon and Billoux before they left. In May they returned east, and the former took a copy of the Duclos article to Browder's Manhattan office. Browder sent it to the *Daily Worker*'s foreign desk; when the translation arrived, he found that he faced the crisis of his career.

In a long, acrimonious meeting, Frachon, who knew little about the United States, instructed Browder to imitate the PCF's actions: call a mass conference and demand entry into the national government. Frachon refused to see that the war had strengthened the United States enormously and had devastated all rivals. His childish views irritated Browder greatly. Billoux had asked Browder to hold their talk in Washington, where he had a busy diplomatic schedule. Accordingly, shortly thereafter the two, plus Foster and Eugene Dennis, huddled in a capital hotel room from early evening until dawn. Browder found Billoux congenial, serious, and responsible. Their interchange, however, proved even more distressing. Billoux revealed that PCF leaders had not discussed the Duclos essay at all; they had received it ready-made from Moscow. Browder moaned that he would be "cleaned out" of CPA leadership if he accepted Duclos's charges and asked why the PCF was interfering with

American Marxism. Billoux simply denied any such intention. Browder told him of his "indirect but personal" pipeline to the White House. Billoux responded that the PCF already knew "in a general way," so Browder concluded that the Russians did also. He never understood how silly the reference to Josephine Adams sounded now that Truman sat in the Oval Office.[8]

In Washington Foster resumed his vocal opposition. Over the years since his nervous breakdown his discontent with Browder's leadership had grown from annoyance and peevishness to strong anger. By now it had reached an obsessive level; Foster was determined to destroy his adversary. Dennis, previously the staunchest Browder loyalist, immediately became Foster's lieutenant and treated the Duclos article as holy writ. The three returned to New York and sat on the essay, quarreling over how to present it to the membership. Foster increased the pressure on May 16. He handed Browder a six-hundred-word message he sought to cable to Duclos. The proposed telegram would "accept the basic content, if not all" of his criticisms. At the same time it declared that the organization's "main line" had been correct. Foster detailed CPA errors and stated disingenuously that the 1944 transformation had sparked considerable Political Committee opposition. He announced that the American and French Communists were now traveling similar paths. Browder refused to send the cable.[9]

The capitalist press shattered the Marxist leaders' public silence. On May 21 *New York World-Telegram* reporter Nelson Frank phoned Sam Darcy and revealed that he had the Duclos article. He summarized its contents and asked for a response. Momentarily stunned, Darcy said little. Instead, he fixated on his sudden opportunity to return and help run the Communist movement. Quickly terminating the conversation, he dialed Foster, who had not contacted him since presiding over his expulsion. Surprised, Foster feigned interest and claimed that he had wondered how to get in touch. Darcy ignored the insincerity and urged the CPA to publish the Duclos piece before opponents did.[10] The next day, the *World-Telegram* featured it prominently.

That night a badly traumatized National Board began an emergency meeting that lasted nearly twenty-four hours. A majority wanted to pay lip service to Duclos's criticisms, admit their mistakes, yet continue under Browder's leadership. The prewar Browder might have ridden out the storm. More modest and pliable then, he had always skillfully trimmed his sails and steered his Americanized Communism within the international movement's narrow tideway, hoisting his own colors all the while.

The 1945 line change proved different, however. He was emotionally unable to accept criticism of his Teheran Thesis, which, friend Philip Jaffe noted, Browder considered "his greatest achievement as a Marxist."[11]

Straining to preserve his authority, Browder proposed publishing the tract in the *Daily Worker.* As CPA president and the newspaper's chief editor, he would preface it with a forward he had already written. It reminded readers that the CPUSA had in 1940 left the Comintern, which itself was dissolved three years later. Grasping at straws, Browder asserted the press constituted the only channel of discussion remaining. Unwilling to acknowledge his familiarity with Soviet intelligence channels or his shortwave link to Dimitrov, he argued that for two years no medium for international Communist discussion had existed. Inevitably, therefore, different approaches emerged. Lying, Browder insisted that he had known that the war's end would require review of all CPA policies. The Duclos article could now "provide a starting point," but the organization remained autonomous and would conduct its own business. Upcoming discussions would be "free in the fullest sense," and the *Daily Worker* would report faithfully the details of the National Board's next deliberations on June 2. Next he revealed Foster's May 16 telegram. Browder pronounced the PCF's line valid only for French Communists. Finally he offered a single concession. Hereafter he would present views "different from" his past opinions.[12]

Now, however, for the first time since 1939, he faced stiff challenges. Dennis attacked his Teheran Thesis as non-Marxist. Gil Green apologized for his previous, vigorous support of the program. Jumping in also was new board member Robert Thompson, a hardliner never among Browder's admirers. He suggested that the CPA look to Foster for future leadership. Bobbing and weaving, Browder conceded that the Duclos article had convinced a "decided majority" that they had "made fundamental errors" in following his innovations. Although he did not feel prepared to make a formal presentation, he took the floor when Dennis and Thompson had finished speaking. Browder's "extemporaneous" remarks filled nearly twenty-three stenogram pages.[13]

Displaying no signs of contrition, he admitted only minor errors. The transformation to the CPA had not inspired European Communist parties emerging from Nazi domination. He had underemphasized the postwar proletarian struggle. He did not guard adequately against oversimplifications of his Teheran Thesis. Browder conceded nothing substantive, however. He accused his colleagues of "making decisions blindly." His program had been necessary for wartime unity; inaccurately, he contended that it was "in no way a repudiation or revision" of Marxism. Defensively, he lectured that he had always believed "long-term peace" could exist "on the single condition" that the East–West alliance survived. If his associates rejected all class collaboration, logically they could not continue supporting the Labor-Management Charter. Turning to recent foreign criticism, he argued that American Communism could not be successful merely by reflecting the European movement. In a final, weary effort to sound regnant yet flexible, Browder offered one of his bromides, "You will find me proceeding very circumspectly, to make sure that the correction of one error is not the production of three new ones."[14]

Throughout the speech Foster and Green heckled him. Foster, however, chastened by a decade of humiliation, avoided a personal showdown; he had seen Browder adjust to international line changes before. Cautiously he opined that "everybody in this room" wanted "Earl to continue" as CPA head if he would just mend his ways. In a rare flash of petulance, Browder retorted he was not at all concerned with his future. As he stumbled, the power-hungry Foster felt a surge of energy and shot back instantly, "But we are, Earl." Browder, aware his command was slipping away, regained his composure somewhat. Sounding like a schoolmaster plagued by unruly pupils, he announced that he would never become "a political zombie" and asked sarcastically if he had to explain the term. The pedestrian Dennis, truly puzzled, broke in, "Yes, what is it?" In a hectoring tone Browder answered that it was "a modern myth about a dead person who has been raised by some magical process and walks around under the control of another mind."[15]

Browder remained convinced that he was so important that he could debate Duclos or whoever wrote the essay. Immodestly, he compared himself with Chinese CP giant Chou En-lai and boasted of addressing indigenous radical needs. Never in 1945 did Browder consider seriously that the message might have come from Stalin. Confident he still enjoyed Soviet support because of his shortwave's silence, Browder vowed not to form a faction. Yet, the antagonism that he and Foster shared mitigated against compromise and cemented his intransigence. Browder could never again work beside Foster; serving under him once more was out of the question. By now the two Communists hated each other more than they did the capitalists.

Although Browder's sway had weakened dramatically, several colleagues spoke on his behalf. Elizabeth Gurley Flynn, the country's leading active woman Communist, responded to Thompson's virtual nomination of Foster, declaring that "nothing would be so disastrous as

William Z. Foster and Browder in New York,
March 23, 1945, just before the CPUSA leadership crisis.
(Courtesy of *People's Weekly World.* Used by permission.)

having Earl Browder's leadership called into question." She also ripped
Green and John Williamson for acquiescing to Duclos's charges so rapidly. Roy Hudson, a left-wing labor leader, declared that Browder was still
chief. Hasty changes might disorient trade union cadres. New York City
Councilman Benjamin J. Davis, Jr., the best known African American

Communist, asserted that Browder had saved the CPUSA from neglecting black problems during the early war years.[16]

The members reached a rough consensus. They would publish the Duclos message with Browder's introduction and quash Foster's telegram. A National Committee meeting would be called after a few weeks' discussion. Thus Browder retained control precariously. Had he been willing to do proper penance, he still could have continued as leader. The board, recognizing the seriousness of the crisis nevertheless, created a five-person subcommittee to draft a response to Duclos. The subcommittee included Browder, Foster, Dennis, Williamson, and "Comrade J," a trade unionist whose name was too prominent to entrust to the stenogram.

Before adjourning, the board addressed a related problem: Giuseppe Berti and Ambrogio Donini's latest activities. Sporadically they had published, in Italian and English, a newsletter called *Italy Today*. On May 23 they had put out their first issue in five months. Attempting to ruin Browder, they now called themselves the "Delegation of the Italian Communist Party in North America." Printing the Duclos article with acid editorial comment, they berated the CPA for not grasping immediately the French essay's significance.[17] The periodical's sudden reemergence had a strong impact on American Communist circles and enraged Browder. He accused Berti of leaking the Duclos article to the *World-Telegram* and intimated that his opponents on the board were plotting with the exiles.

The Duclos essay finally appeared in the *Daily Worker* on May 24, bringing the crisis into every Communist family's home. It prompted a rare public discussion of the movement's basic policies. News of Browder's 1944 suppression of Foster angered many; perhaps an equal number resented the uninvited foreign intervention. For nine more days the board remained adjourned. Slowly CPA members began to grasp the article's true consequence: another change in the international line was taking place. Browder, like Jay Lovestone in 1929, might well prove expendable.

Suddenly Browder attempted an accommodation. Sounding as he had during the era of the Nazi–Soviet pact, he attacked the Truman administration and British imperialism. On May 24 he told a radio audience that the American government had abandoned FDR's foreign policy. It had allowed Churchill to break the Big Three's unity, seize the initiative, and recast international relations. The new "pattern" featured "a world polarized around American–Soviet antagonism," with the British Empire resuming its ancient balance-of-power role. Accordingly, the United States was losing much of the international moral leadership it had gained under Roosevelt. Browder and the domestic Communists would "awaken the American people" to insist on Teheran's fulfillment. He also condemned Britain's suppression of Greek leftists and deprecated President Truman for supporting UN membership for Argentina, a dictatorship already sheltering escaped Nazis.[18]

Shortly before the National Board's next meeting, its subcommittee drafted a special resolution titled "The Present Situation and the Next Tasks." It ignored totally Browder's militant address. It offered a program for winning the Pacific war and returning to a peacetime economy without mass unemployment or regressive taxation. The manifesto thanked Duclos for his advice, condemned CPA "errors," and praised Foster's contributions "to the struggle against opportunism." Finally it urged all members to examine critically the organization's "policies and leadership."[19]

The board met again on June 2. Here Thompson launched a ferocious assault on Browder. Other members hedged until Dennis and Foster joined. Then Green fell in line. Eventually, even the slow-witted Robert Minor, Browder's closest associate, turned against him. The vilification rankled the general secretary worse than anything he had faced previously. He delivered a lengthy theoretical speech on peaceful coexistence but spurned the subcommittee's resolution. Under questioning, however, he indicated that he could support it with an amendment on foreign markets. Simple dignity, of course, prevented his endorsing Duclos's vicious onslaught. Browder made it clear that he would not put up with the kind of browbeating he had inflicted on Foster.[20]

At this point the elder statesman rushed in to prevent any compromise settlement. Pouring oil on the flames, Foster exclaimed that the old Comintern would not have taken "fifty-fifty votes" and neither should the CPA. Turning directly to Browder, he warned, "The comrades here are not afraid to fight you. . . . If you vote against this resolution you commit political suicide in this party."[21] Browder would have to swallow all personal pride. This was simply too much for someone who still considered himself a presidential advisor. Nearly everyone voted for the program while Browder stood alone against it. William Schneiderman absented himself and Roy Hudson abstained. On June 5 even the latter's independence melted, and he decided to support the resolution fully. The *Daily Worker* published the voting results, revealing Browder's opposition. Not since 1929 had American Communists admitted internal dissention publicly. Some rank and filers, with varying degrees of sincerity, urged Browder to place his point of view before the membership, but he remained determined to outdebate his opponents.[22] Over the next two and one-half weeks he displayed remarkable bravado. Although the odds against him increased, he continued to expect victory. Never an advocate of intraparty democracy, he concentrated his efforts on the highest ranking cadres.

Of more significance, Browder had already begun planning his appeal to Moscow, still the ultimate source of authority. For more than two decades the Russians had supported him virtually every time the CPUSA had sought adjudication. With the European war over and travel restrictions easing, he anticipated vindication once again on Soviet soil. On June 4 he addressed six thousand CPA members at a sold-out Manhattan Center meeting. He told them that the association's difficulties would lead to greater Communist unity despite the capitalist press's dismal predictions. Far from being treated as a repudiated leader, he received a thunderous ovation. Browder urged resistance to the "avaricious, grasping capitalist class" of the United States. He charged that the Truman administration had abandoned cooperation pledges FDR had given the Soviets at Yalta. Current policy could only lead to war.[23] Thus Browder had made all policy adjustments the new Moscow line demanded. His swollen pride and Foster's ambitious need for revenge prevented any fraternal solution, however. Obsessed with retribution, Foster wanted blood. Browder, considering himself a valiant international Communist general, was willing to offer some of his own if necessary to keep his commission, but would not surrender.

Browder met his Waterloo, however, at the National Committee's three-day, mid-June meeting. Fifty-four members, including specially invited union leaders, gathered at the Hank Forbes Auditorium in the CPA headquarters. Foster opened on the eighteenth with an unrestrained attack. His contorted face red with rage, he termed Browder "very slow in learning" the Duclos lessons. He decried the cult of personality and "flood of adulation" Browder had encouraged. Browder had long angled for Foster's expulsion and "would have acted upon the slightest provocation." These words were especially effective because they contained truths many cadres had recognized but feared to voice. Skillfully, Foster fused his purge of Browder with demands of young U.S. Communist war veterans for recognition. He made it clear that he wanted to promote Robert Thompson, John Gates, Irving Goff, and others seeking a generational change in the CPA's leadership.[24]

Browder responded with a twenty-thousand-word defense that took more than two hours to deliver. His presentation, filled with lengthy quotations all had heard before, made no pretense of trying to convince any-one. Instead, like a lawyer, Browder summarized his case for the record and hinted broadly that he would appeal to a higher court. On finishing, he retired to his ninth-floor office, infuriating members all the more. De-spite pleas that he return, he remained there throughout that afternoon's discussions and all the next day.

Meanwhile, an incredible spectacle was taking place downstairs. Forty leading cadres, all trying to salvage their jobs, network of associates, and lifestyles, were turning the Leninist self-criticism tradition into self-flagellation. In long speeches they apologized for virtually every contact they had ever had with Browder. They attacked him for a multitude of sins, real and imagined, going back to the mid-1930s. Elizabeth G. Flynn had come to the New York meeting to defend Browder from Duclos's on-slaught until she learned that no other National Committee members would join her. She then denounced his superciliousness in quoting his own writings and offered, "We have all contributed to making Earl Brow-der believe himself infallible." Thereupon she unleashed a series of ad hominem accusations. His susceptibility to revisionism stemmed from his introversion, which had isolated his mind. He was too fond of solitary research and study. When he did put aside his books, he preferred court-ing influential persons to meeting the masses. Sarcastically she recom-mended he tour the country "alone, unknown, unhonored and unsung," come to know the common folk, "and learn to be one of them" again.[25]

Of all the ignominy heaped on Browder, this charge hurt the most be-cause it hit home. Although he could address large hostile crowds, he re-mained simply too diffident to approach strangers on an individual basis. Browder learned of Flynn's words and considered them a poltroonish at-tack on a personality weakness he could not change suddenly at age fifty-four. On June 20 Browder returned, apologized for staying away, and denied being "arrogant." He also made a final pitch for a face-saving "support of American markets." He then spent the remainder of the day listening to abusive oratory from former comrades. "Slumped far down in his chair," according to witness Louis Budenz, Browder "sometimes put his head between his hands as the flood of criticism poured out."[26]

That Browder swallowed his pride and reappeared to hear the invec-tive took discipline. It did not require great selflessness, however. Green later observed that although Browder had never followed Soviet policy "blindly," an "umbilical cord" of loyalty still tied him to Moscow. Having served faithfully for a quarter-century, he had nowhere else to go politi-cally. Henceforth, he looked solely to the USSR for redemption. After all, unlike previous purge victims James Cannon and Jay Lovestone, Browder had never resisted Stalin's authority. Stubbornly he closed his mind to the possibility that the Russians also had abandoned him. That evening the National Committee ratified "The Present Situation and the Next Tasks." Browder cast the sole negative vote.[27] The group then named a new secretariat of Foster, Dennis, and Williamson. It summoned a special emergency convention to New York and scheduled its meeting for July 26–28 to reestablish the CPUSA. Browder's career lay in ashes.

World events seemed to underscore Browderism's sudden irrelevance. On July 17 Allied leaders convened at Potsdam, outside Berlin, for World War II's final conference. There none of the conviviality of Teheran or Yalta brightened the meeting. With Hitler's regime destroyed, painful questions about the administration of liberated Europe loomed large. One day before the gathering opened, the United States detonated the first of three experimental atomic bombs in the New Mexico desert. The remaining two could now be dropped on Japan. Russian assistance in the Pacific was no longer necessary, and President Truman's attitude made that clear. Disagreements over governing postwar Poland and Germany would be settled by fait accompli. The USSR continued to suppress anti-Communist elements in Romania and Bulgaria. The United States blocked Soviet interests in Iran. Accord was limited to reaffirming previous understandings: Germany would be disarmed and demilitarized, and its leaders would be tried for war crimes. A Cold War that would last beyond Browder's lifetime had begun. If Truman was trying to intimidate Stalin, as historians Gar Alperovitz, Martin J. Sherwin, and others have contended, the effort proved futile. The tough Soviet dictator realized that the Americans could not have many of the new weapons. The Red Army already occupied the territory in dispute. Deaths of millions of people did not bother him. A sophisticated Russian research program, aided by espionage, would break America's atomic monopoly within four years.[28]

On July 21 and 22 the CPA's largest state organization, New York, held a boisterous convention at Manhattan Center. For the first time in nearly twenty years, Browder did not attend. Green led one thousand raucous delegates who roared unanimous approval of resolutions condemning the CPA's creation and urging the CPUSA's reconstitution. Foster identified the enemy, proclaiming that they would not tolerate factionalism from "Browder or anyone else."[29]

The ex-leader ventilated his pain and pent-up anger for the first time in a *Daily Worker* article. Printed July 24, it marked his only action approaching a direct appeal to the rank and file that year. The working class should strive for East–West détente, it argued, because Red scares made the United States more reactionary and antilabor. By contrast, a United States friendly with the Soviet Union became a freer, more "liberal" country. Too late, Browder noted Duclos's faulty logic. The PCF had helped prevent a civil war once the Nazi-led Vichy government had collapsed. Now the Communists were forging French unity not with a program of socialism but by helping restore the capitalist economy. Therefore, any revisionism, Browder insisted, had originated in Europe. His anguish led him to foolish hyperbole. The CPA, he argued, had secured President Roosevelt's 1944 reelection by splitting the big bourgeoisie. Browder acknowledged that he and Foster had quarreled for at least eight years. The latter had now returned to his pre-1921 anarcho-syndicalist roots. Browder saved his most contemptuous denunciation for Flynn, whose personal remarks had piqued him worst. She enjoyed the temporary absence of a party line because it made one opinion "as good as another." Now she could babble freely without having Comrade Browder "rebuke her any more for her mistakes." Scornfully, he predicted she would soon resent a new, wrong line's restraints much as she had chafed at a correct one. Browder's defiance of his colleagues did as much to turn the rank and file against him as did his ideological unorthodoxy. Joseph Starobin has noted that "Communists were accustomed to the complete subordination of differences in the interests of unity. Browder would not, however, recant."[30]

The next day Foster repaid Browder's vituperations with a merciless newspaper attack of his own. Browder had learned nothing from the CPA's "profound" public discussion "except to hide his bourgeois reformist line under more skillful phrases." He was irresponsibly peddling "intellectual trash" in Marxism's name. Foster lampooned the notion that progressive capitalists had helped reelect FDR. Foster had discovered that Browder's revisionism possessed a heretofore unnoticed imperialistic content. For American capitalists to develop a $40-billion yearly export trade, they would need a virtual world monopoly. Foster believed that nothing could prevent a postwar economic collapse and claimed that Stalin shared his view. Big business's hatred of Socialism outweighed even the lure of immediate profits. Workers faced a long, complicated struggle at home and abroad.[31]

The special national convention, held July 26–29, reestablished the CPUSA unanimously. Meeting at Manhattan's Fraternal Clubhouse, the gathering, to which Browder was not a delegate, chose a new secretariat of Foster, Dennis, Williamson, and Thompson. Foster clearly dominated, however. They permitted Browder to address one opening-day session. By now only a sackcloth-and-ashes repentance could have salvaged his career. Instead, in a one-hour speech he offered even more vigorous defiance and enraged his audience by vowing to take his case to a higher court. He termed "naive" the notion that the convention would settle the issue and argued that avoidance of international discussion would constitute "American exceptionalism with a vengeance."[32] Defeated but not humbled, he now placed his faith in friends abroad who had never let him down.

Did Moscow ever demand Browder's removal from leadership? Beyond the Duclos article's use of the term "former secretary," there is no direct evidence to suggest this. The Soviets may simply have shelved Browder for possible use at a time that never arrived. More likely they sought to chastise him severely, believing that he would ultimately fall in line. Whatever their plans, Philip Jaffe noted, before December 1945 no Russian CP organ criticized Browder. Georgi Dimitrov and Yugoslav Communist Edouard Kardelj later stated they regretted the way things turned out.[33] Most likely Browder's disgrace was the product of both principled independence and less noble aspects of his personality. The former probably guaranteed conflict at some time, given the international Communist movement's undemocratic nature. The latter, which included Browder's overweening vanity and long-standing animosity toward Foster, would not allow him to backpedal sufficiently in 1945.

## THE PARIAH

Rapidly the USSR's changing exigencies and Browder's stubbornness made him a relic of the bygone Grand Alliance era. Dropping quickly into obscurity, he retained his illusions and inflated self-regard. He sorely missed the limelight: contact with celebrities, Madison Square Garden rallies, and *Daily Worker* headlines. Sometimes, he even longed for *New York Times* interviews, although the paper's reporters had not always been kind. Isolation had profound effects on Browder. In some ways they resembled his troubled response to the stresses of Atlanta Penitentiary. Workaholics do not often handle idleness well, and in 1945 Browder entered a psychological depression from which he never fully recovered. His postconvention actions and words brought even more misery. Reduced to the ranks, he sought to preserve his membership while preparing his Moscow appeal. On July 28, just two days after his pugnacious speech, he sent the convention a careful letter apologizing for his personal attacks. He did not, however, disavow his Teheran views.

On August 3 the *Times* announced that *Pravda* had reported on American Communism's crisis without comment. The news heartened Browder and inspired further illusions. Now he posited that lesser Kremlin bureaucrats had masterminded the Duclos article.[34] He planned to visit Moscow in person, ascertain the situation, and seek reinstatement. On August 6 and 8 the United States unleashed atomic weapons on Hiroshima and Nagasaki, bringing surrender shortly thereafter. Every American radical group protested, except the Communists, who were still clinging to a vanishing hope that U.S.–Soviet cooperation might survive somehow. In this Browder did not differ from his former comrades.

Next he faced a more prosaic but nevertheless pressing task. After his annual August vacation, he would be off the organization's payroll for the first time since 1921. At age fifty-five he suddenly needed a livelihood. The CPUSA's National Board offered to discuss future work if he would recant fully. Seeking to control Browder's activities, it planned to offer him, at his regular salary, a research position. He also received employment offers from textile importer Alfred Kohlberg and right-wing zealot Gerald L. K. Smith. The latter promised to book speeches in cities across the land if Browder would expose fully all CPUSA–Kremlin ties.[35]

For an alleged opportunist, Browder displayed remarkable resistance to temptation. Unwilling to knuckle under to Foster, work for capitalists, or crusade for anti-Communist fanatics, he decided to spread his own Teheran views instead. He contacted wealthy supporters he had attracted during happier days. With their sponsorship he began preparing an amateurish weekly newsletter on economics, politics, and world markets titled *Distributors Guide*. Its first issue appeared on January 5, 1946, and was described by Jaffe as "mimeographed on letter-sized paper and stitched in a blue cover," costing an exorbitant $100 per year.[36] Subscribers included only a handful of friends and followers.

Although the bulletin reached few people, it obviously violated party discipline. Accordingly, on February 5 the CPUSA expelled him. Browder responded impetuously, alienating many erstwhile followers. Using old CPA mailing lists, he sent out an unwrapped, lengthy "Appeal to Members of the Communist Party, USA." It prompted a flood of angry letters from those who had since left the organization and rank and filers fearing FBI scrutiny.[37] Beyond doubt, Browder would enjoy no comeback. Even his dentist and insurance agent asked him to find replacements.

Although scorned, Browder did not despair. Certain he had done nothing wrong, he stepped up his campaign to visit Moscow. After his expulsion, every *Distributors Guide* issue praised Roosevelt, Stalin, and the USSR. Browder applied for a U.S. passport and, after two months' waiting, received one. The next day he telephoned the Soviet Union's New York consulate and made an appointment. A cordial reception ensued; within a week he had a visa, although similar requests by Foster were refused during this time. Browder dropped *Distributors Guide* with the April 27, 1946, issue and, to ascertain his true status, made the costly journey to the USSR at his own expense. Aware that Stalin's government had executed Lenin's contemporaries, the Old Bolsheviks, Browder displayed life-threatening courage and boundless self-confidence nevertheless. Although his passport protected him, it is doubtful that a Cold War U.S. government would have protested greatly had his revisionism run afoul of Stalin's laws.

He arrived in Leningrad on May 2 and left for Moscow the following day. In both cities comrades from previous years extended warm and seemingly sincere welcomes. He later told Jaffe that all "studiously avoided discussing politics" except his old, close friend Solomon A. Lozovsky, now Soviet Information Bureau chief. Lozovsky talked with Browder for more than ten days and had him sum up his views in a series of memoranda. There was no chance that the unforgiving Stalin, whom Browder had offended during the 1920s, would see him or read the material. Accordingly, Lozovsky sent it to Foreign Minister Vyacheslav Molotov, then at a meeting in Paris.[38]

At once Molotov cabled Lozovsky to have Browder remain in the Soviet capital. On May 20 he returned to Moscow and summoned Browder to visit his office at 10 o'clock that night. They met for two and one-half hours. Molotov, who acted solicitous, listened patiently while Browder did all the talking. Too eager to please his famous host, Browder asked no embarrassing questions about the Duclos affair. Although Browder did not make the best use of his opportunity, the meetings seemed significant. Such treatment for a deposed Communist leader was unprecedented; it astounded and confused his American enemies. They feared a renewed leadership crisis. The State Department believed that he remained in good standing with the world movement, that his expulsion was only a stratagem, and that covert work awaited.[39]

Reality, however, proved less exciting. Browder's high profile made him a poor Soviet espionage candidate despite the experiences of his brother and sister. He met no physical harm in Moscow, but Molotov cold-bloodedly offered him a token post of distributing Soviet nonfiction in the United States. On his way home Browder had intended to call on his old friend Dimitrov in Bulgaria, tour Yugoslavia, and then see Paris, but Lozovsky and Molotov cruelly vetoed his plans.[40]

The Russians wanted to consume Browder's energies so he could not launch an opposition CP faction as Jay Lovestone had done after 1929. Foolishly, Browder allowed hunger for redemption to override good sense. He returned directly to New York and registered as a foreign agent. In July he began receiving English translations of Russian books and articles that he tried to place with American publishers. He also met monthly in hotel dining rooms with the Soviet Embassy's second secretary. Here Browder presented memoranda insisting that Foster's leadership was destroying the CPUSA. The exercise fed Browder's illusions and gave the USSR a clear idea of his thinking and ambitions. He also published a book, *War or Peace with Russia?*, and a pamphlet, *World Communism and U.S. Foreign Policy*, both seeking to thaw the Cold War.[41]

Instead, an icy chill swept the planet. In March 1947 the Truman Doctrine was announced, which sent $659 million in aid to Greece and Turkey. Justified as protecting free peoples resisting external aggression and armed minorities, its sweeping terms quickly led to U.S. defense pacts with more than fifty nations. At home the president issued an executive order that required loyalty oaths by all government employees. The first Republican-dominated Congress since 1930 introduced the Taft-Hartley bill, designed to weaken labor unions aided by the New Deal, and enacted it over Truman's veto in June. That month also brought announcement of the Marshall Plan, which, over three years, sent $12 billion to rebuild Western Europe and prevent the spread of Communism.

Browder, insisting he had never disobeyed Moscow, still awaited a call from the CPUSA. He found employment advising Transport Workers Union president Michael J. Quill. In April 1948, over Quill's signature Browder sent a three-thousand-word letter to ranking Italian Communist party figure Luigi Longo. It labeled Foster a "short-sighted factionalist drunk with power" and denounced his "rule or ruin" leadership. The message recalled that "intervention from abroad" had given Foster his position and urged more of the same to remove him.[42]

Early that summer millionaire backer Abe Heller, who had left the U.S. Communist movement after Browder's fall, went to Paris to see Duclos himself. The latter dominated the conversation; Heller raised questions but put forth no effective defense of Browder. Yet by July the repudiated leader, undismayed and confident he had completed a successful drive for his rehabilitation, applied for CPUSA membership. He employed the tortured logic that Marshal Tito's independent Communist government in Yugoslavia posed a mortal threat to Soviet-style Marxism. The danger necessitated abandoning old intramural quarrels. The party rebuffed Browder and, despite his support for Moscow, began linking his name with Titoism. Indeed, Starobin recalls "some of the bitterest party polemics against him date from this period." Stubbornly, he refused to accept his fate. Privately he published a series of pamphlets that offered the Communists unsolicited advice. All attacked Foster vitriolically.[43]

Although Browder was politically dead, Browderism, to the degree that it meant coalition building, was not. Indeed, in 1946, to combat monopoly capital, Foster called for an alliance "beyond anything in Roosevelt's time." By 1948 the party, which had shrunk to fifty thousand members after the Duclos article, swelled to seventy thousand. Nineteen hundred lived in the South, once a Communist desert. Although the CP had not matched its 1939 size of nearly 100,000, its financial resources and influence in progressive circles were impressive. That year former Vice-President Henry Wallace, who opposed the Cold War, launched a third-party bid for the White House. Many unions feared that he might split the liberal vote, help elect a Republican, and usher in more antilabor legislation. The Communists backed him directly, however, much as they, behind Browder, had supported FDR in 1944. The tactic led the exiled Sam Darcy to declare later that such policies continued until the CPUSA had become a "scarecrow."

Browderism without Browder proved a disaster. Actually, however, Foster and Eugene Dennis practiced it ineptly. In June 1948 Wallace, eyeing Vermont newspaper polls, announced that if the Communists would field a "ticket of their own, the new party would lose 100,000 votes but gain 4 million." The calculated comment, repeated thereafter at Center Sandwich, New Hampshire, harkened back to Browder's successful 1936 token effort against Roosevelt, but the CPUSA rejected the idea in August. By contrast, Browder, who loved back-room machinations, would probably have obliged Wallace in return for a face-to-face meeting. This could have given the movement more bargaining chips had Wallace cared to cash them in by withdrawing. Instead, the Communists continued supporting him vocally, and he fought on. In November he received a disappointing 1.1 million popular ballots, no electoral votes, and no concessions from the Democrats. The bipartisan Cold War foreign policy would last another twenty years.[44]

The era's mounting hysteria found predictable domestic targets. The

CIO began expelling CP-aligned unions, wrecking more than a decade's efforts at penetrating the labor movement. The federal government indicted the Communists' entire National Board in 1948, and members' trials consumed the whole following year. The Justice Department, terming the CPUSA's restoration a revolutionary conspiracy, invoked the same Smith Act previously used with the *Daily Worker*'s blessings against the Trotskyists during the war. According to historian Gerald Horne, the Communist leaders believed that they "were really jailed for overthrowing Browder and reading and teaching Marxism and Leninism." The former general secretary offered magnanimously in 1949 to testify for the defense, but the party spurned him.[45] That same year Abe Heller trotted off to confer with Duclos's superior, PCF chief Maurice Thorez, to no avail.

The American Communists unwittingly greased their slide into obscurity. Gripped by an internal panic, the party launched a ruthless search for informers. Urged on by Foster, it purged "revisionists" and "white chauvinists." Faithful, but inactive, members found themselves dropped from the rolls and eyed suspiciously. Cadres by the score went underground, depriving local organizations of their experience and talents.

For Browder repeated rejection finally began to take its toll. In 1949 he resigned his Soviet sales representative position. Three years of trying to peddle material that was chiefly Russian propaganda had left his meager life's savings depleted as he reached age fifty-eight.[46] Thereafter he gradually realized the futility of his rehabilitation crusade, and disillusionment set in. A sense of monstrous injustice replaced his desperate longing for atonement, though at times he felt both. East European events helped strip away remaining chimeras. In show trials reminiscent of those of the 1930s, Hungarian and Czechoslovak courts convicted and ordered the execution of defendants allegedly guilty of "Browderism." Such actions obviously had Moscow's sanction.

While foreign Communists were killing those who echoed Browder's doctrines, the capitalist government at home trapped his family in a vicious crossfire. The military draft, which at the time generally took only uneducated young men in prime physical condition, snared his son Felix, who possessed a doctorate and flat feet. The president of the Massachusetts Institute of Technology considered Felix a mathematical genius and asked Felix's commanding officer to place him where his talents could benefit the nation. Sent to the electronics laboratory at Fort Monmouth, New Jersey, Felix remained there until the FBI, through informers, determined that "he had the same political views as his father." Shortly thereafter Lieutenant General John Murphy arranged Felix's transfer to the army finance center for two years of tedium. The INS renewed the old crusade against Raissa, forcing her and Earl to answer questions again in 1949. Three years later the Justice Department, aided by Senator Joseph McCarthy's henchman Roy Cohn, indicted them both for perjury.[47]

All of this incensed Browder further. After much agonizing, he abandoned the CPUSA, which had long forsaken him. The new decade brought the worst of times. It saw the U.S. armed forces battle Communists in Korea. At home Wisconsin's Senator Joseph McCarthy led the most vicious Red scare ever. Right-wingers, and the politicians who feared their voting power, sought to identify and prosecute anyone who had ever carried a party card. Ex-Marxists James Burnham and Max Eastman became Cold War conservatives. For the first time since 1900, the American left had no influential organization anywhere. Most radicals joined Norman Thomas's denunciations of "red fascism." Only the minuscule Trotskyist sects seemed capable of a rational neutralism. James Cannon's Socialist Workers party and Max Shachtman's Independent Socialist League (formerly the Workers party) condemned both Russia's new imperialism and America's more subtle attempts at world economic domination. Congressional investigations came to feature former revolutionaries "naming names" of erstwhile comrades. Although few individuals had more reason to do so than Browder, he never yielded to the temptation to, as he put it, howl "with the official pack of hunting dogs."[48]

By this statement the ex-Communist Browder meant that he would never testify against friend or foe. Neither would he support capitalism or the Cold War. Such sentiments, though noble, did not constitute a coherent ideological position, however. Yet, enough of his vanity remained that he agreed to sharpen his rhetorical skills at Max Shachtman's expense. As CPUSA leader Browder had repeatedly spurned the Trotskyist's challenges to debate, but now time wore heavily on his hands. He missed public speaking terribly. In addition to regularly scheduled CPUSA rallies, on several occasions in the 1930s he had held his own against Norman Thomas before thousands in Madison Square Garden. On March 30, 1950, in front of twelve hundred left-wing spectators in Manhattan's Webster Hall, Browder and Shachtman squared off. The moderator was Columbia University's radical sociologist C. Wright Mills, who would later write a book arguing that a "power elite" ruled the United States.

Despite Browder's experienced composure and the bitter Shachtman's long-repressed rage, the contest was the worst of Browder's life. For years thereafter left-wing anti-Communists recalled it with glee. The ex-CP head underestimated his opponent and delivered a message notable for its muddled thinking.

The evening's topic asked whether Russia was a socialist community, and Browder took the affirmative position. Instead of citing examples of communal life and relative economic equality, however, he used his most scholarly tones to tout Soviet industrial development: its "productive forces" had reached "a stage higher than capitalism." Wrapped up in the ongoing Cold War, he labored to assure Americans of the Soviet Union's peaceful nature. The country did not impose its system on "unwilling and unprepared nations" because socialism was not "a commodity for export." Russian government was based on "the free choice of conscious people." Such claims left Shachtman with the simple task of showing that the USSR was neither socialist nor democratic. Although angry because the haughty Browder refused to address him by name, Shachtman offered a compelling indictment. Using Soviet government statistics, he underscored the significant gap separating the lowest-paid workers from the highest and asked his audience to imagine the gulf between them and "bureaucrats of all varieties, stripes, ranks, sizes and weights." Sardonically he asked why a "majority of the commission that wrote the Stalin Constitution, the most democratic in the world," had sold themselves to Nazis and other imperialists. As the end neared, Shachtman began reciting names of purge victims. The momentum built as he enumerated general secretaries of Communist parties: Rajk of Hungary, Gomulka in Poland, and Bulgaria's Kostov. Moderator Mills interrupted to tell Shachtman that his time had expired. Shachtman ignored him and turned toward the ashen Browder. Pointing an accusing finger, he thundered that when he first saw Browder at the podium, he had told himself "There—there but for an accident of geography stands a corpse."[49]

Totally defeated, Browder somnambulated through the rebuttal sessions and went home wondering what he could learn from his abasement. How could he avoid similar humiliations in the future? Still unwilling to denounce the USSR's travesty of socialism, he concluded after much thought that he had to become more aggressive. Shortly thereafter, he reasserted his dignity dramatically and courageously during two final appearances in the Washington spotlight.

On April 26, 1950, a subpoenaed Browder stood before a subcommittee of the Senate Foreign Relations Committee. Its chairman, Maryland

Democrat Millard E. Tydings, who anticipated an onerous reelection battle that November, considered him an easy target and tried to win votes by grilling him. Joe McCarthy and more accomplished Red-baiters looked on as spectators. Browder, displaying better bravado than judgment, appeared without legal counsel and fielded three hundred queries. Although many were designed to trap him, he disdained using the Fifth Amendment. Answering all but sixteen questions put to him by Republican minority member Bourke Hickenlooper, he enraged the legislators by refusing to identify persons visiting Tung Pi-wu, a Chinese Communist United Nations delegate, at sympathizer Philip Jaffe's residence in 1945. Bitterly, Browder termed the hearing a hysteria campaign against China. The next day McCarthy harangued the committee until it charged Browder with sixteen counts of contempt. An indictment soon followed.[50]

In the autumn Tydings had to face a hostile electorate that resented Korean War casualties, feared China might enter the conflict, and held him, as Senate Armed Services Committee chairman, partially responsible for military reverses. A conservative Democrat, Tydings also met opposition from labor and blacks, a rise in Republican registrations, and voters angry at an incumbent governor who had signed Maryland's first sales tax into law. McCarthy, however, administered the coup de grace by attacking Tydings's anti-Communist credentials and circulating a doctored fifteen-year-old photograph of Tydings seeming to enjoy casual conversation with Browder.[51]

In March 1951 Browder returned to the front pages like a ghost from a previous age. When tried for contempt of Congress, he again insisted on defending himself personally. To everyone's amazement, an assertive, animated Browder seized the initiative and exploited the bad blood between Tydings and McCarthy. He summoned the latter as a defense witness. The egomaniacal McCarthy stole the spotlight by waiving his senatorial immunity against subpoenas and appearing without warning the final day. Browder the counselor, relying on a correspondence school law degree he had earned nearly four decades earlier, asked McCarthy whether Chairman Tydings had coddled Browder, the supposedly unresponsive witness. McCarthy, more concerned over finishing off his ex-colleague's career than about bashing a broken ex-Communist, answered yes. The senator, reminding the court that he was a former judge, gave his opinion that Tydings had conducted a whitewash of Marxists in high places and that Browder had said exactly what Tydings had wanted him to say. McCarthy believed that Browder would have answered any question with the proper hint from Tydings. Under government cross-examination he underscored that Tydings had never ordered Browder to answer Hickenlooper's queries. Finally, Judge F. Dickinson Letts accepted Browder's motion for acquittal.[52] In a strange sense the dissident Trotskyist Shachtman had inadvertently taught the repudiated Communist Browder the tactics he needed to stay out of jail. Browder also learned from his trial the obvious wisdom of hiring an attorney and invoking constitutional protection. Future Congressional committee and courtroom appearances brought yawns instead of headlines.

The 1950s gave consensus politics an enormous boost. Republican strategist Kevin Phillips has observed astutely that "military Keynesianism" bought support for government spending in the conservative South and Southwest. Training camps and other installations stimulated the local civilian economy and helped reduce fiscal conservatism. The spread of suburbia as a broad national phenomenon doomed older working-class communities. Now almost no one had to live near a factory, and, it seemed, few people wanted to do so. Even many assembly-line workers identified themselves as middle-class. For those left behind, the dream of someday owning a home often replaced the struggle for equality. The existence of an idle wealthy elite became bearable to comfortable proletarians and those with aspirations. At times during this period, however, workers could still show themselves to be militant and aggressive; class consciousness and activism were not totally forgotten. In any case the Communist party's only real influence, with its top cadres in prison after Smith Act convictions, lay in a pacifistic antinuclear movement.

Browder's trial proved the last major victory in a life spiraling rapidly downhill. Forlorn and isolated in 1953, he finally spoke out against the Soviet Union but not his idol, Joseph Stalin. In a series of published interviews that spring, he decried Russia's anti-Semitism and castigated East European Communists for behaving like puppets. Matching the decline in Browder's public fortunes was his melancholy personal life. Actively courted by McCarthyites, he maintained friendly dialogue to ward off total isolation but refused to join their crusade.[53]

Even in his heyday Browder had been unromantic. As hardships accumulated, he became positively saturnine. Raissa contracted cancer, but both the INS and the FBI continued to hound her. Once the world Communist movement defined Browderism as a high crime, she feared nothing as much as being deported to the USSR. While she lay dying in 1955, the government issued a warrant for her expulsion. After her passing, lugubriosity became a permanent feature of Browder's personality. He displayed the solicitousness of an intensely lonely person but no sense of

Federal agent and Browder, September 30, 1952.
(Courtesy of National Republic Collection, Hoover Institution
Archives, Stanford University. Used by permission of Corbis
Bettmann, L.L.C., 902 Broadway, New York, New York, 10010.)

humor.[54] Browder passed up lucrative offers from publishers who wanted
him to reveal his full knowledge of Soviet covert activities in the United
States and foreign domination of the CPUSA. Following Raissa's death,
he sent some of her clothes to Lilly Blum, wife of retired Comintern operative Rudolf Blum (Rudy Baker).[55]

In 1956 Soviet Premier Nikita Khrushchev confirmed two decades of
accusations by Trotskyists and others by revealing Stalin's paranoia and

the existence of slave labor camps. Later that year the USSR crushed a national Communist revolution in Hungary. These events prompted tens of thousands in the CPUSA, a full three-quarters of the members, to abandon the organization. Browder's name circulated briefly among party haunts. He entertained one last flicker of hope that Moscow would intervene in his favor. American Communists who might have considered Browder an improvement over Foster and Dennis deserted the movement instead. By 1958 the CPUSA had a mere three thousand members. *Pravda* settled the issue by hailing Foster and reviling Browder as an opportunist.

Craving the public notice he had once received regularly, an empty Browder sought to join Norman Thomas's Socialists. Almost nobody trusted him, however. During the late 1950s Browder called himself a free-lance writer and professional lecturer. He announced his admiration for Tito and even visited Yugoslavia. Browder expanded a series of talks he gave at Rutgers University into a book titled *Marx and America*, which attacked the concept of absolute working-class impoverishment and Lenin's view that imperialism constituted capitalism's final stage.[56]

Browder's speeches and writings could not pay his rent, however. Likening himself to Marx, who had relied on Frederick Engels for financial support, Browder depended on five or six patrons who usually contributed $100 per month. According to Philip Jaffe, Abe Heller, a generous CPUSA supporter during the 1940s, by now possessed "very little" and gave "much less." Jaffe, who admitted having "more than the others," gave more than $20,000, then a significant sum, during a five-year period after 1954. Thereafter Browder's three sons, all university professors, supported him.[57]

About this time Junius Irving Scales, another ex-Communist twenty-nine years Browder's junior, came to know him on a first-name basis. He found Browder a "very decent and thoughtful man," who had not totally lost his legendary reserve and whose plight was "quite poignant." Scales opined that the vituperation Browder had experienced "must have cut him like a knife." Browder listened patiently and empathetically to the tribulations of other former members. Indeed, some felt embarrassed to tell tales of woe to one who had suffered vastly more. Browder's thinking retained a schematic nature not unknown in the party. He looked for "categories to drop everything into" and stereotypic answers to many questions, though he tried to overcome this tendency.[58]

In the 1960s a New Left arose. It was composed chiefly of southern blacks and white middle-class youth whom historian Milton Cantor

characterized as "sensitive to the paradox of a national creed of social equality and the grim facts of bigotry; the myth of affluence and the
realities of poverty; the pronouncements of peaceful goals and the preparations for nuclear conflict." Virtually all of its tens of thousands of members sought to end racial segregation, the military draft, and the anti-
Communist colonial war in Vietnam that the United States had assumed
when the French departed. The New Left, which included feminists preparing to launch their own movement, Cantor noted, expressed hostility
toward the "dominant ethos of consumerism, materialism, and personal
success"—the very things Browder had always endorsed. This intuitive,
emotional generation displayed a suspicion of reason—the cornerstone of
depression-era radicalism. Not surprisingly, its members did not call on
Browder for advice. He admitted that he shared little with young people
save a deep loathing of President Richard Nixon.[59] Although Browder
constantly reviewed his personal history, he displayed no introspection
and offered simple rationalizations of his words and deeds. Late in life
he even repudiated Marx, leaving yet another void in his existence. Browder never found another ideological home.

Historian Nick Salvatore has noted that when Eugene V. Debs died in
1926, thousands of men and women from across the land came to view
his body at the Labor Temple in Terre Haute, Indiana, and then the front
parlor of his Eighth Street home in Terre Haute. Memorial meetings took
place in "every large city and a thousand hamlets," according to early
biographer Ray Ginger. Debs's funeral audience included "famous writers, wealthy attorneys and businessmen," as well as ordinary people
"with the grease of a lifetime ground into their thumbnails."[60]

Browder's heart failed on June 27, 1973. Not one Communist newspaper in the world printed his obituary. Philip Jaffe recalled that, although
Browder had spoken "on innumerable occasions before crowds of
20,000," a mere handful attended his memorial service. His attempts to
reconcile Joseph Stalin and American radicalism, repudiated in the
1940s, lay forgotten in the 1970s.[61]

# EPILOGUE

■

## *Could We Have Been All?*

Earl Browder, arguably the preeminent twentieth-century Communist leader in the United States, is one of the more tragic figures in American radicalism's history. A Kansas native and veteran of numerous left-wing movements, he was peculiarly fitted by circumstance and temperament to head the party during its heyday. A complex and flawed personality, he did what was necessary to rise atop the hierarchy but possessed an independent streak that ultimately proved his undoing. Still, he could never quite bring the CPUSA legitimacy because he lacked the vision and courage to separate himself and the organization totally from a foreign monster.

Yet as David J. Garrow has noted, Browder, "all of his shortcomings and limitations notwithstanding, was indeed the only CPUSA figure who ever offered a significant promise of creating a party that *might* have been able to play an enduring role in American life. That *even* Browder too in the end was unable to overcome and supersede the CPUSA's Stalinist orientation and lifeline simply highlights how" he is a considerably more empathetic figure than William Z. Foster, Ben Davis, or Eugene Dennis.[1]

Browder, as the linchpin between the USSR's shifting exigencies and CPUSA's indigenous needs, offers instruction on several levels. Historiographically, his life suggests a middle ground (however narrow) between two competing interpretations of the party. The traditional view, developed in the 1950s, has stressed the Soviet-dominated mind-set of CP leaders and understated the significance of his tactical innovations as prelude to later unorthodox Marxism. By contrast, a revisionist school, dominant among academic historians between 1975 and 1997, has emphasized home-grown roots and domestic concerns. Yet it too has neglected Browder, perhaps finding his desire to emulate Joseph Stalin and his delusions of grandeur embarrassing. Neither school of CPUSA studies has fully appreciated how deftly Browder blended elements of both for more than a decade. Under him the party was foreign in purpose, with all strategic shifts emanating from Moscow. Often, however, the organization addressed domestic radicalism through Browder's innovations (at times high-minded and at other times self-serving); misjudgments of the movement's nature; simple failure to appreciate Stalin's global exigencies; spotty implementation of orders; and flexible tactics born out of local initiative, for which Browder was usually eager to take credit.

His career shows that one could be both a Soviet-style Communist leader and an indigenous radical during two brief historical interludes: the Popular Front and World War II. No one before or since did more to harmonize the Third International and the American reform tradition. Browder tried diligently to make his organization less foreign (though no less authoritarian or bureaucratic). Admittedly he had undertaken an impossible task. Yet before 1945 the idealistic, optimistic Browder enjoyed success that confounded his anti-Communist critics and intraparty rivals. Certainly, having Georgi Dimitrov, Solomon Lozovsky, and other powerful friends in Moscow gave him an advantage over his perennial challenger Foster and other opponents.

Between 1934 and 1945 Browder rode simultaneously two horses yoked together by historical accident. He was the CPUSA's most liberal and nationalistic leader, yet he always enjoyed Moscow's support in his showdowns with Foster, perhaps in part because of his role as NKVD talent spotter.[2] Bestriding both steeds, Browder never pondered seriously their ultimate destination. He slipped between them during the Nazi–Soviet pact era. He hesitated for weeks, and the U.S. government ultimately acted before he could. The Grand Alliance, however, returned Browder to his precarious perch.

Nevertheless, in 1945, the two equines diverged permanently. Browder's facile and dysfunctional answer was to deny reality. He insisted that the two could remain conjoined even as they ripped his career apart. There is no evidence that he ever considered resisting Jacques Duclos's edict over purely American concerns. Browder insisted that Franklin Roosevelt's old policy of Soviet–U.S. friendship, which Harry S. Truman had abandoned, must be resumed. The beleaguered Communist leader refused to recognize Stalin's role in helping terminate East–West cooperation.

Here one has to find both Browder and his erstwhile supporters culpable for placing Moscow's approval above domestic radical needs. This goes deeper than the CPUSA's complicity with the covert work of Soviet intelligence agencies. Browder, despite his decade-long crusade to Americanize the CPUSA, waited months and journeyed to Moscow after his expulsion seeking vindication. The cadres and rank and filers had made sincere attempts at every level to become a genuine and accepted part of U.S. political life. Yet, when all was said and done, they were willing to abandon their greatest leader at the drop of a French Marxist's decree. "Browderism," as the 1944 policies became known, can best be described as a mutant strain of mid-twentieth-century Communism. Pragmatic and ideologically vague, it attempted to blend Great Plains radicalism with loyalty to Joseph Stalin.

On a different plane, Browder and the Communist party, with their Soviet orientation, had several things to offer. The Comintern's change of line to the Popular Front was a major cause of the CPUSA's successes during the mid-1930s. Before 1944, members always stressed capitalism's limitations. Cadres and rank and filers displayed a dedication and selflessness even their worst enemies envied, while offering a preview of modern multiculturalism. Browder's leadership provided a willingness to avoid publicity when it might hurt the cause. Conspiring to build influence within other organizations, it manifested a readiness to forego recognition so as to further larger goals. In a political culture in which hyperbole is not limited to pre-election boasts and forecasts, this proved no small sacrifice. As an unintended, but nevertheless real, contribution, the CPUSA offered thunder to steal. At one point Browder seemed to recognize this vaguely. In 1933 he asked rhetorically what effect two million Communist votes the previous November might have had on Congress's generosity in enacting emergency relief measures. In several limited areas the USSR provided a model worthy of emulation. It offered a narrowed gap between the haves and have-nots and the rhetoric of reducing it further. It provided better public education and greater upward mobility within a single generation for the masses, not merely a fortunate few. It enunciated the ethos of common gain and denigrated selfishness.

Had the USSR been a humanistic, Social Democratic state, Browder's divided loyalty might have been more understandable. Soviet Communism's drawbacks, however, help explain the rout of the CPUSA, the era's largest radical party. Failure to achieve political and social legitimacy gave reactionaries a stigma to hurl at all left-wing reform. Thereafter not only conservatives but also liberals flexed their patriotic muscle by pounding Communists. Red-baiting seemed to become part of the American creed by 1949 and remained a common practice for twenty years thereafter. Nothing hurt the CP as much as its extrinsic domination. The social history of rank and filers might not reflect it, but actions of leaders seeking to further the USSR's foreign policy devastated the party.

A disastrous decision by the CPUSA appeared even in the purely domestic context. In 1948 Progressive party presidential candidate Henry Wallace suggested that the Communists run their own ticket to draw hostility away from his candidacy. Perhaps because this smacked too much of Browder's 1936 tactics, the CP refused and supported Wallace openly. This cost the Communists their base in CIO unions, which feared splitting the liberal vote and electing a hostile Republican administration.

As if these mistakes were not enough to destroy Communism's influence in American life, massive government repression hastened the process. Indeed, any foreign connection creates a vulnerability to officially inspired hysteria. In 1948 and thereafter the U.S. government attempted to criminalize the CPUSA. Although the party was permitted to continue functioning legally and its press remained unmuzzled, most of its top and many of its secondary leaders faced indictment and imprisonment. As Richard Nixon's administration would teach the New Left a generation later, a movement that has to spend its time and effort raising legal defense funds cannot prosper.

In 1956 Nikita Khrushchev's revelation of Stalin's atrocities and his own crime in violently suppressing a reform Communist movement in Hungary ended the CPUSA's existence as an organization of substantive import. Few Americans, left or right, are willing to follow any movement that has killed millions of people. Association with a foreign, terrorist state ultimately sickened many rank and filers.

Beyond the domestic blunders, foreign domination, and government persecution lay more subtle causes of the CPUSA's failure. At a fundamental level the party expressed an impatience with the glacial nature of reform in the United States. Although displaying stout spirit, the Communists failed to appreciate how thoroughly conservative the American polity is. Nearly a century ago Woodrow Wilson wrote that only once in a generation does the opportunity for significant reform appear. That positive social change (in contrast to technological wizardry) has so little occasion is not a good thing, but it seems a more or less permanent feature of U.S. political life. Marxism-Leninism's calls for sudden, dramatic transformation were alien to most of American culture. One need not deny the pitifully inadequate results of the reform tradition to recognize its durability. By contrast advocacy of Marxism-Leninism has led to isolation for every domestic group that has ever preached it.

No evaluation of CP failure can ignore the New Deal's misleading nature. On the surface its tolerant, ameliorative administration seemed to offer a rich soil for radicalism's growth. At a bedrock level, however, FDR, despite his brave rhetoric, provided the minimum amount of change necessary to win and keep the hearts of America's working people. He stole the thunder of dissenting movements far larger than the CPUSA: those led by Dr. Francis Townsend, a proponent of generous pensions for the elderly, and Senator Huey Long, who sought to redistribute America's wealth through progressive taxation. Knowing that the Communists could go nowhere without the labor movement, to whom FDR was a hero, Browder tried to build a CPUSA annex on to the New Deal structure. It is no accident that the party's most successful leader most closely approximated a progressive reformer. Americanizing Communism was his greatest achievement. Browder seemed to recognize that patriotism, for many, is an extension of individual and group egos whose strength commands respect.

The CPUSA's experience shows other things as well. The whole emphasis on inevitability, derived of course from the international movement, was a mistake. Intellectuals Reinhold Niebuhr and Dwight Macdonald had long argued that Marxism inherited and extended the liberal illusion that humanity could depend on modern science to promote progress and reason. History may have seemed on morality's side in Karl Marx's day. The twentieth century, however, brought horrors he never imagined: Hitler, the Holocaust, Hiroshima.

Late in life Browder contended that his followers had squandered "the opportunity to weld the best of Communism with the best of the American tradition."[3] His own reliance on the USSR was a curious way to achieve such a fusion, however. In attempting to champion American nationalism and Soviet foreign policy interests simultaneously, Browder was not so much insincere as deluded. For the United States and USSR, extending the Grand Alliance beyond the Axis defeat would have been preferable to the Cold War, but, given generation-long suspicions on both sides, it was highly improbable without a common enemy.

Ever since the Socialist party fragmented in 1919, the American left has needed a large, united, and well-organized democratic movement to challenge the hegemony of capitalist values. Browder and his comrades seemed capable of building one between 1934 and 1945. His tragedy and their tragedy are two of many reasons why twentieth-century America never achieved it and why the CPUSA's failure was a prelude to the collapse of world Communism.

# NOTES

■

## ABBREVIATIONS

| | |
|---|---|
| AH | *American Heritage* |
| AM | *American Magazine* |
| AP | Robert J. Alexander papers (private collection), Department of Economics, Rutgers University, New Brunswick, N.J. |
| BC | Daniel Bell collection, Box 46, Tamiment Library, New York University, New York |
| BP | Earl Browder papers, Syracuse University Library, Department of Special Collections, 600 Bird Library, Syracuse University, Syracuse, N.Y. |
| CB | *Current Biography* |
| CH | *Current History* |
| Columbia | Earl Browder interview, Oral History Project, Columbia University, New York |
| Comintern | Communist International files, fond 495, Russian Center for the Preservation and Study of Documents of Recent History, Moscow, Russian Federation |
| CPUSA-Comintern | American Communist Party files, fond 515, Russian Center for the Preservation and Study of Documents of Recent History, Moscow, Russian Federation |
| DW | *Daily Worker* |
| Dies Committee | House of Representatives, Special Committee on Un-American Activities, Public Hearings (Congress and session as listed) |
| DJ | Department of Justice, Criminal Division; Freedom of Information Act (FOIA) documents |
| DJNA | Department of Justice, National Archives file (FOIA documents), numbers 71–112, 40–51–19, and 202–600, sub. 2840 |
| DS | Department of State files (FOIA documents) |
| ECB | Elizabeth Churchill Brown papers, Hoover Institution Archives, Stanford, Calif. |
| FBI-EB | Federal Bureau of Investigation files on Earl Browder (FOIA documents) |
| FBI-MB | Federal Bureau of Investigation files on Margaret Browder (FOIA documents) |
| FBI-RB | Federal Bureau of Investigation files on Raissa Berkmann Luganovskaya Browder (FOIA documents) |
| FDRL | Franklin D. Roosevelt Library, Hyde Park, New York |
| HLB | Hugo L. Black papers, Supreme Court file, Library of Congress, Washington, D.C. |
| INS | Immigration and Naturalization Service, file on Raissa Browder number A-4280774 (FOIA documents) |
| IS | *Indianapolis Star* |
| IT | *Indianapolis Times* |

| | |
|---|---|
| JGR | Author's interview |
| LD | *Literary Digest* |
| McN | Paul V. McNutt papers, Archives Division, Indiana State Library, Indianapolis, Ind. |
| NM | *New Masses* |
| NR | *New Republic* |
| NRC | *National Republic* collection, Hoover Institution Archives, Stanford, Calif. |
| NY | *New Yorker* |
| NYT | *New York Times* |
| NYP | *New York Post* |
| NYWT | *New York World Telegram* |
| PA | Office of the Pardon Attorney, file #66–373 (FOIA documents) |
| PJJ | Philip J. Jaffe papers, Special Collections Department, Robert W. Woodruff Library, Emory University, Atlanta, Ga. |
| PW | *People's World* |
| RJA | Robert J. Alexander's interview, Robert J. Alexander papers (private collection), Department of Economics, Rutgers University, New Brunswick, N.J. |
| SR | Stanley Reed papers, Margaret I. King Library, University of Kentucky, Lexington, Ky. |
| TD | Theodore Draper's interview, TDP |
| TDP | Theodore Draper papers, Special Collections Department, Robert W. Woodruff Library, Emory University, Atlanta, Ga. |
| THS | *Terre Haute Star* |
| THT | *Terre Haute Tribune* |
| USBP | Federal Bureau of Prisons file #60140-A (FOIA documents) |
| WOD | William O. Douglas papers, Supreme Court file, Library of Congress, Washington, D.C. |

### INTRODUCTION. THE MAN FROM KANSAS

1. John Earl Haynes to James Ryan, July 20, 1994.
2. Gary Gerstle, *Working-Class Americanism* (New York: Cambridge University Press, 1989); Harvey Klehr, *The Heyday of American Communism: The Depression Decade* (New York: Basic Books, 1984), xi, 373, 413, 304.

### 1. FROM FIELD TO OFFICE (1891–1930)

1. M. L. Olgin, *That Man Browder* (New York: Workers' Library Publishers, 1936), 3 (short campaign tract).
2. Earl Browder, unfinished autobiographical manuscript, 21–22; BP; Joseph North, "Earl Browder: A Profile," NM, April 30, 1935, 13; Earl and his brother William followed the genealogist's lead and explored their father's family tree through extensive correspondence. See D. P. Browder to William, October 25, 1935; Frank G. Browder to Earl, September 22, 1936; Ruth Browder to "Mr. Browder," January 10, 1936, BP. Extensive records on Earl's nuclear family appear in PA.
3. John Tipple, "Big Businessmen and a New Economy," in H. Wayne Morgan, *The Gilded Age* (Syracuse: Syracuse University Press, 1970), 13–30; Ruth Rosen, *The Lost Sisterhood* (Baltimore: Johns Hopkins University Press, 1982), 39.
4. Browder, autobiographical manuscript, 23–26, BP; Hubert Kelley, "Our No. 1 Communist," AM 121 (February 1936), 114; Craig Miner, *Wichita, the Magic City* (Wichita: Sedg-

wick County Historical Museum Association, 1988), 90. Local lore puts Earl Browder's birthplace at 628 S. Fern Street, a wooden structure raised in 1990 for highway development. See Beccy Tanner, *Bear Grease, Builders and Bandits* (Wichita: Wichita Eagle and Beacon, 1991), 93.

5. Miner, *Wichita, the Magic City*, 1–87.

6. Lawrence Goodwyn, *Democratic Promise* (New York: Oxford University Press, 1976), 4–557.

7. Browder, autobiographical manuscript, 3a, 27–29, BP.

8. Miner, *Wichita, the Magic City*, 113; Hortense T. Null, "Life of Carry Nation" (M. A. thesis, University of Wichita, 1930); R. L. Taylor, *Vessel of Wrath* (New York: New American Library, 1966).

9. Browder, autobiographical manuscript, 26, 27, BP. In his Soviet personnel file Browder claimed "one brother and one sister active Party workers, others sympathizers," six-page typewritten document titled "Autobiography," opis 261, delo 16(1), CPUSA-Comintern.

10. Only the October 1936 edition of CH (no author listed) cites William Browder's illness as such; PA, 3a–3b; Browder, autobiographical manuscript, 28, BP.

11. Nick Salvatore, *Eugene V. Debs: Citizen and Socialist* (Urbana: University of Illinois Press, 1982), 155–247.

12. John Patrick Diggins, *The Rise and Fall of the American Left* (New York: Norton, 1992), 88–100.

13. Gerhart Niemeyer, "The Second International: 1889–1914," in Milorad M. Drachkovitch, *The Revolutionary Internationals, 1864–1943* (Stanford: Hoover Institution on War, Revolution and Peace, 1966), 95–127; Georges Haupt, *Socialism and the Great War* (Oxford: Oxford University Press, 1972).

14. PA, 3a and 3b; Browder, autobiographical manuscript, 28; Browder to Draper, February 29, 1956, TDP; Kansas City office report, December 17, 1945, file 100–287645–24, FBI-MB; Browder, Soviet autobiography, opis 261, delo 16(1), 1, CPUSA-Comintern.

15. Browder, autobiographical manuscript, 44, BP; he received a Bachelor of Law degree from Lincoln-Jefferson College in Wichita (PA, 3a); Browder, Soviet autobiography, opis 261, delo 16(1), 2, CPUSA-Comintern.

16. "Browder Interview VI," October 22, 1954; Browder to Draper, February 29, 1956, TDP; Browder, autobiographical manuscript, 39, 70, BP; Theodore Draper, *The Roots of American Communism* (New York: Viking, 1957), 308–9.

17. Salvatore, *Eugene V. Debs: Citizen and Socialist*, 280–85.

18. John Higham, *Strangers in the Land* (New York: Atheneum, 1963), chap. 8; Browder, autobiographical manuscript, 72; United States Penitentiary, Leavenworth Kansas, admission summary, n.d., USBP; Sullivan married Margaret, the younger sister of Earl and William, around 1921. "Memorandum for FBI Director from the Special Agent in Charge, New York," January 30, 1958, file 100–287645–141, FBI-MB; "Interview Report," April 24, 1958, file 100–287645–144, FBI-MB.

19. Zechariah Chafee, Jr., *Free Speech in the United States* (Cambridge: Harvard University Press, 1941); William Preston, Jr., *Aliens and Dissenters* (New York: Harper & Row, 1963); record clerk Carl F. Zarter to Assistant Solicitor General John H. Hudson, April 26, 1935, USBP; Browder, autobiographical manuscript, 72–87, BP.

20. Milly Bennett and A. Tom Grunfeld, ed., *On Her Own* (Armonk, N.Y.: Sharpe, 1993), 196–97; Hubert Kelley, "Our No. 1 Communist," 112.

21. Salvatore, *Eugene V. Debs: Citizen and Socialist*, 286.

22. Draper, *Roots of American Communism*, 309.

23. "Browder Interview VI," October 22, 1954, TDP; open letter on *Worker's World* stationery by Ella Reeve Bloor requesting subscriptions, July 22, 1919, BP; JGR/Browder, March 13, 1972.

24. Gladys Browder to James Ryan, December 21, 1976; PA, 3–3c; Kelley, "Our No. 1 Communist," 114.

25. Gladys Browder to Ryan, December 21, 1976; warden to Gladys, August 7, 1919, and July 15, 1920; Gladys to warden, July 9, 1929, USBP; Gladys to Ryan, December 21, 1976.
26. Browder, autobiographical manuscript, chap. IV, 10, 101, BP; JGR/John W. Roberts, Bureau of Prisons Archivist, March 4, 1993. Mr. Roberts's guidance in researching federal prison history is especially appreciated.
27. PA, 3–3c; Leavenworth Penitentiary's "Admission Summary," and "Individual Daily Labor Record," USBP.
28. Bennett, *On Her Own*, 197; Browder, autobiographical manuscript, 94–107, BP.
29. Browder, autobiographical manuscript, 109, BP; parole board president to Browder, November 11, 1920, USBP.
30. Browder testimony, Dies Committee, 76th Congress, 1st Session, Vol. 7, 4439–94; Gladys Browder to Ryan, December 21, 1976; PA, 3–3c.
31. James R. Green, *The World of the Worker* (New York: Hill & Wang, 1982), 101.
32. Browder, autobiographical manuscript, 19, 101–21, BP.
33. Draper, *Roots of American Communism*, 310, 251.
34. Browder, autobiographical manuscript, 122, BP; James P. Cannon, *The First Ten Years of American Communism* (New York: Lyle Stuart, 1962), 111.
35. Draper, *Roots of American Communism*, 310–20.
36. Browder, Soviet autobiography, opis 261, delo 16(1), 3, CPUSA-Comintern; Daniel Bell, *Marxian Socialism in the United States* (Princeton: Princeton University Press, 1967), 125.
37. Browder, autobiographical manuscript, chap. IV, 10, BP.
38. File No. 146–1–11–350, DJ.
39. Harvey A. Levenstein, *Communism, Anticommunism and the CIO* (Westport, Conn.: Greenwood, 1981), 6–7.
40. Edward P. Johanningsmeier, *Forging American Communism: The Life of William Z. Foster* (Princeton: Princeton University Press, 1994), 165–66; Browder, autobiographical manuscript, 168, BP; Cannon, *First Ten Years of American Communism*, 109, CB (December 1944), 10–14.
41. Diggins, *The Rise and Fall of the American Left*, 122.
42. Johanningsmeier, *Forging American Communism*, 181.
43. Browder, autobiographical manuscript, 168, BP; Browder to Draper, March 9, 1956, and February 29, 1956, TDP.
44. "Admission Summary," Atlanta Penitentiary file 66–373, 48, "medical," PA.
45. Browder, Soviet autobiography, opis 261, delo 16(1), 2, CPUSA-Comintern.
46. Kelley, "Our No. 1 Communist," 115.
47. Theodore Draper, *American Communism and Soviet Russia: The Formative Period* (New York: Viking, 1960), 227.
48. Harvey Klehr, *The Heyday of American Communism*, 23; Browder, autobiographical manuscript, 39–40, BP.
49. Browder, autobiographical manuscript, 37–40, BP.
50. Draper, *American Communism and Soviet Russia*, 226; Dimitri Volkogónov, *Stalin: Triumph and Tragedy*, trans. Harold Shikman (New York: Grove Weidenfeld, 1991), 45.
51. Raissa Browder, Soviet autobiography, opis 261, delo 3264, trans. Leon Luxemburg, CPUSA-Comintern; Robert Conquest, *Harvest of Sorrow* (New York: Oxford University Press, 1986), 53–56.
52. Samuel Darcy to Ryan, March 4, 1994.
53. Earl Browder, *Civil War in Nationalist China* (Chicago: Labor Unity Publishing Association, 1927), 9, 46.
54. Browder, Columbia, 2–4; Joseph North, "Earl Browder: A Profile," 13–15.
55. Harvey Klehr, John Earl Haynes, and Fridrikh Igorevich Firsov, *The Secret World of American Communism* (New Haven: Yale University Press, 1995), 42.

56. Browder, Columbia, 194; Bennett, *On Her Own*, 184.

57. Bennett, *On Her Own*, 216; Browder, Columbia, 267.

58. Passport Services office, DS file on Katherine Harrison; passport application, with photograph, November 22, 1927; "Memorandum to London," November 11, 1932 (National Archives, Washington, D.C.), 1–3; opis 72, delo 5242, December 9, 1927 (identification ribbon for concealing in clothing, a frequent Comintern covert activities practice), signed by CPUSA representative J. Louis Engdahl, July 11, 1928, despite her supposed transfer to the Russian CP, opis 72, delo 5242, Comintern; Shanghai Municipal Police, *Security Classified Records Relating to Espionage Activities in Shanghai 1926–1948*, Vol. 7, 92–93 (National Archives, Washington, D.C.); Darcy to Ryan, June 12, 1994. Ex-Communist Benjamin Gitlow later contended that Soviet agent Nicholas Dozenberg had brought a $10,000 bill to Harrison in the United States. She allegedly gave it to Browder, who, on a side venture to the Philippines, tried to cash it. This attracted counterespionage agents, who supposedly followed him to his secret hideaway in Shanghai, smashed a spy ring there, and destroyed Stalin's work in China. Gitlow also claimed that the Comintern criticized Browder severely for this (*I Confess: The Truth about American Communism* [New York: Dutton, 1940], 536–37). Browder denied the charges under oath before the Dies Committee (76th Congress, 1st Session, Vol. 7, 4275–528). In James G. Ryan, "The Making of Native Marxist: The Early Career of Earl Browder," *Review of Politics* 39 (July 1977), 354, n. 51, the writer unintentionally but nevertheless erroneously implied that Philip Jaffe knew firsthand about Harrison and the largenote caper. Mr. Jaffe, to whom I expressed my profound regret in a letter, replied: "You are mistaken that I know how Browder obtained the $10,000 bill. I never met [Harrison] and know of her only through other sources" (Jaffe to Ryan, October 11, 1977). Concerning Harrison, Jaffe remained tight-lipped.

59. Darcy to Ryan, March 4, 1994; Memorandum on Katherine Harrison, November 11, 1932, National Archives; Klehr, Haynes, and Firsov, *Secret World of American Communism*, 45–46. The English-dominated Shanghai Municipal Police was an organization created by British, French, American, and Japanese forces to guard colonialist interests in the city's commercial center.

60. Attaché's Report Blank, ONI, February 5, 1929, file 40–3798–1; O. H. Luhring to Hoover, April 24, 1929, file 40–3798–1; Hoover to C. D. McKean, April 29, 1929, file 40–3798–1; Hoover to L. C. Schilder, July 8, 1929, file 40–3798–11; Hoover to McKean, July 8, 1929, file 40–3798; Report of H. Fink, September 4, 1929, file 40–3798–17; Report of Fink, March 17, 1930, file 40–3798–22, all FBI-EB.

61. Philip J. Jaffe, *The Rise and Fall of American Communism* (New York: Horizon Press, 1975), 29; Klehr, Haynes, and Firsov, *Secret World of American Communism*, 50–51; I am grateful to Harvey Klehr for stressing this final point in a December 12, 1992, conversation.

62. Bert Cochran, *Labor and Communism* (Princeton: Princeton University Press, 1977), 31.

63. The new federation described itself as being organized in Cleveland, August 31, 1929, a "reorganization and expansion of the old Trade Union Educational League." See Trade Union Unity League, *The Trade Union Unity League: Its Program, Structure, Methods and History* (New York: TUUL, n.d.[circa 1929]).

64. Bert Cochran, *Labor and Communism*, 31–36.

65. Draper, *American Communism and Soviet Russia*, 279–310; Harvey Klehr and John Haynes, *The American Communist Movement: Storming Heaven Itself* (New York: Twayne, 1992), 45.

66. Cochran, *Labor and Communism*, 31–36.

67. "Additional Organizational Measures on the American Question," May 17, 1929, opis 37 delo 47, Comintern; telegram from ECCI Presidium to "Victoria," declaring that Moscow "can no longer tolerate increasing factional struggle," March 7, 1929, opis 37, delo 51, Comintern; "Telegram sent to our delegation in America," April 3, 1929," declaring "Ap-

peals by either faction . . . we consider absolutely impermissible," opis 37, delo 51, Comintern; Draper, *American Communism and Soviet Russia*, 397, 430; Jaffe, *Rise and Fall of American Communism*, 31.

68. Klehr, *Heyday of American Communism*, 18, 24, 419; TD/Browder, September 29, 1953, and June 28, 1955, TDP; Browder, Columbia, 225–26; DW, October 15, 1929.

69. *Communist* (April 1930) listed the new secretariat in its statement of ownership (290) to avoid legal problems; Darcy to Ryan, March 4, 1994; "Interview with Earl Browder, May 19, 1953," TDP; Browder, Soviet autobiography, opis 261, delo 16(1), 5, CPUSA-Comintern.

## 2. NO MORE TRADITION'S CHAIN
## SHALL BIND US (1930–1933)

1. Samuel A. Darcy to James Ryan, March 4, 1994; NYT, March 7, 1930 (DW gave far higher figures); Irving Bernstein, *The Lean Years* (Boston: Houghton, Mifflin, 1966), 427.

2. J. Peters, "Confidential Report to the Anglo-American Secretariat" June 8, 1932, opis 1, delo 2623, CPUSA-Comintern. Klehr, Haynes, and Firsov, *The Secret World of American Communism*, 73–95, have reproduced documents showing that Peters later returned to the United States to direct the CPUSA's secret apparatus from late 1932 to June 1938. See also "Party and Masses Work, Strong and Weak Points," referent J. Barnett, August 20, 1932, opis 1, delo 2623, CPUSA-Comintern.

3. "Party and Mass Work"; NYT, March 8, 1932.

4. Levenstein, *Communism, Anticommunism and the CIO*, 20.

5. On July 23, 1933, the Comintern's Anglo-American Secretariat (AAS) advised the CPUSA to "utilize the Scottsboro case for building up" the International Labor Defense (ILD), a supposedly independent body. Dutifully the American Polburo published a resolution, but it revealed too nakedly the ILD-CPUSA "inner connection." It brought immediate, angry denunciation as a "serious political error" from Helen Stassova, an Old Bolshevik who headed the ILD's parent organization, the International Red Aid for Class War Prisoners (also known by the Russian abbreviation MOPR). On July 26 the secretariat reprimanded the CPUSA for failing to remember "that the ILD is a non-Party organization and therefore it is to be led only through the Party fraction." See the minutes of the AAS bureau meeting of July 23, 1933; Stassova's undated letter to the secretariat, and minutes of AAS bureau meeting, July 26, opis 72, delo 204, Comintern. Seven months later she voiced a similar complaint, and the secretariat sent a reprimand to Browder through Gerhart Eisler. Stassova to the AAS, February 9, 1934; letter to Eisler and Browder [in German], February 15, opis 72, delo 274, Comintern. I thank Herbert Romerstein for these materials. Klehr and Haynes, *The American Communist Movement*, 63.

6. NYT, March 3, 1930; April 4, 1931.

7. Louis Kovess, "Immigrants in the CPUSA and Tasks of the CP," June 25, 1932, opis 1, delo 2623, CPUSA-Comintern; "Speech of Comrade Gusev," April 4, 1933, opis 72, delo 225, Comintern.

8. Browder speech, June 21, 1930, opis 1, delo 1878, CPUSA-Comintern.

9. Baldwin to the secretariat, January 23, 1930; Browder to Baldwin, January 27, 1930; "Proposed Statement" and cover letter to Browder, February 7, 1930, all BP.

10. Browder, Columbia, 226, 340, 350; JGR/Browder, March 13, 1972; DW, April 19, 1930.

11. Darcy to Ryan, March 4, 1994; for an argument that Foster was also a "reluctant agitator," see Johanningsmeier, *Forging American Communism*, 249–71.

12. Weinstone speech, April 4, 1933, opis 72, delo 225, Comintern.

13. NYT, June 21, 1930; James Weinstein, *Ambiguous Legacy* (New York: New Viewpoints, 1975), 73.

14. NYT, June 21, 1930.

15. Browder, report to the Polburo, November 22, 1930, reprinted, *Communist* (January 1931), 8–9, 22–23.

16. Darcy to Ryan, March 4, 1994.

17. Minutes of bureau meeting, January 23, 1931, opis 72, delo 147, Comintern.

18. Browder speech, January 3, 1932, opis 72, delo 164, Comintern.

19. "Party and Masses Work," referent J. Barnett, August 20, 1932, opis 1, delo 2623, CPUSA-Comintern; "Discussion," March 14, 1932, opis 1, delo 2671, CPUSA-Comintern; "Discussion Summary, Polburo" March 22, opis 1, delo 2671, CPUSA-Comintern; Browder speech to Polburo, December 11, opis 1, delo 2674, CPUSA-Comintern; "Report of Comrade Randolph," June 26, opis 72, delo 150, Comintern.

20. Matthew Josephson, *Infidel in the Temple* (New York: Knopf, 1967), 132; "On the Questions Raised by Comrade Gusev," April 8, opis 72, delo 184, Comintern.

21. Gusev questions, April 8, 1932, opis 72, delo 184, Comintern; Browder speech, March 14, opis 1, delo 2671, CPUSA-Comintern; "Discussion Summary, Polburo," March 22, opis 1, delo 2671, CPUSA-Comintern.

22. Browder speech, February 10, 1932, opis 72, delo 142; "Organization Directives," February 22, opis 72, delo 2601, both Comintern.

23. "Discussion Summary, Polburo," March 22, opis 72, delo 2671; "Speech of Comrade Gusev," April 4, 1933, opis 72, delo 225, both Comintern.

24. Browder speech, August 27, opis 72, delo 2668, CPUSA-Comintern; DW, June 5; Browder speech, September 20, opis 1, delo 2683, CPUSA-Comintern.

25. Report of Randolph, June 26, opis 72, delo 150, Comintern, and June 28, opis 72, delo 152, CPUSA-Comintern. "Randolph" was the generic name for America's Comintern representative in Moscow.

26. Polburo minutes, July 7, 1932, opis 1, delo 2672; Browder speech, August 18, opis 1, delo 2672; Newton speech, August 27, opis 1, delo 2672, CPUSA-Comintern.

27. Browder speech, August 27, opis 1, delo 2657; Polburo notes, August 29, opis 1, delo 2673, CPUSA-Comintern.

28. Allen speech, "General Political Report and Additional Remarks," August 27, opis 1, delo 2672, CPUSA-Comintern.

29. CI rep to Moscow, August 31, opis 1, delo 2673, CPUSA-Comintern.

30. Foster to Dr. S. Bernstein, September 7, and Bernstein to R. Saltzman of International Workers' Order, September 8, opis 1, delo 2710; untitled memo on Foster's travels, opis 1, delo 2710; Bernstein to Browder, September 17, opis 1, delo 2710; "To Whom It May Concern," October 7, opis 1, delo 2710, all CPUSA-Comintern; Johanningsmeier, *Forging American Communism*, 266; DW, September 15, 1932, January 19, 1934; and January 22, 1934.

31. Undated Allen telegram (before September 14, 1932) to Anglo-American Secretariat, opis 1, delo 2692; Allen to same, September 15, 1932, opis 1, delo 2611, CPUSA-Comintern.

32. Browder memorandum to the Polburo, September 13, opis 1, delo 2673, CPUSA-Comintern.

33. Weinstone speech to Polburo, September 19, 1932, opis 1, delo 2683, CPUSA-Comintern.

34. Browder speech, ibid.; Browder speech to Polburo, September 20, opis 1, delo 2683, CPUSA-Comintern.

35. Weinstone to Polburo, September 20, opis 1, delo 2683, CPUSA-Comintern.

36. Notations on Anglo-American Secretariat closed meetings, September 22, 1932, September 25, October 5, opis 1, delo 148; Polburo minutes, November 12, opis 1, delo 2684; Johnstone report, November 12, opis 1, delo 2679, all CPUSA-Comintern.

37. "Report on 12th Plenum of ECCI by Gebert," November 13, 1932, opis 1, delo 2679, CPUSA-Comintern; Browder speech to Polburo, November 13, opis 1, delo 2679, ibid.

38. "Political Report and Additional Remarks," August 27, 1932, opis 1, delo 2657, CPUSA-Comintern.

39. Committee to L. Platt, October 12, 1932, opis 1, delo 2961; Browder speech to Polburo (relating Kuusinen's remark), December 11, opis 1, delo 2674; Browder speech to Polburo, December 14, opis 1, delo 2680, all CPUSA-Comintern.

40. All membership figures from "Additional Memorandum on Problems of CPUSA," March 23, 1937, opis 1 delo 4066, CPUSA-Comintern.

41. "To the Central Committee of the CPUSA," September 27, 1932, opis 261, delo 3264, Comintern.

42. Letter from New York to Moscow, signed "Lena," December 13, 1932, opis 1, delo 2615, CPUSA-Comintern.

43. Polburo minutes, November 25, 1932, opis 1, delo 2679, CPUSA-Comintern.

44. DW, December 6, 1932; TD/Browder, July 15, 1955, 12–13, TDP.

45. Klehr, *The Heyday of American Communism*, 67–68; *Congressional Record*, House of Representatives, December 7, 1932, 134–35; DW, December 7, 1932; Klehr, *Heyday of American Communism*, 68.

46. Allen to the Anglo-American Secretariat, December 6, 1932, opis 1, delo 2611, CPUSA-Comintern; Browder, "The Revisionism of Sidney Hook," *Communist* (February 1933), 133–46; ibid. (March 1933), 285–300; Diggins, *The Rise and Fall of the American Left*, 160.

47. Browder, "The End of Relative Capitalist Stabilization and Tasks of Our Party," reprinted, *Communist* (March 1933), 233.

48. Speeches of Browder, March 28, 1933, opis 72, delo 221; Amis, April 2, opis 72, delo 223, both Comintern.

49. Speech of Weinstone, April 4, opis 72, delo 225, Comintern.

50. Speech of Gusev, April 4, ibid.

51. Ibid.

52. Speech of Browder, April 8, opis 72, delo 227; Bedacht, August 18, opis 72, delo 229; Kuusinen, April 26, opis 72, delo 233, all Comintern.

53. Speech of Kuusinen, April 26, opis 72, delo 223, Comintern.

54. Levenstein, *Communism, Anticommunism and the CIO*, 22; DW, July 8, 1933.

55. Minutes, Bureau Meeting, Anglo-American Secretariat, April 22, April 27, and May 11, opis 72, delo 204, all Comintern. I thank Herbert Romerstein for these documents.

56. Minutes of CPUSA Extraordinary Conference, July 7–10, opis 72, delo 3103; "Browder Summary," July 10, opis 72, delo 3106; "Immediate Tasks," July 10, opis 72, delo 3109, all Comintern.

57. Maurice Isserman, *Which Side Were You On?* (Middletown, Conn.: Wesleyan University Press, 1982), 10–11.

58. Darcy to Ryan, March 4, 1994.

59. JGR/Gil Green, December 31, 1992.

60. DW, August 5, 1933.

61. TD/Earl Browder, June 23, 1953, and September 29, 1953, TDP.

62. Roger Keeran, *The Communist Party and the Auto Workers Unions* (Bloomington: Indiana University Press, 1980), 93.

## 3. A BETTER MOVEMENT IN BIRTH? (1934–1935)

1. E. H. Carr, *Twilight of the Comintern: 1930–1935* (New York: Pantheon, 1982), 120–22.

2. Ibid., 125; Helen Graham and Paul Preston, *The Popular Front in Europe* (New York: St. Martin's Press, 1987), 2.

3. Samuel Darcy, "Autobiography," TDP; Stella Blagoeva, *Georgi Dimitrov: A Biographical Sketch*, trans. Marjorie Pojarlieva (Sofia: Foreign Language Press, 1961); Fritz Tobias, *The Reichstag Fire* (New York: Putnam, 1964), 214. Stephen Koch in *Double Lives* (New York: Free Press, 1994) relies on thin evidence to argue unconvincingly that the entire Popular Front

of the 1930s was a charade used by Stalin and Hitler alike to discredit and destroy their respective domestic opponents.

4. Jaffe, *The Rise and Fall of American Communism*, 17, 39; Browder to Draper, October 13, 1957, TDP; Jaffe to Ryan, June 12, 1977; Carr, *Twilight of the Comintern*, 101–17.

5. Carr, *Twilight of the Comintern*, 125.

6. Volkogônôv, *Stalin: Triumph and Tragedy*, 337.

7. Carr, *Twilight of the Comintern*, 125, 126, 127.

8. Ibid., 127.

9. TD/Browder, June 23, 1955 (second portion), 2, TDP; RJA/Browder, April 4–5, 1954, AP.

10. Carr, *Twilight of the Comintern*, 154; *Communist International*, No. 12, 14–21 and No. 14, 24–31.

11. Carr, *Twilight of the Comintern*, 151.

12. Robert S. McElvaine, *The Great Depression* (New York: Times Books, 1984), 236.

13. Robert H. Zieger, *American Workers, American Unions, 1920–1985* (Baltimore: Johns Hopkins University Press, 1986), 28.

14. CPUSA Political Bureau, "Directives on Work within the AFL and Independent Trade Unions," *Communist* 13, no. 1 (January 1934), 113–15.

15. Levenstein, *Communism, Anticommunism and the CIO*, 24.

16. Cochran, *Labor and Communism*, 84.

17. Keeran, *The Communist Party and the Auto Workers Unions*, 114; for proof that Bridges was a CP member, see CPUSA Central Committee list, opis 74, delo 467, Comintern. For discussion of the issue, see Harvey Klehr and John Haynes, "Communists and the CIO: From the Soviet Archives," *Labor History* 35 (Summer 1994), 442–46; Green, *The World of the Worker*, 144; Gerstle, *Working-Class Americanism*, 127–29.

18. Raissa Browder, Soviet autobiography, opis 261, delo 3264, CPUSA-Comintern; she listed the dates of her sons' births for an immigration inspector, October 10, 1939, DS; Earl to Georgi Dimitrov, January 19, 1938, opis 74, delo 469, Comintern (I thank Herbert Romerstein for this document).

19. James L. Houghteling (INS Commissioner), "Memorandum," December 7, 1939, INS; T. B. Shoemaker, "Memorandum," December 8, 1939, and Houghteling to the Solicitor General, June 6, 1940, 3, file 56013/511, FBI-RB; JGR/Philip J. Jaffe, August 1, 1977; Kelley did not include the incident in his article but told the FBI about it six years later; L. B. Nichols, "Memorandum for Mr. Tolson," January 28, 1941, file 40–3718–28, FBI-EB; Raissa Browder, DW, June 27, 1936; May 23, 1938, "For a Correct Approach to the Problems of the National Groups," *Communist* (September 1938); "Problems of the National Groups in the United States," *Communist* (May 1939); "The National Groups in the Fight for Democracy," *Communist* (July 1939).

20. JGR/Gil Green, December 31, 1992; JGR/A. B. Magil, January 6, 1993.

21. Klehr, Haynes, and Firsov, 243–49.

22. AAS Buro minutes, January 13, 1934; March 8, opis 72, delo 257, Comintern. I thank Herbert Romerstein for these documents; Klehr, Haynes, and Firsov, *Secret World of American Communism*, 87–90, 71–188.

23. Gil Green, *Young Communists and the Unity of Youth* (New York: Youth Publishers, 1935), 6; Thomas speech reported in DW August 20 and August 25, 1934; Fraser Ottanelli, *The Communist Party of the United States* (New Brunswick, N.J.: Rutgers University Press, 1991), 92.

24. The CPUSA, which has repeatedly refused to discuss Earl Browder, reports the four Americans as John Reed, Charles Ruthenberg, Big Bill Haywood, and Louis Engdahl; Johanningsmeier, *Forging American Communism*, 283; Daniel Aaron, *Writers on the Left* (New York: Avon, 1961), 315.

25. Aaron, *Writers on the Left*, 298–99.

26. J. Joseph Huthmacher, *Senator Robert F. Wagner and the Rise of Urban Liberalism* (New York: Atheneum, 1971), 182.

27. JGR/Robert J. Alexander, November 25, 1986.

28. Earl Browder, "New Developments and New Tasks in the USA," *Communist* (February 1935), 101-3, 113-16.

29. TD/Browder, June 23, 1955 (second portion), 2, 3, and June 6, 1953, 2, TDP; DW, January 21, 1935, and February 16, 1935; SP "Convention Memo No. 6 'United Front,' " 15, BP.

30. Klehr and Haynes, *The American Communist Movement*, 72-73; Cochran, *Labor and Communism*, 75; Levenstein, *Communism, Anticommunism and the CIO*, 25; Green, *World of the Worker*, 147.

31. NM, January 22, 1935; Browder, "Communism in Literature," in Henry Hart, ed., *American Writers Congress* (New York: International Publishers, 1935), 66-71; Max Eastman, *Artists in Uniform* (New York: Knopf, 1934).

32. Hart, *American Writers Congress*, 71.

33. Aaron, *Writers on the Left*, 303; Josephson, *Infidel in the Temple*, 364.

34. Joseph North, *William Z. Foster: An Appreciation* (New York: International Publishers, 1955), 35; TD/David Ramsey, January 15, 1957, 1; March 27, 1957, 5, TDP.

35. Green, *World of the Worker*, 150.

36. Darcy to Ryan, March 4, 1994; March 13, 1994.

37. Darcy, autobiographical manuscript, 234, TDP.

38. Ibid., 233.

39. Ibid., 233.

40. Ibid., 233; Georgi Dimitrov, *The United Front* (New York: International Publishers, 1938), 99.

41. Ibid., 11-109.

42. Ibid., 47-48.

43. Ibid., 47-109; Kermit McKenzie, *The Comintern and World Revolution* (New York: Columbia University Press, 1964), 288.

44. Dimitrov, *United Front*, 93.

45. DW, August 12, 1935; Dimitrov, *United Front*, 42-43; NYT, August 12.

46. "From the Seventh World Congress" (typewritten quotations), BP.

47. Ibid.

48. *Sunday Worker*, October 11, 1936.

49. DW, October 8, 1936.

50. NYT, September 19, 1935.

51. TD/Browder, June 23, 1955, TDP; John Earl Haynes, *Dubious Alliance* (Minneapolis: University of Minnesota Press, 1984), 15-16.

52. Ottanelli, *Communist Party of the United States*, 92, 61.

53. Klehr, Haynes, and Firsov, *Secret World of American Communism*, 59-63; "Questions of the Anglo-American Lander-Secretariat for the Meeting of the Secretariat of the ECCI," n.d. [1935], opis 14, delo 1, Comintern. I thank Herbert Romerstein for this document.

54. Zieger, *American Workers, American Unions, 1920-1985*, 49; Melvyn Dubofsky and Warren Van Tine, *John L. Lewis* (New York: Quadrangle, 1977), 220-21.

55. Browder, *Build the United People's Front* (New York: Workers Library Publishers, 1936), 51; TD/Browder, June 23, 1955, TDP; Klehr, Haynes, and Firsov, *Secret World of American Communism*, 106.

56. Browder speech, April 10, 1936, opis 14, delo 63, Comintern. Fragmentary evidence suggests that before the CIO existed, the Communists sought to create, along industrial lines, an Independent Federation of Labor to unite workers unwilling to go into the AFL. "On the Work of Forming an Independant Federation of Labor in the USA," February 25, 1934, opis 5, delo 408, Comintern. I thank Herbert Romerstein for both documents.

57. Johanningsmeier, *Forging American Communism*, 276.

58. DW, November 29, 1935; NYT, November 28, 1935.

59. DW, November 29, 1935; NYT, November 28, 1935.

## 4. NATIVE RADICALISM (1936)

1. Frank A. Warren, *Liberals and Communism* (Bloomington: Indiana University Press, 1966), 116.

2. Philip J. Jaffe to James Ryan, January 24, 1977; Jaffe, *The Rise and Fall of American Communism*, 17; Stein, "Marx's Disenchanted Salesman," AH 33 (December 1971), 102.

3. George Charney, *A Long Journey* (Chicago: Quadrangle, 1968), 140; Jaffe, *Rise and Fall of American Communism*, 17, 138; JGR/Robert J. Alexander, November 25, 1986.

4. RJA/Browder, April 1, 1950; March 23, 1953, AP; Volkogónòv, *Stalin: Triumph and Tragedy*, 114; JGR/Gil Green, December 31, 1992.

5. Earl Browder, *The People's Front* (New York: International Publishers, 1938), 52; transcript, March 27, 1939, 7, BP; Earl Browder, *The Democratic Front: For Jobs, Security, Democracy and Peace* (New York: Workers' Library Publishers, 1938), 83.

6. Eugene Lyons, *The Red Decade* (New York: Bobbs-Merrill, 1941), 180; Philip J. Jaffe to James Ryan, January 24, 1977.

7. Charney, *A Long Journey*, 60; Dorothy Healey and Maurice Isserman, *Dorothy Healey Remembers* (New York: Oxford University Press, 1990), 60.

8. Earl Browder, *What Is Communism?* (New York: Workers Library, 1936), 154; Browder, *People's Front*, 201.

9. Sharon Hartman Strom, "Challenging 'Woman's Place': Feminism, the Left and Industrial Unionism in the 1930's," *Feminist Studies* 2 (Summer 1983), 359–80; William Chafe, *The American Woman* (New York: Oxford University Press, 1972), 121.

10. Strom, "Challenging 'Woman's Place,' " 379.

11. Ruth Milkman, "Organizing the Sexual Division of Labor: Historical Perspectives on 'Women's Work' and the American Labor Movement," *Socialist Review* 10 (January–February 1980), 119; Philip Foner, *Women and the American Labor Movement: From World War I to the Present* (New York: Free Press, 1980), 300.

12. Robert Shaffer, "Women and the Communist Party, USA, 1930–1940," *Socialist Review* 45 (May–June 1979), 73–118.

13. Elsa Jane Dixler, "The Woman Question: Women and the Communist Party," unpublished dissertation, Yale University, 1974, i–262.

14. Ibid.

15. Earl Browder, *Communism in the United States* (New York: International Publishers, 1935), 101; Earl Browder, *The Communists in the People's Front* (New York: Workers Library, 1937), 4; DW, October 11, 1937; Earl Browder, *A Message to Catholics* (New York: Workers Library, 1938), 9.

16. Browder, *What Is Communism?*, 154, 156; Charney, 74. JGR/A. B. Magil, January 6, 1993.

17. "Additional Memorandum on Problems of CPUSA," March 23, 1937, opis 1, delo 4066, CPUSA-Comintern; HUAC, executive session, 13, BP; Nathan Glazer, *The Social Basis of Communism* (New York: Harcourt, 1961), 90.

18. JGR/Gil Green, December 31, 1992.

19. William Z. Foster, *History of the Communist Party of the United States* (New York: International Publishers, 1952), 349.

20. Ottanelli, *The Communist Party of the United States*, 140–44; Gerald Horne, *Black Liberation/Red Scare* (Newark: University of Delaware Press, 1994), 72–78.

21. Fred Brown, "New Forms of Party Organization Help Us to Win the Masses," *Party*

*Organizer* (July–August 1936), 9; Earl Browder, "Labor vs. Landon," *Worker,* September 13, 1936.

22. Browder, *People's Front,* 235–36; "The Communist Party and Civil Liberties in the United States" [1937], BP.

23. Browder was not the first Communist to remind Americans of their revolutionary traditions. See V. I. Lenin, *Letter to American Workers* (New York: International Publishers, 1934); Bertram D. Wolfe, Jay Lovestone, and William F. Dunne, *Our Heritage from 1776: A Working Class View of the First American Revolution* (New York: Workers' School, 1926).

24. Browder, "What Every Worker Should Know about the NRA" (New York: Workers Library Publishers, 1933).

25. Gerstle, *Working-Class Americanism,* 8.

26. Browder, *People's Front,* 249; the Browder papers contain a typewritten, but by no means comprehensive, list of such talks. It includes "Who Are the Communists?" (1935); "Lincoln and the Communists" (February 12, 1936); "Democracy and the Constitution" (September 1937); "Revolutionary Background of the U.S. Constitution" (September 1937); "American Revolutionary Traditions" (December 1938); "Internationalism: A Tradition of Lincoln and Jefferson" (February 1940); "Rediscovering America" (DW, October 11, 1941); "Jefferson and the People's Revolution" (April 1943); and "Preamble to the CPA Constitution" (May 1944).

27. Earl Browder, "Who Are the Real Americans?" (New York: Workers Library Publishers, 1936), 6; Browder, *What Every Worker Should Know About the NRA,* 4.

28. Browder, *People's Front,* 291.

29. Ibid., 249, 247.

30. Ibid., 256, 254, 192; Gerald Runkle, "Karl Marx and the American Civil War," *Comparative Studies in Society and History* 6 (1964), 117–44.

31. Browder, *People's Front,* 252.

32. Glazer, *Social Basis of Communism,* 130–31.

33. Cochran, *Labor and Communism,* 107.

34. TD/Browder, June 2, 1953, and June 23, 1955; TDP; TD/Samuel A. Darcy, May 15, 1957, TDP.

35. TD/Browder, June 2, 1953, and June 23, 1955; Browder to Draper, October 13, 1957; TD/Darcy, May 15, 1957, TDP. Minor disagreements over details exist, but Browder's and Darcy's accounts are substantially the same. See also Columbia, 249.

36. TD/Browder, June 23, 1955, TDP; Jaffe to Ryan, July 12, 1977.

37. *Communist* (June 1936), 484; *Worker,* May 24, "Convention Memo No. 6, 'United Front,' " 13, BP; TD/Browder, June 23, 1955, TDP.

38. NYT, May 20, 1936; Thomas to Browder, October 22, 2, BP; Waldman quoted in NYT, May 20.

39. "To the National Convention of the Socialist Party of America," May 1936, 1–6, BP; NYT, May 23.

40. DW, December 29, 1934.

41. Undated letter to CPUSA Central Committee; Lovestone sent a copy to Otto Kuusinen in Moscow on January 5, 1935; letters to Browder on January 27, 1936, and January 31, 1936, and an undated missive to the Central Committee blaming the German CP for Hitler's victory, opis 1, delo 4044, CPUSA-Comintern.

42. Lovestone to Central Executive Committee, December 30, 1935, BP; Lovestone to Browder, June 20, 1936, BP; late in life Browder stated, "We never got along." He cited a matter of personality; Lovestone had a "bad character," and Browder had helped expel him. Nevertheless, Browder conceded that he came to adopt a view "close to" Lovestone's American exceptionalism. JGR/Browder, March 13, 1972; Klehr, Haynes, and Firsov, *The Secret World of American Communism,* 128–32.

43. TD/Browder, June 22, 1955; DW, June 4, 1936.

44. "For Dimitrov, Manuilsky, Marty and Randolph from Earl and Edward," April 15, 1936, opis 74, delo 466, Comintern (I thank Herbert Romerstein for this document); Klehr, Haynes, and Firsov, *Secret World of American Communism*, 67–69.

45. NR (July 8, 1936), 252; DW, June 25.

46. William P. Mangold, "The Communist Convention," NR (July 15), 292 (quotations); DW, June 29; NM (July 7).

47. "Election Platform 1936," in Browder, *What Is Communism?*, 180–87.

48. Sandor Voros, *American Commissar* (New York: Chilton, 1961), 264–65; Thomas to Browder, October 22, 1936, BP.

49. CB (no author given), 1944, 11; DW, August 31, September 27, and July 18, 1936.

50. Browder, *People's Front*, 93, 92, 24, 77–78, 102. Browder later explained his belief that campaigning against Landon did not take "many votes away from" the Republican but did ensure that "no left wing votes would go to him." RJA/Browder, December 16, 1971, AP.

51. NYT, March 6, September 4, September 21, and September 12, 1936; DW, September 12; NYT, September 21.

52. NYT and DW, September 13 and 14, 1936. Browder to the president, September 13, DJNA; Cummings to Browder, September 16, 1936, DJNA.

53. NYT, September 20, October 28; DW, September 20; LD, October 31, 10; NYT, May 24, October 26.

54. DW and IS, October 26, 1936; IS, October 24; DW, October 26.

55. THS, October 1 and 2, 1936; NYT, October 1 and 2; DW, October 1–3. The police chief did admit newspersons.

56. Thomas to Browder, October 22, 1936, BP; THT, September 3 and October 1; NYT, October 1 and 2; DW, October 1–3.

57. Reported in NYT, THT, September 30–October 2, 1936; DW, October 1.

58. Charles Stadtfeld (Indiana CPUSA chairman) to the president and Browder to the president, both September 29, 1936. Copies telegraphed from Stephen Early to McNutt, September 30, file No. 3997, FDRL; Foster telegrams to the president and Cummings, September 30, DJNA; Hicks to McNutt, October 1, McN.

59. Assistant Attorney General Brien McMahon to Foster, October 1, 1936, DJNA; Indiana's Assistant Attorney General Ralph E. Hanna's three-page report to McNutt, October 14, McN. I thank Anita Noble for locating this item.

60. DW and NYT, October 2, 1936; THT and THS, October 7.

61. A. Solomon to the U.S. Attorney General, October 1, 1936, DJNA; Daniel K. Schwarz to U.S. Attorney General, September 30; Dr. Lewis A. Sorokin to U.S. Attorney General, October 1, DJNA; Harry Colmery (National Commander) quoted in NYT, October 2; Thomas H. McKee to McNutt, October 1; Hanna to McNutt, October 14, McN; Thomas to the president, October 1, DJNA.

62. IT and the *Erie (PA) Times*, quoted at length, DW, October 19, 1936; *Eugene (OR) Register-Guard; Adrian (MI) Telegram; Utica (NY) Press*, ibid. THS, October 6–7; THT, October 19–20; DW, October 19.

63. IS, October 18; Docket Record, Vigo County, Superior Court No. 32175 and 32177. Suits filed October 7. I thank Hon. C. Joseph Anderson, Judge of the Vigo County Court in Terre Haute, for sending docket sheet copies.

64. THS, NYT, and DW, October 20–22, 1936.

65. THT, THS, DW, NYT, October 19–22, 1936.

66. THT, THS, and IS October 21, 1936; DW, October 23–25.

67. DW, October 22, 1936. Small and Whitlock were identified by reporters Marguerite Young of the NM and Hays Jones of the DW; THT and THS, October 21; DW, October 25; Indiana Workers Alliance to McNutt, October 23, McN.

68. McMahon to Foster, October 21, 1936, DJNA; THT, October 21; NYT, October 22.

69. McNutt to ACLU's H. Path, July 11, 1936, McN; NYT, October 1, 4; DW, October 23; Harold C. Freightner, NYT, October 4.

70. Record of Docket, Superior Court of Vigo County, Indiana, No. 32175 and 32177.

71. Evidence suggests that the CPUSA may have settled with Beecher's and Yates's attorneys informally. Many states have procedures for expunging criminal arrest documents. Terre Haute Police Department files contain no record of Browder's arrest, which suggests that it may have been purged. Such a removal may have served as a quid pro quo for discontinuation of the suits.

72. Thomas, on the ballot in thirty-seven states, received 187,572 votes. Browder, slated in thirty-three states, received 80,159. Edgar E. Robinson, *They Voted for Roosevelt* (Stanford: Stanford University Press, 1947), 187.

## 5. LET EACH STAND IN HIS PLACE (1937-1938)

1. Daniel Nelson, "Origins of the Sit-Down Era: Worker Militancy and Innovation in the Rubber Industry," *Labor History* (Spring 1982), 189; Keeran, *The Communist Party and the Auto Workers Unions*, 155; Cochran, *Labor and Communism*, 108.

2. Keeran, *Communist Party and the Auto Workers Unions*, 149–52, 162, 169; Zieger, *American Workers, American Unions, 1920-1985*, 47.

3. Strom, "Challenging 'Woman's Place,' " 364; Ottanelli, *The Communist Party of the United States*, 144–48.

4. TD/Browder, January 10, 1956, TDP; Klehr, *The Heyday of American Communism*, 245–50; Johanningsmeier, *Forging American Communism*, 282–83.

5. Sidney Fine, *Sit Down: The General Motors Strike of 1936-1937* (Ann Arbor: University of Michigan Press, 1991), 200–201, 341.

6. Ibid., 329–30.

7. Earl Browder, "The American Communist Party in the Thirties," in Rita James Simon, ed., *As We Saw the Thirties* (Urbana: University of Illinois Press, 1967), 329–30; Zieger, *American Workers, American Unions*, 55. On CP influence in the CIO, see Cochran, *Labor and Communism*; Levenstein, *Communism, Anticommunism and the CIO*; and Max Kampelman, *The Communist Party vs. the CIO* (New York: Praeger, 1957).

8. Thorstein Veblen, *The Theory of the Leisure Class* (New York: Viking, 1945); Stuart Ewen, *Captains of Consciousness* (New York: McGraw-Hill, 1976), 27–28, 155, 88, 92; Diggins, *The Rise and Fall of the American Left*, 71.

9. Bruce Nelson, *Workers on the Waterfront* (Urbana: University of Illinois Press, 1990); David Brody, *Steelworkers in America* (New York: Harper Collins, 1970); Melvyn Dubovsky, *When Workers Organize* (Amherst: University of Massachusetts Press, 1968); Robert Zieger, *Madison's Battery Workers* (Ithaca: ILR Press, 1977), 47.

10. Browder, "The Results of the Elections and the People's Front" (text of December report), *Communist* (January 1937), 24; Bittelman, "Review of the Month," *Communist* (December 1936), 1091.

11. Browder, "Results of the Elections and the People's Front," 21, 20, 25.

12. Bittelman, "Review of the Month," *Communist* (April 1937), 295; Hathaway, "The People versus the Supreme Court," *Communist* (April 1937), 311; Hathaway, "Broad People's United Front Needed to Defeat Fascism," DW, May 1, 1937.

13. Browder speech in Moscow, April 8, 1937, opis 1, delo 4058, CPUSA-Comintern.

14. Ibid.

15. "Draft Resolution of the Secretariat of the ECCI on the American Question," opis 1, delo 4064; "Additional Memorandum on Problems of CPUSA," March 23, 1937, opis 1, delo 4065, CPUSA-Comintern.

16. Browder, "The Communists in the People's Front," 598–603.

17. Foster, "Political Leadership and Party Building," *Communist* (July 1937), 720; Bittelman, "Review of the Month," *Communist* (September 1937), 780.

18. Browder, "For a Common Front against the Warmakers," *Communist* (November 1937), 1043.

19. Browder, "The People's Front Moves Forward," *Communist* (December 1937), 1089–90, 1083.

20. TD/Browder, October 10, 1955, 42–43, TDP; Foster, "Congress of the Communist Party of France," *Communist* (February 1938), 121.

21. TD/Browder, October 10, 1955, 26–31, 29, 30, TDP; Foster recalled Browder's charge in "Pre-Plenum meeting of the National Committee," March 23, 1939, 3, PJJ; TD/Browder, October 10, 1955, TDP; "Browder, in American Commission, January 13, 1938," opis 20, delo 530, Comintern. I thank Herbert Romerstein for this document.

22. "Commission Meeting on American Question," January 21, 1938 (uncorrected stenogram of German oral translation), opis 20, delo 528, Comintern. I thank Herbert Romerstein for this document; TD/Browder, October 10, 1955, TDP.

23. "On Building the Democratic Front against the Danger of Fascism," speech delivered January 18, 1938, opis 20, delo 509, Comintern.

24. Hathaway, "The 1938 Elections and Our Tasks," *Communist* (March 1938), 216; Browder, DW, November 20, 1937; Klehr, *Heyday of American Communism*, 207–23.

25. Darcy autobiography (quotation), 533, TDP.

26. The old and increasingly pointless debate between social historians who study the CPUSA from the bottom up and political historians who analyze it from the top down might benefit from a keener appreciation of the party's bifocal nature.

27. "Memorandum to Comrade Dimitrov," January 19, 1938, opis 74, delo 466, Comintern (I thank Herbert Romerstein for this document); Bittelman, "Review of the Month," *Communist* (August 1937), 694; NYT, May 27, 1938, DW, May 27–31; Joseph Starobin, *American Communism in Crisis* (Cambridge: Harvard University Press, 1972), 260–61.

28. Browder, *The Democratic Front for Jobs, Security, Democracy and Peace*, 32–35.

29. Klehr, *Heyday of American Communism*, 210; Klehr writes that the Cuban Communists also employed the Democratic Front concept (448); *Time* magazine, May 30, 1938.

30. Diggins, *The Rise and Fall of the American Left*, 249–60.

31. Nelson, "Origins of the Sit-Down Era," 198–225; Zieger, *American Workers, American Unions, 1920–1985*, 55–59.

32. NYT, August 19, 1988; Mark Hess and Frank Pearson, "The Quiet Man from Kansas" (recording) (New York: Workers Book Shop, 1936). Lyrics reproduced in Robert Leroy Cleath, "Earl Russell Browder, American Spokesman for Communism, 1930–1945," Ph.D. diss., University of Washington, 1963, 27.

33. I thank James R. Barrett for this observation.

34. Steve Nelson, James R. Barrett, and Rob Ruck, *Steve Nelson: American Radical* (Pittsburgh: University of Pittsburgh Press, 1981), 170; JGR/Magil, January 6, 1993; JGR/Scales, June 9, 1995.

35. "Meet Earl Browder" (author not listed), CH (October 1936), 93; Bella Dodd, *School of Darkness* (New York: Devon-Adair, 1954), 68; Reinhold Niebuhr, "The Revised Communist Faith," *Nation*, February 26, 1938, 247.

36. John McCarten, "Party Linesman II," NY, October 1, 1938, 27.

37. JGR/Green, December 31, 1992; JGR/Healey, December 27, 1992; JGR/Magil, January 6, 1993.

38. McCarten, "Party Linesman I," NY, September 24, 1938, 20.

39. "Margaret Browder, was," December 6, 1949, file 100-287645-56, FBI-MB; "Summary of Main File," n.d. [1949], FBI-RB; letter of introduction from Jay Lovestone, December 9, 1927, opis 261, delo 2780, CPUSA-Comintern; "Margaret Browder, was," February 21, 1952, file 100-287645-98, FBI-MB.

40. Special Agent in Charge (SAC), New York, to FBI director, April 8, 1958, file 100–287645-143, FBI-MB.

41. SAC, New York, to FBI director, August 13, 1959, file 100–287645, FBI-MB.

42. "Interview Report," April 21, 1958 (no serialization number on document), FBI-MB; testimony alluded to, SAC, New York, to FBI director, February 3, 1954, file 100–287645-121, FBI-MB.

43. "Interview Report," April 21, 1958 (no serialization number on document), FBI-MB; SAC, New York, to FBI director, May 5, 1958, file 100–287645-144, FBI-MB; SAC, New York, to FBI director, August 24, 1959 (no serialization number on document), FBI-MB; SAC, New York, to FBI director, October 2, 1959, file 100–287645-151, FBI-MB; SAC, New York, to FBI director, October 9, 1959, file 100–287645-152, FBI-MB.

44. SAC, New York, to FBI director, October 13, 1959, file 100–287645-152, FBI-MB; SAC, New York, to FBI director, January 7, 1960 (serialization number obscured), FBI-MB; Walter Krivitsky, *In Stalin's Secret Service* (New York: Harper, 1939), 237.

45. Klehr and Haynes, *The American Communist Movement*, 108.

46. Klehr, Haynes, and Firsov, *The Secret World of American Communism*, 49–57.

47. Ibid., 88–89, 129–30, 231–38; John Apt and Michael Myerson, *Advocate and Activist: Memoirs of an American Communist Lawyer* (Champaign: University of Illinois Press, 1993), 39–179.

48. Browder to Dimitrov, January 19, 1938, opis 74, delo 469, CPUSA-Comintern. I thank Herbert Romerstein for this document.

49. I am indebted to John Haynes for first raising this point in an April 21, 1995, conversation. Indeed, every U.S. government file on Browder has far less documentation before the war's outbreak.

50. McCarten, "Party Linesman II," 26; JGR/Green, December 31, 1992; JGR/Magil, January 6, 1993. Magil found Browder, who visited him at his apartment on East 24th Street occasionally in late 1941 or 1942, an equally charming guest. All meetings had some political purpose; Magil believes the dinners may have preceded *New Masses* fund raisers in private homes or "a public meeting sponsored by the magazine." Such a gathering "would probably have been held at Webster Hall," now a music club. Magil to Ryan, February 7, 1993.

51. "Meet Earl Browder," CH 45 (October 1936), 95; McCarten, "Party Linesman II," 27.

52. Hubert Kelley, "Our No. 1 Communist," 111; McCarten, "Party Linesman II," 26; Jaffe to Ryan, February 3, 1978; RJA/Browder, April 5, 1954, AP; JGR/Alexander, November 25, 1986.

53. "Browder Interview III," June 16, 1953, TDP; TD/Browder, October 12, 1955, 4–5, TDP.

54. JGR/Jaffe, January 3–4, 1977.

55. Diggins, *Rise and Fall of the American Left*, 163.

56. "Browder Interview III," June 16, 1953; TDP; TD/Browder, October 12, 1955, 7–8.

57. McCarten, "Party Linesman II," 26; Kelley, "Our No. 1 Communist," 111.

58. Cleath, "Earl Russell Browder," 272–95.

59. JGR/Magil, January 6, 1993; JGR/Green, December 31, 1992.

60. JGR/Green, December 31, 1992; Jaffe to Ryan, February 13, 1978; Darcy to Ryan, June 12, 1994.

61. JGR/Magil, January 6, 1993.

62. Kelley, "Our No. 1 Communist," 29; special agent in charge, New York, to J. Edgar Hoover, September 26, 1952, file 39–878, FBI-RB; P. E. Foxworth to Hoover, August 19, 1942, file 40–3798-172, FBI-EB; D. M. Ladd to Hoover, September 26, 1952, file 39–878, FBI-RB; two-page document labeled "COMMUNIST," May 18, 1942, file 40–3798-15, FBI-EB; Harold R. Dean to the warden, Atlanta Penitentiary, May 14, 1942, USBP; Jaffe to Ryan, January 12, 1978; special agent in charge, New York, to Hoover, September 26, 1952, file 39–878, FBI-RB. Agents received information on Browder's daily routine from his building superintendent.

63. Kelley, "Our No. 1 Communist," 111; McCarten "Party Linesman II," 26; Jaffe to Ryan, February 3, 1978; JGR/Robert J. Alexander, November 25, 1986; Jaffe to Ryan, January 12, 1978; sworn statement, December 1, 1939, INS; copy of 1938 federal income tax return, BP; 1943 deposition, 1; the CPUSA stated that it had paid Browder the more modest figure of $3,100 in 1938. Notarized letter, April 29, 1939, signed by Roy Hudson, INS; Browder, 1943 deposition, 1-2, BP; TD/Browder, June 6, 1953, 3, TDP; Jaffe persuaded Browder to give her a token payment for a few years so she could qualify for Social Security. She ultimately received a $600 check that she divided among the boys. Jaffe to Ryan, January 12, 1978.

64. Johanningsmeier, *Forging American Communism*, 1-55.

65. Jaffe, *The Rise and Fall of American Communism*, 58.

66. Bloomfield to Dimitrov, August 12, 1938, opis 74, delo 466, Comintern (I thank Herbert Romerstein for this document); Joseph R. Starobin, *American Communism in Crisis, 1943-1957*, 261.

## 6. CRISIS DAYS (1936-1939)

1. Joseph R. Starobin, *American Communism in Crisis, 1943-1957*, 47.

2. Milton Cantor, *The Divided Left* (New York: Hill & Wang, 1978), 114.

3. Earl Browder, "Lenin and Spain," *The People's Front* (New York: International Publishers, 1938), 285; "The Communists in the People's Front," ibid., 165.

4. Hugh Thomas, *The Spanish Civil War* (New York: Harper & Row, 1961), 634-37, 296-98; Peter N. Carroll, *The Odyssey of the Abraham Lincoln Brigade* (Stanford: Stanford University Press, 1994), 12.

5. Klehr, Haynes, and Firsov, *The Secret World of American Communism*, 152.

6. Robert A. Rosenstone, *Crusade of the Left* (New York: Pegasus, 1969), 82; Thomas, *Spanish Civil War*, 637; Carroll, *Odyssey of the Abraham Lincoln Brigade*, 20; Browder placed American deaths at more than one thousand, *Communist* (September 1939), 803.

7. Clarence Hathaway to Ruth B. Shipley, chief of Passport Division, December 24, 1937, DS; Robert D. Murphy, American consul in Paris, to the Secretary of State, December 21, DS.

8. PW, February 15, 1938; Arthur H. Landis, *The Abraham Lincoln Brigade* (New York: Citadel, 1967), 386; Jaffe, *The Rise and Fall of American Communism*, 176.

9. PW, February 15, 1938; Landis, *Abraham Lincoln Brigade*, 386; Jaffe, *Rise and Fall of American Communism*, 176.

10. Rosenstone, *Crusade of the Left*, 336-39.

11. Memorandum, February 24, 1938, DS; Rosenstone, *Crusade of the Left*, 336; R. B. Shipley to White, June 2, BP.

12. Shipley to Browder, August 12, BP; Marty to Browder, n.d. (November or December), BP.

13. Rosenstone, *Crusade of the Left*, 336; Krivitsky, *In Stalin's Secret Service*, 95.

14. DW, April 9, 1937; April 28, 1938.

15. Granville Hicks, "Communism and the American Intellectual" in I. D. Talmadge, ed., *Whose Revolution?* (New York: Howell, 1941); speech by Norman Thomas, March 24 [1937 or 1938], BP.

16. Earl Browder, "Trotskyism against World Peace," in *The People's Front*, 300-310; Earl Browder, "Lessons of the Moscow Trials," in *Fighting For Peace* (New York: International Publishers, 1939), 115-30.

17. Earl Browder, "Stop the Sell Out," NM, September 27, 1938.

18. Earl Browder, "The Munich Betrayal" (delivered November 14, 1938), reprinted in *Fighting for Peace*, 183-84.

19. Jaffe, *Rise and Fall of American Communism*, 39-40.

20. TD/Browder, October 10, 1955, 42-44, TDP; *World News and Views*, October 29, 1938; Browder, *Fighting for Peace*, 167, 168 (quotation).

21. Earl Browder, "For Social and National Security" (speech delivered to CPUSA Na-

tional Committee Meeting, December 3, 1938), reprinted in *Fighting for Peace*, 207; *National Issues* 1 (January 1939), 3.

22. TD/Browder, October 10, 1955, 40; TD/Browder, May 19, 1953, 3, TDP; Browder, "How Stalin Ruined the American Communist Party," *Harpers* (March 1960), 48.

23. "Pre-Plenum Meeting of Political Committee," March 23, 1939, 2–36, PJJ.

24. Ibid.

25. Ibid.

26. Transcript of testimony, March 27, 1939, BP.

27. Browder, Columbia, 371; DW, July 6, 1939.

28. NYT, August 21, 1939; Melech Epstein, *The Jew and Communism* (New York: Trade Union Sponsoring Committee, 1959), 348–50.

29. Isserman, *Which Side Were You On?*, 34; Al Richmond, *A Long View from the Left* (Boston: Houghton, Mifflin, 1973), 283.

30. Epstein, *The Jew and Communism*, 348–51.

31. NYT and DW, August 24, 1939; "Interview with Browder," August 23, 4–10, TDP.

32. Epstein, *The Jew and Communism*, 351.

33. TD/Browder, October 12, 1955, 8, TDP; DW, September 4, 1939.

34. DW, September 2, 7, 4, 5, 12, 1939.

35. TD/Browder, October 12, 1955, 247, TDP; Epstein, *The Jew and Communism*, 353; DW, September 12, 13, 1939.

36. It was contained in a cable quoting a soon-to-appear *Pravda* piece. Fraser Ottanelli claims to have found in the Browder papers a telegram from Moscow dated September 14 that contained "the essence of the Party's shift," *The Communist Party of the United States*, 27. Neither this writer nor the professional archivists at Syracuse University could locate such a telegram.

37. DW, September 13, 1939.

38. TD/Browder, October 12, 1955, 252, TDP.

39. "Discussion by CP National Committee on the International Situation" (stenogram), September 14, 16, 1939, 28–53, 1–3, PJJ. Participants' names suggest that this is a Political Committee transcript.

40. *Communist* (October 1939), 899–904.

41. Isserman, *Which Side Were You On?*, 72; JGR/Green, December 31, 1992; "Ryan's Information" [Eugene Dennis], April 11, 1941, 32–33, opis 261, delo 16, Comintern, trans. Dasha Lotareva; Ottanelli, *Communist Party of the United States*, 189.

42. DW, September 15, 18, 1939; Isserman, *Which Side Were You On?*, 54.

43. Jaffe, *Rise and Fall of American Communism*, 40.

44. Ibid., 44–45.

45. TD/Browder, October 12, 1955, 246, TDP; Herbert Romerstein, *Heroic Victims* (Washington: Council for the Defense of Freedom, 1994), 98. DW, October 22, 1939.

46. Johanningsmeier, *Forging American Communism*, 286, 410.

47. DW, October 28, 1939; Earl Browder, "The War Plans of Roosevelt and Wall Street," in Earl Browder, *The Second Imperialist War* (New York: International Publishers, 1940), 289, 293; Browder, "The Most Peculiar Election Campaign in the History of the Republic," *Communist* (October 1940), 885.

## 7. AGITATOR IN THE HANDS OF
## AN ANGRY GOVERNMENT (1939–1941)

1. Walter Goodman, *The Committee* (New York: Farrar, Straus, & Giroux, 1968), 21.

2. Earl Browder to Georgi Dimitrov, January 19, 1938, reprinted in Herbert Romerstein, "Soviet Archives Confirm Hiss's Guilt," *Human Events* (January 21, 1994), 12; "Prosecutive

Summary Report," September 12, 1952, 20, file 100–287645–104 FBI-MB. Reports of "prospective witnesses," FBI informants, are not known for their veracity. The Browders, however, had no source of capital in 1941, and shortly thereafter Margaret emerged as a partner in a second-hand merchandise store.

3. Browder to Dimitrov, August 1939 (exact date obscured), opis 74, delo 469, Comintern. I thank Herbert Romerstein for this document.

4. Goodman, *The Committee*, 67; NYT, September 10, 1939.

5. Goodman, *The Committee*, 36; DW, September 6, 1939.

6. Browder testimony, Dies Committee, 76th Congress, 1st Session, *Public Hearings*, Vol. 7 (September 5), 4275, 4341, 4463.

7. Ibid., 4338–40, 4323–27.

8. Ibid., 4373; on the statute of limitations, see "Newspaper Summary," September 24, 1939, DJNA. A State Department memo listed the aliases as Nicholas Dozenberg, March 9, 1921; George Morris, November 17, 1927; Albert Henry Richards, November 18, 1931; Richards, November 19, 1933 (A. J. Nichols to John O. Bell, January 10, 1949, DS). On January 13, 1926, Browder had received passport 149817 as "Earl W. Ringrose" (undated document, [post 1946] numbered "54," DS). Browder had also used the names Joseph Dixon, Joseph Ward, Albert Underwood, Earl Russell, and Earl Wingate (Registration Statement, Department of Justice, October 1, 1946, DJ). See also a sheet titled "Factual and Statutory Background," BP; Gitlow testimony, Dies Committee, 76th Congress, 1st Session, *Public Hearings*, Vol. 7 (September 9–11, 1939), 4529–725.

9. Letter to the Justice Department from a "W. B. L." (name deleted), September 28, 1939, DJ.

10. Messersmith to Murphy, October 21, 1939 (citing the referral as April 22, 1929), DS. Three days before Messersmith wrote Murphy, he received a letter from Passport Division chief Ruth B. Shipley. She enclosed an epistle from Pleasantville, New York, demanding Browder's prosecution and accusing the State Department of sympathizing with Communists. She refused to "carry the ball for the Department of Justice" (Shipley to Messersmith, October 18, 1939), DS. Actually Justice had not simply refused to act. The State Department's own records reveal a more complex chain of events. A brief "Memorandum Concerning the Case of Earl Russell Browder" relates that in 1929 the Office of Naval Intelligence alleged that Browder was traveling on the Morris passport. The State Department requested an indictment, but the Justice Department could not locate Browder and eventually closed the case (memorandum sent from an "R. V. H." of the Passport Division to a Mr. Scanlan, September 12, 1935, DS). The State Department had little room to chide the Justice Department for inefficiency. In 1934, when Browder made one of many attempts to acquire a passport in his own name, a clerk failed to check the "refusal list" as well as numerous rejections in Browder's file. As a result valid travel papers were issued. The error went unnoticed until the clerk had found employment elsewhere (R. V. H. to Scanlan, September 12, 1935; memorandum from Division of Eastern European Affairs, August 28; "D. A. S." to Shipley, February 11, all DS); NYT, January 20, 1940; Joseph C. Green, chief, Division of Controls, to Browder, July 27, 1939, DJ; Browder to Green, August 2, BP; Charles W. Yost, acting chief, to Browder, August 8, DJ; Gitlow testimony, Dies Committee, September 7–11, 4529–725.

11. Full text of press release in Browder file, DJNA; Goodman, 270; Ring Lardner, Jr., "My Life on the Blacklist," *Saturday Evening Post*, October 14, 1961, 38–44; George Biehl, a newspaperman, to the attorney general, n.d. (autumn 1939), charging that Thomas maintained a relationship with a bond-sales corporation after his election, DJNA.

12. NYT, October 23, 1939; NYT, August 29, 1942; Irving Howe and Lewis Coser, *The American Communist Party* (Boston: Beacon Press, 1957), 400–401; "Attacks on the Communist Party," *Equal Justice* 13 (February 1940), 7–9.

13. T. J. Fitch, SAC, New York Division, Department of State, to R. C. Bannerman, chief special agent, October 23, 1939, DS; The indictments appear in *Transcript of Record* in case

file "US vs. Earl Russell Browder" (C. R. 106–210), National Archives–Northeast Region; "Newspaper Summary" October 24, DJNA. Attempts to arraign brother William for a similar offense failed (A. J. Nicholas to Assistant U.S. Attorney Lester C. Dunigan, March 29, 1940, DS).

14. "Newspaper Summary," October 24, 1939, DJNA; NYT, October 24; DW, October 24; NYT, October 25; R. B. Shipley to B. W. Butler of the Justice Department's Criminal Division, November 18, DJ; NYT, November 18; Browder statement to the press, October 24, BP; excerpt from the *Boston Herald*, December 8, 1927, describing the incognito travels of a Governor Fuller, BP; see E. A. C. Reed (American consul) to the French official E. H. Van Cauteren, June 27, 1921, BP; October 24, 1939, press statement, BP.

15. O. John Rogge, to Internal Revenue Commissioner Guy T. Helvering, November 3, 1939, DJNA; Treasury Department permission granted, November 8, DJNA; Dingle to Murphy, November 22, DJNA.

16. Henry B. Hazard, assistant to the commissioner, to the district director, August 31, 1939, INS; G. D. Shapp, district director, San Francisco, to the commissioner, September 5, acknowledging a request to investigate, dated August 31, INS; Herbert J. Conley, immigrant inspector, to the district director, October 30, INS; "Memorandum for the Attorney General" from Henry M. Hart, Jr., special attorney, August 26, 1940, DJ; James L. Houghteling, INS commissioner, to the solicitor general, June 6; memorandum by Shipley, November 2, 1939, DS; Hart memo, 2, DJ; Byron H. Uhl, district director, New York, to the inspector, Rouses Point, New York, October 31; Uhl to the commissioner, November 2, INS; Houghteling to the solicitor general, June 6, 1940, INS.

17. Houghteling to the solicitor general, June 6, 1940, INS; "Memorandum for the Solicitor General," O. John Rogge, June 20, file 39–878–2, FBI-RB. Browder may have submitted the petition as late as December 1, 1939. The Hart memo claims that the INS received it December 5, and Attorney General Robert H. Jackson, in a November 28 letter to Eleanor Roosevelt, puts the date as December 1, INS; Rogge, "Memorandum for the Solicitor General," June 20, 1940, file 39–878–2, FBI-RB; Houghteling to the solicitor general, June 6, INS; see two papers in Russian with certified translations by an Isaac Shorr, headed "People's Commissariat of Internal Affairs, USSR, the Division of the Acts of Civil Status," INS.

18. Houghteling, "Memorandum," December 7, 1939, INS; T. B. Shoemaker, deputy commissioner, "Memorandum for the Commissioner," December 8, 1940, INS; Houghteling to the solicitor general, June 6, 3, INS; Houghteling's remark on the State Department's view was based on Shipley to Houghteling, December 21, 1939, DS.

19. Hart memo, 2, DJ; Memoranda by Shipley, November 2, 1939, and June 19, 1940, DS.

20. Jackson to Eleanor Roosevelt, November 26, 1940, INS; Hart memo, 16, DJ; Jackson deportation order, October 30, INS; communication headed Brooklyn, New York, October 25, 1939, signed "Frank Murphy (that's me)" [sic], DJNA; John M. Price to the attorney general, October 25, DJNA; Howard N. Myer to Senator James M. Meade, November 17 (copy sent to Mrs. Roosevelt); Rogge to William Kaplan, November 24, DJNA.

21. Rogge to Cahill, November 9, 1939, DJNA; Morris Shapiro and David L. Clendenin to Cahill, October 28, DJNA; ACLU Director Roger Baldwin to Browder, September 7, BP; Browder's reply apologized for "distortions" by "the public press"; press release, September 8, BP; Jerome Bridchey to Murphy, November 3, DJNA.

22. Rogge to Cahill, November 9, 1939; Cahill to Rogge, November 13; Cahill to ACLU November 13, all DJNA; "Witch Hunting," address by Rogge to New England Conference on Civil Liberties, Boston, January 27, 1940, BP.

23. *Transcript of Record*, 28–48.

24. Ibid., 48–54; copy of Browder's passport application, stamped "Issued September 1, 1934," DS.

25. The employee was Charles Siegel; see "Refusal" sheets in Browder's file, December 8, 1926; December 13, 1928; March 23, 1929; April 17, 1930, DS.

26. Bedacht testimony, *Transcript of Record,* 183–90; Powers, 150–60, 173–83; documents, DJ.

27. Dozenberg, ibid., 132–42; documents, DJ.

28. Browder photograph, NYT, January 23, 1940; Battle's summary, *Transcript of Record,* 223–36; document titled "Summation (Use)," 2, 3, BP.

29. *Transcript of Record,* 236–56.

30. Ibid., 256–62.

31. Ibid., 263.

32. Ibid., 263–77.

33. *Washington Post,* January 23, 1940; NYT, January 23, 1940; the sentence gave Browder a two-year term on each count, to be served consecutively; *United States v. Browder,* 113 F. 2d 97.

34. Raoul Berger to Warner Gardner, special assistant to the attorney general, August 22, 1940, DJ.

35. "Purge by Passport," *Nation,* February 3, 1940, 117.

36. Felix Frankfurter, "Memorandum to the Conference," February 15, 1941, container 261 (Opinions of Other Judges), HLB; *Browder v. United States,* 312 US 335 (1941); container 50, 434, WOD; Ed Parker to Reed, February 18, 1941, SR.

37. NYT, November 29, 1939.

38. "Browder and the Colleges," NYT, November 28, 1939; December 19.

39. Eleanor Roosevelt to a Mrs. Strobell, November 28, 1939, BP.

40. Unidentified speech on creation of an "anti-imperialist people's front," 8, BP.

41. Browder, *The Way Out* (New York: International Publishers, 1941), 235–36; RJA/Browder, April 5, 1954, AP; TD/Browder, October 12, 1955, 11, TDP; Isserman, *Which Side Were You On?,* 65.

42. Press release, "America and the Imperialist War," BP; Browder, *Way Out,* 36; CPUSA to the Extraordinary Party Congress of the Mexican CP, March 11, BP.

43. Earl Browder, *The Jewish People and the War* (New York: International Publishers, 1940); Glazer, *The Social Basis of American Communism,* 154; Jaffe to Ryan, July 12, 1977.

44. *Earl Browder and You* (New York: Campaign Committee, 1940), BP.

45. NYT, February 3, 1940.

46. NYT, January 31, 1940; February 1; February 8.

47. "South of Fourteenth," NYT, February 8, 1940.

48. Rogge, "Memorandum for the Solicitor General," June 20, 1940, file 39–878–2; Solicitor General Francis Biddle to J. Edgar Hoover, June 21, file 39–878–1; Hoover to special agent in charge, New York, July 12, file 39–878–1, all FBI-RB. The government never ruled on the validity of the Browders' marriage. Shortly after Raissa was ordered deported, Hoover received a letter from the Justice Department that advised him to drop the inquiry. Henry M. Hart, Jr., to Hoover, December 23, file 39–878–13, FBI-RB; Hart memo 4, DJ; the official was Major Lemuel B. Schofield, special assistant to the attorney general; see also "Memorandum for the Immigration and Naturalization Service," by Hoover, August 14, file 39–878–2, FBI-RB; E. E. Salisbury, chief, Certifications Branch, INS to Earl Browder, August 11, INS.

49. Alien Registration Act, Section 20 (c); Attorney General Robert H. Jackson noted that Mrs. Browder's case was the first decided under the statute's discretionary provisions (deportation order, October 30, 1940, INS); later Hoover asked Jackson for citations of recent cases on which he had determined that the Communist party advocated revolution ("Memorandum for the Assistant to the Attorney General," November 12, file 39–878–9, FBI-RB); in different documents in Raissa's Soviet personnel file she listed her year of birth as 1894, 1895, and 1896, opis 261, delo 3264, CPUSA-Comintern; Hart memo, 16, DJ.

50. Hart memo, 16, DJ.

51. Browder, *Way Out,* 45–46, 49.

52. NYT, September 5, 1941; see telegrams dated October 8, 1940, 3:55 PM, 4:40 PM, 4:45 PM, October 9, 9:20 AM, 9:30 AM, 1:57 PM, 2:10 PM, and one without a date but conveying the

same message, all DS; quotes from letter, special agent in charge, R. D. Clark to T. F. Fitch, chief special agent, State Department, February 19, 1941, DS.

53. Browder, *Way Out,* 166; Browder, Undated Outline, "The First Half-Year of War," BP.

54. NYT, October 10, October 12, and November 6, 1940.

55. NYT, January 30, 1941; Howe and Coser, *The American Communist Party,* 404; Roy Hudson, "For a Greater Vote and a Stronger Party," *Communist* (August 1940), 709.

56. *Statutes at Large,* 76th Congress, 3rd Session, Chapter 897, 1201–02.

57. "Persecution by Legislation," in Browder, *Way Out,* 64–72; "Minutes of the Special Convention, CPUSA," 3–5, PJJ; Browder, *Way Out,* 184–91.

58. Minutes of Special Convention, Communist party, November 16–17, 1940 (stenogram), PJJ; excerpts from Browder's speech, opis 20, delo 540, CPUSA-Comintern; Browder, *Way Out,* 133; *Draft Resolution, Dissolution of the Communist International,* 2, BP; Dimitrov, opis 20, delo 540, Comintern.

59. JGR/Green, December 31, 1992.

60. Warden Joseph W. Sanford to Hoover, October 1, 1941, FBI-EB; DW, March 25–28; quotations, transcripts of warden's interrogation of Howard Rasmus and Oscar R. Martin, March 29, USBP.

61. Warden's interrogation, USBP.

## 8. TO FREE THE SPIRIT FROM ITS CELL (1941–1944)

1. Earl to Raissa Browder, July 6, 1941, BP; Earl to Felix Browder, July 24, BP; Browder to Minor, August 16; Sanford to Hoover, file 40–3798-1, October 1, FBI-EB; Minor to Browder, August 7, 1942, BP.

2. Nick Salvatore, *Eugene V. Debs, Citizen and Socialist,* 309–15.

3. Annual reports to the attorney general by warden Fred G. Zerbst, 1919 and 1920; H. Park Tucker, "A History of the Atlanta Federal Penitentiary, 1901–1956," unpublished manuscript, 81–178, USBP. I thank John W. Roberts and Anne Diestel for making these materials available to me.

4. Tucker, "History," 345–415.

5. James V. Bennett, *I Chose Prison* (New York: Knopf, 1970), 60–97; JGR/John W. Roberts, March 14, 1994; Tucker, "History," 399.

6. Reports by Dr. Zbranek and the psychologist, April 18, 1941, 4b and following page (also numbered 4b). The bureau deleted their names, but Tucker, "History," 427, reports Zbranek as the only psychiatrist during the era. Reading level, 412.

7. Browder, autobiographical manuscript, 24, BP.

8. Report of J. C. Leonardo, U.S. Penitentiary, Atlanta, Georgia, "Admission Summary," 3c, PA.

9. "Admission Summary," Psychiatric Report, 4b and the following page, PA.

10. Psychological report, 4b, PA.

11. "Release Progress Report," June 15, 1942, USBP.

12. Raissa Browder to E. R. Goodwyn, Jr., acting chief parole officer, Atlanta Penitentiary, April 14, 1941, BP; Johnstone to Earl Browder, May 22, BP; Minor to Browder, August 7, 1942, BP.

13. Col. J. T. Bissel to J. Edgar Hoover, April 17, 1942, file 40–3798-1, FBI-EB; quote from Mary "Molly" Dewson to Eleanor Roosevelt, n.d. (1952), recalling her wartime letter to the president in response to a message from Mrs. Roosevelt, January 3, 1953, all FDRL; Special Progress Report, 2, PA.

14. Acting warden Ben Overstreet, Jr., to Hoover, April 13, 1942, National Archives; Bureau of Prisons, "Release Progress Report," June 15, National Archives; John T. Conolly to

the warden, May 14, USBP; Ray Ginger, *Eugene V. Debs, A Biography* (New York: Collier, 1966), 408.

15. Minor to Raissa Browder, June 15, 1941, BP.

16. Sanford to Hoover, October 1, 1941, file 40–3798–1, FBI-EB; Overstreet to Hoover, November 4, National Archives; Daniel Bell and William Goldsmith/Browder, January 10, 1956, BC.

17. Bell and Goldsmith/Browder, January 10, 1956, BC.

18. Browder, Application for Executive Clemency, 4, 5, PA; Overstreet to Hoover, November 4, 1941, National Archives; Overstreet to Hoover, April 13, 1942, National Archives; Minor to Raissa Browder, August 15, 1941, BP; RJA/Browder, April 4, 1954, AP.

19. Correspondence between Eleanor Roosevelt and Franklin D. Roosevelt, n.d. (1941), FDRL.

20. "Analysis and Summary of All Passport Cases in Southern District, New York, 1918–1941," PA; Attorney General Francis Biddle to the president, December 5, 1941, DJ.

21. Mary van Kleek, "Prisoner Number 60140," excerpt from *The Witness*, April 16, 1942, 6–9, BP; "The Case of Earl Browder," *New Republic*, March 27, 384; Carl Ross, *Let Freedom Ring for Earl Browder* (New York: New Age Publishers, 1942), Box 414, NRC; D. M. Ladd, "Memorandum for the Director," May 19, file 40–3798–107, FBI-EB; Hoover to Major General Edwin M. Watson, September 10, 1941, FDRL; Hoover to the attorney general, September 29, PA; Hoover to the assistant attorney general, September 29, PA; Hoover to the attorney general, April 6, April 21, May 9, 1942, PA; J. T. Bissell, assistant executive officer, Military Intelligence Service, to Hoover, April 17, file 40–3798–1, FBI-EB. Actually the Committee collected an estimated 3,768,000 signatures on its petitions to President Roosevelt. See a document titled "COMMUNIST," May 18, file 40–3798–15, detailing the campaign to free Browder and subsequent events, FBI-EB.

22. Helen C. Camp, *Iron in Her Soul: Elizabeth Gurley Flynn and the American Left* (Pullman: Washington State University Press, 1995), 200, 169.

23. *Worker*, May 17, 1942; "Communist Party, USA," June 3, file 40–3798, FBI-EB; Sanford to James V. Bennett, May 19, National Archives; Release surveillance summary, 1, file 40–3798–2, FBI-EB.

24. "Memorandum for the President from the Attorney General," May 16, FDRL; NYT, May 17, 29; for the FBI's dismay at Browder's release, see Ladd to Hoover, May 19, file 40–3798–154, FBI-EB. On continued surveillance, see Hoover, "Memorandum for the Attorney General," July 31, file 40–3798–174, FBI-EB.

25. Nelson Lichtenstein, *Labor's War at Home* (Cambridge: Cambridge University Press, 1982), 123–24; Green, *The World of the Worker*, 192; Earl Browder, *Victory and After* (New York: International Publishers, 1942), 19; Keeran, *The Communist Party and the Auto Workers Unions*, 230.

26. Browder, *Victory and After*, 86–88, 113.

27. Browder, Columbia, 391; Levenstein, *Communism, Anticommunism and the CIO*; Green, *World of the Worker*, 188.

28. Levenstein, *Communism, Anticommunism and the CIO*, 160–61; Earl Browder, *Production for Victory* (New York: Workers Library Publishers, 1942), 22–24; Lichtenstein, *Labor's War at Home*, 152.

29. Karl G. Yoneda, *Ganbatte: Sixty Year Struggle of a Kibei Worker* (Los Angeles: UCLA Asian-American Studies Center, 1983), 115.

30. Isserman, *Which Side Were You On?*, 141–43; Horne, *Black Liberation/Red Scare*, 11, 97, 138.

31. Romerstein, *Heroic Victims*, 86–87.

32. *Worker*, October 4, 1942; Earl Browder, Memorandum, "China, the State Department and the Communists," April 22, 1950, 2–3, BP. Welles to Browder, October 6, 1942; Browder

302 ■ NOTES TO PAGES 212–220

to Welles, October 8, BP; Browder press statement, October 15, BP; Eighty-first Congress, Second Session, U.S. Senate, Subcommittee of the Committee on Foreign Relations, Hearings Pursuant to S. Res. 231, *A Resolution to Investigate Whether There Are Employees in the State Department Disloyal to the United States*, part 1, 682 (Tydings Committee).

33. DW, October 16, 1942; Hoover to Assistant Secretary of State Adolf A. Berle, Jr., October 24, National Archives; Browder to Welles, December 29; Welles to Browder, January 11, 1943; Browder to Welles, January 15; Browder to Welles, September 10; Welles to Browder, March 26; Browder to Welles, May 13; Welles to Browder, May 15. Browder correspondence, BP.

34. Hoover to Berle, October 24, 1942, National Archives.

35. JGR/Gil Green, December 31, 1992; L. Brent Bozell, "National Trends" (clipping from *National Republic*), NRC; Josephine T. Adams folder, TDP; Isserman, *Which Side Were You On?*, 46; Harvey Klehr, "The Strange Case of Roosevelt's 'Secret Agent,' " *Encounter* (December 1982), 84–88; Joseph P. Lash, *Eleanor and Franklin* (New York: Signet, 1971), 905; TD/Adams and Browder, April 21, 1956 (tape recording) TDP.

36. *Philadelphia Inquirer*, May 23, 1941; TD/Lape, February 13, 1957, TDP.

37. TD/Eleanor Roosevelt, January 17, 1957, TDP; Adams to Roosevelt, December 10, 1941; April 6, 1942; Roosevelt to Adams, April 9, 1942; Adams to Roosevelt, April 20, 1942, all FDRL.

38. Klehr, "The Strange Case of Roosevelt's 'Secret Agent,' " 87; TD/Lape, February 13, 1957, TDP.

39. TD/Browder, March 13, 1957, TDP; Hoover to Eleanor Roosevelt, January 6, 1943, FDRL. Atop the letter is the typed notation, "Copy sent to Miss Adams, 1/8/43."

40. Browder to Welles, May 13, 1943, BP.

41. TD/Eleanor Roosevelt, January 17, 1957, TDP; Roosevelt to Adams, February 12, July 13, October 3, 1944, FDRL; TD/Roosevelt, January 17, 1957, TDP; Lash, *Eleanor and Franklin*, 906. Only one bears proof that the president read it. On a letter concerning a Bolivian political crisis is the handwritten notation: "This should be taken up with the State Dept.-FDR" (Adams to Eleanor Roosevelt, November 28, 1944, FDRL).

42. Klehr, "Strange Case of Roosevelt's 'Secret Agent,' " 87; TD/Browder, March 13, 1957, TDP.

43. JGR/Green, December 31, 1992; TD/Adams and Browder, April 21, 1956 (tape recording), TDP.

44. Isserman, *Which Side Were You On?*, 180–81; Memo of conference, July 23, 1942, BP.

45. Browder to Roosevelt, October 22, 1942, BP; letter to *New York Herald Tribune*, July 16, 1943, BP; Browder to Rev. Hastings Smyth, March 19; Smyth to Browder, March 27, both BP.

46. Isserman, *Which Side Were You On?*, 182.

47. Jaffe, *The Rise and Fall of American Communism*, 85.

48. Earl Browder, "Teheran: History's Greatest Turning Point," text, file 40–3798–25, FBI-EB; Earl Browder, *Teheran and America, Perspectives and Tasks* (New York: Workers' Library, 1944); Earl Browder, *Teheran: Our Path in War and Peace* (New York: International Publishers, 1944).

49. Browder, "Teheran: History's Greatest Turning Point," 1–4.

50. Arthur Schlesinger, Jr., later noted that Morgan "having been dead for some months was in no position to accept the invitation." Schlesinger, *The Vital Center* (Cambridge: Riverside Press, 1949), 110.

51. Browder, *Teheran: Our Path in War and Peace*, 73.

52. Ibid., 73–80.

53. Browder, *Teheran and America*, 46.

54. Browder speech, January 15, 1945 (text), file 40–3798–25, FBI-EB; Browder, *Teheran: Our Path in War and Peace*, 78, 79; Browder, *Teheran and America*, 25; Starobin, *American Communism in Crisis*, 59.

55. Browder, *Teheran: Our Path in War and Peace*, 80–81 (quoting Senate Document No. 106, 78th Congress); Malcolm Sylvers, "The 1944–1945 Upheaval in American Communism," *Internationale Tagung der Historiker der Arbeiterbewegung* 21 Linzer Konferenz, 1985, 258.

56. JGR/A. B. Magil, January 6, 1993.

57. Charney, *A Long Journey*, 257.

58. Isserman, *Which Side Were You On?*, 176, 179; Ottanelli, *The Communist Party of the United States*, 208.

59. Browder, *Teheran and America*, 28.

60. Ibid., 28–44.

61. Ibid., 41.

62. Earl Browder, "Should the American Communist Party Be Liquidated?" (July 11, 1943) transcript, TDP; Starobin, *American Communism in Crisis*, 61; Summary of twenty-two newspaper editorials marked "Add to Garlin Memo on National Convention Publicity," 1944, BP.

63. JGR/A. B. Magil, January 6, 1993; Dodd, *School of Darkness*, 162, 174; Steve Nelson to Elizabeth Gurley Flynn, January 28, October 27, 1944, BP; Junius Irving Scales and Richard Nickson, *Cause at Heart* (Athens: University of Georgia Press, 1987), 139.

## 9. BROWDERISM IN FULL BLOOM (1944-1945)

1. Volkogónòv, *Stalin: Triumph and Tragedy*, 48.

2. Starobin, *American Communism in Crisis, 1943–1957*, 24; Irene Leslie, "Lenin on the Woman Question," *Communist* 15, No. 3 (March 1936), 245–52; Dixler, "The Woman Question: Women and the Communist Party," 252–61.

3. TD/David Ramsey, January 15, 1957, 1, 3; March 27, 5; January 15, 1, 4, all TDP.

4. Foster letter to the National Committee, January 20, 1944, BP; Darcy, autobiographical manuscript, 586–88, TDP; Foster letter to the National Committee, 1, BP.

5. Foster letter to the National Committee, 1–8, BP.

6. Ibid.

7. "Corrected Stenogram of National Board Meeting," February 8, 1944, 1, part 3, 1, PJJ.

8. Childs's speech, ibid., part 1, 1; Green's, part 1, 4; Minor's, part 1, 1; Dennis's, 1; Darcy's, 2; National Board Meeting, part 4, 1, PJJ.

9. National Board Meeting, 2, 3, 4, PJJ.

10. NYWT, March 9, 1944; *U.S. News and World Report*, April 16, 1954, 112–16; "General Intelligence Survey in the United States," August 1944, 73, FDRL; DW, May 10, 1944.

11. Copy, February 29, 1944, BP; Browder to Political Committee, March 5, BP.

12. Jaffe, *The Rise and Fall of American Communism*, 62; Starobin, *American Communism in Crisis*, 74.

13. Dimitrov to Molotov, March 8, 1944, trans. Harry Walsh, opis 74, delo 482, Comintern (I thank Herbert Romerstein for this document).

14. Com. Aerova, "A Brief Review of the Work of the CPUSA Congress and Establishment of the Communist Political Association," September 2, 1944, opis 14, delo 146-A, Comintern (I thank Herbert Romerstein for this document); Aerova to Dimitrov, "On the Communist party of the USA," November 9, opis 1, delo 4698, CPUSA-Comintern; Starobin, *American Communism in Crisis*, 74–75.

15. Darcy to Ryan, May 9, 1994; DW, April 5, 1944; Darcy, autobiographical manuscript, 574, TDP.

16. Diggins, *The Rise and Fall of the American Left*, 187–92.

17. Lichtenstein, *Labor's War at Home*, 178.

18. Marty's letter, written in English, appears in Browder's pamphlet *Answer to Vronsky* (privately published, May 1948), BP; Ottanelli, *The Communist Party of the United States*, 209, 276.

19. *Worker*, May 21, 1944.

20. One should not confuse organizational autonomy with intraparty democracy. Browder's goals included independence from Moscow and proving himself a world-caliber Communist figure; they did not entail empowering rank and filers.

21. Browder, Columbia, 409.

22. JGR/Robert J. Alexander, November 25, 1986; Roca letter, *Political Affairs* 24 (March 1945), 268–85; Horne, *Black Liberation/Red Scare*, 129; Romerstein, *Heroic Victims*, 101.

23. NYT, May 21, 1944.

24. *The Worker* moderated Browder's claims somewhat. It reported seventy thousand registered Communists (including twenty-four thousand recruits), plus nine thousand on military leave, *Worker*, July 16, 1944; DW, May 20; NYT, May 21; *Worker*, May 21.

25. NYT, May 22, 1944; DW, May 23–24.

26. Sylvers, "The 1944–45 Upheaval in American Communism"; Jaffe, *Rise and Fall of American Communism*, 64–68.

27. Leon Friedman, "Election of 1944," in Arthur M. Schlesinger, Jr., ed., *History of American Presidential Elections*, Vol. 4 (New York: McGraw-Hill, 1971), 3009–17; Richard Polenberg, *War and Society* (Philadelphia: Lippincott, 1972), 195–99.

28. Isserman, *Which Side Were You On?*, 208; John Morton Blum, *V Was for Victory* (New York: Harcourt, 1976), 285.

29. Friedman, "Election of 1944," 3026–34; Polenberg, *War and Society*, 207; "Memorandum for the Attorney General," January 14, 1944, FDRL; a departmental memo to J. Edgar Hoover declared that Assistant Secretary of State Adolph A. Berle insisted he had telephone orders from the president to approve the application (Edward A. Tamm to Hoover, June 30, file 39–878–31X, FBI-RB).

30. Goodman, *The Committee*, 166–67.

31. Friedman, "Election of 1944," 3032–33; Isserman, *Which Side Were You On?*, 210; *Time*, November 13, 1944, 23.

32. Browder testified on September 19, 1944. House of Representatives, Special Committee on Campaign Expenditures, 78th Congress, Second Session, Hearings on H. Res. 5510, 194–216.

33. *Biographical Directory of the American Congress, 1774–1971* (Washington, D.C.: U.S. Government Printing Office, 1971), 736; Browder testimony, 231.

34. Browder testimony, 231–35.

35. Friedman, "Election of 1944," 3037–38; Isserman, *Which Side Were You On?*, 207–13; DW, November 9, 1942; Starobin, *American Communism Crisis*, 77, 269.

36. Clifford McAvoy to DW, January 29, 1942, BP; DW, November 9.

37. Klehr, Haynes, and Firsov, *The Secret World of American Communism*, 234–37; Elizabeth Bentley, *Out of Bondage* (New York: Devon-Adair, 1951), 184–263.

38. JGR/Philip J. Jaffe, August 1–3, 1977.

39. For Browder's review of Willkie's book, see *Worker*, April 19, 1943; TD/Josephine Adams and Browder, April 21, 1956, TDP.

40. Jaffe, *Rise and Fall of American Communism*, 56.

41. Browder, *Teheran: Our Path in War and Peace*, 28.

42. Typewritten introduction to *China's New Democracy*, BP.

43. Letter from Mao Tse-tung to Browder written in Chinese on rice paper (translated by Annie Szeto, Syracuse University class of 1977, November 9, 1976), BP; Jaffe, *Rise and Fall of American Communism*, 57.

44. Starobin, *American Communism in Crisis*, 271–72; copy of Sharkey's article, "Why Communist Programs Vary," BP; Browder to Sharkey, March 31, 1945, BP. Gerald Horne notes that the South African CP also "came out openly against Browder's position," *Black Liberation/Red Scare*, 138.

45. TD/Browder, June 28, 1955, side 2, TDP.

46. Arthur M. Schlesinger, Jr., "Origins of the Cold War," *Foreign Affairs* 46 (October 1967), 35; Stephen E. Ambrose, *Rise to Globalism* (Baltimore: Penguin, 1971), 64.

47. Summary of Browder's activities, March 12, 1945, file 40–3798–28, FBI-EB; "Mr. Churchill Treads Dangerous Path," DW, December 12, 1944; "The Crisis in the Coalition," *Worker,* December 31, January 7, 1945.

## 10. BROWDERISM UPROOTED (1945–1973)

1. Starobin, *American Communism in Crisis,* 81–82; Jaffe, *The Rise and Fall of American Communism,* 78.

2. An English translation of the Duclos article appeared in William Z. Foster, et al., *Marxism-Leninism vs. Revisionism* (New York: New Century Publishers, 1946), 21–33; Starobin, *American Communism in Crisis,* 80.

3. Foster, et al., *Marxism-Leninism vs. Revisionism,* 34; Starobin, *American Communism in Crisis,* 80.

4. Foster et al., *Marxism-Leninism vs. Revisionism,* 34.

5. John Gates, *The Story of an American Communist* (New York: Nelson, 1958), 98; Starobin, *American Communism in Crisis,* 80.

6. JGR/Gil Green, December 31, 1992.

7. Arthur M. Schlesinger, Jr., "Origins of the Cold War," 22–52; John Gaddis, *The United States and the Cold War* (New York: Columbia University Press, 1972), 297; Browder, "How Stalin Ruined the American Communist Party," 45.

8. TD/Browder, June 28, 1955, 34. Browder, Columbia, 443; Daniel Bell, William Goldsmith/Browder, January 10, 1956, BC; Browder, Columbia, 443–44; TD/Browder and Josephine T. Adams, April 21, 1956, TDP.

9. Browder, Columbia, 445–46; Maurice Isserman, *Which Side Were You On?,* 221; copy of telegram, BP. Browder revealed the date Foster had given it to him at the National Board meeting (stenogram, May 22–23, 1945), 2, PJJ.

10. TD/Darcy, May 15, 1957, 4, TDP; Starobin, *American Communism in Crisis,* 272.

11. TD/Browder, June 28, 1955, TDP; Jaffe, *Rise and Fall of American Communism,* 84.

12. May 22–23, 1945, stenogram, PJJ; "A Foreword to the Article of Jacques Duclos," BP; DW, May 24; NYT, May 25.

13. May 22–23, 1945 stenogram, 4, quotations, 19–22, PJJ.

14. Isserman, *Which Side Were You On?,* 223; "Browder's First Speech after the Duclos Article," PJJ.

15. Quotations, May 22–23, 1945, stenogram, 21–23, PJJ; JGR/Philip J. Jaffe, August 1–3, 1977.

16. Speeches of Flynn, Hudson, and Davis, May 22–23 stenogram, 23–28, PJJ.

17. Notes, "Foster's revolt and Browder's expulsion," TDP; Starobin, *American Communism in Crisis,* 270; Isserman, *Which Side Were You On?,* 224–28.

18. DW, May 24, 1945; NYT, May 26.

19. "The Present Situation and the Next Tasks," DW, June 4.

20. "Leadership" (Draper's notes on the CPA crisis), TDP; NYT, June 5, 1945, DW, June 4; Starobin, *American Communism in Crisis,* 86–92; Isserman, *Which Side Were You On?,* 228.

21. "Stenogram of National Board Meeting," June 2, PJJ.

22. June 2 Stenogram, PJJ; Starobin, *American Communism in Crisis,* 92; DW June 4, 1945; Israel Amter to Browder, June 4, BP; DW, June 5.

23. NYT and DW, June 6, 1945.

24. Jaffe, *Rise and Fall of American Communism,* 81; National Committee stenogram, June 18–20, 1945, PJJ; Notes, "Foster's revolt and Browder's expulsion," TDP.

25. "Speech by Elizabeth Gurley Flynn," *Political Affairs* (July 1945), 612–19.

26. Starobin, *American Communism in Crisis,* 93–106; Jaffe, *Rise and Fall of American Com-*

*munism*, 82; *Political Affairs* 24 (July 1945), 612-18; Louis F. Budenz, *This Is My Story* (New York: McGraw-Hill, 1947), 298-99.

27. JGR/Gil Green, December 31, 1992; DW, June 22, 1945.

28. Gar Alperovitz, *Atomic Diplomacy* (New York: Simon & Schuster, 1965) and *The Decision to Use the Atomic Bomb* (New York: Knopf, 1995); Martin J. Sherwin, *A World Destroyed* (New York: Knopf, 1975); Barton J. Bernstein, ed., *The Atomic Bomb* (Boston: Little, Brown, 1970).

29. NYT, DW, July 22-23, 1945.

30. Browder quotations, DW, July 24, 1945; Starobin, *American Communism in Crisis*, 104.

31. Foster quotations, DW, July 25, 1945.

32. "Speech of Earl Browder to National Convention, Communist Political Association," July 26, BP.

33. JGR/Robert J. Alexander, November 25, 1986; JGR/Gil Green, December 31, 1992; Jaffe, *Rise and Fall of American Communism*, 84.

34. NYT, August 5, 1945; August 3; Browder, Columbia, 450.

35. The CPUSA's offer reported, NYT, August 5, 1945; Kohlberg to Browder, August 1, 1945; Smith to Browder, September 21; Kohlberg renewed his offer on March 5, 1946, and January 18, 1954, in letters, BP.

36. Jaffe, *Rise and Fall of American Communism*, 138.

37. Browder, "Appeal to Members of the Communist Party, USA," n.d. (1946); "To the Yonkers Club and to all members of the Communist Party," February 1, 1946; he received dozens of angry letters from "Appeal" recipients, including Albert Mudavan, February 24; Eva Berhenholt, February 27; and Nathan Friedman, n.d., all BP.

38. Jaffe, *Rise and Fall of American Communism*, 141; Browder, Columbia, 460.

39. Starobin, *American Communism in Crisis*, 278; unclassified document #77 (memorandum dated January 18, 1946), DS.

40. Jaffe, *Rise and Fall of American Communism*, 142.

41. Ibid., 142-44; Browder, Columbia, 454; *War or Peace with Russia?* (New York: A.A. Wyn, 1947), and *World Communism and U.S. Foreign Policy* (New York: privately printed, 1947).

42. Quill letter addressed "Dear Friend," April 16, 1948, BP; Jaffe, *Rise and Fall of American Communism*, 151-54.

43. Browder to Alexander Trachtenberg, July 6, BP; unpublished Browder letter to DW, July 1, BP; Starobin, *American Communism in Crisis*, 198; Earl Browder, *The Decline of the Left Wing of America Labor* (New York, 1948); *Labor and Socialism in America* (New York: 1948); *Where Do We Go from Here?* (New York, 1948); *Modern Resurrections and Miracles* (New York, 1950), all privately printed.

44. Darcy, autobiographical manuscript, 593, TDP; Starobin, *American Communism in Crisis*, 123, 188-89.

45. Klehr and Haynes, *The American Communist Movement*, 108-9; Horne, *Black Liberation/ Red Scare*, 225; Browder to the CPUSA, March 23, 1949, BP.

46. Starobin, *American Communism in Crisis*, 279; JGR/William Browder, March 13, 1972.

47. Jaffe, *Rise and Fall of American Communism*, 155-56; RJA/Browder, April 5, 1954, AP; Department of Justice press release, September 30, 1952, National Archives; "Lt. Gen. John Murphy," n.d., box 18, folder 11, ECB.

48. Browder to Rudy Blum, March 6, 1953, BP.

49. "Is Russia a Socialist Community?," *New International* 56, no. 3 (May-June 1950), 145-76.

50. Jaffe, *Rise and Fall of American Communism*, 156-57; Browder, autobiographical manuscript, 5, BP.

51. David Oshinsky, *A Conspiracy So Immense* (New York: Free Press, 1983), 176.

52. Earl Browder, *Contempt of Congress: The Trial of Earl Browder* (New York: privately printed, 1951).

53. See letters from Elizabeth Churchill Brown to Browder, June 30, 1954, to November 12, 1965, ECB.

54. JGR/Robert J. Alexander, November 25, 1986.

55. See lengthy Browder–Blum correspondence, BP.

56. Browder to Alexander, March 18, 1957, BP; JGR/Alexander, November 25, 1986; *Marx and America* (New York: Duell Sloan and Pearce, 1958).

57. Jaffe to Ryan, January 13, 1978.

58. JGR/Scales, June 9, 1995.

59. Cantor, *The Divided Left*, 182, 184; JGR/Browder, March 13, 1972.

60. Nick Salvatore, *Eugene V. Debs, Citizen and Socialist*, 340–41; Ginger, *Eugene V. Debs: A Biography*, 479–80.

61. Jaffe, *Rise and Fall of American Communism*, 10.

## EPILOGUE. COULD WE HAVE BEEN ALL?

1. David J. Garrow to Malcolm M. MacDonald, January 2, 1995.

2. Draper, *American Communism and Soviet Russia*; Isserman, *Which Side Were You On?* By the mid-1990s Isserman seemed to recognize the need for a historiographical middle ground: "No more thought-killing dualities. American Communism was not a pure and unblemished expression of democratic, populist and revolutionary traditions, nor was it just an assemblage of Moscow stooges engaged in devious service. The story of the CPUSA is full of contradictions, and it's past time for all concerned to acknowledge and learn to live with them." In "Notes from Underground," *Nation*, June 12, 1995.

3. TD/Earl Browder, June 28, 1955, 43, TDP.

# BIBLIOGRAPHICAL
# ESSAY

■

## PRIMARY SOURCES

The Earl Browder papers at Syracuse University contain Browder's publications, much of his correspondence (more incoming than outgoing), and several drafts of an unpublished autobiography that stops in the mid-1920s. He preserved few items before 1934 and very little concerning his personal life. The Columbia Oral History Project provides a disappointing overview of his career. Although Joseph Starobin, who later wrote a perceptive book on the CPUSA, conducted the interviews, he did not press Browder with probing questions. The Daniel Bell collection interview at the Tamiment Library is smaller, but illuminating. Theodore Draper's papers at Emory University are voluminous, highly informative, and valuable. (His collection at the Hoover Institution Archives deals with Cuba and does not address Browder's career.) Philip J. Jaffe's papers, also at Emory, contain stenograms of CPUSA Political Committee meetings that Jaffe, an inveterate collector though not a party member, saved from destruction. Professor Robert J. Alexander's personal library has interviews taken by one of Browder's Socialist party opponents.

Federal government records with their prosecutorial bias, available through the Freedom of Information Act, counter the often self-serving nature of reminiscences. The State Department files chronicle Browder's successful efforts to obtain a passport in his own name and officials' attempts to have him indicted for using spurious documents. The Justice Department records reveal its battle with the State Department, as both agencies sought to dodge responsibility for not stopping Browder's illegal activities before 1939. The documents from the Justice Department also contain perceptive (and contrasting) legal opinions on the statute of limitations question. The Federal Bureau of Prisons collection is excellent. It contains records on Browder's family life, psychological and psychiatric evaluations, and intelligence test results. Atlanta Penitentiary's larger context is revealed through the warden's annual reports and an unpublished history written by the prison's Protestant chaplain. The Pardon Attorney's Office has Browder's lengthy, detailed petition for executive clemency and material on the CPUSA's campaign to secure his release. Browder's two-thousand-page FBI file reveals extensive government surveillance and J. Edgar Hoover's untiring efforts to prosecute Browder for any possible violation. Raissa Browder's files, kept by the FBI and Immigration and Naturalization Service, detail her lengthy battle to avoid deportation despite obviously disingenuous testimony. They also show the two agencies' anger (most acutely expressed by Hoover) toward President Roosevelt for his leniency. Margaret Browder's 561-page FBI file focuses entirely on the espionage question. The number of informers possessing only hearsay knowledge or being "unwilling to testify" is especially striking. Historian David J. Garrow has pointed out that "in FBI jargon a source who is unwilling (or often 'unavailable') to testify is not an informant at all, but is a 'black bag job,' Bureau-ese for a surreptitious burglary carried out by agents themselves." Such informants "always seem to be those who furnish membership lists, contributor records, or other materials that could have been photographed during an off-hours entry of an office or home" (Garrow to Malcom M. MacDonald, January 2, 1995).

The Comintern and the American party files at the Russian Center for Preservation and Study of Documents of Recent History in Moscow, which include personnel files on Earl and Raissa Browder, provide the real jewel of the research. They offer a priceless record of the Browders' roles as members of an international revolutionary movement. They also detail the vicious struggle between competing CPUSA cadres for Soviet favor.

Some stateside sources are useful in a far more limited sense. Material at the Hoover Institution Archives, including the Elizabeth Churchill Brown papers and National Republic collections, document attempts by the McCarthyite right to recruit ex-Communist Browder during the 1950s. The latter contains a wealth of photographs from Browder's entire career. The Paul V. McNutt papers at the Indiana State Library have material on Browder's 1936 arrest and mobbing in Terre Haute. The Stanley Reed papers at the University of Kentucky and those of William O. Douglas and Hugo L. Black at the Library of Congress deal with Browder's Supreme Court case.

### SECONDARY SOURCES

Although there are no previous Browder biographies, other books on the CPUSA during his era have, of course, discussed aspects of his career. Few academics looked at American Communism before the 1950s. The first scholarly studies appeared during the McCarthy era. Not surprisingly, the Moscow tie received greatest emphasis. Daniel Bell, in a 1952 essay titled "Marxism Socialism in the United States" (published separately by Princeton University Press in 1967), saw American Communism's path as a series of twists and turns directed by the USSR. Irving Howe and Lewis Coser's *American Communist Party: A Critical History* (Boston: Beacon Press, 1957) stressed members' malleability. Max Kampelman's *Communist Party vs the CIO: A Study in Power Politics* (New York: Praeger, 1957) portrayed the CPUSA's role in the labor movement as negative and conspiratorial. That same year Theodore Draper produced the definitive organizational history of the party in the 1920s in *The Roots of American Communism* (New

York: Viking, 1957) and later in *American Communism and Soviet Russia: The Formative Period* (New York: Viking, 1960). Draper set a high scholarly standard and argued persuasively that CP domestic policy from 1922 on served as an appendage of the USSR's revolutionary government.

In the 1960s historians displayed little interest in the CPUSA, but the 1970s brought subtly nuanced historiographical changes. Joseph Starobin's *American Communism in Crisis, 1943–1957* (Cambridge: Harvard University Press, 1972) analyzed the party from Browder's ouster to its near disintegration in 1956. Starobin considered the CPUSA's voluntary attachment to Soviet forms and foreign policy to be the cause of its failure. Philip J. Jaffe's *Rise and Fall of American Communism* (New York: Horizon Press, 1975), part history, part biography, part document collection, analyzed Browder's deliberate and allegedly successful reshaping of his historical image over the twenty-seven-year period from his expulsion until his death. James Weinstein's *Ambiguous Legacy: The Left in American Politics* (New York: New Viewpoints, 1975) and Stanley Aronowitz's *False Promises* (New York: McGraw-Hill, 1973) criticized the CPUSA for emphasizing defense of the Soviet state over building up a strong revolutionary movement in the United States. In their view favorable conditions had appeared during the Great Depression.

In the 1980s, a polarization of historians' attitudes occurred regarding the CPUSA. Maurice Isserman's *Which Side Where You On? The American Communist Party During World War II* (Middletown: Wesleyan University Press, 1982) argued that Browder's Popular Front leadership recruited a generation of domestically oriented ethnic Americans who attempted to build a democratic form of Communism left of the New Deal. His study took direct issue with Draper's viewpoint. The debate between Isserman and Draper began a life of its own, with followers choosing sides and joining in, stimulating a growing scholarly interest in the once-ignored CPUSA. Harvey Klehr's *Heyday of American Communism: The Depression Decade* (New York: Basic Books, 1984), one of the most controversial studies of the subject, shared Draper's perspective and brought his narrative up to 1939. Klehr broadened the focus beyond party leadership, however, to include Communist efforts among labor, farmers, intellectuals, whites, blacks, ethnic groups, youth, and the unemployed. Fraser Ottanelli attempted to refute Klehr in his *Communist Party of the United States: From the Depression to World War II* (New Brunswick, N.J.: Rutgers University Press, 1991). A discipline-wide flowering of a "new social history" was also witnessed in the 1980s. Rejecting (at times castigating) political history as focused on presidents, prime ministers, and kings, it shifted the emphasis toward multicultural and feminist concerns. Studies on American Communism blossomed. Memoirs and monographs explored the party's local, ethnic, and gender roots. Biographies and other studies investigated the movement's contributions to more specialized areas. Such books displayed little interest in the career or life of Browder, a white Anglo-Saxon male who spent his entire party career among the CPUSA's top national hierarchy.

Studies that do not teach us much about Browder but show the direction of scholarship between 1975 and 1995 include: Rosalyn Fraad Baxandall, *Words on Fire: The Biography and Writings of Elizabeth Gurley Flynn* (New Brunswick, N.J.: Rutgers University Press, 1985); Paul Buhle, Mari Jo Buhle, and Ben Georgakas, *Encyclopedia of the American Left* (Urbana: University of Illinois Press, 1992); Paul Buhle, *Marxism in the United States: Remapping the History of the American Left* (London: Verso, 1991); Helen C. Camp, *Iron in Her Soul: Elizabeth Gurley Flynn and the American Left* (Pullman: Washington State University Press, 1995); Peter N. Carroll, *The Odyssey of the American Lincoln Brigade* (Stanford: Stanford University Press, 1994); Bert Cochran, *Labor and Communism* (Princeton: Princeton University Press, 1977); Eugene V. Dennett, *Agitprop: The Life of an American Working-Class Radical, the Autobiography of Eugene V. Dennett* (Albany: State University of New York Press, 1990); Franklin Folsom, *Impatient Armies of the Poor* (Niwot: University Press of Colorado, 1991); Gil Green, *Cold War Fugitive: A Personal Story of the McCarthy Era* (New York: International Publishers, 1984); Dorothy Healey and Maurice Isserman, *Dorothy Healey Remembers: A Life in the American Communist Party* (New York: Oxford University Press, 1990); Gerald Horne, *Black Liberation/ Red Scare: Ben Davis and the Communist Party* (Newark: University of Delaware Press, 1994); Gerald Horne, *Communist Front? The Civil Rights Congress, 1946–1956* (London: Associated University Presses, 1988); Edward P. Johanningsmeier, *Forging American Communism: The Life of William Z. Foster* (Princeton: Princeton University Press, 1994); Christopher Johnson, *Maurice Sugar: Law, Labor and the Left in Detroit, 1912–1950* (Detroit: Wayne State University Press, 1988); Roger Keeran, *The Communist Party and the Auto Workers Unions* (Bloomington: Indiana University Press, 1980); Robin D. G. Kelley, *Hammer and Hoe: Alabama Communists during the Great Depression* (Chapel Hill: University of North Carolina Press, 1990); Aileen S. Kraditor, *"Jimmy Higgins": The Mental World of the American Rank-and-File Communist, 1930–1958* (Westport, Conn.: Greenwood, 1988), a social history that is nevertheless profoundly anti-Communist; Harvey A. Levenstein, *Communism, Anticommunism and the CIO* (Westport, Conn.: Greenwood, 1981); David Leviatin, *Followers of the Trail: Jewish Working-Class Radicals in America* (New Haven: Yale University Press, 1989); Robbie Lieberman, *My Song Is My Weapon: People's Songs, American Communism and the Politics of Culture* (Urbana: University of Illinois Press, 1989); Paul Lyons, *Philadelphia Communists, 1936–1956* (Philadelphia: Temple University Press, 1982); Mark Naison, *Communists in Harlem during the Great Depression* (Urbana: University of Illinois Press, 1983); Steve Nelson, James R. Barrett, and Rob Ruck, *Steve Nelson, American Radical* (Urbana: University of Illinois Press, 1982); Junius Scales and Richard Nickson, *Cause at Heart: A Former Communist Remembers* (Athens: University of Georgia Press, 1987); Ellen W. Schrecker, *No Ivory Tower: McCarthyism and the Universities* (New York: Oxford University Press, 1986); Charles Shipman, *It Had to Be Revolution: Memoirs of an American Radical* (Ithaca: Cornell University Press, 1993); Karl G. Yoneda, *Gambatte: Sixty Years Struggle of a Kibei Worker* (Los Angeles: UCLA Asian-American Studies Center, 1985).

By contrast, Harvey Klehr and John Earl Haynes's *American Communist Movement: Storming Heaven Itself* (New York: Twayne Publishers, 1992) and Guenter Lewy's *Cause That Failed: Communism in American Political Life* (New York: Oxford University Press, 1990) displayed the continued vigor of the traditional political history approach. In the same vein, Robert Cohen's *When the Old Left Was Young* (New York: Oxford University Press, 1993) deserved mention.

The 1992 opening of the Soviet archives at the Russian Center for the Preservation and Study of Documents of Recent History in Moscow provided an undreamed-of opportunity toward reaching a fuller and clearer understanding of American Communism's role in the world revolutionary movement. Materials there offer the possibility of lowering the decibel level of the historiographical debate and finding an approach toward a synthesis. An important first step occurred with the publication of *The Secret World of American Communism* by Harvey Klehr, John Earl Haynes, and Fridrikh Igorevich Firsov (New Haven: Yale University Press, 1995). It contained ninety-two documents concerning the CPUSA's link to Soviet covert activities, interwoven with explanatory narrative. The authors recognized it as merely the tip of an iceberg.

Within months of the *Secret World's* appearance, the National Security Agency and Central Intelligence Agency began releasing nearly 2,200 intercepted World War II–era cables to Moscow. NKVD and GRU agents in the United States had concealed them among Soviet diplomatic telegrams. Mostly between 1947 and 1952, the U.S. Army's Signal Intelligence Service decrypted them. Code named the "Venona," they confirm and reinforce dramatically the thesis propounded by Klehr, Haynes, and Firsov.

No future study of American Communism can ignore or fail to take seriously the archival treasures in Moscow. It is hoped that further research will explain more fully the role played by the conflicting demands of indigenous radicalism and international Communism.

# INDEX

Aaron, Daniel, 77, 80
AAS. *See* Anglo-American Secretariat (AAS)
Abraham Lincoln Brigade, 150–53
ACLU. *See* American Civil Liberties Union (ACLU)
Adams, John, 105
Adams, Josephine Truslow, 201, 212–15, 251
Aerova, Maria, 229
AFL. *See* American Federation of Labor (AFL)
African Americans: attitudes against, during World War I, 13; and Browder, 142; and CPA, 235; and CPUSA, 43–44, 59, 98, 210, 254–55; as Ku Klux Klan's target, 24; migration to cities by, 5, 24; National Negro Congress, 102; and New Deal, 107; and New Left of 1960s, 272–73; and race riots, 210; Roosevelt's program for, 224; Scottsboro Boys, 43, 44, 59; and Spanish civil war, 150; suffrage for, 106
Agriculture Department, 101
Aid to Dependent Children, 97
Alexander, Robert J., 78, 142, 185
Alien Registration Act, 299 (n. 49)
Alperovitz, Gar, 259
Amariglio, David, 153
America First Committee, 171
American Civil Liberties Union (ACLU), 46, 114, 118, 119, 178, 205
American Commonwealth Federation, 111
American Federation of Labor (AFL): aloofness from politics, 125; Browder on, 90; Browder's involvement with, 12; and charter pledging mutual recognition and respect to CIO and U.S. Chamber of Commerce, 245; and CIO formation, 89, 101–2, 123; and Communists' "dual" unions approach, 21; and Communists in Chicago Federation of Labor, 26; at CPUSA convention of 1944, 235; membership of, compared with CIO, 134; in 1920s, 24, 26; in 1930s, 71–72, 78–79, 89; and no-strike policy during World War II, 208; and TUEL, 23; and TUUL,

71–72, 78–79; and women's work in mass-production industries, 97; workers ignored by, 9, 34, 61, 89
Americanization campaign, 103–7, 131, 170, 185, 232, 235, 278
American Labor party, 108, 160, 168, 211
American League Against War and Fascism, 101
American Legionnaires, 114, 117, 118
American Medical Association, 232
American Plan, 21, 24, 104
Americans for Democratic Action, 232
American Student Union, 91
American Workers party, 72
American Writers' Congress, 79–80
American Youth Congress, 76
Amis, B. D., 59
Amter, Israel, 40, 45
Anderson, Clinton P., 240
Anglo-American Secretariat (AAS), 45, 49–54, 58–59, 76, 89, 284 (n. 5)
Antiwar activities: during World War I, 12–15; during World War II, 166, 185–86
*Appeal to Reason*, 9, 13
Aragon, Louis, 79
Argentina, 256
Arnold, Benedict, 105, 155
Aronberg, Philip, 31
Atlanta Penitentiary, 192, 196–202, 197
Atomic weapons, 259, 262
Australian Communist party, 242–43
Austria, 156

Baker, Rudy, 140, 271
Baldwin, Roger, 46–47
Baseball, 145
Bates, Sanford, 198
Battle, G. Gordon, 179–81
Beard, Charles, 106
Bedacht, Max, 37, 46, 60, 180
Beecher, Samuel, 116–19, 292 (n. 71)
Benjamin, Herbert, 41, 57, 229
Bennett, Harry, 43
Bennett, James V., 198
Bennett, John J., Jr., 190
Bennett, Milly, 14, 31–32

Bush, George, 134
Business values during 1920s, 124–25
Byoir, Carl, 214

*Cahiers du Communisme,* 246–47
Cahill, John T., 178–83
*Call,* 63
Calverton, V. F., 77, 154
Camp, Helen C., 205
Canadian Communist party, 94
Cannery and Agricultural Workers Industrial Union, 61
Cannon, James P., 15, 22, 24, 35, 167, 196, 259, 267
Cantor, Milton, 149, 272–73
Carnegie, Andrew, 5
Carpentier, Georges, 198
Carr, E. H., 65, 67, 69
Carroll, Peter N., 151
CBS, 113, 132
CCC. *See* Civilian Conservation Corps (CCC)
Chafe, William, 96–97
Chamberlain, Neville, 156, 165, 166
Charney, George, 96, 220
Chase, Stuart, 21
Chemadonov, V. T., 68
Chernov, Victor, 46
Cheyney, Ralph, 18
Chiang Kai-shek, 30–31, 211, 242
Chicago Federation of Labor, 26
Childs, Morris, 227
China: Browder's trip to, 30–34, 149; Chiang Kai-shek in, 211, 242; Communist party in, 241–42, 253; and Japan, 50, 202, 203, 211; labor organizing work in, 31–32; Mao Tse-tung in, 241–42; State Department policy on, 211–12
Chou En-lai, 253
Church, Ralph E., 239–40
Churchill, Winston, 202, 203, 209, 217, 218, 234, 244, 255
CI. *See* Communist International (CI)
CIO. *See* Committee for Industrial Organization (CIO); Congress of Industrial Organization (CIO)
Citizens' Committee to Free Earl Browder, 204–5, 212, 213
Civilian Conservation Corps (CCC), 97, 113
Clark, John S., 139
Cochran, Bert, 34, 36, 72, 107, 121

Cohn, Roy, 267
Cold War, 243, 249, 250, 259, 264, 265, 267, 278
Collins, H. A., 118
Collins, John, 43
Comintern. *See* Third International (Comintern)
Committee for Industrial Organizations (CIO), 89, 90, 97, 101–2, 107, 121–25, 129, 134. *See also* Congress of Industrial Organizations (CIO)
Commonwealth Federation in Washington State, 127
*Communist,* 27, 49, 225, 247
Communist International (CI), 66, 84, 85, 173
Communist Labor party, 16, 18, 19
Communist League of America, Left Opposition, 38
Communist party (CP), 16, 18, 19, 23, 26. *See also* Communist party of the United States (CPUSA); and specific countries
Communist party, USA (Opposition) (CPO), 110–11
Communist party of the United States (CPUSA): and African Americans, 43–44, 59, 98, 210, 254–55; and Americanization campaign, 103–7, 131, 170, 185, 232, 235, 278; anti-Trotsky heresy hunt by, 35; antiwar position during World War II, 166, 185–86; and Bonus March, 51–54; Browder as General Secretary of, 62, 137; Browder as presidential candidate in 1936, 109, 112–20, 127, 292 (n. 72); and Browder's imprisonment in 1940s, 192, 201–2; Browder's leadership of, in 1930s, 46–59, 73, 76–82, 93–96, 99; Browder's leadership of, in 1940s, 207–9; Browder's plan for peaceful coexistence in 1940s, 221–23; Browder's salary, 146, 295 (n. 63); Browder's siblings in, 8, 281 (n. 9); Browder-Thomas debates, 90–91; and cooperation with Socialist party, 76, 78, 79, 81, 88, 90–91, 109–10; covert operations of, 139–41; decline of, in 1950s, 270, 272; and Democratic Front, 131–34, 160, 162, 163, 166, 168, 172; "dissolution" of, in 1944, 231, 248; domestic policy in 1937–1938, 125–34; and election of 1936, 109, 112–20, 127, 292 (n. 72); and election of 1940, 189–90; and election of 1948, 265, 277; and era of elation from 1936–

CP. *See* Communist party
CPA. *See* Communist Political Association (CPA)
CPO. *See* Communist party, USA (Opposition) (CPO)
CPUSA. *See* Communist party of the United States (CPUSA)
Cuban Communist party, 94, 233, 293 (n. 29)
Cummings, Homer, 114
Curran, Joe, 209
Currie, Lauchlin, 211
Czechoslovakia, 156, 266

*Daily Worker,* 37, 38, 49–51, 58, 61, 62, 90, 123, 127, 128, 142, 151, 159–62, 165, 186, 195–96, 210–12, 222, 244, 247, 250, 252, 255, 256, 259–60
Daladier, Edouard, 165, 166
Darcy, Emma, 32
Darcy, Sam: and Browder's peaceful coexistence plan, 222; Browder's relationship with, 62, 82–83, 132, 135, 229–30; and Browder's support for Roosevelt administration, 130; and Communist party backing of Wallace, 265; demotion of, in CPUSA, 158; on Dimitrov, 66, 83–84; and Duclos article on Browder, 247, 251; and election of 1936, 108; expulsion of, from CPUSA, 229–30, 235; on Katherine Harrison's relationship with Browder, 32; militancy of, 40, 47; personality of, 134; on Raissa Luganovskaya, 30, 49, 143, 145; and Teheran Thesis, 220, 226, 227–28; at World Congress in 1935, 82–84
Davis, Angela, 144
Davis, Benjamin J, Jr., 254–55, 274
Davis, Dave, 235
Debs, Eugene V.: Browder compared with, 2, 94, 99, 186, 192, 197, 198; Darcy's praise for, 229; death of, 25, 118, 273; indictment and imprisonment of, 13, 19, 197–98; as Socialist presidential candidate, 2, 9, 10, 19; Soviet interest in release from prison for, 201
Debs, Theodore, 197
DeCaux, Len, 124
Declaration of Independence, 105
De Gaulle, Charles, 231
De Leon, Daniel, 8
Democratic Front, 131–34, 160–63, 166, 168, 172, 178, 293 (n. 29)

Dempsey, Jack, 198
Denikin, A. I., 30
Dennis, Eugene: and Browder's removal from CPUSA leadership, 250–53, 255, 256, 261, 269; as Browder's supporter, 131, 135, 158, 227; criticism of Foster by, 131, 158, 227; and Democratic Front debate, 163; Garrow on, 274; international reputation of, 34; and Pan-Pacific Trade Union Conference (PPTUS), 31; and protection of Communist parties from government infiltration, 211
Depression. *See* Great Depression
Dewey, John, 21, 58, 154
Dewey, Thomas E., 189, 214, 236, 238, 240
Dewey Commission, 154
Dickstein, Samuel, 171
Dies, Martin, 171, 172, 238
Dies Committee, 171, 172–74, 180, 239
Diggins, John Patrick, 25, 58, 125
DiMaggio, Joe, 145
Dimitrov, Georgi: and Browder as presidential candidate, 109; Browder praised by, 94, 130–31; and Browder's fears for sister Margaret, 171; Browder's friendship with, 66, 88, 94, 275; and Browder's need for shortwave radio receiver/recorder, 157, 166, 252; on Browder's removal from CPUSA leadership, 261; as Comintern head, 67; and Communist parties during World War II, 233; and CPUSA burglary of Lovestone's home, 111; and CPUSA conflict over Teheran Thesis, 229; and CPUSA convention in 1938, 132; and CPUSA's cancellation of affiliation with Comintern, 191; and Farmer-Labor party, 86, 93, 126; and Foster, 130–31, 157–58; and government infiltration of Communist parties, 210–11; at Seventh World Congress, 82–87; and Spanish civil war, 150; support for Browder rather than Foster, 130–31; and support for Roosevelt, 83–84, 108–9; trial of, for Reichstag fire, 65–66, 67; and United Front, 82–87, 91
Dingle, John D., 176
*Distributors Guide,* 262–63
Dixler, Elsa, 98, 225
Dodd, Bella, 222, 235
Dollfuss, Engelbert, 66
Dolson, Jim, 31
Donini, Ambrogio, 243, 250, 255

Turkey, 264
TUUL. *See* Trade Union Unity League (TUUL)
Twain, Mark, 131
Tydings, Millard E., 269–70

UAW. *See* United Auto Workers (UAW)
UMW. *See* United Mine Workers (UMW)
Undjus, Margaret, 31
Unemployed Councils, 41, 63, 102
Unemployment during Great Depression, 40–41, 48, 96
Union party, 108, 120
Unions. *See* Labor movement; and specific unions
Unitarian Church, 8
United Auto Workers (UAW), 122–23, 124, 209
United Communist party, 19, 21
United Electrical, Radio, and Machine Workers, 124
United Front, 65, 68, 69–82, 85–86, 87, 88, 91, 110–11
United Furniture Workers, 43
United Mine Workers (UMW), 89, 90, 107
United Nations, 244, 250, 256, 269
United Rubber Workers, 121
U.S. Chamber of Commerce, 245
U.S. Congress Against War, 101
U.S. Steel, 15, 123
Urban migration, 5, 24
USSR. *See* Soviet Union

Vandenberg, Arthur, 189
Van Kleek, Mary, 57
Van Tine, Warren, 89
Varga, Eugene, 130, 131
Veblen, Thorstein, 124
Vestal, J. A., 14
*Victory and After* (Browder), 207–8
Vietnam War, 273
Violence: Browder's rejection of, 46–47, 87; CPUSA at rallies of other groups, 45, 63; and CPUSA in 1930s, 40–45; demonstrations and riots on unemployment in 1930, 40–41; during election campaign in 1936, 114–15, 118, 119; and labor movement during 1930s, 42, 43, 47, 72–73, 123–24; *Los Angeles Times* building bombing, 10–11; terrorist bombings in 1920, 18–19
*Voice of China*, 89

Volkogónóv, Dimitri, 67, 225
Von Schleicher, Kurt, 67
Voorhis, Jerry, 191
Voorhis Act, 191, 217
Voros, Sandor, 112

Wagner, Robert F., 81
Wagner Act, 123
Wagner-Costigan antilynching bill, 133
Waldman, Louis, 109–10, 133
Waldman, Seymour, 44, 115
Walker, Jimmy, 40
Wallace, Henry A., 236–37, 248, 265, 277
Wang Ching-wei, 30–31
Wang Ming, 67
War Department, 216
Ware group, 140
War Manpower Commission, 206
*War or Peace with Russia?* (Browder), 264
Washington, George, 105, 185, 235
Wayland, Julius, 9
Weaver, James B., 6
Weinstein, James, 48
Weinstock, Louis, 235
Weinstone, William W., 37–38, 46–55, 58–59, 61, 130, 147, 157–58
Weisbord, Albert, 34, 35
Welles, Sumner, 166, 211–12, 214, 241
Whalen, Grover, 40–41
White, David McKelvy, 152
Whitley, Rhea, 173
Whitlock, Charles, 118, 291 (n. 67)
Whitman, Walt, 131
Wichita, Kansas, 5–7
Williams, G. *See* Mikhailov, Boris
Williamson, John, 229, 254, 255, 259, 261
Willkie, Wendell, 189, 211, 236, 241
Wilson, Edmund, 154
Wilson, Woodrow, 12, 13, 15, 277
Wobblies. *See* Industrial Workers of the World (IWW)
Wolfe, Bertram, 36, 58
Woll, Matthew, 79
Women: Browder on women's rights, 96, 98–99, 142–43, 207; Browder's attraction for, 26–27, 29; in Communist Political Association (CPA), 225; CPUSA on rights of, 96, 97–99; CPUSA's reaction to Luganovskaya, 30, 49, 74, 145; employment of, 96–97, 206–7; and Equal Rights Amendment, 97–98, 207; and labor movement, 34, 63, 73, 97, 122; in military dur-

# ABOUT THE AUTHOR

James G. Ryan is associate professor of history at Texas A&M University at Galveston. He received M.A. degrees at the University of Delaware and the University of Notre Dame and a Ph.D. from the University of Notre Dame.